A ROYAL HISTORY
OF ENGLAND

A Royal History of England

ISBN: 9781845358884

First published in Great Britain in 2021 by DC Thomson & Co, Ltd.,
185 Fleet Street London EC4A 2HS.

To purchase this book call: 0800 074 0188, overseas customers: +44 1382 575052,
or visit: www.thisengland.co.uk.

A ROYAL HISTORY
OF ENGLAND

■—— PAUL JAMES ——■

Contents

Foreword   7
Introduction   9

1.   Egbert (828-839)   13
2.   Ethelwulf (c.839-858), Ethelbald (c.858-860) and
Ethelbert (c.860-866)   17
3.   Ethelred (866-871)   21
4.   Alfred the Great (871-899)   25
5.   Edward the Elder (899-924)   31
6.   Athelstan (924-939), Edmund (939-946) and
Edred (946-955)   35
7.   Edwy the Fair (955-959) and
Edgar the Peaceful (959-975)   40
8.   Edward the Martyr (975-978)   46
9.   Ethelred the Unready (978-1016)   50
10.   Edmund Ironside (April 1016-November 1016)   56
11.   Canute (1016-1035)   60
12.   Harold Harefoot (1035-1040) and
Harthacanute (1040-1042)   65
13.   Edward the Confessor (1042-1066)   69
14.   Harold Godwinson (January 1066-October 1066)   76
15.   William I (the Conqueror) (1066-1087)   82
16.   William II (1087-1100)   89
17.   Henry I (1100-1135)   95
18.   Stephen (1135-1154)   101
19.   Henry II (1154-1189)   107
20.   Richard I (1189-1199)   114
21.   John (1199-1216)   120
22.   Henry III (1216-1272)   128
23.   Edward I (1272-1307)   136
24.   Edward II (1307-1327)   144
25.   Edward III (1327-1377)   150
26.   Richard II (1377-1399)   157
27.   Henry IV (1399-1413)   165

28.	Henry V (1413-1422)	172
29.	Henry VI (1422-1461 and 1470-1471)	179
30.	Edward IV (1461-1470 and 1471-1483)	188
31.	Edward V (April 1483-July 1483)	196
32.	Richard III (1483-1485)	202
33.	Henry VII (1485-1509)	211
34.	Henry VIII (1509-1547)	220
35.	Edward VI (1547-1553)	229
36.	Lady Jane Grey (10-19 July 1553)	236
37.	Mary I (1553-1558)	241
38.	Elizabeth I (1558-1603)	249
39.	James I (1603-1625)	264
40.	Charles I (1625-1649)	277
41.	Oliver Cromwell and the Interregnum (1649-1660)	288
42.	Charles II (1660-1685)	298
43.	James II (1685-1688)	311
44.	William III (1689-1702), Mary II (1689-1694)	323
45.	Anne (1702-1714)	331
46.	George I (1714-1727)	340
47.	George II (1727-1760)	348
48.	George III (1760-1820)	354
49.	George IV (1820-1830)	364
50.	William IV (1830-1837)	371
51.	Victoria (1837-1901)	379
52.	Edward VII (1901-1910)	387
53.	George V (1910-1936)	395
54.	Edward VIII (January 1936-December 1936)	404
55.	George VI (1936-1952)	413
56.	Elizabeth II (1952-present)	421

Foreword

Angela Linforth, This England

When I took over as Editor of *This England* in September 2018, Paul James's A Royal History of England series was a jewel in the crown of a magazine filled with gems. It was a feature that explored and celebrated our nation's history and monarchs in a really accessible and anecdotal way – which to my mind brings the story of England vividly to life. That's the reason why, I think, the series has been so popular with our readers over the 14 years it has been running and why our readers have been asking if we would put all 56 parts into one glorious book.

Over the centuries, our Kings and Queens have been at the heart of almost every significant happening in England since Egbert was crowned the first King of the English in 828. They've been at the centre of countless wars and betrayals, but also countless triumphs and great periods of stability and growth. Some have been uniquely suited to the role and have thrived and led with great panache, while others have been completely unsuited and struggled. Yet each and every one of them is fascinating in his or her own way.

I was reading a newspaper columnist recently who spoke of a turbulent time in Parliament over the last five years. Turbulent, I thought – it's nothing compared to the Middle Ages!

We finish, of course, with our most longstanding monarch, Her Majesty Queen Elizabeth II, and it's difficult to think of a more exemplary reign.

I hope you enjoy this book as much as we enjoyed putting it together.

Introduction
Paul James

The Queen smiled directly at me. One of those radiant smiles for which Elizabeth the Second will always be remembered. Her whole face lit up and her eyes twinkled, probably because, as a small boy, I was dressed exactly as Prince Charles had been at the same age – right down to the velvet-collared coat.

At a younger age than most children I became aware of the mystique and magic that surrounds royalty. Born in Norfolk, twelve miles from Sandringham, I used to be taken by my parents to stand outside St Mary Magdalene Church whenever the Queen and the Royal Family were attending the Sunday morning service. In those far off glorious days there were no barriers to keep people at a distance and security seemed to be little more than the local village policemen, so the Queen was quite literally within touching distance. When Her Majesty walked past, as a child I could not help but sense the reaction of the people around me. Here was someone special.

It was not, however, my first introduction to royalty. I was born one month prematurely, and my mother always used to say that on the very day I should have been born, I was taken to the Sandringham Flower Show. Not that I remember it! In an early childhood photograph I am looking, not at the camera, but at my own reflection in the glossy paintwork of the Queen Mother's Daimler. From a very early age, before I could even read, one of my grandmothers would give me coronation books to look at. Not just those from 1953, but also the coronation books of George V and George VI and I would sit in bed drinking in the magnificent pictures of golden coaches, velvet robes, glittering crowns, the orb and sceptres. While other children had fairy stories, I was looking at the real-life fairy tale of Kings and Queens. Once I was able to read, my bookshelves filled with 50 volumes from the Ladybird 561 series on royal and historic figures.

My childhood was spent being taken to see members of the Royal Family at every available opportunity. Their official visits to a local town or to a County Show; we attended Trooping the Colour, stood in the hot sun at Windsor Castle to watch the Garter Procession and waited outside the London Palladium in the pouring rain to see the Queen arrive for the Royal Variety Performance. We would be in The Mall or outside Parliament to view the pageantry of the State Opening or a royal wedding procession.

We knew many people who worked for the Royal Family, heard numerous "behind the scenes" stories, and I would receive itineraries of overseas tours, menus from the Royal Yacht Britannia, plans and guest lists for a state banquet at Buckingham Palace. Growing up in that sort of environment, it was little wonder that my career came to involve royalty. I was subconsciously building up a wealth of background information without even realising it.

For over 40 years as an author and broadcaster I was regularly given the opportunity to appear on radio and television, write dozens of books, hundreds of articles, and commentate on every aspect of royal life. It also enabled me to attend many official royal events. One day I might have been handling papers in Queen Victoria's handwriting, the next broadcasting on radio to Australia or being interviewed for an American television programme, the next following Princess Anne around on various royal visits. Some years I saw the Queen and Prince Philip in the flesh more often than my own parents.

My introduction to *This England* magazine came on the day of Prince Charles's 40th birthday in 1988. I was taking part in a live BBC television programme to celebrate the occasion, hosted by Alan Titchmarsh, and was due to travel from Brighton to the Pebble Mill Studios in Birmingham. To occupy my time on the long train journey, I perused the station bookshop and was drawn to the attractive cover of *This England*. I read every word of that issue while on the train and soon took out a subscription. Over the next couple of years, it struck me that something was missing from the magazine. While celebrating the best of England, it rarely featured the Royal Family.

In 1991 I contacted the then Editor, and founder of *This England*, Roy Faiers. I should perhaps say Mr Faiers, as he was very gentlemanly and was always Mr Faiers; I would never have dared call him Roy! We had recently celebrated the Queen Mother's 90th birthday and it seemed to me that the world knew everything that there was to know about her, yet people knew very little about Prince Philip's mother. She was as much a grandmother to Princess Anne and Princes Charles, Andrew and Edward, as the Queen Mother. So I suggested an article on Princess Alice.

Not only did Mr Faiers say that he felt "the idea worthy of merit", but that he would like me to do an entire series of biographies, which we called Royalty Remembered. The idea was that they would be about past members of the Royal Family who were within living memory. Plus, I was to write additional feature articles for any milestone royal birthdays, anniversaries and Jubilees as they arose. Thus began my long association with *This England* that has now gone on for more than 30 years.

In 2006 I embarked on the series that I had always wanted to write: the fascinating story of England's Kings and Queens, having been interested in our royal history since first reading the Ladybird books of my childhood. Although not a new concept, history books tend to start with William the Conqueror, as if the monarchy in England began in 1066. I wanted to go right back to the beginning, to the earliest ruler to wear a crown, the first to call himself "King of the English". Thus, the series *A Royal History of England* began. Some 1,200 years of history, over 60 monarchs, in 56 articles that would take 15 years to complete for the quarterly magazine.

I am grateful to the late Roy Faiers for originally commissioning the series; his successor Stephen Garnett for continuing to be such an enthusiastic supporter (particularly when the remains of King Richard III were discovered before I wrote the article about him, and the issue in which it appeared was published at the time of his reburial in Leicester – a remarkable coincidence that no one could have foreseen). I'm also grateful to the current Editor, Angela Linforth and Features Editor Isobel King, for taking over the series with equal enthusiasm and, at the suggestion of *This England*'s readers, putting all the articles together in this book.

This was never intended to be an academic series, but a gentle look at England's monarchy. By the very nature of being magazine articles, they could only ever be potted histories due to the limited space. A lot of facts will inevitably have been missed out. I was once giving a talk about Royalty and the Theatre at the Winter Garden in Eastbourne.

As I sat on the stage before the event began, I heard a man in the audience say very loudly, "I'm looking forward to hearing all about William IV and the theatre." My immediate thought was, "But there's nothing in the talk about William IV . . ." At the question-and-answer session at the end of the evening came the inevitable comment: "You didn't say anything about William IV." I could only answer that the talk was just a flavour of the connection between royalty and the theatre, and to include everything would have meant a talk lasting 19 hours! So it is with this book, it can only be a summary of events over the past 1,200 years and includes the facts and stories that I personally found interesting.

It has truly been a labour of love writing the pieces and the greatest satisfaction has been when readers have told me that they always hated history, but found the articles made it accessible and they had enjoyed reading about royal history for the first time in their lives. One *This England* reader* wrote that he "felt a degree of emotion" when the series came to an end. I am delighted, therefore, that the articles have now been put together for the first time in this collection.

England without its Kings and Queens now seems unthinkable, for they have shaped our nation, provided a sense of continuity and invoked a spirit of patriotism. The English landscape is dotted with castles and palaces, battlefields, statues, parks and forests, lasting reminders of our royal past. Monarchs have inspired great literature, such as Shakespeare's plays *Richard III* and *Henry V*; gathered together significant works of art for us to enjoy, and on the most basic of levels have provided names for many of England's public houses. Most of us know a King's Arms, a Queen's Head, a Rose and Crown, or a Queen Victoria pub. At a higher level, many of our laws were originally instigated by England's monarchs. Citizens are invested by them with medals and honours for courage and good works. Coins, banknotes and stamps bear the Sovereign's head. England's monarch is Head of State, Head of the Church, Head of the Armed Forces, it is His or Her Majesty's Government. Our royal history is all around us, even if we take it for granted.

This book ends with the extraordinary life of our longest-reigning monarch Elizabeth II who, as much as any of her predecessors, has provided stability and a focus for national identity. By the very nature of a hereditary monarchy, we already have Charles III, William V and George VII waiting in the wings. For as long as it remains popular, England's royal future is assured.

---

* John Garner, Victoria, Australia, *This England*, summer issue 2021

Chapter 1

Egbert c.775–839
Reign: 828–839

When Queen Elizabeth II was crowned at Westminster Abbey in 1953, it was declared that she was the 42nd sovereign on the throne of England since 1066 and that her ancestry could be traced directly back to William the Conqueror. The ceremony of anointing and crowning performed on that day has been carried out in England since at least the year 828, and the Coronation oath sworn by the Queen had changed little since the time of the Anglo-Saxons. Whenever Her Majesty has visited the Channel Islands, the last of the original Norman possessions, she is still known by the 1,000-year-old title Duke of Normandy. Such is the enduring nature of our hereditary monarchy, woven like a golden thread through the tapestry of England's history.

Whilst each successive ruler has adapted and changed to suit the times, one of the monarchy's greatest strengths is that its roots are so firmly embedded in the past. No other country in the world can boast of such a long and glorious royal chronicle as England.

In 1999 the Queen granted her youngest son, Prince Edward, the title Earl of Wessex. At the time there was criticism in the media that he had been given a Ruritanian title, as if it had been plucked at random from the pages of a Victorian romantic novel or an Ivor Novello musical. Yet the Queen's choice was significant, for she had looked back a millennium-and-a-half to the very origins of the monarchy in this country.

It's said that in the year 519AD a chieftain called Cerdic founded the Kingdom of Wessex, and his descendants have reigned in an almost unbroken family line ever since. Kings from the House of Wessex were crowned on the ancient Coronation Stone at Kingston upon Thames, and previous Earls of Wessex have included King Harold (killed at the Battle of Hastings). The Queen, therefore, bestowed one of the oldest titles on her son and can claim to have Cerdic in her bloodline.

The sovereigns since King Cerdic have each left their mark but who can rightfully be called the first King of England? Many romantic stories of our royal history abound and sometimes it is difficult to separate fact from fiction. Did King Arthur really exist? Was the grave discovered under a platform at King's Cross Station really that of Queen Boudicca? Who was King Offa, responsible for the dyke from the Wye to the Dee to repel raids from Wales?

Although we have come to accept England as one large country, up to the fifth century AD it was a divided land that had been much invaded, most notably by the Romans in 43AD. Evidence of their occupation can still be seen today, from Hadrian's Wall to the famous Roman baths in Bath. Even some of our best-known roads were laid out by the Romans, such as Ermine Street, Fosse Way, and Watling Street.

Invasions by various Teutonic tribes in the fifth century saw the end of Roman domination, and Jutes, Angles and Saxons settled throughout our island and each established their own small kingdoms.

The Jutes invaded first and overtook Kent.

The Saxons later occupied land to the west of Kent, which became the Kingdom of South Saxons (Sussex). East Saxons settled north of the Thames (Essex), while Angles headed for the east coast (East Anglia) and formed two distinct groups: the north folk (Norfolk) and the south folk (Suffolk).

Other Angles settled in the middle of the country (Mercia) and the land north of the Humber (Northumbria), while remaining land in the south, including the Isle of Wight, was occupied by the West Saxons (Wessex). Thus, we can see the very origins of what have become our counties and regions today, and all eventually combined to form Angle-land – or England.

Although none of this happened overnight, and there was more than a century of bloodshed and many battles between the tribes and native Britons over territory, eventually seven distinct Kingdoms were formed. Known as the Heptarchy, they were Northumbria, Mercia, Wessex, Sussex, Essex, Kent and East Anglia, and each had their own ruler or King. There are records of numerous battles, such as one at Deorham (now Dyrham) in

Gloucester in 577, and another at Chester circa 607, where the Britons were defeated while trying to protect their land.

Often villages and hamlets were raided and overtaken, one by one, to slowly extend territorial boundaries. The Kings also fought against each other for supremacy. Æthelfrith, the first King of Northumbria was victorious at Chester, but was killed in a battle with the King of East Anglia who then took over his land.

Gradually the larger kingdoms predominated, with Northumbria being for a period the strongest. But from time to time the balance of power would change until eventually the King of Mercia extended his rule to cover East Anglia and Essex, while Sussex and Kent submitted to the King of Wessex. The seven kingdoms virtually reduced to three, with earlier kingdoms becoming shires to make government easier.

None of the three kingdoms had total supremacy, however, and each still battled to take control. The King of Northumbria was finally defeated by the Mercians in 658; the death of Mercia's King Offa in 796 brought an end to over a hundred years of dominance, and by the year 802 Wessex had become the most significant area with King Egbert at the helm.

After a 26-year reign as King of Wessex, and a major victory at the Battle of Ellendum (now Wroughton, near Swindon) Egbert was crowned King of the English in 828. He was a direct descendant of Cerdic, the very first King of Wessex, and through him could supposedly trace his ancestry back to the god Woden (or Wotan). Later Anglo-Saxon chroniclers fancifully claimed that they could even trace Cerdic back to Adam and Eve, via a son of Noah! An illustrious foundation on which our monarchy has been built.

There is no actual record of Egbert's Coronation, but the earliest known ritual to survive is from the mid-eighth century, which had a solemn blessing and a crowning, probably preceded by an anointing with oil. The ceremony certainly had a Christian basis, and there were Biblical echoes of Solomon's anointing by Zadok the priest and Nathan the prophet.

Saxon kings were crowned at both Kingston upon Thames and Winchester, but the venue for Egbert's Coronation is sadly unrecorded. We do know that he was crowned King of the English (Rex Anglorum), rather than King of England. Almost 400 years were to pass before monarchs began officially calling themselves after their country rather than their people.

King Egbert was born between 770-780AD and was the son of Ealhmund, King of Kent. Egbert has been acknowledged as an outstanding ruler, a competent military leader, and effectively defeated invasions that threatened his kingdom, particularly from the Welsh. By the time he died, on 4 February, 839, probably in his sixties, he had ruled for 37 years and had founded a dynasty that still survives to this day.

He was buried at Winchester in the old Saxon Minster, where his chaplain was St Swithin. Egbert's bones are now preserved at the present Winchester Cathedral in a mortuary chest above the choir screen. Visitors to another great English cathedral, Wells in Somerset, can see an image of Egbert, portrayed in a now weather-beaten statue, still proudly wearing a crown, as an enduring reminder of his place as the very first King of the English 1,200 years ago.

Chapter 2

Ethelwulf   Ethelbald   Ethelbert
c.800–858   c.831–860   c.836–866
Reign: c.839–858   Reign: c.858–860   Reign: c.860–866

King Egbert of Wessex was the first to establish the prospect of a single monarch ruling over the whole of England, but the constant danger of invasion remained. The Vikings from across the North Sea were a particular threat and plagued Egbert's successors for almost two centuries. Only the leadership skills and fortitude of his sons and grandsons preserved our island from Danish ravages and prevented the total conquest of England by Viking invaders.

When King Egbert died in February 839, his eldest son Ethelwulf succeeded to the throne and was crowned at Kingston upon Thames, Surrey, later that year. Little is known of Ethelwulf's early life. He was born around 800 and became Subregulus (or deputy ruler) of Kent, Essex, Sussex and Surrey circa 825, after leading a great army and seizing the region to extend the kingdom of Wessex.

Ethelwulf was not a soldier at heart and, as a devout Roman Catholic, preferred to defend the church rather than fight for territory. Historically Ethelwulf has two main claims to fame: he is best remembered as being the father of Alfred the Great, and his reign is chiefly known for its periods of bad weather.

Very early in Ethelwulf's reign blight fell on the orchards and fields of England, and the King was told of a priest's visitation from an angel with a dire warning. The failure of the crops was due to man's sin and lack of regard for the Lord's Day. Unless the people of England repented and showed respect for holy days, the country would be invaded by heathens in

17

ships who would destroy the land and massacre its inhabitants. Ethelwulf planned to visit Rome, believing that a pilgrimage of prayer and a blessing from the Pope would save his people, but before he could depart the prophecy seemingly came true. The menace of Viking invasion that had plagued England began to escalate. The ninth-century *Anglo-Saxon Chronicle* tells of "great slaughter" in London, Canterbury and Rochester in 839, and the following year that "King Ethelwulf fought at Charmouth with 35 ship's crews, and the Danes remained masters of the place".

Five years passed before the tide seemed to turn and the "men of Somersetshire and Dorsetshire" fought the Danish army near the mouth of the River Parrett at Bridgewater Bay and "obtained the victory". Although the heathen army continued the assault, Ethelwulf's men remained victorious. In 851 a large army was defeated at Sandwich in Kent, with nine ships taken and the rest dispersed. The *Chronicle* reports: "The same year came 350 ships into the mouth of the Thames; the crew of which went upon land, and stormed Canterbury and London, and then marched southward over the Thames into Surrey. Here Ethelwulf, at the head of the West Saxon army, fought with them at Ockley, and made the greatest slaughter of the heathen army that we have ever heard reported to this present day." It was not, however, to be a lasting victory and the Vikings merely bided their time before the next onslaught, setting up camps on the Isles of Thanet and Sheppey.

In the ninth century our island was far from a united kingdom, and the threat was not just from overseas invaders. In the year 853 the Welsh crossed the border to wreak havoc on English land. King Ethelwulf and his army marched into North Wales to subdue the marauders and restore order. In a divided country the king had to be prepared for attack from every quarter, and each region had its own sub-ruler or king just waiting for an opportunity to usurp his position. It was Ethelwulf's strong religious beliefs and formidable family that helped him survive.

In around the year 830 King Ethelwulf had married Osburga of Hampshire. They had four sons, Ethelbald, Ethelbert, Ethelred and Alfred, and one daughter, Ethelswitha. Some sources claim a fifth son, Athelstan, although from what is known of his life it is now generally agreed that this was actually Ethelwulf's brother rather than his son.

Ethelwulf's great ambition had been to make a pilgrimage to Rome, but the constant need to defend his realm forced him to remain in England. Despairing that he would never be able to make the journey, in 853 he sent his youngest son Alfred to receive a blessing from the Pope. The four-year-old boy was despatched with a large escort "of men, noble and simple" to protect him, as the Vikings were destroying and plundering areas of Europe en route to Italy. The royal pilgrim met Pope Leo IV, and the pontiff wrote to King Ethelwulf that he had adopted Alfred as his "spiritual son".

Ethelwulf's health began to deteriorate and he spent much time in prayer. His wife, Queen Osburga, had recently died; Vikings based on the Isle of Sheppey continued to besiege the east and south coasts, and the king no longer had the strength to fight. In 854 Ethelwulf gave a tenth of his land for church and monastic use and for his own everlasting salvation, and finally made plans to visit Rome himself.

Before his departure, news reached England that Pope Leo IV had died and Ethelwulf arrived in Rome during the summer of 855 to greet the newly elected Pope Benedict III. Ethelwulf remained in Rome for 12 months before returning to England via France, where he stayed as a guest of the equally devout Charles the Bald. The two kings formed an alliance against the Vikings. Monasteries and castles had been burnt on the banks of the Seine, treasures had been stolen and people massacred, including 126 monks. Somewhat surprisingly it was announced that the widowed Ethelwulf was to marry Charles's daughter, Judith, who was scarcely more than 13 years old. It can only be assumed that the union was for political reasons.

The wedding took place at Verberie-sur-Oise on 1 October, 856, and at the same time Judith was anointed and crowned Queen of Wessex. Ethelwulf returned to England after more than a year's absence, bringing with him his young bride. The noblemen of England, who did not welcome the French child as their queen, treated this unexpected development with outrage. Ethelwulf's eldest son Ethelbald had taken over his father's role during the long pilgrimage and was now reluctant to relinquish the power. Soon England faced the threat of civil war between Ethelbald's supporters, who wanted him to seize the crown, and those loyal to Ethelwulf who longed to see him resume his rightful place.

Ethelwulf, now weak and in poor health, was not prepared to fight his own son. To put an end to contention over succession, Ethelwulf created a system that existed up to the 20th century, whereby the oldest living son of the monarch would always inherit the throne. This established a ruling dynasty on the basis that the crown could be passed on to a natural successor by birthright, rather than having to win leadership through battle. In theory this should have brought harmony, but it did nothing to stop Ethelbald plotting to overthrow his father.

For the unity of his family and his country, Ethelwulf stood aside and allowed Ethelbald to become king in all but name, while reducing his own authority to govern only the regions of Kent, Essex, Sussex and Surrey. Within two years Ethelwulf was dead. He died on 13 January, 858, and was buried in Winchester Cathedral. His will was characteristically generous, benefiting both the poor and needy in England and the church. Few of King Ethelwulf's possessions are known to have survived, but his ornate gold ring is now at the British Museum in London.

For the only time in English history, the crown passed to each one of the King's four sons in turn and a series of very short reigns followed. First, 24- year old Ethelbald was crowned at Kingston upon Thames in 858.

Unscrupulous and manipulative, he was a very different character from his pious father. Within a short time he had caused a scandal by marrying his stepmother, Judith, at Chester. She was still only 15 years old and this second marriage resulted in even greater outrage than when Ethelwulf had married her. A contemporary document declared that the wedding was "contrary to the law of God and the honour of Christendom" and that "all men in England" were appalled by the development. The marriage was soon annulled, and Ethelbald died on 20 December, 860, after an unhappy reign that lasted less than two years. He was buried at Sherborne Abbey in Dorset.

Ethelwulf's second son Ethelbert was the next to inherit but ruled for just five years. Born around 836, very little information about him survives, other than that he had a unifying effect on his country and had the popularity that his brother lacked. The *Anglo-Saxon Chronicle* states that Ethelbert "succeeded to the whole kingdom and held it in good order and great tranquillity". Early in his reign the Vikings returned with a vengeance, taking Winchester by force, but were driven back by armies from Hampshire and Berkshire under Ethelbert's command. The threat of invasion abated, and England experienced a period of peace. Believing that the enemy had been defeated, Ethelbert was lulled into a false sense of security, not realising that the Vikings were merely changing tactics and far worse was to come. King Ethelbert died unmarried and childless in 866 and was buried beside his brother at Sherborne.

When Ethelwulf's third son, Ethelred, succeeded to the throne, larger armies than ever before were waiting to attack with a renewed determination to conquer. By All Saints' Day 866 the city of York had been overtaken. Soon the great abbeys at Peterborough, Crowland and Ely were in flames, and the battle to save England would cost a king his life.

Chapter 3

Ethelred c.837–871
Reign: 866–871

"And now, new enemies arose, who, for a long time, troubled England sorely. These were the Northmen, the people of Denmark and Norway, whom the English call the Danes. They were a warlike people, quite at home upon the sea; not Christians; very daring and cruel. They came over in ships, and plundered and burned wheresoever they landed. They came back, over and over again, burning and plundering, and laying England waste." Charles Dickens, *A Child's History of England*

England at the end of the ninth century was in a perilous state. The Vikings, who for so long had attacked, destroyed and pillaged during raids, were now determined to conquer. Where previously they had stolen treasures, they now wanted to take land. For the young King Ethelred, still only in his mid-twenties, the Viking invasion would dominate his reign.

Ethelred (not to be confused with Ethelred the Unready) was born around 837, the third son of King Ethelwulf and Queen Osburga. Although his birthplace is unrecorded, the family estate at Wantage, Berkshire (then in the region known as Wessex), a fertile area of farmland, seems the most likely contender. The peace of rural England at this time would have been an idyllic place for children to grow up, but even then there were tales of Viking invaders crossing the nearby Lambourn Downs into Wessex.

His father had only recently been crowned king and the threat to his country and its people must have weighed heavily. During Ethelred's childhood the south-east of England was especially vulnerable, and the sight of Viking "dragon" ships, with their high sterns carved in the shape of fearsome beasts, must have struck terror into many hearts as they approached the shore.

We know little of Ethelred's education, which possibly centred on hunting and the art of battle. It is recorded that Queen Osburga read Anglo-Saxon poetry from a book to her children, which tells us that books were available to them and that there was a degree of literacy in the family. It is also known that Ethelred's father had a secretary called Felix, who was "well versed in Latin" and could have instructed the king's children.

Certainly it is documented that Ethelred's younger brother Alfred struggled to learn Latin, and eventually mastered it in adulthood, so it is possible that Ethelred was taught, too. Doubtless religious texts would also have been studied, as his parents were devout Christians, and as Ethelred grew up his own faith deepened. Because of his piety he is known now as Saint Ethelred.

Ethelred succeeded his brother Ethelbert to the throne in the year 866 and, like his predecessors, was crowned at Kingston upon Thames. Whether or not Ethelred had a Queen at this point is unknown, although he certainly married at around this time. Nothing is known about his wife, thought to be Wulfrida, but they had two sons. The first, Ethelwald, was born around 868, while the second, Ethelhelm, remains an obscure figure.

Some consider him to have been Archbishop Ethelhelm of Canterbury, who died in January 923, but there is no conclusive proof to support this. Considering King Ethelred's strong religious beliefs, the idea of his son becoming Archbishop of Canterbury is not beyond the realms of possibility.

What we do know for certain is that Ethelred inherited a kingdom under threat. In 866 the Danes landed in East Anglia, marched through Lincolnshire, crossed the Humber and on towards the city of York, arriving on All Saints' Day. Civil unrest in Northumbria, the region where York was situated at this time, distracted the people and enabled the Viking leader Ivar the Boneless to sneak in with his army and take control. Only the swift intervention of King Ethelred and his army prevented the invaders from overtaking Nottingham and territory south of the area then known as Mercia.

A visit to the Jorvik Viking Centre in York gives an indication of life during this period of occupation. More than 800 items were uncovered on the site and streets have been recreated, complete with sounds and smells, to give a dramatic impression of life at this time.

They may have been the enemy, but the Vikings were nevertheless a skilled people and set up workshops in textiles, metalwork, bone and antler carving, woodworking, and jewellery. They established a trading community, and their influence can still be seen to this day. Coppergate, for example, was the area of the city where copper goods were crafted. The suffix gate that is so prevalent in York comes from the Viking word gata, meaning street.

Although a relatively peaceful community was established in York, the Vikings continued to wreak havoc in the Fens, destroying abbeys at Peterborough, Crowland and Ely. In the autumn of 869 they captured Edmund, the sub-ruler of East Anglia, tied him to a tree and fired arrows at him. His body, wrote an eye-witness, was like "a thistle covered in prickles".

Edmund had tried to protect his Christian land from the heathens, and martyrdom has made him the subject of many a stained-glass window in churches along the east coast. There his body was enshrined in Suffolk and eventually became Bury St Edmunds where a great abbey was built to house his relics.

Having plundered as far north as the River Tyne, established the city of York as their capital, and taken control of East Anglia, the Vikings now planned to march southwards to conquer the region of Wessex. Throughout 870 they appeared to be living peaceably on farms around East Anglia, and the threat of further invasion seemed to have subsided. But King Ethelred was merely being lulled into a false sense of security.

In December 870, when least expected because of the poor weather conditions, under the command of Halfdan (brother of Ivar the Boneless) the Vikings set up camp to the east of Reading, near Wantage.

The choice of location was deliberate for this area of Berkshire was the royal manor, King Ethelred's own territory. Within three days the infiltrators had begun building a strong defensive wall around their camp and would have become firmly entrenched had a party of Vikings not set out to steal horses and supplies from neighbouring dwellings.

Some became lost due to the weather conditions and lack of local knowledge. Their cover was blown and the alarm went out. King Ethelred mustered his main army and led the attack, killing all Vikings found outside the newly built ramparts, although the Danes maintained possession of their camp.

King Ethelred, with his brother Alfred as second in command, spent the next four days drawing up battle plans to lead his army across the Berkshire Downs. In the contemporary *Anglo-Saxon Chronicle* it is recorded that the area was Ashdown, but where Ethelred actually fought the Vikings has been the subject of conjecture. The Vikings, drawn up in two divisions, were ready to meet them. Ethelred also divided his own men into two forces but then, before battle could commence, the King disappeared.

With the Vikings eager to fight, Alfred sent a messenger out to search for Ethelred. He was found in his tent, with a priest saying Mass. The kneeling King was urged to leave the tent immediately and return to the battlefield, but Ethelred declared that he would never place man before God and refused to leave until the service had ended. Only when the mass was over did the King return to his army.

At first the Vikings seemed to have the advantage. They were in a high position at the top of the Downs and could charge down to Ethelred's army beneath them. The English weather, however, worked against them. The January winds and ice made the slopes hazardous and the Vikings suffered heavy losses as they literally fell at the feet of Ethelred's men.

By nightfall, the men of Wessex were celebrating victory, while the remaining Vikings sought protection behind the walled ramparts and planned their next move. Although Ethelred's men guarded the camp, over the next fortnight the Vikings stealthily slipped out in small groups under the cover of darkness and, probably joined by reinforcements from other parts of the country, set up another base two miles from Basingstoke. By the time Ethelred became aware of this new camp, the Vikings were fully prepared and an attempt to overcome them failed.

Two months passed before King Ethelred attacked again. At the end of March a battle took place at Meretun, some sources say "Marden", which is thought to be the Wiltshire village of Marten near Marlborough. Others, however, believe it to be Martin, near Cranborne in Dorset.

Once again, the *Anglo-Saxon Chronicle* tells us that the Vikings were in two divisions and that there was "much slaughter" on both sides. Heahmund, the Bishop of Sherbourne, was among the men of Wessex killed and King Ethelred was wounded that day, too, although the extent of his injuries is unrecorded. Certainly the English withdrew unexpectedly by evening, a sign that their leader was probably debilitated, and the Vikings began to look increasingly invincible. Within days more Danish ships crossed the Channel and a vast army of invaders marched towards the Viking base camp near Reading.

On 23 April, 871, came the news that King Ethelred was dead. Barely 30 years old, the King whose short reign had been dominated by aggressors was laid to rest in Wimborne Minster, Dorset. It was now left to his brother, Alfred the Great, to take up England's cause.

Chapter 4

Alfred the Great c.849–899
Reign: 871–899

There was not English armour left,
Nor any English thing,
When Alfred came to Athelney
To be an English King.
G. K. Chesterton, *Ballad of the White Horse*

When we think of Alfred the Great today, we instantly remember him as the King who burnt some cakes. It is a story that has been retold for more than 1,000 years, and in the 1940s the Ministry of Food even went so far as to suggest the type of cake that Alfred was baking.

In a leaflet to encourage the patriotic use of home-produced oatmeal in place of flour, particularly when bread became rationed after the war, the Ministry stated: "The cakes that King Alfred burned were, in all probability, oaten cakes." Age-old recipes suddenly became popular once again, and a government subsidy made oatmeal and rolled oats easily affordable.

Although his culinary skills have been questioned, there is little doubt about King Alfred's achievements. He has been credited with establishing the English Navy; he instituted a judicial system of trial by jury that still exists in our courts today, and encouraged education and literacy to give the English people a sense of identity. Because of his own writings, and a contemporary biography written by Bishop Asser at the end of the ninth century, we know far more about Alfred than any of his royal predecessors.

Alfred was born at Wantage, Berkshire, around 849 and as the youngest son of King Ethelwulf and Queen Osburga, it seemed unlikely that he would ever succeed to the crown. At the age of four, following the death of his mother, he was sent to Rome to receive a blessing from Pope Leo IV.

It would seem extraordinary for us today to send such a young child abroad on a pilgrimage, but Alfred was accompanied by a large retinue of men and the experience was undoubtedly character building. Undaunted, Alfred made the long journey to Italy again two years later with his father to meet the newly elected Pope Benedict III. These early experiences formed the foundation of Alfred's lifelong Christian faith.

Back in England, Alfred's formative years were spent on the royal estates at Wantage, Chippenham, Wilton and Winchester, during the successive reigns of his father and three brothers. Education at this time was lacking, with generally greater emphasis placed on the protection of material possessions and lands from the marauding Vikings than on schooling. In adult life Alfred complained that he had not learned to read until he was 12 years old and that there had been no good teachers in the whole of Wessex.

As a small child he had enjoyed listening to his mother reading Anglo-Saxon poems, ballads and battle songs and, although he learned them off by heart, he was frustrated at being unable to read them for himself. As King he wrote, "When I began to reign, I cannot remember one south of the Thames who could explain his service book in English," and that his great desire had been for every youth to "abide at his book till he can well understand English writing."

Although Alfred struggled to learn Latin, and did not master it until the age of 38, he enjoyed looking at illuminated manuscripts and religious texts in Latin. He attended Mass daily, and throughout his life found comfort in the music of the Psalms. He was well acquainted with Bishop Swithin of Winchester, later venerated as a saint, from whom he received wise counsel.

By the time Alfred reached the age of 17 he had developed into a strong character, both physically and mentally. A skilled soldier and hunter, he was a practical and methodical youth, with an eye for detail. It is said that he carried a small notebook with him at all times and jotted down thoughts, stories and prayers, and liked an ordered and disciplined life so that each hour of the day was usefully filled.

He even designed a lantern clock, with rings around a candle inside to mark an hour's burning time (he had 12-inch candles made, each lasting exactly four hours), so that the day could be divided up accurately.

When Ethelred succeeded as King in 866, he did not hesitate to have his young brother Alfred by his side as secundarius, his second-in-command. Gone were the days when brother fought against brother for the crown.

The short reign of King Ethelred was dominated by Viking invasion, with many brutal battles to secure land. Whenever defeat loomed, it was Alfred who gave encouragement to the troops and restored morale. A white horse carved into the chalk of the Berkshire Downs at Uffington is popularly believed to mark the site of Alfred's victory in a battle with the Danes in January 871. Although the figure itself is likely to date back to the Bronze Age, being in the area where the battle was fought and won, the white horse has now become associated with Alfred.

Some nine battles were fought that year, with King Ethelred mortally wounded in March 871. Although Ethelred had two sons, it was twenty-two-year-old Alfred who had won the confidence of the army through his strong leadership skills and was declared King on 23 April, 871.

There is no record of Alfred's Coronation, although it is believed to have taken place at Kingston upon Thames. Alfred had married Ealswyth in 868 and the couple had at least three sons and three daughters. The family were united in a strong Christian faith. One daughter, Ethelgiva, eventually became Abbess of Shaftesbury Abbey, and Queen Ealswyth spent the final years of her life as a nun at St Mary's Abbey, Winchester. Realising the importance of education, Alfred ensured that his children were given formal lessons at court so that all could read and write.

Like his predecessors, Alfred had to be a warrior-king with the prime concern of protecting his country. But weary of fighting, early in his reign Alfred bargained with the invaders and negotiated peace based on a financial settlement – which we have come to know as Danegeld. The Vikings left their base camp at Reading and moved further north, leaving Alfred's homeland in Wessex free from strife for several years.

Lincolnshire, Derbyshire and Northumbria suffered greatly as a result, and by the year 875 the unscrupulous Vikings began to covet the south of England once again. That autumn they set up an impenetrable camp at Wareham, Dorset, where they remained for a year before heading off to Devon and establishing themselves at Exeter.

Alfred pursued them with his army and again negotiated with the leaders. A storm in the English Channel off the coast of Swanage had sunk 120 Viking ships on their way to Devon and, without the back-up he needed, the leader Guthrum agreed to peace and relocated his army to Gloucester.

It was only a temporary truce and shortly after Twelfth Night, 878, Guthrum made a surprise attack on King Alfred's royal palace at

Chippenham. Alfred, Ealswyth and their children fled to avoid capture. At the same time a new fleet of Viking ships reached the Devon coast.

The contemporary *Anglo-Saxon Chronicle* records that Alfred "uneasily sought the woods and fastnesses of the moors", and took refuge on the Isle of Athelney, amid the Somerset marshes.

While at Athelney, King Alfred burned the cakes! Unrecognised by the local people, who could have no idea what their monarch looked like, Alfred and his family were able to take shelter anonymously at a peasant cottage. Sources vary as to whether it was a cowherd's, swineherd's or woodcutter's cottage, but one day the wife asked Alfred to watch some cakes that she had left baking on the hearth, and the preoccupied King unwittingly allowed them to burn. The wife severely scolded him on her return, unaware of his identity. Alfred later rewarded his hosts generously for their hospitality and we can only guess at the wife's reaction when she discovered that she had shouted at the King.

Alfred gathered an army of local men around him and a campaign of attack was formulated from his Athelney hideaway, with messages being spread across the land to the King's loyal supporters to be ready for the fight. Good news eventually reached Alfred that a Saxon army led by the Earl of Devon had defeated another Danish attack, with more than 1,000 Vikings slaughtered. A legend from this period is that Alfred disguised himself as a minstrel and played at a Viking camp to try and gain information about his enemy.

Seven weeks after Easter, 878, Alfred's supporters were summoned to Egbert's Stone in the Forest of Selwood, from where the King marched his men to regain the royal lands at Chippenham. The *Anglo-Saxon Chronicle* tells us that "there came to meet him all the people of Somersetshire, and Wiltshire, and that part of Hampshire which is on the side of the sea; and they rejoiced to see him" and that they "put the Danish army to flight"'. After 14 days, it is said that the Vikings were "terrified by hunger and cold and fear" and surrendered, even offering hostages as a guarantee of peace.

A treaty was agreed at Wedmore, which ensured withdrawal of enemy forces from Wessex, and established territorial boundaries. Incredibly, the animosity that had for so long existed between Alfred and his enemy Guthrum seemed to disappear. It is recorded that there was a celebratory feast and merrymaking between the Saxons and Danes, and that Guthrum became a Christian, was baptised with Alfred as his godfather, and went to live peacefully in East Anglia. Guthrum set up bases at Cambridge and Thetford, where his troops became farmers.

Peace was not, however, enjoyed by the whole of England. More Vikings attacked Kent and tried to take over Rochester. In 886 Alfred had to fight to secure London as Vikings sailed up the Thames. He fortified the city by developing "boroughs", whereby settlers received plots of land and in return manned the defences in times of attack.

As a result of Alfred's planning, London's streets were formulated. If he could glance at a map of London today, particularly in the area between Cheapside and the River Thames, he would still recognise his street plan. In other parts of England Alfred negotiated a partition treaty with the Danes, using the Roman Watling Street as a boundary line, allowing them to have certain areas of northern and eastern England.

In 893 more Vikings sailed across to Kent and Sussex. It took Alfred some four years to overcome this invasion and restore order. Alfred realised that the invaders had to cross the Channel to reach us, and if he could thwart them at sea they could be prevented from reaching our shores. Alfred built bigger ships to defend our island, which were double the length and had twice as many oars as Viking ships, and formed the first English Navy.

With a Navy to protect the coast, Alfred turned his attention to the land. He had 25 key towns fortified with garrisons that could repel any attack at the outset, before invaders could establish a stronghold. He also instituted an early form of Home Guard called the fyrd, whereby working men could be called upon as soldiers in times of emergency and return to their occupation when not required.

Using a rota basis, Alfred was always sure of a supply of men to defend his kingdom, and during a long military campaign this meant that people's livelihoods continued. This form of protection proved so successful that in the final years of Alfred's reign all attempts at invasion were thwarted.

Not having to continually fight battles saved money and Alfred spent half the revenue on improving education. He set up schools, employing the best teachers he could find so that literacy would be widespread in England. Conscious that the published works of English writers at the time were poetical, he encouraged the writing of prose and translated books himself from Latin into Anglo-Saxon, including works by Orosius and the Venerable Bede. As a result, he has been called the creator of English Literature. With a firm belief in the importance of history, Alfred initiated the *Anglo-Saxon Chronicle* so that the history of England could be recorded for posterity. Backdated to Julius Caesar's raid of 55BC, the *Chronicle* continued until 1154.

Because of his religious beliefs, Alfred paid for churches and monasteries that had been ruined by the Vikings to be restored. He also founded Shaftesbury Abbey and designed the New Minster at Winchester. With a sense of justice and morality, he reshaped English laws to bring stability and order to his people. He extended the production of coinage, establishing a Royal Mint at Winchester, with coins from that period referring to Alfred as King of the English.

He encouraged craftsmanship, particularly gold and silverwork, and an elaborately decorated jewel found near Athelney in 1693 bears the inscription "Alfred had me made". Thought to have belonged to Alfred himself, it can now be seen at the Ashmolean Museum in Oxford.

Many places in England still have reminders of King Alfred today. There are well known statues of him at Wantage (Oxfordshire), Winchester (Dorset) and Pewsey (Wiltshire). His image can be seen in a stained-glass window at Portsmouth Cathedral, and many heroic portraits have been painted over the centuries. A copy of King Alfred's will is kept at Arreton Manor on the Isle of Wight, the original house having been left to his son Ethelward, and coins from his reign have been unearthed.

The most unusual item to be associated with him must be the Blowing Stone at the village of Kingston Lisle in Oxfordshire. Tradition says that Alfred blew through holes in the stone, making a trumpet-like sound to summon his troops to battle. The stone was moved to its present location in the mid-18th century, where it remains as a curiosity for tourists.

King Alfred died on 26 October, 899, at the age of 50. and was initially buried in the Old Minster at Winchester, before being transferred to the New Minster once building work was completed around 903. In the 12th century his remains were removed to Hyde Abbey, which was later destroyed during the Reformation. In 1999 a Community Archaeology Project run by Winchester Museums managed to confirm the site of the royal tomb, although his bones had been scattered and the search for them is ongoing.

Never actually called "Great" in his own lifetime, Alfred's epitaph could be his own words: "So long as I have lived, I have striven to live worthily."

Chapter 5

Edward the Elder c.874–924
Reign: 899–924

As the son and successor of Alfred the Great, Edward had a very hard act to follow. Rather than be overshadowed by his father's achievements, he strove instead to carry forward many of Alfred's plans. Edward proved to be a strong military leader in the ongoing campaign to defeat Viking invaders and re-conquered much of England from them, something his predecessors had been unable to achieve.

By the end of his reign he had gained authority over all Danish-held land as far north as the Humber and established an administrative framework for the whole of England. He also has the distinction of having fathered more children than any other English monarch, ensuring that the bloodline of Alfred the Great would continue.

A 12th-century manuscript tells how Edward was summoned to his father's deathbed and was "earnestly bade to love God" and to place all his hope in Him. Not only did Edward fulfil his father's desire to build a new Minster at Winchester, and restore churches desecrated by the Vikings, but in 907 he founded Romsey Abbey in Hampshire which is still thriving more than 1,100 years later.

Edward's exact birth date is unknown, but he is believed to have been born around 874 in Wessex, the second child and eldest son of King Alfred and Queen Ealswyth. Much of his early life is unrecorded, but in 893 he married a noblewoman called Egwina, with whom he had two sons and a daughter. Later, when he became King, the marriage was annulled and Egwina was cast aside.

Even though he was the eldest son, Edward's pathway to the throne was not automatically guaranteed. Towards the end of Alfred the Great's reign, Edward had been appointed sub-King of Kent, but Alfred did not actually name a successor, and on his death in 899 a rebellion broke out in favour of Edward's cousin Ethelwald (son of Alfred's brother King Ethelred). With two contenders for the throne, the Witan (the national council or parliament of Saxon England) voted in favour of Edward.

Ethelwald did not accept this decision. He and his supporters seized the royal palace at Wimborne and lands at Christchurch. Immediately Edward gathered together his army and headed south. Fearing defeat, the cowardly Ethelwald slipped away under the cover of darkness and headed to Northumbria where he sought refuge among the Norsemen of York. Edward was crowned at Kingston upon Thames on 8 June, 900.

Shortly afterwards Edward married for a second time, taking Elfleda from Wiltshire as his wife. The couple had two sons and eight daughters, but King Edward certainly could not settle into a life of domestic bliss. In the north of England his cousin Ethelwald was still plotting to overthrow him and take the throne for himself.

Ever since Alfred the Great's treaty with the Danish leader Guthrum, the Vikings had kept to their agreed territory north of Watling Street, known as Danelaw, but now Ethelwald encouraged them to invade Edward's kingdom. He joined forces with Guthrum's son, Eric, and attacked both Mercia and Wessex.

King Edward's retaliation had an element of surprise. Rather than defending his land in the south, he marched his army northwards and invaded the Viking's own territory instead, reclaiming that part of the country for himself. Then, as he returned home, he confronted the Viking army on their way back. Both Ethelwald and Eric were killed in the subsequent Battle of Holme.

This did not, however, bring an end to the Viking problem. In 906 Edward defeated a large Danish force that had invaded Kent and Essex, and the following year signed a peace treaty with both the Danes of East Anglia and the Kingdom of York (at that time Northumbria). The contemporary *Anglo-Saxon Chronicle* also reveals that Edward rebuilt Chester, which implies that the city had been beseiged.

In his attempt to defend the country, Edward was aided by his formidable sister Ethelfleda – known as the Lady of Mercia – and with her help regained the Midlands and south east of England. Ethelfleda oversaw the building of many defensive fortresses (burghs) throughout the land, which became both garrison strongholds from which to launch attacks and places of refuge when under siege. Advancing along the boundary of the River Trent, she fortified Tamworth and Stafford before turning southwards, securing the valley of Avon with a fort at Warwick.

She then forced the Vikings out of Derby and Leicester. By the year 910 the *Chronicle* tells us that "King Edward took possession of London, and of Oxford", and a great fleet of Vikings from Brittany were "greatly ravaged" and perished at sea.

For the next eight years Edward and Ethelfleda pushed the boundaries of Wessex and Mercia northwards to gain full control of England. William of Malmesbury, writing in the 12th century, has left us with a fascinating portrait of Ethelfleda:

"She was the delight of his subjects, the dread of his enemies, a woman of an enlarged soul . . . this spirited heroine assisted her brother greatly with her advice, was of equal service in building cities, nor could you easily discern whether it was more owing to fortune or her own exertions, that a woman should be able to protect men at home, and to intimidate them abroad."

Ethelfleda died at her Tamworth home in 918, and was laid to rest in St Peter's Abbey, Gloucester, where the Cathedral now stands. By this time Edward was in a strong position. Soon the kings of Wales and the Welsh people gave him their allegiance. Then the kings of the north – Donald of Strathclyde and Constantine II of the Scots – submitted to Edward and accepted him as overlord. It is significant that Edward took the title King of the Angles and Saxons. His predecessors may have considered themselves rulers of the English people, but in reality were really Kings of Wessex. Edward clearly regarded himself to be King of all England.

Although the region of Mercia had long been independent and was now ruled by Ethelfleda's daughter Elfwinn, Edward soon deposed her and sent her to a nunnery, to gain total sovereignty himself, absorbing Mercia into his own kingdom.

In 919 Edward married for a third time, taking Edgiva, daughter of Ealdorman Sigehelm of Kent, as his bride. They had two sons and three daughters. This means that Edward fathered at least 18 children, and probably more that did not survive infancy. Three of his sons succeeded as kings of England, six daughters became nuns, and the remaining daughters entered dynastic marriages. Edward's sons-in-law included four kings, two dukes, a French count, and Holy Roman Emperor Otto the Great.

Although conflict with the Vikings did not cease, there were no further major battles during his reign. Forts, city walls, and sea defences did much to repel invaders. By restoring Danelaw to Saxon rule, Edward established a more united country and was said to have spread "English influence" through his laws.

Although he lacked his father's religious conviction, he reorganised the church, creating many new bishoprics, including Wells. As an outstanding military leader, raising three new armies every year, Edward defeated the Vikings through a policy of sheer aggression. To him, attack was the best form of defence.

In 924 Edward was forced to lead his army northwards to put down a Cambro-Mercian rebellion in Cheshire. He died at Farndon-on-Dee, Cheshire, on 17 July, 924, and was succeeded by his son Athelstan, the first child from his first marriage. Some 55 years after his death he was given the title Edward the Elder to distinguish him from the murdered Edward the Martyr.

Edward was buried in the new Minster at Winchester, which he had built. After the Norman Conquest, the Minster was replaced by Hyde Abbey to the north of the city and, in 1110, Edward's coffin and that of his father and mother were carried through the streets in procession and buried in front of the high altar. The Abbey was later destroyed during Henry VIII's dissolution of the monasteries and the King's last resting place today is unknown, but is certainly within the newly developed Hyde Abbey Garden site created in 2003, where the outline of the old abbey can now be seen.

Chapter 6

Athelstan	Edmund	Edred
c.894–939	c.921–946	c.923–955
Reign: 924–939	Reign: 939–946	Reign: 946–955

King Athelstan has gone down in English history as one of our more heroic monarchs. Singled out by his grandfather, Alfred the Great, as having strong leadership qualities, he never lost a battle and is known as Athelstan the Glorious. Many scholars consider him to be the first true King of All England, while others even go as far as to suggest that Athelstan and the legendary King Arthur were one and the same.

William of Malmesbury, writing in the 12th century, tells us that King Alfred embraced Athelstan affectionately "when he was a boy of astonishing beauty and graceful manners . . . and made him a knight unusually early, giving him a scarlet cloak, a belt studded with diamonds, and a Saxon sword with a golden scabbard."

Athelstan carried the sword for life, using it victoriously in battle as his Excalibur. William of Malmesbury's description of Athelstan as a slim, blond youth – "His hair, as we ourselves have seen from his relics, flaxon, mingled with gold threads" – adds to the romantic image.

Factually we know that Athelstan was a successful ruler. He secured peace for the country, laid down laws that made life easier for his people and is said to have given the English a sense of identity. He established the concept of monarchy as we would recognise it today and cultivated the image of being "royal". Athelstan was the first of our kings to be pictured on coins wearing a crown and, like so many of his successors, he amassed a great collection of jewellery and works of art.

He also received international recognition, had extensive contact with foreign monarchs and formed alliances by arranging marriages for five of his sisters to European kings. Several foreign princes were sent to England to be educated at his court; the King of Norway even presented Athelstan with a ship as a gift of thanks for the way in which his son had been taught by English tutors.

Athelstan was born in the year 894, a son of King Edward the Elder and Queen Egwina. At the time of his birth Egwina was his father's mistress and so technically Athelstan was illegitimate. He grew up and was educated in the home of his redoubtable aunt, Ethelfleda, and had a particular interest in geometry and science.

Like his grandfather, he had a great love of literature, was an avid reader and throughout his life enjoyed the company of poets and writers. He also encouraged the translation of the Bible into English.

Athelstan became King at around the age of 30 after his father's death in 924 and was crowned at Kingston upon Thames the following year. The Saxon Coronation Stone which now stands outside the Guildhall is carved with Athelstan's name to record the event.

One of the great achievements of his reign was to extend the boundaries of his kingdom. At a ceremony in 927 at Eamont Bridge near Penrith, where Dacre Castle stands today, rulers of Scotland and the north acknowledged Athelstan as overlord. At Hereford in 930 five Welsh kings did the same, establishing the river Wye as the Anglo-Welsh border, and paid him in gold, silver, cattle, hunting dogs and falcons as a gesture of submission. Thus, the country of England was formed.

Particularly interested in building and architecture, Athelstan encouraged the development of new towns and gave tax benefits to the inhabitants, making it more attractive to live in built-up areas than in the country. He established a formal organisation for stonemasons who were involved in building work. This eventually led to the formation of the Freemasons. He took control of the currency and regulated the weight of gold and silver in coins to try and prevent fraud. As a religious man, he also banned Sunday trading and imposed harsh penalties on anyone who broke the law.

The chronicler Simon of Durham made an unusual comment about Athelstan, claiming that in 933 he had ordered his half-brother Edwin to be drowned at sea. Tradition has it that a malicious member of the royal household had it rumoured that Edwin was plotting to overthrow Athelstan and claim the crown for himself.

Although Edwin robustly denied this, Athelstan was concerned that his own illegitimacy might lose him the kingdom. He needed Edwin out of the way, but to have him murdered or executed would draw attention to the situation and Athelstan did not want blood on his hands.

Instead he had Edwin cast adrift in an empty boat, without food or water, or any means of steering the boat towards land. The idea being that Edwin would die from natural causes and Athelstan would not personally have killed him. Faced with the prospect of a slow death, Edwin jumped into the sea and drowned. Filled with remorse, Athelstan founded Milton Abbey in Dorset, where daily masses were said for Edwin's soul.

Athelstan was devoted to the church and established many monasteries during his reign. He also rebuilt churches that had been destroyed by the Vikings, particularly in Exeter and York.

An ancient manuscript says that he "built himself churches of great honour, wherein to worship God with all his might."

Athelstan also collected a number of religious relics, which were supposed to have included part of the cross on which Christ died, the crown of thorns, and even the lance which had pierced the side of Jesus as he hung on the cross. Other relics were St Samson's arm and St Branwaladr's head. These were kept at Milton Abbey, but were destroyed by fire in 1309 when lightning struck the church during a violent storm.

The focal point of Athelstan's reign for historians is the Battle of Brunanburh, which was a day-long battle that took place somewhere between Solway and the Mersey in the autumn of 937. (After extensive research in 2004, Professor Steve Harding concluded that the site of the battle is now a golf course in Bebington, a suburb of Birkenhead. Previously Bromborough in Cheshire had been the commonly accepted location.)

A coalition of enemies from Wales, Scotland, Ireland and the Vikings, who had resented having to submit to Athelstan at Eamont Bridge a decade earlier, invaded England. Athelstan defended his land in what is considered to be the bloodiest battle of that century, with some reports stating that as many as 60,000 men took part in the fight.

Although he lost two nephews, Athelstan won a decisive victory. As the *Anglo Saxon Chronicle* tells us, "Never before in this island was an army put to greater slaughter by the sword since the time when the Angles and Saxons landed. King Athelstan, lord of warriors, ring-giver of men, with his royal brother Edmund, won undying glory with the edges of swords. The Scots and the host from the ships fell doomed."

Athelstan remained active right up to the time of his death, dying in his palace at Gloucester from an unrecorded disease on 27 October, 939, and was buried at Malmesbury Abbey in Wiltshire. Although the tomb that can be seen today in the north aisle dates only from the 15th century, it bears a fitting inscription:

> *Struck his enemies with fear,*
> *by terror of his name alone.*
> *A royal son prolonged a noble line,*
> *when a splendid gem lit up our darkness.*
> *Great Athelstan, glory of the country,*
> *way of rectitude, noble integrity,*
> *unswervable from the truth.*

Over 1,000 years since his death, Athelstan is commemorated throughout England in towns such as Margate, Folkestone, Kettering, Southampton and Dorchester, where many roads and streets bear his name. In the shadow of St Paul's Cathedral is Addle Hill, where Athelstan (sometimes spelled Adelstan) once had a palace in London.

As a bachelor king with no children, Athelstan was succeeded by his 18-year-old half-brother Edmund, who had been his second-in-command at Brunanburh. Known as "the Magnificent" because of his love of jewels and fine clothes, and also "the Deed Doer", the young Edmund I was crowned at Kingston upon Thames on 29 November, 939. Scarcely had the holy oil dried on Edmund's brow than England came under renewed attack from the Vikings.

Olaf Guthfrithsson (King Olaf I of Dublin), one of Athelstan's enemies who had been defeated at the Battle of Brunanburh, overtook Northumbria by military force and began heading southwards to conquer the Midlands. It took King Edmund some two years to win back his land in the Midlands and regain the five boroughs of Derby, Leicester, Lincoln, Nottingham and Stamford.

In 944 he finally reclaimed York and Northumbria and so became ruler of the whole of England. A year later he conquered the independent kingdom of Strathclyde, although later gave it back to King Malcolm I of Scotland on the basis that they would be allies, and so established for the first time a safe border between England and Scotland.

King Edmund married twice. Firstly, Elgiva in around 940, with whom he had two sons and a daughter. Elgiva died some four years later, possibly in childbirth, and Edmund married Ethelfleda from Wiltshire. The marriage was to last only a short time, for on 26 May, 946, King Edmund was unexpectedly murdered by a robber in his palace at Pucklechurch, south

Gloucestershire. The 24-year-old king was laid to rest at Glastonbury Abbey by Abbot Dunston, later an Archbishop of Canterbury. Edmund had reigned for just six years.

With Edmund's sons still infants and therefore too young to rule, a third brother came to the throne of England. King Edred was the youngest son of Edward the Elder and his wife Edgiva, and had been born in the year 923.

Like his brothers before him, he was crowned at Kingston upon Thames in Surrey, proved to be a strong military leader, and was deeply religious. Unlike them, however, Edred suffered from very poor health, had a weak digestion and could barely swallow solid food.

Possibly aware of King Edred's physical weaknesses, the Vikings attempted to regain the north of England. They set fire to Ripon and defeated English forces at Castleford in 948. Erik Bloodaxe, the ruthless King of Norway, took control of York and tried to take over Northumbria, but was eventually defeated by Edred's army.

Erik had the backing of Wulftsan, the Archbishop of York, which gave him political power. King Edred therefore had Wulftsan captured, imprisoning him in the castle of Judanburh. Support for Erik immediately collapsed. He fled across the Pennines, but was ambushed and killed at Rey Cross, Stainmore, on the site of an old Roman camp.

With Erik Bloodaxe out of the way, peace was restored and Edred became King of All England once again, just as his brothers Athelstan and Edmund had been. His chief advisor was the faithful St Dunstan, who influenced many of Edred's policies, and even persuaded the king to be scourged as a penance for his sins. Unmarried, Edred devoted his life to God and the people of England, leaving large amounts of money in his will to help the poor and needy.

A small, slight figure, King Edred never recovered from the wasting disease that plagued his life. He died at Frome in Somerset on 23 November, 955, at the age of 32, the last of Edward the Elder's sons. Edred's bones lie today in a mortuary chest at Winchester Cathedral. "He endured with patience his frequent bodily pains," wrote William of Malmesbury, "and his death was accompanied with the utmost grief of men and joy of angels."

Chapter 7

Edwy the Fair
c.941–959
Reign: 955–959

Edgar the Peaceful
c.943–975
Reign: 959–975

In the middle of the 10th century two brothers ruled over England and they could not have been more different in character. Edwy, sometimes known as Eadwig, was a pale and sickly youth, who had a divided kingdom and died soon after his 18th birthday, while his brother Edgar has been described as having the strength and vitality of earlier Saxon kings, and brought peace and unity back to the country.

Edwy, born around 941, and Edgar, born around 943, were sons of King Edmund. They were just infants when their father was murdered and so Edred, their uncle, became king in their place. When Edred died, unmarried and childless in November 955, it was the 14-year-old Edwy who succeeded to the throne as King Edmund's elder son.

Although not in the best of health, Edwy was a fair-haired, handsome youth with an eye for the ladies. At a banquet which followed the Coronation at Kingston upon Thames in January 956, Odo the Archbishop of Canterbury noticed that the newly crowned king was missing. The young Edwy had become bored with the celebrations and escaped with his cousin Elgiva and her mother. The angry Archbishop sent Dunstan, Abbot of Glastonbury, and Cynesige, Bishop of Lichfield, to find the king and bring him back to the table. They discovered Edwy in a bedchamber, seated on a couch between the two ladies, his bejewelled crown lying beside him on the floor.

It is said that Dunstan severely reprimanded the boy, replaced the crown on his head, and literally dragged him by force back to the banquet. King

Edwy never forgave the Abbot for humiliating him in front of the guests.

King Edwy shocked the Archbishop and the Abbot further by announcing that he intended to marry his cousin. When objections were raised by the church, with claims that the union was uncanonical, Edwy hit back by mounting an investigation into Abbot Dunstan's finances.

Dunstan was unwilling to account for large sums of the church's money that had mysteriously disappeared, saying that it was a matter between him and God. Consequently, King Edwy banished Dunstan from the country and he took refuge at a monastery in Flanders. It was a short-lived triumph for Edwy, however, as Dunstan plotted against him from across the Channel. Monks in England were encouraged to oppose Edwy at every available opportunity and it became a battle between the monarch and the church.

Refusing to be browbeaten, Edwy went ahead and married his cousin Elgiva. This only exacerbated the feud with Abbot Dunstan, who hatched a plot with the clergy from Northumbria and Mercia to oust Edwy from the throne and replace him with his brother Edgar.

A rumour was put about that a statue of Christ had spoken, commanding that Edwy's authority be reduced to the area of Wessex only and that Edgar should be king over the rest of England. Not surprisingly, this heavenly directive just happened to coincide with the wishes of Dunstan.

Abbot Dunstan and the Archbishop of Canterbury joined forces to make life as difficult as possible for King Edwy and, because they were so opposed to his marriage, they arranged to have Queen Elgiva kidnapped. Legend has it that she was branded on the forehead before being shipped off to Ireland as a slave.

Once there, the story concerning her true identity was believed and a small band of loyal supporters helped transport her back to England to resume her rightful place beside the King. Dunstan's followers, however, became aware of the situation and ambushed Elgiva's convoy as it reached Gloucester in September 959. Elgiva was tied up, stabbed repeatedly with a sword, and left to die.

It is said that when King Edwy received the news of his young wife's murder, he sank into a deep depression and, having a weak constitution anyway, died of a broken heart at Gloucester on 1 October, 959. The fact that he died at Gloucester, where Elgiva was killed, suggests that he might have travelled there to collect her body.

Some historians consider that the broken heart story may have been put about by Dunstan at a later date, and that Edwy could actually have been murdered. Some contemporary chroniclers state that Edwy's marriage was annulled because the couple were "too related", but again this could have been a story to cover up Elgiva's murder. Still others say that Elgiva was not murdered but lived on in exile after Edwy's death.

During his very short reign, Edwy was not a popular king. He imposed high taxes on his people, granted great privileges to his friends, and was said to have shown favouritism to the region of Wessex over the rest of England. He was, however, generous in making grants to the church and various religious institutions. Particularly charitable, considering how he had been treated by some members of the clergy.

After Edwy's untimely death, whatever the cause, his brother Edgar acceded to the throne. Dunstan returned to England from exile and made the claim that he had seen Edwy's soul in a vision being carried away by demons, but that through his prayers Edwy had been spared the descent into hell. This seemed to vindicate him and, with no blot on his copybook, Dunstan soon became Bishop of Worcester, then London, and eventually Archbishop of Canterbury. He was later made a saint.

Dunstan acted as the 17-year-old King's advisor. Edgar had the great fortune that the Vikings, who had so dominated the reigns of his predecessors, seemed unusually quiet and England experienced a period of tranquillity. Consequently, Edgar has been known as the Pacificus, translated variously as the Peaceful or the Peaceable. Because his brother had concentrated his attentions on Wessex, Edgar tried to unite the whole country by introducing new laws that applied "to every province in my dominion". Such was the discontent with Edwy, that Edgar had been declared King "north of the Thames" by a conclave of Mercian nobles in the year before he actually acceded to the throne.

King Edgar's Coronation in Bath Abbey did not take place until Whit Sunday, 11 May, 973 – 14 years into his reign. It was devised by Archbishop Dunstan following the European form of service. Whereas earlier ceremonies in England had placed great emphasis on the actual moment of crowning, the new service put much more importance on the anointing with holy oil.

As the Archbishop of Canterbury did the actual anointing, it showed the significant link between the church and the crown, and strengthened the message that the King's authority came from God. This part of the Coronation service has been treated with magnitude ever since. At Queen Elizabeth II's Coronation in 1953, the anointing was treated with such solemnity that television cameras were forbidden to show it.

Another part of the ceremony devised by Dunstan was the ritual rowing of the King down the River Dee at Chester by the Kings of Scotland, Wales and the Isle of Man as an act of homage and allegiance, symbolising the unity of the country and total acceptance of Edgar as ruler.

In his private life, King Edgar married Ethelfleda, known as "the white duck", in around 961 and they had one son, named Edward. Ethelfleda's fate is unknown, but some reports say that she died in childbirth, which was not uncommon at this time. In the early days of his marriage, Edgar also acquired a mistress, Wulfrida, the Abbess of Wilton, with whom he had a daughter, Edith (later Abbess of Barking and Nunnaminster) in 962.

Within a short time of his first wife's death, Edgar embarked on a relationship with Elfrida, the daughter of Ordgar, Ealdorman of Devon. It is said that Edgar had heard reports of Elfrida's beauty and sent one of his closest friends, Ethelwold, to Devon to see if she lived up to her reputation.

When Ethelwold arrived he found that Elfrida was indeed a great beauty, and decided that he would like to marry her himself, so reported back to the King that Elfrida was unattractive and feeble-minded. Ethelwold duly married her, but this naturally created problems as he had to keep her hidden from the King. Edgar must have known of the marriage and probably considered it a strange union if Elfrida was as unappealing as Ethelwold claimed.

Inevitably the day came when King Edgar was hunting near his friend's home at Wherwell, Hampshire, and asked to spend the night. Ethelwold could not refuse a visit from the King, and so was forced to confess to Elfrida what he had done.

He asked her to maintain the charade by making herself look as unattractive as possible and to act as if she were simple. Angered by her husband's deceit, and realising that he had prevented her from being Queen, she did the exact opposite.

From Richard Grafton's 16th-century *Chronicles of England*, we learn that Elfrida dressed herself in her very best clothes and "if Dame Nature had anything forgotten or misprinted in her, she left not what might be done by woman's help to have it amended and reformed".

King Edgar was overcome by Elfrida's beauty and immediately realised the deceit. Pretending that all was well, he invited Ethelwold to join him on the hunt. Later in nearby woods, Ethelwold was struck by a spear and died from the injury. Elfrida was told that her husband had fallen from his horse.

In around 964 Edgar took Elfrida as his bride and the couple later had two sons, Edmund and Ethelred. Edmund died in childhood and was buried in Romsey Abbey, Hampshire. Ethelred, the Unready, later became King. In 973 Elfrida was crowned with her husband at Bath, the first recorded instance of the Coronation of a Queen Consort in England.

Influenced by Dunstan, one of King Edgar's achievements was to reform the church, and to ensure that all monasteries had the same degree of order and discipline, following Benedictine principles. Many corrupt priests were banished, and church lands and wealth increased greatly, partly through new laws which enforced a system of people giving a tenth of their income, or tithe, to the church, with heavy penalties if they failed to pay. He also founded 40 new monasteries and repaired many more that had been ravaged during earlier Viking invasions.

Edgar tightened administrative practices in the provinces to ensure the enforcement of laws within the shires and boroughs, each shire having its own law court. It is recorded that he once introduced a "Wolf Tax", whereby the Welsh King Hywel agreed to give Edgar 300 wolves a year as a sign of submission, but this proved impractical as there were simply not enough wolves available in Wales.

Edgar regulated weights and measures throughout the land and introduced new coinage, recalling old coins to be melted down and reminted, which remained virtually unchanged for the next 300 years. He reorganised the English navy to strengthen the country's defences from coastal invasion and initiated a form of conscription to ensure that the ships had enough sailors.

As the *Anglo-Saxon Chronicle* of the period recorded: "No fleet however proud, no host however strong, was able to win booty for itself in England while that noble King occupied the throne."

Art and culture flourished under King Edgar, with an abundance of paintings, sculptures, decorative metalwork, illuminated manuscripts, and delicate carvings being produced, and monasteries and churches in particular were beautified with artworks. London became the centre of commerce and traders from other countries established businesses to sell their wares.

Edgar died at Winchester on 8 July 975 and was buried at Glastonbury Abbey, Somerset, because of its connection with St Dunstan. He was originally laid to rest in the Chapter House, but in 1052 was transferred to a Chapel named after him at the far eastern end of the Abbey. His name also lives on in the neighbouring parish of Edgarley. He was later canonised and St Edgar's feast day is celebrated on 8 July.

In January 2020 it was reported that remains of the Anglo-Saxon abbey in Bath, where Edgar's coronation had taken place over 1,000 years ago, had been unearthed by a team from Wessex Archaeology whilst restoration work was being undertaken on Bath Abbey's unstable floor.

Because his was a peaceful reign, it has been described as a Golden Age in Anglo-Saxon history. While King Edgar's predecessors fought for and established the Kingdom of England, it was he who brought unity and an end to the different regions of Northumbria, Mercia and Wessex battling for supremacy. England had finally become one country.

Chapter 8

Edward the Martyr c.962–978
Reign: 975–978

No worse deed than this was ever done among the English nation
since they first sought the land of Britain.
Men murdered him but God has magnified him;
He was in life an earthly king –
He is now after death a heavenly saint.
Anglo-Saxon Chronicle

King Edward the Martyr has often been described as one of the least significant monarchs in English history. Yet, due to the manner of his death and the events that followed, he is still remembered and commemorated with an annual feast day, and many churches in England bear his name.

The son of King Edgar the Peaceful and his first wife Ethelfleda, Edward was born around the year 962 and came to the throne when his father died unexpectedly 13 years later. Edward was said to be very volatile and liable to violent outbursts. His stepmother Elfrida (King Edgar's second wife) who wanted her own son Ethelred to reign instead, spread the rumour that Edward was mentally unstable and not fit to be king.

Although she had many supporters, ultimately it was agreed that Edward had the rightful claim. Archbishop Dunstan declared that he was "A young man of great devotion and excellent conduct", and the Witan (the Parliament of the day) met on the royal estate at Calne, Wiltshire, and after much debate elected him King. Tradition has it that during the discussions, the floor of the meeting room collapsed and only Dunstan and Edward's supporters survived, but this was almost certainly put about by Edward's enemies to explain how he came to be chosen in favour of Ethelred.

At the beginning of his reign in 975 a comet was seen in the sky, which was thought to be a particularly bad omen, and the following year there was a very poor harvest in England. A great famine followed, causing considerable suffering and hardship amongst the people. Not an illustrious start. Because of Edward's devotion to the church, noblemen who opposed his accession made a series of violent attacks on monasteries by setting fire to the buildings and slaughtering the monks.

Edward's achievements during his reign were few, but he continued his father's policies and was guided by Dunstan, the Archbishop of Canterbury, to reform the church and support the Benedictine monasteries. He was said to have lived a "good and holy life", was generous to the poor, and won the affection of the English people, although was known by those closest to him to still have outbursts of rage.

On 18 March, 978, King Edward was hunting at Wareham in Dorset with friends, and that evening visited his stepmother, Elfrida, and half-brother, Ethelred, at Corfe Castle. Unwisely, he left his entourage in the woods and arrived at the castle alone. There are various reports of what happened next, but while still seated on his horse, Edward was offered a goblet of mead and was stabbed in the back as he drank it. No-one was ever convicted of the murder and so the mystery of his attacker's identity remains.

In the 12th century William of Malmesbury blamed Elfrida, writing that she had signalled to one of her servants to stab him. Other writers at that time went further still and claimed that the widowed Queen had herself been wielding the dagger. As the assassination of Edward placed his half-brother Ethelred on the throne, some sources even claim that Ethelred was himself the culprit, but as he was only around ten years old at the time, it seems unlikely. Historians feel that it is more probable that one of Ethelred's supporters carried out the attack, but at the instigation of Elfrida.

The stabbing startled Edward's horse, which bolted from the castle, and the wounded King fell from the saddle and with one foot caught in the stirrup was dragged behind the horse and died on the road. Eventually his body fell into a stream at the foot of Corfe Castle. The stream was afterwards found to have healing properties.

Not wishing to be implicated, Elfrida ordered the corpse to be hidden in a cottage opposite the castle, which belonged to a woman who had been blind since birth and would not see what she was hiding. However, a heavenly light appeared to the woman during the night and her sight was miraculously restored. Seeing the body, she ran out into the street screaming.

Elfrida quickly had the corpse buried in a local marsh and hoped that the evidence was now gone for ever, but one year later a pillar of fire appeared over the grave and could be seen by all the inhabitants of the village. The body was exhumed and immediately a healing spring of clear water rose out of the ground. King Edward's body was transferred to the Church of the Most Holy Mother of God in Wareham and was interred without any royal honours, as Elfrida hoped that his name would soon be forgotten. Later, maybe repenting her crime, Elfrida built two monasteries at Wherwell (Hampshire) and Amesbury (Wiltshire) and ended her days as a nun.

After a series of miracles, Edward's body was moved to the chancel of Shaftesbury Abbey on 13 February, 981, in a great procession and was buried with full royal honours on the north side of the altar. As his coffin in the procession passed by people who were crippled and lame, they were immediately restored to full health and soon his tomb became a place of pilgrimage. It was reported that lepers were healed and the blind regained their sight on touching King Edward's gravestone.

In the year 1001 his tomb was regularly seen to rise several inches from the ground and Edward was declared a saint and martyr on 20 June. Even if not physically involved in Edward's murder, it is said that Ethelred had feelings of remorse over the manner in which he had inherited the crown, and the process of canonisation for the dead King Edward began to help assuage Ethelred's conscience. Shaftesbury was renamed Edwardstowe in his honour, and only reverted to its former name after the Reformation. Edward was officially made a saint in 1008.

St Edward is said to have appeared in the dreams of a devout man saying that he did not wish to lie in this particular grave, and that was why his tomb appeared to levitate miraculously. So King Ethelred ordered his half-brother's body to be moved once again to a more prominent place amongst holy relics in the Abbey. When bishops opened the tomb a beautiful fragrance issued from it, described by them as the aroma of Paradise.

The teenage king was not allowed to lie in peace, for when Henry VIII dissolved the monasteries in the 16th century, and many buildings and relics were desecrated, monks hid St Edward's bones for safekeeping and their whereabouts was not discovered for almost 400 years.

In 1930 the Wilson-Claridge family acquired the site on which the ruins of Shaftesbury Abbey stood. A year later, an excavation in the area that was once the north transept unearthed a Tudor casket made of lead. It contained bones and part of a skull, believed to be the remains of Edward the Martyr.

The casket was retained by the Wilson-Claridges, eventually leading to a dispute between two elderly brothers in the 1970s when one wanted the bones to be reburied at Shaftesbury Abbey and the other wanted to donate them to a small sect of the Russian Orthodox Church in exile, which had promised to purchase some disused mortuary buildings at Brookwood cemetery, Woking, and establish a new shrine.

The identity of the remains was finally confirmed by an eminent osteologist as being those of Edward, based on historical, anatomical and surgical grounds. In September 1979 a Synod of Bishops accepted without reservations the authenticity of the relics, and they were placed in the strong-room of a Woking bank for a decision on their fate. Eventually the Russian Orthodox Church Outside Russia was granted the relics and a church at Brookwood cemetery adopted St Edward's name. A formal ceremony of enshrinement took place in September 1984 and Edward's remains at last had a final resting place, over 900 years after his death.

The St Edward Brotherhood of Monks was established and in the Orthodox Church today he is recognised as a Passion-bearer saint, one who accepts death out of love for Christ, and his feast day is celebrated on 18 March, the day on which he was murdered. In March 2001 a special service was held to mark the 1,000th anniversary of Edward first being revered as a saint, and people still make pilgrimages to England from all over the world to venerate this holy martyr at his shrine.

At Corfe in Dorset where Edward died, the church of St Edward the Martyr was built in the 13th century. It's believed the church stands on the site of the blind woman's cottage, where Edward's body was taken after the murder. Everything but the tower was demolished in 1859 and a new gothic-style church was built, but the church bearing his name is still in use.

In Cambridge the Church of St Edward King and Martyr also dates back to the 13th century, and on Christmas Eve 1525 the first openly evangelical sermon to be preached at any church in England was made from the pulpit. Other churches are dedicated to the King, including those at Castle Donington (Leicestershire), Athelhampton (Dorset), Goathurst (Somerset) and even as far afield as Manhattan in New York. A shrine also stands within the ruins of Shaftesbury Abbey to commemorate where he was first laid to rest a millennium ago.

In art, Edward is generally depicted with a cup in one hand and a dagger in the other, often with a falcon on his arm as a reference to the hunt on that final ill-fated day. This King of England, it seems, will always be remembered for his death rather than his life.

Chapter 9

Ethelred the Unready c.968–1016
Reign: 978–1016

If one single fact about King Ethelred II is remembered today it is his association with the suffix "Unready", a nickname which is now often misinterpreted. The name Ethelred, or Æþelræd, in the old English language, meant "noble counsel", and a pun on his name was Unræd meaning "without counsel" or "badly advised". The joke, therefore, was based on the fact that King Ethelred was given poor advice by the people around him, rather than being unprepared.

It would be true, nevertheless, to say that Ethelred was certainly unready to inherit the crown. He came to throne at around just ten years old following the murder of his half-brother, Edward. It was an ominous way to begin a reign. Ethelred wept uncontrollably on hearing the news, which infuriated his mother, Elfrida, who was implicated in the murder.

She grabbed a large candle and beat Ethelred so hard that for the rest of his life he had a fear of candles and would not allow one to be lit in his presence. Not surprisingly, William of Malmesbury later wrote of the hapless monarch that "the career of his life is said to have been cruel in the beginning, wretched in the middle, and disgraceful in the end."

Ethelred was born in the year 968, the son of King Edgar the Peaceful and his second wife, Elfrida. At his baptism, the baby Ethelred had an "accident" in the font, angering the bishops gathered around through his defilement of the holy water. Dunstan, the Archbishop of Canterbury, declared, "By God, and his mother, this will be a sorry fellow!"

The odds seemed to be against him from the start. Ethelred became King on 18 March, 978. He was crowned a month later at Kingston upon Thames, with Archbishop Dunstan predicting a disastrous reign because of the events that had led to Ethelred's succession.

When enemies realised that there was a child on the throne of England, invasions intensified. Although the English navy was enlarged, it proved impossible to keep the marauders at bay as the kingdoms of Denmark, Sweden and Norway joined forces against them.

Because of his youth and inexperience, King Ethelred inevitably had to rely on the advice of others which was not always beneficial. By 982 Southampton, Thanet and Cheshire had been ravaged, a raid had been made on Portland, and the coasts of Devon and Cornwall were overtaken by Vikings.

In 991 Olaf Tryggvason, heir to the crown of Norway, led 93 ships up the Blackwater estuary in Essex, preparing to conquer the south-east of England. Before attacking, however, Olaf tried to bargain with the English. He was willing to call off the assault in return for gold and armour, saying: "Better for you all that you should buy off this onslaught of spears with tribute money, than that we should join battle so grievously."

The Ealdorman of Essex, Byrhtnoth, was not prepared to be held to ransom and refused. England would fight the Vikings instead. The Battle of Maldon took place in August that year, which proved disastrous for the English as the Vikings vastly outnumbered them. Byrhtnoth, at 6' 9" tall, was a brave and inspiring leader, but was struck by an axe in the heat of battle and lost his head. Although buried in Ely Cathedral, he is commemorated today with a memorial window at St Mary's Church, Maldon, depicting his dying prayer.

His statue guards the door to All Saint's Church in the high street, and in 2006 another impressive bronze statue of him was erected on the promenade. A tapestry depicting the battle can be seen at the Maeldune Centre in the town, made in 1991 to mark the 1,000th anniversary. Many English soldiers were slain on that day, but the Battle of Maldon is remembered for its heroic losers rather than the now forgotten victors.

By this time Sigeric, the then Archbishop of Canterbury, advised King Ethelred that they should pay off the Vikings to try and bring an end to the constant threat. King Alfred the Great had previously obtained peace through a financial settlement, and so Ethelred agreed to follow suit and pay protection money to the Vikings – a system known as Danegeld.

To gather sufficient funds, a tax was levied on all English subjects and collectors were sent to towns and villages to accumulate £10,000. This was an enormous sum in those days, when the average annual income was a matter of pence, and a high price to pay for peace. The Bishop of Dorchester made up the shortfall, receiving land in return. The whole Viking army gathered at Southampton for the winter, probably laughing at the foolishness of Ethelred in paying them off.

It proved to be a disastrous policy for Ethelred. Despite being paid another £16,000 in 994, the south-east of England suffered further invasions, when the Danish King Sweyn Forkbeard led an attack with nearly 100 ships full of Viking warriors, ravaging large areas of Essex, Kent, Surrey and Hampshire. Each time the Vikings were paid money, they withdrew for only a short time before returning for even larger sums. It became a vicious circle, resulting in a saying: "Once you have paid him the Danegeld, you never get rid of the Dane."

It set a dangerous precedent too. The 12th-century historian Henry of Huntingdon wrote, "And this infliction has continued to this present day, and, unless God's mercy interposes, will still continue, for we now pay to our Kings, from custom, the tax which was levied by the Danes from intolerable fear."

England was militarily weak and at the beginning of the 11th century Ethelred decided that the only way to overcome the intruders was to mount a surprise attack. He sent secret letters to every town in England announcing that a massacre of all Danes – men, women and children – would take place on St Brice's Day, 13 November, 1002. English citizens were told that all Vikings should be slaughtered on the same day, wherever they were in the country.

As a result, many Viking communities were destroyed in the unanticipated uprising. In a charter of 1004 Ethelred justified the slaughter writing, "A decree was sent out by me, with the counsel of my leading men and magnates, to the effect that all the Danes who had sprung up in this island, sprouting like cockle amongst the wheat, were to be destroyed by a most just extermination."

Unfortunately, many peaceful Danish settlers were also killed, simply because of their birthplace rather than because they posed any threat. It gave Ethelred a reputation for being rash and ruthless. Unluckily for Ethelred, King Sweyn's sister, Gunhilda, was one of those killed in the massacre, which further incurred the wrath of the Danes. Sweyn wanted revenge and in 1003 came to England himself with his son, Canute.

Sweyn commanded a vast fleet of ships, landing some of his army in Kent before sailing round to East Anglia, from where the rest of his men marched into the Midlands and Northumbria, eventually heading southwards into Wessex. Within a year Wilton, Salisbury, Norwich and Thetford had suffered greatly through attacks, which involved great loss of life and the burning down of buildings. Soon some 16 shires had been overtaken.

Kent suffered yet again with a further Viking raid in the autumn of 1011, when Canterbury was sacked and the Cathedral set on fire. Alphege, the Archbishop of Canterbury, was taken to Greenwich as a hostage and was murdered on Easter Day, 1012. He was later canonised, and the church of St Alphege now stands on the spot where he died.

The following summer, Sweyn gained submission of much of the country, helped by the fact that there was great disunity by this time. Feudal lords had created their own private domains and the united kingdom that monarchs since the reign of Alfred the Great had fought so hard to maintain was destroyed. People had become so disillusioned with Ethelred that they were prepared to accept Sweyn as their King, as long as it meant a return to a peaceful way of life. The Vikings had finally won and the Danish Sweyn became recognised as King of England on Christmas Day 1013, although was never crowned.

Ethelred and his Queen, Emma, were forced into exile in France, seeking the sanctuary of her brother, Richard, Duke of Normandy. King Sweyn's rule was short-lived, for just six weeks later he fell from his horse and died at Gainsborough on 3 February, 1014. He was initially buried in England, but his remains were later moved to Roskild Cathedral in Denmark.

Although Sweyn's son Canute was chosen by the Danes to take his father's place, English noblemen invited Ethelred to return as their monarch instead. The *Anglo-Saxon Chronicle* tells us that: "All the councillors who were in England . . . determined to send for King Ethelred, and they said that no lord was dearer to them than their natural lord, if he would govern them more justly than he did before. Then the King . . . said that he would be a gracious lord to them and reform all the things which they hated . . . (and) during the spring King Ethelred came home to his own people."

Canute reluctantly went back to Scandinavia, biding his time.

Ethelred's reinstatement was brief. His health deteriorated and he died of an unrecorded illness on 23 April, 1016, aged 48. He was buried at St Paul's Cathedral, where 650 years later his tomb was destroyed in the Great Fire of London: a final ignominy that even his body did not rest in peace.

The struggles that Ethelred endured during the early years of his reign stemmed from his youth and inexperience. Because of the epithet

"Unready" it is easy to think of Ethelred as a completely ineffective monarch, but he did have some accomplishments. He proved himself to be a good administrator, and reformed the judicial system based on the premise that people were innocent until proven guilty, and introduced what would eventually become the grand jury as an impartial panel to advise whether a case should go to trial. This practice continued in England until 1933. He also standardised the coinage and reduced the number of mints producing coins in an attempt to prevent counterfeiting, which was rife at the time.

Ethelred's weakness was that he tended to rely on favourites at court, who were elevated to high positions not because of their abilities, but because they happened to be his friends.

Impulsive by nature, he often accepted unsuitable advice without question and was easily led astray. A particular favourite called Ethelsine had considerable influence over the young monarch and directed him to sanction many acts of oppression over the English people.

On his advice, for example, Ethelred was wrongly led to believe that he owned land occupied by the Bishop of Rochester. This resulted in an unnecessarily violent siege in an attempt to claim it. Ethelred was unsuccessful and was denounced by the Archbishop of Canterbury for avarice but it was a foolish act fuelled by irresponsible advice from a greedy counsellor. As any church land seized was redistributed amongst noblemen at court, the Bishop of Rochester's loss would have been Ethelsine's gain.

In 993 Ethelred admitted that advisors had taken advantage of his lack of knowledge. In 997 he conceded before Parliament the sins of his youth, and restored land that he felt he had taken unlawfully. He blamed Ethelsine for badly advising him and took away his position and wealth. Unfortunately, Ethelred then received poor advice from an equally unworthy confidant, a traitor called Leofsige. Before long, Ethelred realised the error of his ways and banished Leofsige from court. He in turn was replaced by Wulfgeat who treacherously colluded with the Danes, causing England to be continually ravaged as a result.

Once unmasked, Wulfgeat had all his possessions taken from him as punishment for the bad advice that he had given the King. Matters did not improve, as for the last ten years of his reign, Ethelred's chief advisor was a notorious turncoat called Eadric Streona, described by William of Malmesbury as "the refuse of mankind and a reproach unto the English".

No contemporary portraits exist of King Ethelred, but he was described by those who knew him as being good-looking and having graceful manners. His main home was in Oxfordshire and according to the *Anglo-Saxon Chronicle*, he built a palace at Headington. Today a cul-de-sac called Ethelred Court is thought to mark the original site, although excavations continue periodically for further evidence. In the 17th century "considerable foundations" were discovered by a Dr Plot in a field called Court Close.

Ethelred married twice, firstly to Elfleda in around 985, although no record exists as to where. The couple had eight sons and five daughters. After Elfleda's death, he married Emma of Normandy on 5 April, 1002, at Winchester Cathedral, with whom he had two sons and a daughter. Each of Ethelred's sons was given the name of a previous King of England.

This second marriage proved to be an unhappy one and it was an unfavourable union as far as the English people were concerned. It did nothing to improve Ethelred's popularity and the long-term consequences for the country were dire. Emma was the great-aunt to William of Normandy who eventually conquered England at the Battle of Hastings in 1066. As a final affront, when Ethelred died, Emma married his enemy, Canute.

It is said that King Ethelred has one of the worst reputations of any monarch in England, because he lost most of his country to the Vikings, which his forebears had fought so hard to preserve. Even as Ethelred lay dying, the Danish King Canute was said to be hammering on the gates of London's city walls. It was left to his son Edmund to fight Canute for the Kingdom.

Chapter 10

Edmund Ironside c.989–1016
Reign: April 1016–November 1016

Compared to many Kings of England, little has been recorded about the life of Edmund, yet few forget his nickname: Ironside. There are conflicting opinions as to how it came about. Some say that it was on account of the armour he wore; others believe it resulted from his powerful stature and legendary strength, but most claim that it was because of his military leadership. This is born out by an 11th-century historian who described Edmund Ironside as "a brave soldier and an able general".

Edmund was the second son of King Ethelred the Unready and his first wife Elfleda, and was born around the year 989. His elder brother died in 1014, leaving him heir to the throne. Edmund was very different in character to his badly advised father. Headstrong and determined, he followed his own heart even if it meant going against his father's wishes.

In August 1015 he married Edith at Malmesbury in Wiltshire, deliberately defying his father, for Edith was the widow of King Ethelred's sworn enemy Sigeferth. Following a power struggle over the north of England, Sigeferth had been murdered on Ethelred's orders, so it can have done little for family harmony when Edmund married Edith. He even abducted her from a nunnery to claim her as his wife just to antagonise his father. The couple eventually had two sons, Edward and Edmund.

In the month of Edmund's marriage, the Danish King Canute had landed at Poole harbour with a fleet of more than 200 ships, each with 80 men on board, going on to attack areas of Dorset, Wiltshire and Somerset, before heading to Warwickshire.

The *Anglo-Saxon Chronicle* records that they "plundered, and burned, and slew all they met . . . Canute went out through Buckinghamshire to Bedfordshire; thence to Huntingdonshire; and so into Northamptonshire along the fens to Stamford. Thence into Lincolnshire. Thence to Nottinghamshire; and so into Northumbria toward York." Canute finally marched his men back down to Wessex, arriving on 1 April, 1016, before heading to London.

An 11th-century English monk, Florence of Worcester, wrote that Edmund Ironside mustered an army but gained little support from the people of England. Edmund therefore attacked those who refused to fight against the Danish army and many English villages were destroyed in the process, although it has been suggested that the villages were destroyed simply to prevent the Danes from getting supplies of food and extra horses.

On 23 April, 1016, just as Canute and his army reached London, King Ethelred died. Edmund succeeded to the throne and was crowned that same month at the old St Paul's Cathedral. He inherited a country under attack and with divided loyalties amongst the people.

Although accepted by the citizens and nobles of London as King, nobles and churchmen in Southampton turned their allegiance to Canute instead. Canute had greater military strength and began to lay siege to London. Soon a deep trench had been dug around the city so that Canute's men could control who went in and out. Before London was completely surrounded, Edmund escaped and fled to Wessex to gather his own army.

As King, Edmund was now able to muster a supportive army and many battles with the Vikings followed to gain control of England. The English defeated the Danes at Pen on the Somerset-Wiltshire border (now known as Penselwood), at Brentford (London) and Otford (Kent).

After midsummer there was one particularly bloody yet indecisive two-day battle at Sherston in Wiltshire. A local man called John Rattlebone fought on Edmund's side against Canute. Although mortally wounded, Rattlebone simply clasped a stone tile to his side to staunch the flow of blood and carried on fighting, dying as the Danes retreated. Today the Rattlebone Inn in the village of Sherston is named in his honour, and in the church is a chest carved with the initials RB that is reputed to have once held his armour. A weather-beaten Saxon figure outside the church porch is believed by some to be an image of John Rattlebone, clutching a stone to his wound.

It was during the Battle of Sherston that Edmund's brother-in-law, and supposed supporter, Edric Streona suddenly turned traitor and changed his allegiance to Canute. He viciously cut off the head of a man named Osmear, whose face and hair were very like King Edmund's, held it up and declared:

"Oh, ye men of Dorsetshire, Devonshire and Wiltshire, flee quickly; ye have lost your leader: Lo! Here I hold the head of your lord and King, Edmund. Flee with all speed!" The soldiers, believing that the King had been slain, were terrified until they realised it was a trick, and that Edmund was still alive. In spite of Edric's support, Canute was unable to win the battle. The Danes withdrew under the cover of darkness and returned to London, "slaying and burning whatsoever they overtook, as their custom is". On 18 October, 1016, Canute finally gained a victory over Edmund at the Battle of Ashingdon. The Danes, with a smaller army, were inferior in strength, but had greater determination to win.

Unfortunately for Edmund, he was again double-crossed by the treacherous Edric Streona, who weakened the English army's morale and the battle was lost. Edric "betrayed his natural lord and all the people of England," declares the *Anglo-Saxon Chronicle*. "There had Canute the victory, though all England fought against him!" The *Chronicle* continues that, "all the nobility of the English nation were destroyed."

Called the Battle of Assandune in the 11th century, Ashingdon in the Rochford district of Essex, south of the river Crouch, and Ashdon in north Essex both lay claim to being the battle site. The ghostly moaning of dying soldiers has been heard at Ashingdon, and at Bloodstained Hill where the battle supposedly took place, it was said that no grass would ever grow again, although today there is grass! At Woodham Mortimer near Ashingdon, graves of Danish soldiers have been unearthed, and it is known that a church built by King Canute to commemorate his victory once stood in the neighbouring village of Hockley. Four years after the battle Canute returned to Ashingdon, accompanied by Archbishop Wulfstan, to consecrate a church "for the souls of the men who had been slain". The 13th-century St Andrew's Church stands on the site today.

After his defeat at the Battle of Ashingdon, King Edmund and his army retreated to Gloucestershire but were soon followed by Canute. Legend has it that Edmund challenged Canute to single combat, believing that it would save unnecessary loss of life. The conflict was, after all, between the two of them over the crown. In a fight to the death, the victor would become King of England. Canute was much smaller in stature than Edmund and, realising that he could lose his life, suggested a peaceful resolution to the situation instead. The two met at Deerhurst, Gloucestershire, on an island known as Olney, formed by the River Severn and Naight Brook. The two kings sailed over from opposite sides in fishing boats, and negotiated a peace settlement, virtually dividing the country in half, whereby Edmund kept the areas known as Wessex, Essex, East Anglia and London, while Canute ruled over the land north of the River Thames.

It was agreed that whoever lived the longest would gain the territory of the other, and thereby rule the whole country. Florence of Worcester wrote, "Afterwards, having exchanged presents of arms and robes, they separated."

On 30 November, less than six weeks after this agreement was made, Edmund died mysteriously in London or Oxford and Canute became King of All England. The cause of Edmund's death is unrecorded. Canute's supporters put about the story that Edmund had died through illness, although inevitably there is the suspicion that he was assassinated.

Henry of Huntingdon wrote that Edmund "was treasonably slain. Thus it happened: one night, this great and good king, having occasion to retire to the house for relieving the call of nature, the son of the ealdorman Edric Streona, by his father's contrivance, concealed himself in the pit, and stabbed the King twice from beneath with a sharp dagger, and leaving the weapon fixed in his bowels, made his escape. Edric then presented himself to Canute, and saluted him, saying, 'Hail! Thou art sole King of England!' Having explained what had taken place, Canute replied, 'For this deed I will exalt you, as it merits, higher than all the nobles of England.' He then commanded that Edric should be decapitated and his head placed upon a pole on the highest battlement."

Edmund was buried at Glastonbury Abbey, Somerset, near his grandfather King Edgar, although his tomb was destroyed during the Dissolution of the Monasteries. After his death, Canute sent Edmund's two sons to Sweden with orders for them to be murdered, but their lives were spared.

One controversy surrounds Edmund to this day. An anonymous Elizabethan play called *Edmund Ironside*, telling the story of Edmund, Canute, and a traitorous nobleman Edricus, is believed by many scholars to be an early work of William Shakespeare. The manuscript, now in the British Museum, is said to contain over 250 words and phrases that appear for the first time in Shakespeare's writings, more than 600 rare words used by him, there are some 2,000 parallels with the known plays, and it contains many unusual themes and even errors that occur in the Bard of Avon's other works. Some have even gone as far as to suggest that *Edmund Ironside* could be the first drama that Shakespeare ever wrote.

But, like much of the real Edmund's life, it is a mystery forever lost.

Chapter 11

Canute c.994–1035

Reign: 1016–1035

Ask anyone about King Canute and they immediately conjure up an image of him sitting on the shore commanding the tide to turn, as the waves lapped unyieldingly around his feet. The famous story leaves us with the impression of a power-crazed monarch, who thought that he could control the sea, and yet the popular legend is falsely recounted.

The King was surrounded by flatterers and sycophants at court who told him that he was so powerful that even the sea would obey him. To show that he was a mere mortal with limited royal powers, Canute took his courtiers to the water's edge to prove that he could not control the tide.

In 1140 the Anglo-Norman chronicler Geoffrey Gaimar wrote in his *History of the English* that Canute was at Westminster in London beside the River Thames, where he "held his sceptre in his hand, and he said to the tide: 'Return back, flee from me lest I strike thee.' The sea did not retire for him, more and more the tide rose. The king remained and struck the water with his sceptre. The river retired not for that, so it reached the king and wetted him." Canute had proved his human fallibility.

Henry of Huntingdon, another 12th-century chronicler, records that King Canute retreated from the waves saying, "Let all men know how empty and worthless is the power of kings, for there is none worthy of the name, but He whom heaven, earth and sea obey by eternal laws." It is reported that the King later hung his crown on a crucifix at Winchester and never wore it again.

Others record the historic episode as having taken place at Bosham in

Sussex, where Canute's eight-year-old daughter accidentally drowned and is buried in the middle of the nave of Bosham church. The legend may have developed from the fact that Canute built a dyke near the harbour to reclaim land for farming. The dyke was unsuccessful, did not keep back the sea, and at very high tides the land flooded. The Anglo-Saxon word for dyke was char, and over the centuries the story developed of King Canute sitting in a chair trying to control the tide.

Although Canute came from a warmongering family and had joined his father Sweyn Forkbeard of Denmark on many Viking raids of England, he came to the throne peaceably, with Edmund Ironside ruling the southern counties and Canute everything north of the river Thames. When Ironside died suddenly in 1016, Canute was left as King of All England. Frequently portrayed in art as a bearded elderly man, he was just 21 years of age when he came to the throne.

Once he was king, Canute was no longer England's enemy, ruled competently and it has been written by his contemporaries that he "had a heart of gold". Canute was born in Denmark around the year 994, although the exact date is unrecorded, a son of King Sweyn and his wife Queen Gunhilde of Poland. Some historians claim that Canute's mother was the notorious Swedish figure Sigrid the Haughty, but she is now generally believed to be a mythical character.

Little is known of Canute's early life, other than from historic Danish writings which state that he was taught fighting skills by a chieftain called Thorkell the Tall. He first came to England as part of a Viking raid in 1013, eventually took control of his father's base camp in Lincolnshire, and was also put in charge of the great Viking fleet. Given such great responsibility at a relatively young age says much about his strength of character and abilities.

He divided England into four earldoms: Wessex, East Anglia, Northumbria and Mercia. His aim was to have four loyal Lords taking care of his interests and uniting the country, especially in his absence. Canute was in an unusual position as he was not only ruler of England but he also became King of Denmark, and later Norway and parts of Sweden. More than any previous monarch of England, this made him very powerful within Western Europe.

He tried to make laws that were suitable for all his kingdoms, which had a unifying result, but they were based very much on the earlier English laws of King Edgar. No longer did the Danes invade England, because they both had the same king, and the Viking raids that had plagued this country for centuries finally came to an end.

As an enemy of England, Canute had collected Danegeld – protection money supposedly in return for peace. But once king of this country it became Heregeld – an "army tax" to pay for soldiers. Whereas Danegeld had weakened England and sapped finances, Heregeld actually strengthened England and ensured that there was a mighty army in case of attack.

Such was the security of England that between 1019 and 1028 Canute was able to make at least four missions to Europe with his English army to increase his territory, which included seizing Norway from its ruler King Olaf. With a certain irony, the Scandinavian races that had long invaded England, were now themselves invaded by a former Viking leader and an English army. The tables had turned. Canute eventually installed two of his sons on the thrones of Denmark and Norway.

In 1027 he made a long state visit through Europe, ending in Rome. He attended the Coronation of the Holy Roman Emperor, Conrad II, at the old St Peter's Basilica on 26 March that year and had an audience with Pope John XIX. Canute negotiated a trade treaty with Emperor Conrad, which reduced the rates in tolls and taxes that English traders had to pay when crossing borders, and through the Pope he secured certain privileges for the English clergy, and made it easier for pilgrims visiting Rome.

He was the first English king since Alfred the Great to make this kind of pilgrimage and a proclamation was made to the people of England on his return, outlining his achievements. This greatly increased his popularity. Ultimately he was seen as a great king, and is often referred to as Canute the Great or the Mighty. This inevitably led to adulation and sycophancy at court, which resulted in his legendary commanding of the tide to prove his limitations.

Overall, though, King Canute brought much needed economic stability to the country and took control of trade routes through the North Sea and the English Channel, which opened up the market for English goods. He brought peace throughout England and wrote that he wanted his people to "have no war to fear on any side or the hostility of individuals". Although violent clashes were to continue for many centuries across the Scottish boundary, during Canute's reign he received "without bloodshed" the submission of three kings of Scotland.

There is no evidence that religion played any part in his life until he came to England, but as king he was guided by Christian values and principles, and encouraged the teaching of Christianity. Monasteries flourished during his reign and churches that had been destroyed by the Vikings were rebuilt at his own expense and any money plundered was returned. He turned to

Wulfstan, Archbishop of York, for spiritual advice when drawing up new laws, and was keen for his people to receive justice, and for wrongs to be put right.

Although he became a deeply religious man, he was not above using his close relationship with the clergy to his own advantage. The church appeared to turn a blind eye to that fact that Canute had two wives. He married firstly Elgiva of Northampton and fathered two sons.

Yet one of his first acts on becoming king was to marry Queen Emma, the widow of King Ethelred the Unready. Not only did this align him directly to the English dynasty of monarchs, but as Emma was originally from Normandy it also formed a better relationship with France and saved England from a Norman invasion during his reign.

We cannot now know the true nature of the union, but it appears that Canute's heart was really with Elgiva, for he kept up his relationship with her even though married to Emma. It seems probable that he married Emma simply for dynastic purposes, and maybe she went along with the arrangement as it enabled her to resume her position as Queen Consort.

As part of the marriage contract Emma insisted that any children she had by Canute would succeed to the throne, rather than the two sons he already had with Elgiva. She also spread doubts throughout the royal court that Canute was even the father of Elgiva's children. Canute overcame any suggestion of bigamy by claiming that Elgiva was his "handfast" wife, in accordance with Danish custom, and so he was not legally married to her.

Both wives outlived King Canute, who died at Shaftesbury, Dorset, on 12 November, 1035, aged around 40. His remains now lie in a mortuary chest at Winchester Cathedral along with those of his lawful wife, Queen Emma.

As with many of our early kings, Canute's personal possessions have long since disappeared, but one unusual object associated with him remains. In the Victoria and Albert Museum in London there is a ceremonial drinking vessel known as the Pusey Horn.

The Manor of Pusey, now in Oxfordshire, was given to a William Pusey by King Canute as a mark of gratitude for warning him of an impending attack. It is a two-foot-long ox horn with silver-gilt decoration, which can be used either to drink from or be blown as a hunting horn. It bears an inscription stating that it was a gift from King Canute, and it remained in the Pusey family for some 900 years before being given to the museum in 1938.

Canute's first glimpse of England was the port of Sandwich in Kent as the Viking long ships landed. The *Anglo-Saxon Chronicle* claims that in

1031, four years before he died, King Canute "gave to Christ's church in Canterbury, the haven of Sandwich, together with all the dues that there accrue from both sides of the harbour, so that whenever the tide is at its highest and fullest, and a ship is afloat in closest proximity to the shore, and a man is standing on that ship with a small axe in his hand, the monastery shall receive the dues from as far inland as can be reached by a small axe thrown from the ship."

This was just one of many tokens to make amends for his youthful attacks on England with his father. Throughout his reign he strove to wipe out the memory of the horror and bloodshed that had paved his way to the throne and atone for the cruelty inflicted by his forebears on the English. In a complete turnaround, the man who was once England's adversary eventually became England's saviour, bringing decades of peace and prosperity. After his death, much of his work was undone by his sons, and the peaceful empire that he had established began to disintegrate.

Chapter 12

Harold Harefoot   Harthacanute
c.1016–1040   c.1018–1042
Reign: 1035–1040   Reign: 1040–1042

After many centuries of conflict between the Anglo-Saxons of England and the Vikings of Denmark, King Canute brought peace between the warring nations. By placing one of his sons, Harthacanute, on the throne of Denmark and naming another son, Harold, as his successor in England, he hoped that he had achieved a lasting peace.

But as soon as King Canute died in 1035, there was an immediate dispute between his two sons, and the security of England was once again in peril.

With King Canute's complex personal life, having, in effect, two wives, Queen Emma, the widow of Ethelred the Unready, was the mother of Harthacanute and Elgiva of Northampton, whom he took as his "handfast" wife, was the mother of Harold.

Although Queen Emma had insisted that her children should take precedence over Elgiva's, King Canute wanted Harold to be the next monarch of England. After his death, this created a complicated situation over who should succeed. Not only were two sons at odds, but two mothers were as well.

Queen Emma and the influential Earl Godwin wanted Harthacanute on the English throne and campaigned fiercely. Elgiva bribed key figures in an attempt to secure Harold's position. Many powerful noblemen took opposing sides, and the ensuing dispute over who should be the next king almost led to civil war in England.

The parliament of the day, the Witan, held talks at Oxford, and finally

Harold, the elder son, was chosen as monarch, in accordance with King Canute's wishes. They also considered that Harthacanute had been out of England for too long.

This caused great bitterness between the two brothers and Harthacanute immediately began plotting an invasion of England. English kings had long fought to keep the Vikings out of the country, and now a dispute within the very heart of the Royal Family threatened to spark conflict between England and Denmark once again.

As if this was not enough, there were two other claimants to the throne. Queen Emma had more sons, Edward and Alfred, by her first marriage to King Ethelred. They ventured over from their home in Normandy, probably at her instigation, to ensure that she had a son on the throne.

But Alfred, known as the Atheling, was murdered by Earl Godwin to take him out of the equation. In his 12th-century *History of the English*, Geoffrey Gaimer writes that Earl Godwin took the ill-fated Alfred "under his protection and led him into the town of Guildford" where he lodged him overnight. The next morning he had Alfred stripped, tied to a horse, and ridden to Ely where "they put out his eyes". Alfred the Atheling died as a result of his injuries.

"Never was a bloodier deed done in the land since the Danes came," ran a popular song of the day. After Alfred's murder, Edward fled back to France for fear that the same fate should befall him.

King Harold was crowned at Oxford in 1036, although contemporary sources say that the Archbishop of Canterbury refused to undertake the crowning himself. Harold later gave his richly embroidered Coronation robe to Croyland Abbey in Lincolnshire.

Very little is known about King Harold. He was born around 1016, probably in Northampton, and as he grew up developed a love of hunting. He particularly enjoyed boar hunts, which were popular at the time, and being very quick on his feet, earned for himself the nickname Harefoot. No record of a marriage exists, although he fathered an illegitimate son, Elfwine, who became a monk. Elfwine founded Sainte-Foi Abbey in Aquitaine.

Harold Harefoot has been described by historians as a weak and nondescript character with very little influence. He was barely 19 when his father died, and Elgiva became very much the power behind the throne and ruler on her son's behalf. The outflanked Queen Emma went to live quietly in Winchester but had all her treasures stolen by King Harold's supporters and so in 1037 fled to Flanders for safety. Her great-nephew was William of Normandy, who would play a significant part in English history in 1066.

King Harold Harefoot died at Oxford on 17 March, 1040, at the age of just 23, having ruled England for only four years and 16 weeks. He was buried in the old Abbey Church of St Peter at Westminster.

News of Harold's death reached Harthacanute in Denmark just as he was about to embark on an invasion of England with a fleet of 62 warships. Seven days before midsummer, Harthacanute landed peacefully at Sandwich in Kent to claim the English crown, but it was not with a spirit of reconciliation. He immediately had King Harold's corpse disinterred, decapitated and thrown into a ditch.

It was later retrieved from the River Thames by a fisherman. Harold was reburied in the 9th-century church of St Clement Danes in the Strand, London. One theory about the church's name is that it honoured Harold's Danish family.

The Coronation of Harthacanute took place at Canterbury Cathedral in June 1040, so we can assume that the Archbishop of Canterbury's allegiance was to Harthacanute rather than Harold. Once crowned, however, Harthacanute was not a favourable king.

To pay for his navy he revived the Danegeld, a heavy tax on the English people, which made him extremely unpopular. Although many different versions exist, the story of Lady Godiva riding naked on horseback through the streets of Coventry to appeal against oppressive taxation stems from this period in our history. When two of his tax collectors entered Worcester in 1041, they were set upon and killed by protesters. Harthacanute refused to countenance any insurrection and had his men devastate Worcester as a punishment, setting fire to many buildings. The English came to detest their new king.

Harthacanute's heart was really in Denmark and his concern was more for the Scandinavians than the English. Food prices rose in England and the cost of wheat was 55 pence a sester (approximately eight bushels). Like his half-brother, he is not credited with any significant accomplishment and it is said that he spent most of his reign "drinking and roistering". The *Anglo-Saxon Chronicle* forthrightly declares: "He never accomplished anything kingly as long as he ruled."

Once Harthacanute was on the throne, his mother, Queen Emma, returned from her self-imposed exile and had more influence and power than the King. She firmly believed that until her son married and had a queen of his own, then she had every right to be a co-ruler and act as if she were his consort.

She particularly controlled the Treasury, and had an account of her life written, called *Encomium Emmae*, showing her in a good light so that history would look upon her sympathetically. It is a biased account of her life as the wife of King Canute, and neglects to mention that she was previously married to King Ethelred the Unready. A copy of the manuscript made in 1043 still exists and is in the British Library today.

In June 1042, having reigned for less than two years, Harthacanute attended the wedding of his standard-bearer, Towed the Proud, in Lambeth. The *Anglo-Saxon Chronicle* tells us that while at the wedding feast Harthacanute "stood drinking, he fell suddenly to the earth with a tremendous struggle; but those who were nigh at hand took him up, and he spoke not a word afterwards, but expired on the sixth day before the ides of June."

He was buried with many of his predecessors in Winchester Cathedral.

With the deaths of Harold and Harthacanute, Danish rule of England finally came to an end. Edward the Confessor, from the Saxon house of Wessex and a direct descendent of Alfred the Great, now succeeded and the crown passed back to the English line of kings.

Chapter 13

Edward the Confessor c.1003–1066
Reign: 1042–1066

One of the most enduring symbols of monarchy in this country must be the magnificent Crown Jewels, which are housed today in the Tower of London. Although kings had traditionally worn crowns of varying styles, the idea of Coronation regalia was introduced to England by Edward the Confessor in 1043. He was the first of our kings to be pictured on a throne holding a sceptre in one hand and an orb in the other, both surmounted with a cross. He also had a staff with a dove on top, a jewelled sword of state, and wore a Coronation ring. This form of ornamentation has now been used at every Coronation in England for more than 900 years.

The last English monarch to be made a saint, Saint Edward the Confessor's name is now inextricably linked with the coronation of our kings and queens. The climax of the ceremony comes when the Archbishop of Canterbury places on the monarch's head, St Edward's Crown, which is also known as the Crown of England. Although the present crown dates only from the reign of Charles II – Oliver Cromwell having had the Crown Jewels broken up – it was created in 1661 using the same design as Edward the Confessor's own crown.

The gold staff carried in procession is called St Edward's Staff, which is laid on the altar to represent the Sovereign as God's chosen ruler of the people. The Coronation Throne on which the king or queen sits throughout the proceedings is also known as St Edward's Chair, and for centuries was housed at Westminster Abbey in the Chapel of St Edward the Confessor, before being moved in 1998.

The Imperial State Crown was made for Queen Victoria's Coronation in 1838 using many historic jewels and contains a sapphire that once belonged to Edward the Confessor. Legend has it that the King was attending the consecration of a chapel dedicated to St John the Evangelist, when he was approached by a beggar asking for alms. The King had already given away the money that he had with him that day, so he took off his sapphire ring and gave it to the beggar as a gift.

The King was visited by two pilgrims 23 years later, who to his surprise gave him back the sapphire ring. They claimed that they had been travelling in the Holy Land, where they met a very old man who told them that he was St John the Evangelist. He said that he had once disguised himself as a beggar and had been given the ring. He now asked for it to be returned to its original owner.

So Edward the Confessor received his ring back and declared it to be a holy relic. He died shortly afterwards and the ring was buried with him. Nearly a century later on 13 October, 1163, when his body was being moved, the sapphire was taken from the ring still on his finger, in the presence of King Henry II. Today it can be seen at the centre of the cross at the top of the Imperial State Crown, seen every year at the State Opening of Parliament.

Not only was Edward the Confessor the inspiration behind the Crown Jewels, but he also founded Westminster Abbey where 38 English monarchs have had their Coronation. A small monastery had been established on the site during the reign of King Edgar a century earlier, but it was Edward who had a large stone church erected in its place. He gave a tenth of his fortune to cover the cost of the building and it became the earliest example of Norman architecture in England.

Built on marshy land called Thorney Island, it was west of the old St Paul's Cathedral and so became known as the "west minster". While still a child Edward had vowed that he would one day make a pilgrimage to St Peter's in Rome, but he never actually got to make the journey, and so he dedicated Westminster Abbey to St Peter instead.

Consecrated on Holy Innocents' Day, 28 December, 1065, it is the final resting place of 17 monarchs, including Edward himself. King Henry III was said to be so devoted to the memory of Edward the Confessor that he wanted an even more magnificent building to house his shrine. In the 13th century Henry had Westminster Abbey reconstructed into the gothic style that we see today.

Edward was born around the year 1003 in Islip, Oxfordshire, a son of

King Ethelred the Unready and Queen Emma of Normandy. England was under fierce attack from the Vikings at the time and King Ethelred and his family were eventually forced into exile in France in 1013, where they found sanctuary with Queen Emma's brother, Duke Richard of Normandy.

Edward's childhood was therefore spent in his mother's homeland. This gave him a French upbringing and he had no thoughts of inheriting the kingdom of England. After the death of his father, when the Danish King Canute claimed the throne, Edward and his brother Alfred remained in France for their own safety. It is recorded that when his cousin, Duke Robert, went on a pilgrimage to the Holy Land, Edward became a guardian to Robert's son, William of Normandy.

Edward's half-brother Harthacanute succeeded to the throne in March 1040 on the death of Harold Harefoot. As they both had the same mother, Queen Emma, Edward was invited to come back to the land of his birth as one of the new King's family. But Edward had not been living in England long when King Harthacanute died suddenly. This left a question as to who should accede as the next King of England.

Harthacanute was unmarried and had no direct heir. King Magnus of Norway claimed that he and Harthacanute had made a pact that if either of them should die without an heir, they would inherit the other's kingdom. But nobles and church leaders in England wanted Edward to be the next monarch, as he was a son of Ethelred the Unready and the last direct descendant of Alfred the Great.

The *Anglo-Saxon Chronicle* says that even before Harthacanute had been buried, Edward was chosen by "all the people of London as king". He came to the throne in a wave of great popularity and was crowned on 3 April, 1043, in Winchester Cathedral.

Strangely, Edward did not have the support of his own mother, who wanted Magnus of Norway to be king instead. It is said that Queen Emma had no affection for the children from her first marriage, and Edward resented her second marriage to King Canute after his father's death. Edward had her arrested and later put to trial on a charge of committing adultery with a bishop. He took away her property and jewellery, leaving her in poverty.

Although described as being idle and too fond of sport when a young man, Edward was almost 40 by the time he became King and had matured greatly. Physically he was portrayed by those who knew him as "a very proper figure of a man – of outstanding height and distinguished by his milky white hair and beard, full face and rosy cheeks, thin white hands, and long translucent fingers; in all the rest of his body he was an unblemished royal person."

His was not a particularly significant reign in English history, but he brought peace and prosperity to the country. England's gold work and embroidery became especially popular in the markets of Flanders and France. He was concerned for the welfare of his people and brought an end to the unpopular Danegeld tax. He also managed to avoid war during his reign, with little threat of invasion other than the occasional skirmish with the Welsh.

The main problem that Edward encountered was that he had divided loyalties between England and Normandy. Although a peace-loving man, he faced intense opposition from several high-ranking men because of his background. Having lived so long in France, Edward spoke Norman French as his main language, he wore Norman style clothes, and his favourites at court were Normans. This did not always endear him to the English people.

Throughout the early part of Edward's reign three earls were formidable opponents: Earl Leofric of Mercia and Earl Siward of Northumbria, who were extremely influential in the north of England, and Earl Godwin of Wessex, who was one of the most powerful men in the south at the time and acted as if he were king himself. All three were anti-Norman and suspicious of Edward because of his obvious bias.

An extremely ambitious and ruthless man, Earl Godwin encouraged Edward to marry his daughter, Edith, as this would place him in an even stronger position. The couple were wed on 23 January, 1045, but why Edward went along with the marriage remains a mystery. He was fully aware that his new father-in-law had murdered his brother Alfred the Atheling, although Earl Godwin consistently denied it.

Throughout their married life Edward and Edith had no children and some historians have suggested that this was deliberate on Edward's part. It put an end to Godwin's dreams of having a grandson on the throne.

Matters came to a head in September 1051 when Edward appointed a Norman as Archbishop of Canterbury – Robert of Jumièges. Godwin was fiercely opposed to this, but Edward took the upper hand and stood up to his father-in-law, forcing the earl and his family into exile.

Edward said that Godwin could only return to England if he brought his brother Alfred back with him. Obviously this was not possible. At the same time Edward sent Edith into a nunnery at Whirwell in Hampshire feeling the banishment of Godwin gave him an excuse to get rid of his wife as well.

Although the king thought that this was the end of the troublesome earl,

Godwin gathered himself an army, plus some strong supporters amongst the English, and returned a year later, coercing Edward to accept him back into the Royal Court.

Edward reluctantly gave Godwin back his lands, allowed Queen Edith to return, sent all Norman advisers back home to France, and kowtowed to him to avoid civil war. But the circumstances behind the death of his brother Alfred still rankled with the King. On 15 April, 1053, whilst celebrating Easter, Earl Godwin swore an oath that he had not murdered Alfred the Atheling. He then choked to death. The scene was later described by Henry of Huntingdon:

"In the twelfth year of Edward's reign, when the King was at Winchester where he often resided, and was sitting at table with his father-in-law, Godwin, who had conspired against him, the Earl said to him, 'Sir, King, I have been often accused of harbouring traitorous designs against you, but as God in heaven is just and true, may this morsel of bread choke me if even in thought I have ever been false to you.' But God, who is just and true, heard the words of the traitor, for the bread stuck in his throat and choked him, so that death presently followed."

With Godwin gone, Edward lived the rest of his reign peaceably, and piously as a very religious man. Today he is known as the Confessor because of his strong faith. Its meaning is "one who bears witness to Christ through his life". Having reigned for 24 years, he died in the early hours of 5 January 1066 at the Palace of Westminster aged around 62, following a stroke. He was buried in the newly consecrated Westminster Abbey. His burial procession is depicted in the Bayeux Tapestry.

With no heirs, Edward was succeeded by his brother-in-law, Harold, Earl of Wessex. There had been several contenders for the throne but Harold, the son of Earl Godwin, claimed that as Edward drew his final breath, he had stretched out his hand to him as a sign that he was to be the next King of England.

Others were convinced that Edward would not have wanted a relative of Earl Godwin's on the throne, but Harold had his Coronation within 24 hours of Edward's death so that no-one could oppose him. Three months later, Halley's Comet appeared in the sky and remained there for 15 days. Astrologers said that it was a portent to show the transfer of a kingdom. Many saw it as an ill omen.

In 1161, nearly a century after his death, Edward was made a saint by Pope Alexander III, and his feast day is celebrated annually on 13 October. He is the only King of England to be canonised and the first sovereign reported to "touch for the King's Evil" (scrofula). An example is given in *Vita Aedwardi Regis*, written by an anonymous monk in the 11th century.

"A certain young woman had an infection of the throat and of those parts under the jaw which, from their likeness to an acorn, are called glands. These had so disfigured her face with an evil smelling disease that she could scarcely speak to anyone without great embarrassment. She was informed in a dream that if she were washed in water by King Edward she would be cured of the most troublesome pox . . . and when the king heard of it, he did not disdain to help the weaker sex, for he had the sweetest nature, and was always charming to all suitors. A dish of water was brought; the king dipped in his hands, and with the tips of his fingers anointed the face of the young woman and the places infected with the disease. Those diseased parts that had been treated by the smearing of the King softened and separated from the skin. Hardly had she been at court a week, when all foulness washed away, and the grace of God moulded her with beauty."

Edward is the only English saint whose remains still rest in their medieval shrine, although his body has been moved several times within Westminster Abbey. Originally he was laid to rest in front of the high altar in 1066, but once canonised, his remains were transferred to a shrine on 13 October, 1163. A century later, King Henry III rebuilt the Abbey and had a more elaborate shrine constructed out of Italian marble and semi-precious stones, which Edward's remains were moved to in 1269. This shrine became a place of pilgrimage and many claimed to have been healed simply by touching the stonework.

During Henry VIII's dissolution of the monasteries, Edward's shrine was vandalised and his body was removed once again for safety, and was hidden within the Abbey until the reign of Queen Mary I. She had the shrine reconstructed, although much of it had disappeared by this time, so it became much smaller and less elaborate than it had originally been.

The Confessor's coffin was finally returned to the inner cavity, where it has remained since 1557. Nearby is a stone screen depicting 14 scenes from his life, and the shrine itself is said to mark the very centre of the Abbey.

In October 2005, over 1,000 years after Edward's birth, the exact location of his original burial chamber was discovered by archaeologists using radar equipment. Because medieval records state that he was buried in front of the high altar of Westminster Abbey, the location of the tomb was believed to be in that position. But the combination of archaeological investigation and 21st-century technology has revealed that the high altar was moved in

13th century by King Henry III, and Edward the Confessor's first tomb was actually ten feet behind the present altar.

Today Edward the Confessor is known as the patron saint of the Royal Family, difficult marriages and separated spouses. From the reign of Henry II he was also the patron Saint of England, replaced after 1348 by Saint George. But the Crown Jewels and Westminster Abbey remain as his tangible and resplendent legacy to England.

Chapter 14

Harold Godwinson c.1022–1066
Reign: January 1066–October 1066

If we know anything at all about King Harold, we recall that he was shot in the eye with an arrow at the Battle of Hastings. The scene is depicted on the 11th-century Bayeux Tapestry, and if you visit Battle Abbey in Sussex it is even possible to stand on a stone marking the very spot where Harold reputedly died. And who can forget Stanley Holloway's rendition of Marriott Edgar's famous monologue, in which they found Harold at the end of the battle "so stately and grand, sitting there with an eye-full of arrow, on his 'orse with his 'awk in his 'and."

As with so many historical events, it is difficult to separate fact from legend. Experts now claim that Harold might not have been shot in the eye, for what appears to be an arrow on the tapestry could actually be a later addition when it was repaired in the 19th century. In an engraving of the Bayeux Tapestry made in 1729 there is no arrow. Others say that in medieval imagery, those guilty of perjury were put to death by being stabbed in the eye. So the tapestry could merely be a piece of political propaganda, portraying Harold as an oath breaker and showing William of Normandy as the rightful king.

A contemporary account of the Battle of Hastings by Guy, Bishop of Amiens, states that four knights killed Harold with swords. This is backed up by William of Poitiers who, writing in the 1070s, said that Harold "all dignity lost, was recognised not by his face but by certain indications . . ." But whatever the reality, an arrow in the eye will always be the most popular story.

Harold was our last Saxon king, and also has the unfortunate claim to fame of being one of only two Kings of England to have been killed in battle. Little is known about his early life, but he was born at Bosham, West Sussex, around the year 1022, a son of the ruthless and powerful Earl Godwin of Wessex, and his wife Gytha Thorkelsdóttir of Denmark, a sister-in-law of King Canute.

As a youth he would certainly have been trained in military matters. A contemporary chronicler, Orderic Vitalis, wrote of Harold: "This Englishman was very tall and handsome, remarkable for his physical strength, his courage and eloquence, his ready jests and acts of valour." It is recorded that he once rescued two soldiers from quicksand. He is also known to have had a deep religious faith.

Harold's older sister, Edith, married King Edward the Confessor, placing the Godwin family in a very high position. In 1045 Harold was created Earl of East Anglia and, on the death of his father, he succeeded as Earl of Wessex in 1053. The Earl of Wessex was said to be the most important man in England after the monarch. Harold received a further title five years later when he became Earl of Hereford, and by 1064 was being styled as Duke of the English.

Around the year 1058, Harold embarked on a pilgrimage to Rome, where he had an audience with Pope Benedict X. While in Italy, Harold acquired a number of holy relics which he brought back to England. On the journey he was attacked by outlaws and almost lost his sacred treasures. But, as a soldier, he was able to fight them off and returned to England with the relics intact. He had a church at Waltham Abbey in Essex rebuilt to house them, and the building was dedicated by the Archbishop of York in 1060. Harold visited Waltham Abbey on many occasions for spiritual inspiration in times of trouble.

Harold further improved his standing with the King in 1062, when he lead several successful forays into Wales and strengthened the English border to repel raids. Everywhere the Welsh were defeated, a stone monument was erected, emblazoned with the phrase: "Here Harold was victorious."

Harold's downfall, however, began in 1064 when he made a trip across the English Channel, setting sail from either Bosham or Selsey Bill, and was shipwrecked off the coast of France. He was captured by a French Count, Guy of Ponthieu, and held hostage. He was soon rescued by William of Normandy but, in return, he was pressed into making an oath.

A contemporary reported that "Harold took an oath of fealty to William in a religious ceremony" and of his own free will agreed to be William's proxy at the court of Edward the Confessor. More significantly, he promised that when the King died "he would use all his influence and resources to secure the English throne for William . . ."

Harold made the pledge over a small leather box, called a phylactery, containing saintly relics. The Normans considered that this gave the oath religious significance and so was binding. Harold's supporters claimed that he was tricked into making this oath, and it was, therefore, invalid, because it was made under duress.

When Edward the Confessor died in January 1066, childless and without an heir, there were actually four claimants to the throne of England. Edward's nephew, Edgar Atheling, was probably the closest heir as a grandson of King Edmund Ironside. But he was still a youth and a strong leader was needed.

King Harald Hardrada of Norway said that he had a claim through an earlier agreement made between King Harthacanute of England and his father, King Magnus of Norway. But he could not substantiate this claim.

Edward the Confessor's cousin, William of Normandy, obviously insisted that he had been promised the crown through the oath sworn by Harold.

But ultimately it was Harold himself, as a powerful Earl in England and brother-in-law to the late King, who had the upper hand. He was crowned King in London on 6 January, the first Coronation to take place in the newly built Westminster Abbey, although this was not the building that we know today. The swiftness of the ceremony perhaps reflects Harold's concern that there might be a change of heart, or another claimant could beat him to it.

Not surprisingly, Harold's accession to the throne caused a storm in Normandy. William felt that Harold had gone back on his promise and swore that he would take his rightful crown by force. This eventually led to the Norman invasion, which changed the course of England's history.

In his private life, there was another change for Harold. His great love was a woman called Edith Swanneshals (Edith of the Swan Neck), with whom he had at least five children. She was his common-law or "handfast" wife, a civil partnership in the Danish manner, but this union was not recognised by the church in England. In January 1066, possibly on Coronation Day itself, Harold legally married Edith, a daughter of the Earl of Mercia. As monarch he needed Edith to be recognised as Queen and to have legitimate heirs.

Because of the threat from William of Normandy, from the earliest days of his reign King Harold had his men keep watch on the south coast of England for fear of invasion from France. But the spring and summer of 1066 went by and no invaders appeared.

Harold had another unfortunate enemy, his own brother Tostig Godwinson, the Earl of Northumbria. Harold felt that his brother had imposed unfair taxation on the Northumbrian citizenry. And when Tostig faced a revolt from the people, Harold did nothing to help him, which led to a family rift.

Then in September 1066, England was unexpectedly invaded in the north rather than the south. King Harald Hardrada (Harald the Ruthless) of Norway, having failed to win the crown of England, decided to take the country by force instead. His 300 boats containing 15,000 men stealthily entered the River Humber and made their way towards York. Tostig sided with the invader against his brother.

At the time, Harold was suffering with a very painful leg. Worried by the news of this unforeseen invasion in Yorkshire, Harold spent the night in prayer. He is said to have seen a vision of Edward the Confessor in his dreams, telling him that he would be victorious. In the morning, Harold's leg was better. He immediately headed north with his army to halt the Norwegian invasion.

On arrival, he offered his brother a third of his kingdom if they could put aside their differences, and if Tostig and his followers would swear allegiance to the English crown. When Tostig asked what Harald Hardrada would receive from this agreement, King Harold replied, "Seven feet of ground." Harald Hardrada happened to be seven feet tall, so was actually being offered only a grave. Tostig simply turned his back on his brother, and the hostilities commenced.

The fighting was fierce for many hours. The clash of axes was said to sound as if a thousand anvils were being struck at exactly the same time. King Harold and his army eventually defeated the Norwegians at Stamford Bridge on 25 September. Hardrada and Tostig both lost their lives in the ensuing battle, as did thousands of men from the Norwegian army. It is said that the battlefield was bleached white with bones for the next 50 years.

King Harold's victory was short-lived. Just three days later news reached him that William and his Norman army, in a fleet of several hundred ships, had landed on the Sussex coast near Pevensey Bay on 28 September. Harold marched his men back from Yorkshire to Sussex in less than two weeks, no mean feat in the 11th century, averaging some 30 miles per day.

At Senlac Hill, north of Hastings, Harold's Saxon army finally came face to face with the Norman invaders at around 9am on Saturday 14 October, 1066.

Mounted on his horse, King Harold addressed his men with the words, "Stand firm, and victory shall be yours. Let no man leave the ranks until I give the order. Instead, do you all stand shoulder to shoulder like a rock against which the sea beats in vain. So shall the enemy waste their strength upon you, and in the end suffer defeat."

William had a formidable force of many hundred mounted knights and thousands of archers and foot soldiers – estimated at between 5,000 and 7,000 men. Harold was said to have had a number to match his enemy, but his men were exhausted after the long march from Yorkshire. Just as William had tricked Harold into signing an oath, so he now duped him on the battlefield.

After many hours of fierce fighting, William ordered some of his men to flee. Harold's army wrongly thought that the Normans were retreating, broke rank and charged after them. Disobeying Harold's instructions to remain "shoulder to shoulder", this left a gap in the English lines, and Norman soldiers were able to infiltrate and attack the Saxons mercilessly with axes and swords.

At sunset, William ordered his archers to fire arrows into the air directly on to the weakened and greatly depleted army. A shower of hundreds of sharp arrows fell from the skies, and with one final charge from the Normans on horseback, the Battle of Hastings was won. As dusk descended, thousands of Saxons lay dead, including King Harold.

The most probable scenario is that Harold was injured with an arrow in the eye, causing him to fall from his horse. Once helpless on the ground, he was fatally attacked by swordsmen. Harold's mother, Gytha, and his wife, Queen Edith, actually watched the battle from an oak tree, and Edith had the dreadful task of identifying his body. It was said to be so mutilated that she had to open his chainmail and look for recognizable marks on his body to be certain that it was him.

Harold's final resting place remains a much-debated mystery. His mother offered William the weight of her son in gold if she could have his body, but William rebuffed her. Harold was reputedly buried on a Sussex beach, as William refused to allow him a proper Christian burial and did not want a tomb that might become a martyr's shrine, although legend has it that his body was later returned to Bosham – the place of his birth.

In 1954 an Anglo-Saxon stone sarcophagus was discovered by workmen beneath the chancel arch in Holy Trinity Church, Bosham. The dismembered bones inside, with a limb and the head missing, appeared to be from someone injured in battle. The suspicion was that it could be the body of King Harold.

The grave was covered over again and remains untouched. With the advent of carbon dating and DNA testing since that time, a petition was made as recently as 2003 for the coffin to be reopened and the bones examined. However, the Chichester Diocese refused to allow the grave to be excavated on the basis that it would be impossible to prove that the remains were those of King Harold. A living direct descendant would need to be found to compare DNA samples, and the likelihood of that was considered improbable.

Another long-held belief is that Harold's body was reburied in a marble tomb at Waltham Abbey in Essex. The building of his day has long since gone, but two stones outside the present Waltham Abbey Church bear the inscriptions: "This stone marks the position of the High Altar, behind which King Harold is said to have been buried 1066" and "Harold, King of England, obit 1066". As with the arrow in the eye legend, the mystery of his final resting place will probably never be resolved.

Chapter 15

William I (the Conqueror) c.1028–1087
Reign: 1066–1087

One of the most memorable dates in English history must surely be 1066, the year of the Battle of Hastings, when William of Normandy brought an end to Anglo-Saxon rule and changed the path of our monarchy for ever. Despite his eventual achievements, William's arrival on the shores of England prior to the Battle of Hastings seemed inauspicious.

As he stepped off his boat near Pevensey Bay in Sussex, he fell flat on his face. Refusing to be embarrassed, he immediately turned it to his advantage by grabbing two handfuls of sand and pebbles, and loudly declaring, "By the splendour of God, thus do I hold England in my hands!"

Guillaume de Normandie, as he was known in his lifetime, was the illegitimate son and only child of Robert I, Duke of Normandy, and his mistress Arlette (sometimes called Herleva), the daughter of a tanner. Robert is said to have fallen in love with her whilst spying on her as she washed linen in a stream. Although William was born around 1028 at Falaise Castle, seat of the Dukes of Normandy, he was largely raised by his mother elsewhere as she was deemed socially inferior. Later in life William was mocked by his enemies for being the descendant of a humble tanner.

When his father died whilst on a pilgrimage to the Holy Land in July 1035, the eight-year-old William inherited the title Duke of Normandy and so was elevated to the aristocracy. Because of his youth, he was protected by four noblemen but by the time he reached maturity others, including King Henry I of France, were looking enviously at his inheritance and tried to take over his duchy.

All four of his guardians were gradually assassinated. William, however, fought back and not only protected his lands but also expanded his territory by the time he was 20. It was an early clue to the "conqueror" that he would become.

Above average in height, with grey eyes and dark hair, William was said to be powerfully built. Both physically and mentally strong, he proved himself to be a tenacious soldier and it was noted that he could draw and fire his bow while his horse was at full gallop. He was ruthless and had a strong determination to succeed.

At a time when the church and the state had almost equal authority, William cultivated allies within the church, as he knew that this would strengthen his position in the long term. Although William supported the reforms of Pope Leo IX, the pontiff did not reciprocate. When William wanted to marry Matilda of Flanders, the Pope tried to prevent the union on the grounds that they were distant cousins.

William went ahead with the wedding anyway, and around 1051 married Matilda in the Notre Dame chapel of Eu Castle, at Seine-Maritime in Normandy. It proved to be an incredibly happy marriage and a later Pope, Nicholas II, finally gave the couple the Papal blessing in 1059. Because William was around 5ft 10in tall and Matilda was only 4ft 2in they appeared physically unsuited, yet there is only one recorded disagreement during their 32-year marriage. They had at least nine children, two of them eventually becoming Kings of England.

Although based in France, William's great ambition was to rule England, and he felt that he had a genuine right to the crown. His great-aunt Emma had married both King Ethelred II and King Canute, and his own wife, Matilda, was a direct descendant of King Alfred the Great. Most importantly he based his claim on the fact that King Edward the Confessor, his second cousin, had once stated that he wanted William to be his successor.

This was later reinforced by Harold Godwinson, who had sworn an oath to back William's claim at court. When Harold later reneged, William was incensed. When news reached Normandy that Harold had actually been crowned king in January 1066, just hours after Edward the Confessor's death, William could speak to no-one until he was able to control himself. Enraged at what he considered to be a betrayal, William determined to come to England to take by force what he considered to be his rightful position.

On 28 September, 1066, William sailed for England with hundreds of ships and thousands of men. For many centuries England had been invaded by the Vikings, but they had always been repelled. Now England was taken over by the Normans. Ironically, the Normans got their name through being "men from the north" or Norsemen, and were originally Vikings who had settled in an area north of the River Seine in around 900AD. So the Vikings finally succeeded after all, when, after the ferocious battle of Hastings on 14 October, 1066, Harold was killed and his forces were routed, William emerged victorious.

We tend to think that William immediately became King, but after Harold's death Parliament chose Edgar Atheling as successor. Edgar was just 15 years old, but as a grandson of King Edmund Ironside was considered a legitimate heir to the throne as the only living male relative from the line of English monarchs.

However, William, as victor at the Battle of Hastings, declared himself to be the new King of England. In the end, Parliament backed down and Edgar, conscious of his youthful weaknesses, personally relinquished the throne to William in a meeting at Berkhamsted. It was in this small Hertfordshire town that William of Normandy became William the Conqueror. Soon work began on building a castle at Berkhamsted, which became a favourite retreat for our first Norman monarch. William also founded Battle Abbey on the site of his victory at Senlac Hill.

William's Coronation took place at Westminster Abbey on Christmas Day, 1066. The service was conducted in both English and French by Archbishop Ealdred of York and Bishop Geoffrey of Coutances. When they jointly asked the congregation if they would accept William as their king, the people all shouted lustily in agreement – but in their own languages. The Norman guards posted outside heard the cacophony and wrongly assumed that there was a revolt. They immediately panicked and set fire to some outhouses, which quickly spread, and soon there was pandemonium as crowds rushed from the church to safety.

William was left trembling in the sanctuary, with only the bishops and a few clergy remaining to complete the ceremony. So William has the unique distinction of being crowned in a virtually empty Abbey. Word of the chaos spread amongst the English people, almost as quickly as the fire had done, and they became very suspicious and distrustful of the Normans.

To William's surprise, the English were not prepared to submit easily. For the next decade there was constant civil unrest and resistance against the Norman invasion. Some insurrections were led by the thwarted Edgar Atheling. Rebellions quickly broke out in East Anglia, the Midlands, Northumbria, York, Worcester, Gloucester and Exeter. One by one, William's soldiers quashed them, often destroying whole towns and villages and 100,000 people lost their lives trying to protect their homes.

All but two Anglo-Saxon noblemen lost their positions, power, and lands. William had initially hoped that English noblemen would work with him, but instead he had to oust the most influential and replace them with Norman barons instead. He was ruthless in his approach and determined to prove that his conquest of England was total. As far as he was concerned, all land now belonged to the crown. Gradually he distributed the estates of the Saxon aristocracy to his supporting French barons. England now had a ruling class that did not actually speak English.

William's aim was to bring an end to the practice that existed in England whereby nobles and landowners controlled their vassals and serfs. He introduced instead his own feudal system, meaning that (apart from inheritable estates which he gave to friends, family and loyal followers) the Crown owned most of the land in the country, and leased it to barons, knights and farmers.

Every tenant of land now had to swear an oath of allegiance to the King, and more or less give him whatever he asked for, whether it was taxes or military service. This law applied to everyone, no matter who they were.

When William discovered that his half-brother, Odo, was collecting money for the Church rather than the crown, he had him arrested and imprisoned. An ancient English chronicler recorded, "Stark he was to men that withstood him. Earls that did aught against his bidding, he cast into bonds; bishops he stripped of their bishoprics, abbots of their abbacies. He spared not his own brother: first he was in the land, but the King cast him into bondage. If a man would live and hold his lands, need it were that he followed the King's will."

King William and his barons built castles and strongholds for themselves out of stone, rather than the traditional wooden buildings which were predominant at the time, possibly as much to protect themselves from the local people as to repel foreign invaders.

England is said to have had only one stone castle before William came to the throne, and 27 by the time of his death, including those at Rochester, Chepstow and Dover. The first to be constructed by the new King was Hastings Castle, and the most enduring must be Windsor – begun during William's reign – which is now the oldest castle in the world in continuous occupation. The symbols of our monarchy, the Crown Jewels, are now kept at the Tower of London, which has William the Conqueror's White Tower at its very heart.

Some 500 motte-and-bailey castles were also built during his reign, consisting of a high mound of earth with a wooden or stone keep on the top.

Architecturally, new buildings in William's reign inevitably had a Norman style, with rounded arches and doorways. This can particularly be seen in churches and cathedrals of the period, such as at St Albans, Winchester, Ely and Durham. Although the Norman influence can still be seen in many ancient buildings, the two most remarkable items that survive from this period are the Bayeux Tapestry and the Domesday Book.

The tapestry was commissioned by William's half-brother, Odo, who was Bishop of Bayeux, and it was possibly intended for the new cathedral at Bayeux that was being built at the time. The 230-foot tapestry depicts scenes leading up to the Norman Conquest. In an era when many were illiterate, it was a piece of visual propaganda and included scenes that reinforced William's right to be King of England. It is sometimes known as the Tapesty of Queen Matilda as William's wife is said to have worked on some of the embroidery.

The Domesday Book is considered to be one of the greatest documents in our history, providing a unique picture of England in the 11th century. The idea came to William whilst spending Christmas at Gloucester in 1085, and was really intended as a survey of the country, so that he could have an accurate record of his subjects and their assets, and ultimately know how much he could raise in taxes. He called it "The Description of All England". It recorded who owned every piece of land and how much it was worth. It is said that each ox, cow and pig in the country was accounted for, and even every plough. Astonishingly, it was completed in just eight months and contains the records of 13,418 settlements in 40 counties of England. Nearly every town, village and hamlet mentioned in the Domesday Book can still be found on a 21-century map of England.

The original 413-page book, handwritten in red ink by one un-named man, still survives in the National Archives at Kew. A second volume of 475 pages, known as "Little Domesday", was compiled later, with additional information missed from the main book.

Although these may be considered as relics, William's influence can still be seen in many areas of our lives to this day. For example, at his Coronation he became King William I, and our monarchs are numbered from his reign. So, although we had Edward the Elder, Edward the Martyr, and Edward the Confessor prior to the Norman invasion, it was the Edward on the throne after William's time that we know as King Edward I (reign 1272-1307).

During William's reign our language changed, with French replacing

Anglo-Saxon at court. Gradually, many French words were introduced into everyday speech, so that by the year 1100, Middle English had begun to develop, which forms the basis of our vocabulary today. The Norman word caboche, for example, became cabbage in English. The Norman pouquette became pocket; caundèle developed into candle, and so on.

William set up a new bureaucracy in England, which really formed the basis of our Civil Service. Administration was carried out in each shire or county, overseen by sheriffs acting on the King's behalf. This gave the monarch extra control in the way the country was governed, and the sheriffs ensured that law and order was kept, and that taxes were paid. William's aim was that the monarchy should become more powerful than the church.

William boasted that during his reign, only one lawbreaker was executed. This might give the impression of benevolence on his part, but he was actually ruthless in punishing wrong-doers, and his preferred method was to have criminals blinded or maimed, rather than hanged.

Parts of the English landscape were permanently changed by William, too. Vast areas were cleared in Hampshire in 1079 to create a habitation for deer – not because of William's fondness for the creatures, but because of his love of hunting. Nova Foresta, as it is called in The Domesday Book, became a royal hunting ground, even though it meant destroying many villages and settlements in the process. It is said that 36 parishes disappeared when the New Forest was cleared for the King's sport, and the inhabitants were evicted. By the end of his reign, the Crown owned 69 forests, which covered a third of the kingdom, depriving former owners of any rights.

Although he was undoubtedly a ruthless and self-centered monarch, peace in England was restored by the end of William's reign. The *Anglo-Saxon Chronicle* of the period tells us that "We must not forget the good order he kept in the land, so that a man of any substance could travel unmolested throughout the country with his bosom full of gold. No man dared to slay another, no matter what evil the other might have done him."

In spite of making many enemies on both sides of the English Channel, William lived to be nearly 60, when the average life span was less than 45 years. As he grew older, his hairline receded until he had lost most of his hair at the front, and he was said to be stout, with a large stomach that made him look as if he was pregnant. In his latter years he spent much of his time in his homeland in northern France but had lost none of his fighting spirit.

In August 1087 he and his army raided the town of Mantes-la-Jolie in a territorial dispute with King Philip I of France. Soldiers destroyed the town by fire but, whilst riding down a steep hill, William's horse slipped on some hot ashes and, as the animal fell, the King was crushed against the saddle and suffered severe abdominal injuries. He never recovered, and spent his final weeks being nursed by monks at the Convent of St Gervais, near Rouen, and died on 9 September. William bequeathed Normandy to his eldest son, Robert. His second son, William, hurried to England with his father's ring and was proclaimed King.

William the Conqueror was buried at St Stephen's Church, L'Abbaye-aux-Hommes, at Caen. In an unfortunate repeat of the King's Coronation, fire broke out during the funeral, causing many to disperse in panic. A local resident then claimed that the abbey was built on land owned by his father, which had not been paid for. The debt had to be settled on the spot by William's son Henry before the funeral could continue. Then, because of William's large girth, and the swelling of his abdomen due to his fatal injury, his body would not fit into the stone tomb. Monks forced the body in, with unpleasant results, as it burst open, and the few remaining mourners fled due to the foul stench.

As with many of his predecessors, William the Conqueror did not rest in peace. His grave was defiled and vandalised several times over the centuries and his remains were finally scattered by a Calvanist mob in 1562. Legend has it that only a thigh bone could be found afterwards. His original tomb, said to be of gold and silver decorated with precious stones, was finally destroyed during the French Revolution in 1793. An investigation in the 20th century found that there was indeed a single thigh bone in the old tomb and a new stone was placed over it on 9 September, 1987, the 900th anniversary of his death.

Nine European monarchs can now trace their ancestry directly back to William the Conqueror, including Queen Elizabeth II (who is his great granddaughter 22 times). When the Queen was in Normandy on 6 June, 1984 to commemorate the 40th anniversary of D-Day, she took the opportunity to visit the tomb of her ancestor.

The Normandy Landings on D-Day were a turning point in World War II, and ultimately led to Hitler's defeat, saving us from invasion. A Latin inscription on the Bayeux War Memorial, erected by the British to honour all those who died during the Battle of Normandy and the advance to the Seine in 1944, reads: "We, once conquered by William, have now set free the Conqueror's native land".

Despite various threats over the centuries, all who love our country can take pride in the fact that there has been no successful invasion of England since the Norman Conquest of 1066.

Chapter 16

William II c.1056–1100
Reign: 1087–1100

William II has been described as the worst monarch ever to sit on the English throne, and it is often said that he has received more insults than any other King of England. The Victorian historian and Bishop of Oxford, William Stubbs, called him "a foul incarnation of selfishness in its most abhorrent form, the enemy of God and man." An 11th-century Archbishop of Canterbury said that William was "as dangerous as an untamed bull", and the *Anglo-Saxon Chronicle* tells us that he was "loathsome to well nigh all his people."

Today we refer to him as William Rufus or "the Red" because of his strawberry blond hair, which he wore long and flowing, with a centre parting. He was also reported to be very red-faced, so the nickname could be a result of his ruddy complexion.

William was born in Normandy in 1056, the third son of William the Conqueror and Queen Matilda. Little is recorded about his early life, other than that he was educated by an Abbott called Lanfranc, who later came to England and was appointed Archbishop of Canterbury. In adulthood, William was reported to be smaller than average in height, and William of Malmesbury records that he was thick-set and pot-bellied, with piercing blue eyes which had sparkling flecks of white that flashed whenever he was angry.

Not only was William physically unattractive, his character was none too pleasant, either. He lacked confidence in public and spoke loudly when nervous, which made him appear intimidating and arrogant. Quick to take offence, he was vindictive towards anyone who upset him. Orderic Vitalis, a contemporary chronicler, described him as being violent at times, when he would become "swollen with anger".

William only really seemed at ease with people of noble birth and had no rapport at all with the ordinary folk. The only records of him appearing relaxed and having fun are when he was with his closest friends. Little wonder that his public reputation was of a cold and ruthless man.

The fashion of William's day was to wear shoes or boots with pointed toes curved over like a scorpion's tail, and men began to equal women in their mode of dress. They wore full-length robes with trains that swept the ground as they walked, with long wide sleeves that covered their hands.

"Impeded by these frivolities," wrote Orderic Vitalis in the early 12th century, "they are almost incapable of walking or doing any kind of useful work." Men curled their hair with hot irons and wore very feminine caps. William of Malmesbury, writing in 1125, tells us, "Then the model for young men was to rival women in delicacy of person, to mince their gait, and to walk with loose gesture."

William was extremely vain and wore these fashions with relish. He was what might in a later period have been called a "dandy". His clothes were extravagant, and he insisted that they were of a high price. On one occasion he was putting on some new boots and asked a servant how much they had cost. When he was told that the price was three shillings, he became angry and demanded a pair that were "worth a mark of silver". The disgruntled servant went off and brought the king back a much cheaper pair but told him that they were very expensive. "These are much more suitable to royal majesty," said William.

On the death of his father on 9 September, 1087, William ascended the throne of England, but it was not a straightforward inheritance. William the Conqueror actually had four sons: Robert, Richard, William and Henry. He always had a very poor relationship with his eldest son Robert, and so bequeathed him a lesser title; Richard had died young in a hunting accident, and so it was the third son, William, who he chose to become the next King of England.

The fourth son, Henry, received an inheritance of £5,000 of silver, but no further title or power. This situation inevitably created animosity between them. Even in childhood there was disharmony amongst the brothers, William and Henry once emptying the contents of a chamber pot over Robert's head!

When William the Conqueror died near Rouen, William Rufus

immediately sailed for England with his father's ring to secure what he considered to be his rightful place. Within weeks he was crowned on 28 September in Westminster Abbey as King William II.

Robert remained in France as the new Duke of Normandy. Rivalry between the two brothers continued, with several military campaigns against each other. Since the Conquest of 1066 many Normans had lands in both England and France, and this acrimony placed them in an awkward situation. Whichever brother they showed allegiance to inevitably meant offending the other.

Eventually relations seemed to soften when William gave his brother a mortgage of £10,000 on the Duchy of Normandy, so that Robert had sufficient funds to go on a crusade to the Holy Lands. Although this appeared to be a generous gesture, it actually gave William power as he had control over the finances, and also effectively became ruler of Normandy while Robert was away.

The money that he handed over to Robert was not from his own coffers, either. William had claimed that he needed to assemble an army of 20,000 soldiers, making every shire in England send a particular number of men, with each man having ten shillings to "cover expenses". William then simply took all the shillings, which amounted to £10,000, and sent the men away again. It was an easy, if underhand, way of raising funds.

William's first act on becoming King was to go to the Royal Treasury in Winchester and seize the keys. Here he found his father's riches, amounting to some £60,000 in coins and jewels, with which he filled his own coffers. So, from the outset, he gained a reputation for greed, which made him very unpopular with the English people.

Soon he promised them fair laws but changed nothing. He pledged to lower taxes, but only raised them, and faced many civil rebellions as a result. Throughout his reign many barons tried to overthrow him, but William always managed to thwart them, sometimes by military might, often with empty promises. He came to be regarded as a bully and an oppressor.

Forest laws became harsher, and anyone found hunting on the King's land was hung with his own bowstring. No-one was allowed to keep a dog anywhere near his royal lands. He himself kept mastiffs to guard his households, but the dogs had their front claws removed so that they could not easily run away.

Between 1091 and 1093 William had battles with the Scots and managed to repel several invasions led by King Malcolm III of Scotland. Malcolm was killed at the Battle of Alnwick after trying to take control of Northumbria. The knight who led the attack was Robert de Mowbray, Earl of Northumbria, then one of the most powerful barons in England. Afterwards de Mowbray led a conspiracy to try and depose William, but the King discovered the plot and had him dispossessed and imprisoned for life.

William faced further rebellions and in 1098 invaded North Wales to suppress an attack by Welsh aggressors. He continued his father's practice of building castles and strongholds, notably Carlisle Castle, to protect his territory.

One of William II's legacies to us was the rebuilding and enlargement of the magnificent Westminster Hall, now the most ancient part of the Palace of Westminster. When William first inspected the newly built great hall, which is the length of four cricket pitches end-to-end, it was typical of him that he complained that it was not large enough and looked much smaller than he had planned.

It was here that Parliament used to meet, and where many important men have been honoured, such as Sir Winston Churchill on his 80th birthday in 1954. It is where Nelson Mandela addressed both houses of Parliament in 1996, and where royalty have lain in state, including Queen Elizabeth the Queen Mother in 2002.

Although not a great supporter of the church, one of England's magnificent cathedrals, Durham, was begun during his reign in 1093. William had previously confiscated a lot of church property to give to his friends, which led to many disputes with the church. When Bishops and Abbotts died, William did nothing about appointing successors, leaving churches and abbeys in a vulnerable position, and saving himself money.

As England's historians at this time were mostly monks, it could account for why we are now left with such a poor view of his life. For some four years there was no Archbishop of Canterbury, but in 1093 William became very ill and almost died, which prompted him to turn to the church for comfort. He sent for an Italian Benedictine monk called Anselm and appointed him Archbishop of Canterbury. Once William recovered, though, he turned away from God.

William quarreled with Archbishop Anselm in 1097, and told one of his courtiers to inform the Archbishop that he "hated him much yesterday, that he hated him much today, and that he would hate him more and more tomorrow and every other day." The saintly Anselm responded, "I would rather have you angry with me than God angry with you." Anselm went to

Rome in self-imposed exile, and William seized all his land in England and divided it up amongst his friends.

After a reign of just 13 years, William died on Thursday 2 August, 1100. He is the only adult English king not to have married, and he died without fathering an heir. As with several English monarchs, uncertainty still surrounds his death and, after 900 years, it is a mystery that can never be resolved.

On the eve of his death he was staying at a hunting lodge in the New Forest with friends when he had a terrible nightmare. He is said to have had a vision of his own death and in the dream his blood blotted out the sun. The next morning he awoke feeling ill, not made any better by the arrival of a monk who warned him that he had also dreamed that the King was about to die.

Later that afternoon, while out hunting stags in the forest, the King was shot in the chest with an arrow and died immediately. Whether accident or murder has long been debated. Just before the hunt, the King had been sharing a meal at the lodge with his associates, when a blacksmith arrived with six new arrows. William gave two to his close friend Sir Walter Tyrrell, saying "It is only right that the sharpest should be given to the man who knows how to shoot the deadliest shots." Within hours the King was shot by one of those two arrows.

The official story was that Frenchman Walter Tyrrell had been aiming at a stag, but accidentally hit an oak tree instead. The arrow ricocheted off the tree and plunged into the King's chest. As he was supposed to be an expert marksman who could fire the "deadliest" of shots, it seems unlikely that he would mistakenly hit a tree.

Tyrrell later denied having fired that fatal shot, and other contemporary accounts state that he had not even been in the New Forest that day at all. Other reports say that he immediately fled back to France, for fear that he should be hanged for murder, supposedly stopping at a blacksmith's on the way to have his horse shod with backward facing horseshoes so that his tracks could not be followed.

Whether Tyrrell was an assassin, or simply framed for the murder by another, is something that cannot be proven. William's younger brother Henry was present at the time, and succeeded to the throne as Henry I. Some believe that William was shot on Henry's orders. That Henry's Coronation took place within days may imply some involvement, and a determination on his part to be crowned as quickly as possible.

Although the King was out on a shooting party with friends, nobody seemed overly concerned about his disappearance, and a local charcoal burner named Purkis later found the body. William of Malmesbury relates that a few countrymen helped lift the corpse on to Purkis's cart, and it was pushed unceremoniously to Winchester Cathedral for burial, "with blood dripping from it all the way". Out of respect for his position as King of England, William was buried beneath the tower at the centre of the cathedral.

Seven years later the tower collapsed on top of the tomb, although William of Malmesbury is quick to point out that the tower might have collapsed anyway, even if William Rufus had not been buried there, but many considered it to be "divine judgement".

The King's body was then said to have been moved to the Lady Chapel, although his original 12th-century tomb remains to this day in the middle of the choir stalls under the present tower. His bones now lie in a mortuary chest in the cathedral.

The spot where William is said to have died in the New Forest is marked by the Rufus Stone, which was placed there by John, Lord Delaware, so that the event might never be forgotten. By Victorian times the original stone had become so worn and defaced that a new, iron-clad stone with inscriptions on three sides was erected in 1841, which stands there today between the Hampshire villages of Stoney Cross and Cadnam. About 200 yards from the stone stands an English public house named the Sir Walter Tyrrell. A local joke is that it is just an arrow shot away from the Rufus Stone.

The King was not widely mourned, and the *Anglo-Saxon Chronicle* has left us with a far from glowing obituary, saying that during William's reign "Righteousness declined and evil of every kind towards God and man put up its head. Therefore, he was hated by almost all his people and abhorrent to God. This his end testified, for he died in the midst of his sins without repentance or any atonement for his evil deeds."

In 1929 the English novelist and humorist Edmund Clerihew Bentley summed up the image that is left of this unlamented monarch, writing:

> *There exists no proof as*
> *To who shot William Rufus*
> *But shooting him would seem*
> *To have been quite a sound scheme.*

Chapter 17

Henry I 1068–1135
Reign: 1100–1135

Some Kings of England have a lasting reputation for being good and loved by the people, while others are remembered as ruthless and hated by their subjects. King Henry I, however, was a monarch of contrasts with a relatively good public image, yet often hardhearted and abhorrent in private. "He seemed the most fortunate of kings," wrote 12th-century chronicler Henry of Huntingdon, "he was in truth the most miserable."

Born in Selby, North Yorkshire, in 1068, he was the youngest and only English-born son of William the Conqueror and Queen Matilda. The site where Henry was born, near the river at Church Hill, is now permanently commemorated by a blue plaque, provided by Selby Civic Society, which was unveiled by the High Steward of Selby on St George's Day 2010.

Henry was educated entirely in England and was known for being particularly intelligent. Contemporary chroniclers praised him for his wisdom, and he was nicknamed Beauclerc because he loved studying and had a thirst for knowledge. He was said to have been better educated than his French-born brothers Robert and William Rufus; he could speak three languages and was the first King of England since Alfred the Great who could read and write fluently.

Physically it is recorded that in adulthood he was dark haired with a receding hairline, which he disguised by combing it forward into a fringe. As he grew older, he developed the same figure as his father, with a large paunch.

Very conflicting pictures of his character are left to us by contemporary accounts. Some chroniclers try to praise him, saying that he was a very different king from his predecessors, and he is invariably described as "peace loving". Robert de Torigny, writing in 1149, even went as far as to say that Henry was "the peace and glory of the earth".

Yet others claim that he was pitiless, callous and cruel – more brutal than any other monarch of the period. When, for example, it was found that some men minting England's coinage were manufacturing fake coins to line their own pockets, Henry had every single one of those at the mint tortured. Both the innocent and the guilty were made to suffer, which included having their right hands removed.

Even before becoming king, Henry had in 1090 pushed a man who had offended him off the top of Rouen Castle. More shockingly, he once gave orders for two of his own grandchildren to be blinded and to have their noses cut off. Juliana, one of his illegitimate daughters, was married to a man whom Henry considered was disloyal to him and so he took revenge on their children. This act almost drove Juliana insane and she wounded Henry by firing an arrow directly at him. Henry, it seems, was not so kind and peace loving as his supporters liked to make out.

To add to the contradiction, William of Malmesbury, writing in the early 12th century, claimed that "throughout his life he was wholly free from carnal desires", yet Henry is much more widely known to have been lustful and he admitted to having fathered more than 20 illegitimate children from at least six different mistresses. He holds the record for having more acknowledged illegitimate children than any other English monarch.

He was known to be avaricious, enjoying his wealth and possessions. Some condemned him for his extravagant, decadent lifestyle, although if Henry heard of any criticism, the person responsible would be mysteriously mutilated or murdered. Life could be dangerous for any detractors.

There was a lifelong rivalry between Henry and his elder brothers Robert and William. When King William II was killed in August 1100, Robert was away on a crusade at the time, so Henry immediately claimed the throne before his elder brother could return. And, as William had done, he rode straight to the Royal Treasury at Winchester and demanded the keys, using threats of violence to obtain them. Once he had control of England's finances, he rode on to London to organise his Coronation.

The new King Henry I issued a Charter of Liberties, a forerunner of the Magna Carta, and promised to abolished any injustices of his predecessors, and to ensure peace for his subjects, which immediately made him popular with the people.

In July 1101, his brother Robert of Normandy invaded England, landing with his army at Portsmouth. Many English barons supported Robert's claim to the throne, and English and Norman armies gathered at Alton in Hampshire ready to fight, although no actual battle took place. Henry and Robert drew up a treaty to settle their dispute amicably and the two agreed to keep the peace. Henry said that he would make no claim upon Normandy if Robert renounced his claim to the English crown. Henry agreed to pay his brother an annuity of £2,000 in silver as recompense, and Robert returned home to France.

Henry, however, had no intention of keeping his word and soon reneged on his side of the bargain. He vindictively had every English nobleman who had supported Robert's claim to the throne swiftly executed and began plotting to take Normandy by force.

He invaded in 1105 and again a year later, eventually defeating Robert at Tinchebrai in 1106. Robert was imprisoned, first at Devizes and later in Cardiff Castle for almost 30 years, until his death. Legend has it that after Robert made an unsuccessful attempt to escape, Henry blinded him with a red-hot poker. Robert now rests in Gloucester Cathedral, where there is an impressive tomb with a painted wooden effigy, dressed in armour.

Although fighting his own brother for territory seemed coldblooded, it actually made Henry popular in England. The people saw it as retribution for the Battle of Hastings, as an English king had now conquered Normandy. By a strange quirk of fate, the Battle of Tinchebrai was fought in September, 1106, the 40th anniversary of the Norman invasion of England. Since that day the English Sovereign has always held the title Duke of Normandy, and in the Channel Islands Queen Elizabeth II is still toasted at official functions as "the Duke of Normandy, our Queen!"

Within months of being crowned, Henry found himself a bride. His choice was tactical rather than a love match, for he married Edith, the daughter of King Malcolm III of Scotland and his queen, Margaret, who was a great-granddaughter of King Edmund Ironside. It was a very astute move as this made peace with Scotland, and also linked the Normans to the English house of Wessex. Edith was a Saxon name and so she became known as Matilda instead, as it was more acceptable to the Normans.

Henry had four legitimate children by this marriage: William, Matilda, Euphemia and Richard, the latter two dying young. The surviving daughter, Matilda, was married twice, first to the Emperor of Germany and, after his death, to Geoffrey of Anjou. Geoffrey wore a sprig of yellow broom in his helmet, which has the Latin name Planta Genista. As a result, he was known by the surname Plantagenet, creating a dynasty that would one day rule over England.

Henry's only surviving legitimate son and heir, William, died at the age of 17 on a ship that sank in the English Channel on 25 November, 1120. The Prince had been on a visit to Normandy with members of the court and the royal family but came home on a separate ship.

Henry arrived safely, but the *White Ship* carrying the Prince had a drunken helmsman, who struck a rock. The ship sank quickly with its 300 passengers. All onboard were drowned, except a butcher named Berold, who had to inform the court of the tragedy. Henry collapsed on hearing of his son's death and it is said that he never smiled again. Some of Henry's illegitimate sons and daughters also perished in the wreck.

Henry's wife Queen Matilda died on 1 May, 1118, and was buried in Westminster Abbey. He then married Adela of Brabant and Louvain at Windsor Castle on 2 February, 1121, but had no children with her.

As with some of his predecessors and successors, there were conflicts with the church during his reign, particularly when the church tried to free itself from the secular control of the King. Anselm, Archbishop of Canterbury, who had returned to England from exile following the death of William II, refused Henry the right to appoint Bishops.

Bishops were major landowners in England at the time, and so Henry needed to be in control and appoint loyal supporters. Eventually Anselm was exiled in 1103 for a second time, although King and Archbishop were reconciled four years later when a treaty was drawn up, under which Bishops had to pay homage to the King in return for their land.

When Anselm died shortly afterwards, Henry kept the position of Archbishop of Canterbury vacant for five years. It was no coincidence, perhaps, that when the church was trying to disassociate itself from the monarchy, Henry suddenly developed healing powers and was said to be able to cure people of the "King's Evil" by simply touching them.

In a more positive move, Henry invited a group of monks from Cisteaux in France to set up monasteries in England, and they became known as the Cistercians. Henry gave them the land on which they built Tintern Abbey.

It was through the church that Henry also brought about a change in men's fashions during his reign. After he had heard a sermon by a French Bishop, condemning long hair in men as being too feminine and long beards as resembling a "he-goat", he made all the men in his court cut their hair short. So, a fashion for a more clean-cut look came into being and Henry's own hair and beard were trimmed by the Bishop.

The reign of Henry I particularly stands out as period of peace. Although he fought wars overseas, such as two with King Louis VI of France over the ownership of Normandy, in England there were none. Warfare also changed under Henry and noblemen now wore heavy armour to protect them when fighting and were much more likely to be taken prisoner than killed.

Although Henry taxed his subjects heavily, he tried to make the system of taxation fairer and appointed England's first Chancellor of the Exchequer. Accounting was undertaken on a table covered by a cloth in the chequered pattern of a chess board, so that the columns could easily be used for calculations and the business of adding up the figures took place behind a screen called a cancellum, which is the origin of the title.

Sheriffs from all over England had to go to Winchester at Easter and Michaelmas every year to present the taxes that they had collected. The money was placed within the various boxes on the chequered table, so that the amounts paid could be seen instantly, and any shortfall was immediately apparent. Sheriffs' jobs were at risk if they failed to produce the full amount of taxes due.

Tally sticks were also used at this time, bone or wooden sticks with notches carved on them, as a device for the sheriffs to record figures. The 12th-century instructions describe the manner of cutting as, "at the top of the tally a cut is made, the thickness of the palm of the hand, to represent a thousand pounds; then a hundred pounds by a cut the breadth of a thumb; twenty pounds, the breadth of the little finger; a single pound, the width of a swollen barleycorn; a shilling, rather narrower than a penny is marked by a single cut without removing any wood." Tally sticks were used by the Exchequer until 1826. Eight years later it was decided that all surviving tally sticks should be burned at the Palace of Westminster. The resulting fire got out of control and the Houses of Parliament burned down!

Henry also reorganised the legal system in England so that set penalties were established, rather than the arbitrary punishments of earlier reigns. Some were very severe, such as the death penalty for crimes against property, but he did re-establish the former Shire Courts so that people could receive a fair hearing. He brought an end to ordeals by fire and water as a method of deciding whether a person was guilty or innocent, and encouraged fines instead. As a result, Henry became known as The Lion of Justice.

Henry encouraged sheep rearing in England, which did much to boost the woollen trade. He also set up trade guilds as associations to protect craftsmen, a precursor to the later trade unions, and many Guildhalls were built as meeting places.

King Henry I has one unusual claim to fame in that he established England's first zoo. At his hunting lodge at Woodstock in Oxfordshire he gathered together a range of exotic animals, including lions and leopards, and even a camel, which had all been brought back on boats by returning crusaders as gifts for the King.

He had a seven-mile-long wall built to keep the animals in, and the people out. Later monarchs moved the menagerie to the Tower of London, and finally to Regent's Park, where there is still a zoo to this day.

Another legacy of Henry's to us is a unit of measurement. The length of the King's arm, from his shoulder to the tip of his thumb, was established as being "one yard".

Henry had a longer reign than any of his predecessors and died on 2 December, 1135, at Lyons-la-Fôret in Normandy. He had eaten a large dish of lampreys, similar to eels, after a day's hunting. He became ill with dysentery or food poisoning as a result and died. The phrase "a surfeit of lampreys" has entered the English language as the cause of his death.

He was buried in front of the altar at Reading Abbey, which he had founded in 1121 "for the salvation of my soul", although the tomb was destroyed during the Reformation. Some of his internal organs, including his brain, were buried at Rouen in Normandy.

After his death, Henry had wanted his daughter Matilda to succeed him, but his nephew Stephen (the son of his sister Adela) claimed the crown instead. Although he had made his barons swear to accept Matilda as Queen, once Henry was dead the barons changed their support to Stephen. The 35 years of peace that Henry I had brought to England soon came to an end. Ahead lay an unsettled period in our history that would become known as "The Anarchy" or "The Nineteen-Year Winter".

Chapter 18

Stephen c.1096–1154
Reign: 1135–1154

Kind, generous, and benevolent might seem like positive adjectives with which to describe a king, but in the early 12th century such qualities were seen as a sign of weakness. The last of our Norman monarchs lacked the ruthlessness of his predecessors and it was said that King Stephen reigned, but did not rule.

Stephen was born in Blois, France, in around 1096. He was the third son of Count Stephen of Blois and Champagne, and Adela, a daughter of William the Conqueror. The Count was killed during a Crusade to the Holy Land and in 1106 Adela sent ten-year-old Stephen, and his younger brother, Henry of Blois, to live in England with their uncle, King Henry I, so that they could be educated at the royal court. As well as formal subjects, Stephen was trained in martial arts and became a skilful soldier.

King Henry became very fond of his nephew and made him Count of Mortain when he reached the age of 18, and gave him valuable estates in Normandy, and the south-east and north-west of England. In adulthood Stephen was said to be one of the wealthiest men in England. In 1125 he married a daughter of Eustace III, Count of Boulogne. She had inherited her father's money and estates, so the union increased Stephen's wealth still further.

When Henry I died on 1 December, 1135, the crown should have gone to his daughter Matilda, but there were claims that on his death bed he had named his nephew Stephen as his successor. Matilda was hated by the powerful barons, who did not like the idea of a woman on the throne and they also detested her husband, Geoffrey Plantagenet, Count of Anjou. Plus, she had left England at the age of six, whereas Stephen had been in the country since childhood.

Matilda was a strong and formidable woman, whereas Stephen was known for his gentleness and charm. A contemporary chronicler wrote, "By his good nature and by the way he jested and enjoyed himself, even in the company of his inferiors, Stephen earned an affection that can hardly be imagined." Tall, blond and blue eyed, he was said to be the "handsomest man in all England".

He had a particular advantage in that his younger brother was now the Bishop of Winchester, who secured support from the church and persuaded the Archbishop of Canterbury to crown him. "Aldermen and wise folk gathered the folkmoot" (Anglo-Saxon for "assembly" or "meeting of the people") "and these providing at their own will for the good of the realm, unanimously resolved to choose a king."

Stephen was selected instead of Matilda, and was crowned at Westminster Abbey on Thursday 26 December, 1135, which appropriately also happens to be St Stephen's Day. The citizens swore to defend the King with "money and blood", while Stephen promised to "apply his whole strength" to maintaining peace and strong government of his realm.

He toured the country in 1136, granting any requests that were put to him, even restoring the freedom of the forests which his grandfather William the Conqueror had taken away from the people. But instead of the promised peace and stability, England soon entered a time of civil war and anarchy.

There was friction between those who supported Stephen and those who had wanted Matilda as Queen. Within a year of Stephen's accession feudal barons were doing exactly as they liked to line their own coffers. They built castles to protect themselves and began terrorizing the people, devising all kinds of unspeakable tortures to extract money and land.

When the people had no more to give, whole villages were burned to the ground. Writings of the period leave us with a vivid and horrific picture of the misery that the English people suffered at the hands of the barons.

"They hanged up men by their feet and smoked them with foul smoke. Some were hanged up by their thumbs, others by the head, and burning things were hung on to their feet. They put knotted strings about men's heads and writhed them until they went into the brain. They put men into prisons where adders and snakes and toads were crawling, and so they tormented them.

"Some they put into a chest, short and narrow and not deep, and that had sharp stones within, and forced men therein that they broke all their limbs. In many of the castles were hateful and grim things called 'rachentenges', which two or three men had enough to do to carry. It was thus made: it was fastened to a beam and had a sharp iron to go about a man's neck and throat, so that he might no way sit, or lie, or sleep, but he bore all the iron. Many thousands they starved with hunger."

One contemporary chronicler wrote that it was a time in our history when "Christ and His saints slept". If Stephen had been a stronger king, he would have nipped the barons' behaviour in the bud, but he allowed matters to get out of hand and his authority was destroyed.

When Stephen suffered a period of ill health, Matilda's uncle, King David I of Scotland, took advantage and invaded England. Although Stephen left his sickbed to protect his land, instead of being able to fight back as he might have done in good health, he was forced to allow King David to take Northumberland, Westmorland and Cumberland.

With Stephen now gaining a reputation as a weak and ineffective king, the Scots returned in 1138 to extend their territory still further, but this time the people of the north fought them in Yorkshire. Known as the Battle of the Standard, the sacred banners of Saints Cuthbert of Durham, Peter of York, John of Beverley and Wilfrid of Ripon were hung from a four-wheeled cart in the middle of the battlefield at Northallerton.

The English army took up their position behind this impressive cart on the morning of 22 August and swore to defend the standard to the death. It was a fierce battle with some 12,000 lives lost, but within two hours King David's army was forced to retreat towards the Tyne, and soon returned to Scotland.

It was not a time to celebrate victory, for England seemed to be constantly under attack from both without and within. Although Stephen successfully fought back against the Welsh as they tried to cross the border, and thwarted insurrections as they occurred throughout the land, the greatest threat came from across the English Channel.

The furious Matilda was not prepared to take rejection and gathered an army of her own. She invaded England on 30 September, 1139 with her half-brother Robert, Earl of Gloucester. He made his base in Bristol, while Matilda settled in Arundel and soon established her own court in the West Country.

Stephen's efforts to prevent her proved ineffectual and his problems only increased. He never knew who he could trust, as often nobles changed their allegiance, supporting Stephen if he appeared to be in control, and Matilda if it looked as if she had the upper hand.

Soon he discovered that his Chancellor, the Bishop of Ely, and his Treasurer, the Bishop of Lincoln, were amongst those in league with Robert, Earl of Gloucester. Even his own brother, Henry, Bishop of Winchester, turned against him because Stephen refused to make him Archbishop of Canterbury.

In February 1141 Stephen faced a rebellion in Lincoln, led by Robert of Gloucester and the Earl of Chester. Before the battle on Candlemas Day, King Stephen attended Holy Communion.

"As he placed in the hands of Bishop Alexander the taper of wax, the usual royal offering, it broke," wrote Henry of Huntingdon. "The Pix also, which contained Christ's body, snapped its fastening and fell on the altar while the Bishop was celebrating; a sign of the King's fall from power."

That day Stephen was captured during a battle outside Lincoln. Although he is reported to have fought like a lion, attacking with his sword until it broke, he was hit on the head with a stone, knocked unconscious and taken captive. He was held in chains at Bristol castle.

Matilda now had control and set off for London to claim the throne for herself. Stephen was officially deposed on 10 April and a Church Council declared that Matilda was Queen of England. The Bishop of Winchester announced that all who supported her would be blessed, and those against her would be cursed.

Matilda was on the verge of being crowned when her haughtiness began to alienate her followers. "With stern eye and knitted brow, her countenance losing any semblance of feminine gentleness, she broke into a furious rage driving them away," wrote one chronicler of the time.

When she began demanding money from the people of London and increased taxes, they became hostile, forcing her to escape to Devizes on 24 June. From there she was taken to Gloucester disguised as a corpse. Dressed in grave clothes, she was tied to a bier and was transported unheeded.

Support now turned back to King Stephen. His wife, also called Matilda, took up his cause. At Winchester, she led an army into battle and had Earl Robert taken hostage. Using him as a bargaining tool, she offered Robert in return for her husband. Stephen was released from captivity on 1 November, 1141 and was restored to the throne. He was crowned again on 25 December at Canterbury Cathedral, and in 1146 another "crown-wearing ceremony" took place at Lincoln Cathedral. So Stephen had three Coronations.

In November 1142 King Stephen and his army laid siege to Oxford Castle where his enemy Matilda came close to being captured, but she escaped by being lowered down the castle walls on a rope. Being winter, she managed to escape at night by crossing the frozen River Thames. It is said that she wore a white robe which hid her against the snow. Although she survived and set up a base at Abingdon, her power and support had faded.

In October 1147 Robert of Gloucester died and Matilda finally gave up the fight, leaving England the following spring, and never returning. Even without his old adversaries, Stephen still faced unrest, with many now supporting Matilda's 15-year-old son Henry Plantagenet instead.

Not wanting Henry Plantagenet to rule England, Stephen had a plan to relinquish the throne to his own eldest surviving son, Eustace. He felt that if he could see his son crowned, then the future of the monarchy would be secure. But there was opposition, not least from the church. Without the backing of the Archbishop of Canterbury, the plan was scuppered and England never saw a King Eustace.

Henry Plantagenet, although only young, made a dashing attempt to seize the crown and arrived on the south coast with a few knights to help him. His money quickly ran out but, with the brazenness of youth, he asked Stephen for cash to help him pay his soldiers.

It was a measure of King Stephen's kindness and generosity that he actually acceded to this request and gave Henry the money. So, through his compassionate nature, Stephen was literally funding his own enemy. Fortunately for him, Henry soon abandoned his quest and returned to France.

In 1149 Henry Plantagenet was given the Dukedom of Normandy by his father, and in 1152 married Eleanor of Aquitaine, effectively becoming ruler of a region from Normandy to the Mediterranean. In January 1153, now older and wiser, he set out to invade England once again, as a previous Duke of Normandy had in 1066.

The two armies met at Malmesbury and were preparing to do battle when strong winds and heavy rain forced them all to seek shelter and the fight was abandoned until later in the year.

By this time Stephen had no fight left in him and eventually met Henry amicably at Wallingford on the River Thames. With just the river separating the two enemy camps, Henry and Stephen bargained across the water for two days until an agreement was reached.

A treaty was drawn up to finally end the argument over succession once and for all, with an agreement that Henry would succeed to the throne after Stephen's death. This pact gave stability and brought an end to what is known as the "Nineteen-Year Winter".

Stephen was in very low spirits at this point in his life. His wife of more than 25 years had died at Hedingham Castle, Essex, in May 1152, and when his son Eustace died in August 1153, Stephen seemed to lose the will to live. He died at Dover on 25 October, 1154, at the age of 56. Some say it was of a broken heart, although the official cause recorded at the time was "his old complaint, the emrods with the iliac passion" – dysentry, intestinal obstruction and haemorrhoids.

Stephen was buried next to his wife, Queen Matilda, and their son Eustace at Faversham Abbey, which he had founded. The tombs were destroyed during the Reformation but were rediscovered during excavations in 1964. Their bones are now thought to rest in an uninscribed canopied tomb within the Parish Church of St Mary of Charity, Faversham.

Much liked as a man, Stephen ultimately proved ineffective as a king. His 19 years on the English throne were judged by medieval commentators as being not a reign but simply one long war of succession.

Chapter 19

Henry II 1133–1189
Reign: 1154–1189

The first of our monarchs to call himself King of England, rather than King of the English, Henry II was a great-grandson of William the Conqueror and the first of 14 Plantagenet kings on the English throne. Named after the yellow broom flower Planta Genista worn by his father, and which appears in the family coat of arms, the name Plantagenet for the royal house was not actually used until after the War of the Roses in the 15th century, some 300 years after Henry's death.

The family was simply known in England as the Angevins, after their homeland of Anjou. Henry's nickname during his lifetime was Curtmantle, because of the short robe that he used to wear, shorter than anything worn by his predecessors – a garment sometimes known as the Anjou mantle.

Of all the events in his 35-year reign, King Henry II's name will be forever associated with one main episode: a quarrel with his Archbishop of Canterbury, Thomas Becket. Originally Thomas was his Chancellor, and they had been great friends, described as being of "one heart and one mind", with much banter and joshing between them. One day they were out riding together in London when they saw a frail old man with a ragged coat.

"Would it not be an act of charity to give him a thick warm cloak?" suggested Henry.

"It would indeed; and right that you should attend to it, my king," replied Becket.

"You shall have the credit for this act of charity," said the King, and laughingly wrestled Thomas Becket to the ground, pulled off his new cloak and gave it to the old man.

When Archbishop Theobald of Canterbury died in April 1161 after a long illness, Henry pushed to have Becket, then an archdeacon, elected as successor, naturally thinking that he would have a friend and ally in the senior position of the Church of England.

Thomas, however, wanted to prove that he was worthy of the role and that he had not been given the job simply because he was the King's friend. "You will soon hate me as much as you love me now," Thomas told the King, "for you assume an authority in the affairs of the church to which I shall never assent."

Thomas changed from the moment he became Archbishop of Canterbury in June 1162, and the two men quarreled constantly. Some 700 years later, in his tragic play, *Becket*, the poet Tennyson summed up the relationship:

> "*I served our Theobald well when I was with him;*
> *I served King Henry well as Chancellor;*
> *I am his no more, and must serve the Church.*"

Until Henry's reign, the Church of England was extremely powerful, with its own courts and laws and was answerable to the Pope rather than the monarch. The church now wanted even greater independence but Henry was determined to maintain control and insisted, for example, that the election of bishops and abbots was to take place before royal officers, in the King's Chapel, with His Majesty's assent.

The King and Becket argued over the ending of clergy's immunity from prosecution. Henry did not want priests to be above the law and felt that they should be tried in a secular court if they had committed an offence. In January 1164 he introduced the Constitutions of Clarendon with 16 proposals which limited the church's power. Becket fought against it but did not have the support of all his bishops, and general opinion was in the King's favour.

In October 1164, Archbishop Thomas Becket was summoned to Northampton by the King to attend a Great Council, where he was found guilty of treason. Becket fled to France and remained in exile for six years, under the protection of the Pope.

In order to secure the line of succession in England, in 1170 Henry had his eldest son, also called Henry, crowned in a ceremony to make him "the young king". This type of Coronation of an heir apparent was a French custom and had never happened before in England. It only served to anger Becket in exile, as normally the Archbishop of Canterbury would preside over such a royal ritual. The Pope and the French King were also outraged, and the Pope threatened to veto Henry's French provinces.

Henry had little option but to allow Becket to return to Canterbury.

When Becket finally returned to England he received a great welcome in Kent, but immediately proceeded to infuriate the King by excommunicating the Bishops of Salisbury and Lincoln who had taken part in the crowning of the young Prince Henry.

"What a parcel of fools have I in my Court, that not one of them will avenge me of this one turbulent priest!" the King declared. Chroniclers vary in their account of Henry's words, with some saying "troublesome priest", others "upstart clerk", but whatever the King really said, four of his knights misinterpreted Henry's comment.

They murdered Becket in Canterbury Cathedral on 29 December, 1170, wrongly believing that they were carrying out Henry's wishes. As a result, Henry appeared to be the villain, and Thomas Becket was raised to the position of saint and martyr.

The King was so shocked by the murder that it was written, "for three days he would eat nothing nor speak to anyone, and for five more weeks his doors were closed and he led a solitary life." As penance, Henry walked to Canterbury barefooted and was flogged by the priests there. His battle with the church was lost. Henry's reputation suffered irreparably as a result and his reign is for ever tainted by the murder of Becket.

Henry was born at Le Mans in France on 5 March, 1133, the eldest son of Count Geoffrey of Anjou and Empress Matilda, a daughter of King Henry I. He spent some of his childhood in England while his mother was trying to lay claim to the English throne, which she considered was hers by right. Henry received a full-time education until the age of 12, studying at Bristol, Bath and Normandy, and some of the best scholars were employed to teach him.

He developed a love of reading, and particularly enjoyed studying the history of the Roman Empire and became fluent in Latin. As a teenager he came to England again with a band of mercenaries to continue his mother's claim to the throne but was unsuccessful.

On the Feast of the Epiphany in January 1153, now aged 20, Henry tried again. When King Stephen died in October 1154, Henry acceded to the throne without any opposition. He was crowned King Henry II at Westminster Abbey just two months later on 19 December.

We perhaps know more about Henry's character and appearance than any previous monarch, as so many 12th-century writers have left personal accounts for posterity. He was said to be strong-willed, down-to-earth, and disliked the pomp and ceremony associated with his royal position. He cared little for his appearance and so shunned sumptuous materials and elaborate jewellery for more practical clothing, hence his simple short robes.

An expert in dogs and birds, Henry loved hunting and it was said that in his hands he either had a bow, a sword, a spear or an arrow, unless at rest or writing. "His hands show by their coarseness that he is careless and pays little attention to his person," says a 12th-century account, "for he never wears gloves, except when he goes hawking."

He was impulsive and changed his mind quickly, expecting everyone around him to keep up with his plans. If he said that he was staying somewhere for a whole day, he would suddenly decide to leave early in the morning and throw all arrangements in disarray.

If he was meant to be departing from a place in the morning, he would sleep until midday and not leave until evening. "I believe that in truth he took delight in seeing what a fix he put us in," wrote Peter of Blois, one of Henry's courtiers, in a letter.

Many recollections tell us that he could not remain still and always had to be doing something. Even in church he took documents to read, an arrow to mend or would be writing notes, so that he could occupy any quiet moments in the service.

One chronicler wrote that, "On his return home in the evenings he would seldom sit down, either before he took his supper or after. He passed nights without sleep and was untiring in his activities." It was said that Henry would vault over a table rather than walk round it. In 1177 it was recorded: "In a single day, if need be, he can travel the length of four or five day-marches. Thus outsmarting his enemies, he often mocks their plots with a sudden appearance."

Physically, Henry had a wrestler's build with a broad chest and muscular arms. His complexion was ruddy, and some say that he had freckled skin and a "lion-like" face, possibly based on the fact that he had a large round head with a mane of auburn hair. It is also recorded that, "He had an enormous paunch by the fault of nature rather than over-eating." Henry battled constantly with his weight, eating frugally for fear of becoming too fat.

His voice was said to be "harsh and cracked" due to much shouting, and he had a very violent temper. Henry could become so enraged that his courtiers felt that he had something of the Devil in him.

Before his accession, Henry had married the beautiful and rich Eleanor of Aquitaine on 18 May, 1152, at Bordeaux Cathedral. She was the former wife of King Louis VII of France, whom she had divorced after 15 years of marriage. Nine years older than Henry, she was a strong-minded woman, which led to clashes with her husband because of his short temper, so theirs was a very tempestuous relationship.

The couple had at least five sons: William (who died at the age of 3), Henry, Geoffrey, Richard and John, plus three daughters: Matilda, Eleanor and Joan. Henry also had several illegitimate children, including Geoffrey (a Bishop of Lincoln) and Morgan (a Bishop of Durham) whose mother has never been confirmed, and William Longespée (who became Earl of Salisbury), the son of his mistress Ida de Tosny, the Countess of Norfolk. But the true love of Henry's life was really "Fair" Rosamund Clifford, who was famed for her beauty. She died in 1176, and legend has it that she was poisoned on the instructions of Queen Eleanor.

Henry's aim on becoming King was to restore order in England and to undo the harm that his predecessor had done to the monarchy and the country. He refused to tolerate the barons who had become too powerful, and demolished the castles that had been built by rebellious noblemen in King Stephen's reign, replacing then with manor houses.

He passed more laws than any previous monarch, and raised taxes for landowners, introducing a fairer system in which the richest people paid the most. By end of his reign, the English were accustomed to paying taxes.

Henry developed an English militia force, in addition to his mercenary army, which meant that his subjects in general did not have to do compulsory military service. The only time that men took up arms was competitively in tournaments. This gave people more time to develop their trades and agriculture began to flourish in England.

He overhauled the judicial system in what he considered to be a fairer approach to the law. He discovered that over 100 murderers had escaped execution because they had claimed the right to be tried in a church court, which was unable to impose any violent sentence.

Trial by ordeal was still a common practice in the 12th century, with thieves, for example, often made to hold a red hot iron bar in their hands. If the skin blistered, they were considered guilty of the crime. Henry introduced Assize Courts with a trial judge and twelve local men to administer the law. The jury was not made up of impartial people to reach a verdict, as today, but consisted of witnesses to the crime. Henry's system evolved, resulting in central control over the administration of justice, so that only royal courts could try criminal cases.

By the end of the 12th century people were more likely to take an issue to court to be resolved than resort to violence or take matters into their own hands. Property laws were also made more uniform, with the introduction of primogeniture which meant that the eldest son inherited his father's land.

Henry's territory was vast and stretched throughout England and France; in fact he owned more land in France than the King of France. Henry's was the largest kingdom in Europe at the time, reaching from the Somme to the Pyrenees, and from the Scottish border to the Mediterranean. Later he added Ireland to his territory.

Henry had wanted his kingdom to be divided amongst his four sons at his death, with the largest portion going to his oldest surviving son and heir, Prince Henry. But the brothers fell out amongst themselves over the division and, spurred on by their mother, became allied to King Philip II of France.

Eventually Eleanor plotted to have Henry ousted as king, but once her scheme was discovered, he had Eleanor imprisoned for the last 15 years of his reign – albeit in a French Château, which gave her some measure of freedom. Two of their surviving sons subsequently died, leaving only Richard and John to fight over the succession.

When Henry heard that even his favourite son, John, no longer supported him, he lost the will to live. It is said that Henry turned his face towards the wall, saying, "Now let all things have their way; I care no more for myself nor for the world. Shame, shame on a conquered king."

He died ten days later at Château de Chinon in France on 6 July, 1189, aged 56. He was buried at Fontevrault Abbey, where his carved and painted tomb can still be seen.

Twelfth-century chronicler Roger of Howden recorded that on the day after his death, Henry was carried out for burial, "adorned with regal pomp, a golden crown on his head, gloves on his hands, a gold ring on his finger, holding a sceptre, wearing shoes of gold fabric, with spurs on his feet and girded with a sword." When his son Richard viewed his father's body, many present saw that blood came from Henry's nose, which was believed to be a sign of indignation at the betrayal that had hastened his death.

Although King Henry II's reign began well, it ended badly. The once-powerful barons began to rebel, angry that their authority had been taken from them. Relations with his wife deteriorated as she colluded with their sons against him, and Henry's reputation obviously suffered because of Thomas Becket.

Throughout the centuries his reputation has never recovered, with each successive generation keeping the memory of Becket alive through legend, art, and literature. For the Canterbury Festival of June 1935, for example, T.S. Eliot was commissioned to write a play immortalising one of the most significant events in the city's history. He called it *Murder in the Cathedral*.

While there is a statue of Henry II at Canterbury Cathedral, it is Becket who permeates the great building with many reminders of the former Archbishop, from a stained-glass window in the north ambulatory made of medieval glass to Antony Gormley's striking artwork *Transport*, which was unveiled in January 2011 and hovers over the site of Becket's original tomb.

For Henry II, it seems, there will never be any escape from the troublesome priest.

Chapter 20

Richard I 1157–1199
Reign: 1189–1199

In the centuries-old tales of Robin Hood and his Merry Men, many recount that King Richard the Lionheart returned from the crusades and met with the famous outlaw in Sherwood Forest. Visitors to Nottingham Castle Art Gallery can see Daniel MacLise's famous painting depicting the event.

Yet Richard spent barely six months of his ten-year reign in England. His whereabouts during these visits are well documented, and there were very few occasions on which the two legends could really have met. Their encounter, like the very existence of Robin Hood, is destined to remain a mystery.

England's first King Richard has been variously described as an icon, a warrior, and a national hero ranking alongside Saint George, but he was actually considered to be a much better soldier than he was a king. A bronze statue of him now stands outside the House of Lords at Westminster, a crown on his head and a sword raised high in his hand.

On the plinth is carved Coeur de Lion rather than Lionheart – which is perhaps appropriate for a man who spent more time in France than in England, and whom some historians believe could not even speak English.

Although he has been called a national hero, Richard appeared to have had little affection for England and complained that the country was cold, and it was always raining. During his relatively short reign, England became little more than a source of revenue to enable him to fund his fighting in the crusades.

"I would have sold London itself if I had found a buyer rich enough," he confessed. He sold many of his English possessions, including lands and property, and even some of the Crown Jewels, to fund his military campaigns.

Richard may have been French at heart, but he was born in England at Beaumont Palace, Oxford, on 8 September, 1157. He was the third son of King Henry II and Queen Eleanor of Aquitaine. Physically he was extremely handsome, with reddish blond hair and striking blue eyes, and as a child was always tall for his age. In adulthood he reached the height of 6ft 5in.

Speaking only French at home, Richard received a good education, studied Latin, enjoyed writing poetry and loved music. He wrote songs and conducted choristers in the royal chapel. But his artistic pursuits belied a nasty temper and a cruel streak, and his main interest was in military matters. He trained as a soldier and took part in many tournaments in his youth.

Overall, he was a strong character, very decisive and as a young man was nicknamed "Richard Yay and Nay" as he always seemed to have an answer for everything. As he matured, Richard developed into a strong military leader and succeeded in ruthlessly quashing many internal revolts in Aquitaine. But he lost popularity through his cruel punishments to those who rebelled against him.

The marriage of Henry II and Eleanor of Acquitaine was tempestuous and the couple separated. Richard went to live with his mother at Poitiers in France and was created Duke of Acquitaine in June 1171. Eleanor soon manipulated her son to rebel against his father and encouraged Richard to try and oust Henry II from the throne.

In May 1174 Richard led a campaign and sailed to England, but he was still only 16 and had no hope of success against Henry, who had an army of some 20,000 mercenaries. Eventually Richard met with his father and begged forgiveness.

On the death of his elder brother in 1183, Richard became heir to the throne of England but was soon at odds with his father again over the size of his inheritance. Henry II planned to divide up his kingdom, so that Richard's younger brother John would also inherit land, but this would inevitably mean a reduction in the size of Richard's domain. Soon Richard was at war with his father and joined forces with the 22-year-old King Philip II of France, eventually forcing Henry II to accept Richard's demand to be the sole heir. Within days Henry II had lost the will to live and died on 6 July, 1189.

King Richard I was crowned in a magnificent ceremony at Westminster

Abbey on 3 September, 1189, on a purple carpet beneath a canopy of silk, but the celebration was marred by bloodshed. With a belief at the time that Jews had the power of sorcery, all Jewish people were banned from Westminster during the Coronation for fear that a spell would be put on the new monarch.

A number of prominent Jews arrived at the Abbey, bearing gifts for the King, but were turned away. Soon there was violence in the streets, with soldiers slaughtering Jewish families and burning down their houses. News of the outrage reached Richard at the Coronation banquet in Westminster Hall and, although he tried to restore order, a wave of anti-Semitism spread to other cities across England. Mobs were incited to pillage and massacre Jewish communities throughout the land, notably at Clifford's Tower, York, in March, 1190. Thousands of innocent people perished at this time.

Not only was there strife within his kingdom, but Richard succeeded to the throne during a period when there was trouble in the Holy Land. When news reached Europe in October 1187 that the Saracen leader, Saladin, had defeated a crusader army and captured the city of Jerusalem, King Henry II had intended to undertake a crusade to free the city and at the same time cleanse himself of guilt following the murder of Thomas Becket at Canterbury Cathedral. But he failed to do so and his successor, Richard, took on the challenge instead.

Crusades were military expeditions undertaken between the 11th and 13th century to free the Holy Land from the Saracens. There had been constant battles over territory, but for more than a century the Christians had control of Jerusalem. Now it was lost, with reports that the "True Cross of Christ" had been placed across the main gateway of Baghdad so that the Saracens trampled on it each time they passed. Richard intended to restore Jerusalem to the Christians.

Richard sailed for Palestine on 12 December, 1189, with King Philip II of France and Emperor Frederick of Germany, on what was to be the Third Crusade to the Holy Land. It was not long, however, before Richard was the only remaining leader of the army. It had always rankled with Philip that Richard owned more French land than the King of France, and soon a quarrel began resulting in Philip's withdrawal from the crusade. Then the German Emperor accidentally drowned en route, which left Richard in sole charge. Encountering bad weather, Richard spent the winter in Sicily with his sister Joan before continuing on towards the Holy Land. He conquered Cyprus on the way, and while there married Berengaria of Navarre at the Chapel of St George, Limassol, on 12 May, 1191.

Described as "more learned than beautiful", she was also crowned Queen Consort of England at the same time. She has traditionally been declared to be "the only English Queen never to set foot in the country", but there is evidence that she visited later in life when she was a widow. In the early 20th century the Cunard shipping line named a liner *RMS Berengaria*, their first to be named after a British Queen. Originally launched in 1912, the ship was later captained by Arthur Rostron, who had been captain of the *Carpathia* during the rescue of passengers from the Titanic.

Richard and his men continued to the ancient city of Acre in the Holy Land. The crusaders successfully besieged Acre in July 1191 and two months later Richard defeated Saladin at Arsuf, near Jaffa. Although it was a bloodthirsty and violent victory, in which 2,700 men with their wives and children were slaughtered, Richard received praise and honour amongst Christians for taking Jaffa.

Richard hoped to regain Jerusalem, but his army was weakened through lack of food, bad weather, poor living conditions and low morale, and he eventually had to admit defeat. He made peace with Saladin, agreeing a three-year truce. Although Richard's crusade failed, it resulted in easier access to the Holy Land for pilgrims.

On the return journey to England, Richard was shipwrecked and had to continue the journey overland through Austria. He had fallen out with former ally Duke Leopold of Austria when Richard tore down the Duke's banner from the walls of Acre, saying that only kings had the right to raise their standards in victory.

To travel safely through Austria, Richard disguised himself as a merchant, but was recognised and captured near Vienna by Duke Leopold's men. He was identified by his gold ring, which was far more valuable than a merchant could ever have afforded. Richard was later sold to Emperor Henry VI of Germany and was held hostage for 14 months until a ransom of 150,000 marks was paid for his release.

Legend has it that his whereabouts were discovered by his minstrel, Blondel, who travelled across Europe in search of his master, singing outside every castle he could find. Richard, imprisoned in a dungeon, heard his minstrel singing a song that they had composed together, and the King made his presence known by joining in the song.

The ransom money was raised in England through the sale of church lands and town charters, and huge tax increases for property owners. When released, Richard was able to return to his kingdom, landing at Sandwich in Kent on 13 March, 1194.

While away on the crusade Richard had left England in the hands of William Longchamp, the Bishop of Ely (who was appointed Chancellor) and his youngest brother, Prince John Lackland. John was a traitor and colluded with King Philip II of France, and together they plotted to overthrow Richard. But when Richard returned, he reasserted his authority, and to prove to the people that he was their true King, he underwent a second Coronation ceremony at Winchester on 17 April, 1194. He forgave his brother but seized Prince John's castle in Nottingham – supposedly spending a day in Sherwood Forest, where maybe he did meet Robin Hood, after all!

In May 1194 Richard left England for the last time and spent five years fighting Philip II in Normandy in an attempt to recover lands seized during his absence in the Holy Land. At the Battle of Gisors he shouted the battle cry "Dieu et mon droit" ("God and my right"), later adopted by King Henry V as the motto of England. It is now on the coat of arms of the United Kingdom to show the divine right of the monarch to govern. In 1199 his adversary Philip II was killed in battle, but it was to be a short-lived victory for Richard.

Richard the Lionheart was killed by a crossbow wound whilst besieging a castle at Châlus-Chabrol near Limoges on 6 April, 1199, aged just 42. The arrow wound in his shoulder need not have proved fatal, but a soldier called Marchedès attending to the king removed only the wooden shaft and left the iron arrowhead deep in the flesh. Richard later died from gangrene.

On his deathbed he sent for the bowman, gave him 100 shillings and pardoned him, saying, "I forgive you my death. To the conquered faction now let there be bright hopes, and the example of myself."

After the king's death, however, Marchedès had the bowman flayed alive and hanged. Some chroniclers referred to the circumstances of Richard's death as "the Lion killed by an Ant". He was buried at the feet of his father at Fontevrault Abbey. His heart was preserved in a casket at Rouen Cathedral in Normandy, and his brain was buried at Charroux Abbey in western France.

Opinion about Richard is divided. His upbringing was in Aquitaine and he showed far greater interest in his French territory than he ever did in England. His absence weakened the crown in England and did little for the country's economy, but at least by embarking on a crusade to the Holy Land he felt that he had fulfilled his duty as a Christian monarch.

The nickname Coeur de Lion is said to originate from a story that he had once thrust his arm into the mouth of a lion and pulled out its heart, although that is likely to be a fabrication to symbolise his courage as a soldier.

Today he is one of the few Kings of England to be remembered by his epithet "Lionheart" rather than his regnal number. With no legitimate children as heirs, on Richard's death the crown passed into the hands of another monarch to feature in the legend of Robin Hood: the villainous King John.

Chapter 21

John 1167–1216

Reign: 1199–1216

King John has one of the worst reputations of any English monarch. Only the infamous Richard III ranks alongside him in the unpopularity stakes. Historians have variously described John as evil, avaricious, selfish, idle, untrustworthy, treacherous, tyrannical, and possessing few redeeming qualities. He had children slaughtered, men and women crushed or starved to death, and those who crossed him were hanged.

Any good that he did in his life has been overshadowed by his wicked deeds and he is now remembered by the epithet Bad King John. It has often been said that he neither feared God, nor respected man, and Charles Dickens wrote, "I doubt whether the crown could possibly have been put on the head of a meaner coward, or a more detestable villain, if England had been searched from end to end to find him out."

John was born at Beaumont Palace, Oxford, around Christmas Eve, 1167. He was the fifth and youngest son of King Henry II and Queen Eleanor of Aquitaine. His parents separated soon after he was born and he was brought up by his father, and also spent time as part of the household of the King's chief minister Ranulf de Glanvill.

From this minister, John began to take an interest in administrative and legal affairs, although he was lazy and no great scholar. As he grew up John's greatest passion was hunting, a sport he enjoyed at Kinver and Feckenham in the Midlands, and he became obsessed with personal hygiene, even paying a "bath man" to help him wash as often as possible.

Said to be Henry II's favourite son, John was spoiled and immature. In

1185 he was sent to rule Ireland as Governor (Henry's ultimate aim was to have him crowned King of Ireland) but at the age of just 18 he was too young and inexperienced to make a success of it. He very quickly alienated the locals, laughing at and even tugging the beards of the Irish chieftains as they paid homage to him, and within months John returned home with his tail between his legs.

In Henry II's final years John turned against his father and tried to have him ousted from the throne. At the root of this treachery lay the fact that King Henry had bequeathed land to his elder surviving sons Henry, Richard and Geoffrey, and yet nothing to his youngest son John, who was supposed to be his favourite.

This clearly rankled and was not made any easier when he acquired the nickname "John Lackland". King Henry's reasoning was that he did not have enough territory to divide between the four, but it led to a family feud.

When John's brother, Richard, acceded to the throne in 1189, he tried to make amends for their father's neglect. Richard gave John the high-ranking Norman title Count of Mortain, which brought him an income. Later, Richard gave John land in Northamptonshire, two manors in Suffolk, and the profits from two forests, Sherwood and Andover, plus the revenue from six counties of England: Derbyshire, Devon, Dorset, Cornwall, Nottinghamshire and Somerset. This was to make up for John's previous lack of land, and Richard hoped to gain John's loyalty in return.

On the surface, all seemed well between the two brothers as a result, until Richard went off on the Crusades. John then discovered that Richard had named their nephew, Prince Arthur of Brittany, as his heir. Once again John seemed to have been overlooked and was said to be "white with anger".

Prince Arthur was the son of their late brother Geoffrey, and so had a rightful place in the line of succession. But, taking advantage of Richard's absence on the Crusades, John conspired with King Philip II of France to have Richard ousted as King. The scheme failed when King Richard returned to England. Despite the fact that John had tried to depose him, Richard excused his brother, saying that John was "only a child" – even though John was 27 at the time. Possibly King Richard simply saw his brother's actions as an ongoing sign of his immaturity. He actually forgave his brother and named John as his successor.

King Richard continued to honour his one surviving brother and in 1199 John was invested as Duke of Normandy, but did not take the ceremony seriously, giggled throughout and accidentally dropped the ceremonial sceptre as it was handed to him.

John married twice, but it was typical of his character that these relationships were not straightforward. When he still had no land of his own and only a small income, John became betrothed to a wealthy heiress, Isabella of Gloucester, also known as "Hawise". The couple married at Marlborough Castle, Wiltshire, in August 1189. She was entitled to the Earldom of Gloucester, which brought John a large income, but it proved to be an unhappy, childless marriage and they were divorced ten years later.

After his divorce, John married Isabella of Angoulême at Bordeaux Cathedral, Gascony in August 1200. She was another wealthy heiress and was aged just 14 when they married. She was actually betrothed to Hugh de Lusingnan when John first met her, and so he made yet another enemy when he stole her away from her fiancé. After John's death, Isabella finally married Hugh, her first love.

John and Isabella had five children, and he had at least 12 illegitimate children by various mothers. This second marriage was not a happy one either. Isabella eventually tired of her husband's adulterous behaviour and began to take lovers herself. When John discovered this, he had two of the men hanged above Isabella's bed, leaving an appalling sight for her to discover when she entered her chamber.

Richard the Lionheart was killed in 1199, and John succeeded his brother as King. Many backed Prince Arthur of Brittany's claim to the throne but the powerful English barons preferred the English-born John. Fearing that Prince Arthur might try and usurp him, John eventually had Arthur imprisoned and secretly murdered. One report says that John cut Arthur's throat himself, tied a heavy stone to the body and threw it in the River Seine.

King John was crowned at Westminster Abbey on 27 May, 1199. Aged 32, he had a vast territory that stretched from England to the south of France, yet strangely he soon lost his mother's homeland – the Duchy of Aquitaine – which his family had worked so hard to protect, and within a few years his empire had diminished rapidly.

During various failed military campaigns John lost Normandy, Maine, Anjou, Touraine, followed by northern Aquitaine, and he spent the next decade trying to reclaim them. His epithet Lackland seemed very apt. It has been said that King John's reputation would have been better if his foreign policy had not been so disastrous. His military defeats actually earned him another disparaging nickname, John Softsword.

In England, John imposed high taxes to fund these unsuccessful wars which made him unpopular amongst his people, particularly in the north of

England. Prices rose steeply and many families suffered great hardship as a result. He then introduced even higher taxes in order to raise money to fund yet more military campaigns to try and win back the French lands he had lost. Scutage, which was a form of tax by which a knight could buy himself out of military service, was raised 11 times during John's reign.

Not only did John upset the citizens of England but he also had a very bad relationship with the church. Soon after his succession he agreed to make a holy offering of 12 gold pieces to a Bishop but delayed the ceremony of handing over the money by playing with the coins and eyeing them covetously.

The irritated Bishop demanded that John leave his church. On another occasion he was at mass on Easter Day and interrupted the Bishop's sermon three times, saying that he was hungry and wanted his breakfast. Eventually the King walked out of the church without receiving Holy Communion.

Following the death of Hubert Walter, Archbishop of Canterbury, in 1205 John had a major disagreement with the Pope over the election of a new archbishop. The Pope rejected John's candidate John de Grey, Bishop of Norwich, and instead chose Stephen Langton – a cardinal-priest at San Crisogno in Rome. John refused to allow Langton to set foot on English soil and declared that anyone who acknowledged Langton as Archbishop of Canterbury was a traitor and an enemy.

In retaliation, Pope Innocent III closed all churches in England and forbade any public celebration of sacred rites. No-one could get married and even funerals could not be held. The Pope excommunicated John and joined forces with King Philip II of France to have John ejected from the throne. Bishops and clergy could have stood by their king but instead they supported the Pope.

Refusing to back down, John confiscated all clergy lands as retribution. When the Archdeacon of Norwich withdrew from the King's service, he was crushed to death "under a cope of lead" as a punishment and as an example to prevent other clergy and noblemen following suit. Noblemen who disobeyed King John had their wives and children imprisoned, where they were starved to death.

This dispute with the church caused John to be so unpopular in England, that in the end he was forced to back down and swear an oath of allegiance to the Pope and pay him an annual levy of 10,000 marks – a huge sum in those days.

"On the 15 May, 1213," recorded an ancient chronicler, "King John knelt before the legate, Pandulf, surrendered his kingdom to the Roman See;

took it back again as a tributary vassal, swore fealty and did liege homage to the Pope." This did not go down well with the people of England, and the common feeling was that he had become the Pope's puppet. "He has forfeited the very name of King," wrote another chronicler, "from a free man he has degraded himself into a serf."

John's relationship with the Church did not improve and many clergy felt that the King was too autonomous and out of control. An assembly met at St Albans in 1213 to discuss the issue, and the Archbishop himself read out Henry I's Charter of Liberties at St Paul's Cathedral, which had limited the monarch's power.

The dispute reached its climax at Runnymead on 15 June, 1215, when King John was forced to put his seal on a document called Magna Carta, which contained 63 clauses that he was, in theory, compelled to accept. The aim of Magna Carta was to directly challenge the monarch's authority and to reduce his powers. In short, the charter stated that the King could no longer do just as he wished, raising taxes or seizing property at a whim, but had to accept the law of the land.

Twenty-five barons enforced the Charter, and John felt outnumbered, complaining that he was in effect up against twenty-five kings. Although he smiled during the sealing, so angry was he, that he threw himself on the ground at Windsor and began chewing the rush matting through rage. The 13th-century chronicler Matthew Paris recorded that following Magna Carta, King John was "constantly raging, biting and tearing his nails, muttering and gnashing his teeth, and cursing his father and mother."

There is a popular misconception that King John "signed" Magna Carta at Runnymede, but there were no signatures on the original document. The King simply placed his seal on it, in front of witnesses as a mark of authentication. Although a significant document in English history, surprisingly it was annulled within weeks, being declared null and void on 24 August, 1215. Magna Carta is now remembered because later monarchs had the charter rewritten, having removed clauses that challenged their power.

Although Magna Carta still forms part of English law, it is the much modified 1297 version issued during the reign of King Edward I that is the basis, not King John's of 1215. It was because of Magna Carta that people were given, for example, the right of a fair trial by jury. One clause even forms the basis of the US Bill of Rights: No person shall be . . . deprived of life, liberty or property, without due process of law. Because of King John's wrangles with the Church, one particular clause from Magna Carta still remains on the statute roll to this day: "We have granted to God, and by this our present Charter have confirmed, for Us and our Heirs for ever, that the Church of England shall be free, and shall have all her whole Rights and Liberties inviolable. We have granted also, and given to all the Freemen of our Realm, for Us and our Heirs for ever, these Liberties under-written, to have and to hold to them and their Heirs, of Us and our Heirs for ever."

Another states: "The City of London shall have all the old Liberties and Customs [which it hath been used to have]. Moreover We will and grant, that all other Cities, Boroughs, Towns, and the Barons of the Five Ports, and all other Ports, shall have all their Liberties and free Customs."

Unfortunately the original Magna Carta sealed by King John has not survived, and may even have been destroyed by him, but as there were copies at the time for each county of England, for the Barons of the Cinque Ports, and for the royal archives, some are still in existence.

Four of the 1215 versions are on public display today. One survived with its original seal intact and was discovered at Dover Castle in 1630, but this was subsequently severely damaged by fire. Two are held by the British Library, one is in Lincoln Cathedral (this copy was stored at Fort Knox during World War II), and the best-preserved example belongs to Salisbury Cathedral. Later versions of Magna Carta are held at Durham Cathedral, Hereford Cathedral, and the Bodleian Library in Oxford.

In 2006 the BBC held a poll so that members of the public could recommend a date for a proposed National Day for Britain. The date on which King John sealed Magna Carta, 15 June, received the most votes, more even than D-Day or VE Day. Although the then Chancellor, Gordon Brown, supported the idea of a National Day, a public Bank Holiday for Magna Carta Day has not yet materalised.

The barons knew only too well that King John would never be controlled by Magna Carta and so they actively began to seek a new King. Within a few years England was facing civil unrest, which became known as the First Barons' War. The Barons invited the Dauphin Louis of France (the future King Louis VIII) to come and replace John as their leader.

He sailed across the Channel with a large fleet in the hope of seizing the crown by force, but the people of England refused to be vanquished. Shakespeare's play *King John* ends with the words:

"This England never did, nor never shall,

Lie at the proud foot of a conqueror."

During the resulting civil war King John and his followers began to wreak havoc across England, setting fire to monasteries, destroying and pillaging churches as they progressed across the country. In the most famous incident of this period, King John's own possessions, including the Crown Jewels, were supposedly lost in the Wash. Contemporary reports tell us that the King was travelling from Spalding in Lincolnshire to Bishop's Lynn (later renamed King's Lynn) in Norfolk, when he was taken ill and decided to return.

While his party went back via Wisbech, the carts carrying his baggage took another route along the Wash and were caught by the incoming tide. Various locations are reputed to be the scene of the disaster, in which many men, horses, carriages and personal effects were lost. Older accounts claim that it was "near Sutton Bridge, on the River Nene", others that it was at a crossing on the Welland Estuary at Fosdyke.

Nothing has ever been recovered, despite many searches over the past 800 years, leading some historians to suggest that the Crown Jewels were in fact stolen or sold and never ended up in the Wash at all. That King John died so quickly after the event adds fuel to the theory of foul play and, until his glittering crown is pulled from the mud, the doubts will always remain.

On 12 October, 1216, King John arrived at Swineshead, Lincolnshire, where he spent the night at a Cistercian abbey. On 14 October he reached Sleaford, where his illness grew steadily worse, before moving on to Newark-on-Trent, Nottinghamshire, two days later. He died at Newark Castle during the night of 18/19 October, reputedly from dysentery which had been brought on by eating a surfeit of eels and a new type of beer. Others suggest that the King was deliberately poisoned following the theft of the Crown Jewels. Whatever the cause of death, the King was not lamented. A contemporary wrote: "Foul as it is, hell itself is defiled by the fouler presence of John."

In accordance with instructions in the codicil of John's will, he was buried in Worcester Cathedral which he had visited many times. Although John had a poor relationship with clergymen and the church, he was frequently seen praying at the shrine of St Wulfstan at Worcester, and the saint is now featured along with St Oswald on John's Purbeck marble tomb in the Choir.

John's tomb has been opened twice, firstly in 1529 when the tomb was raised above ground and made more elaborate, and later during repairs to Winchester Cathedral in 1797. On this second occasion, an eyewitness account reveals that the King's "teeth were quite perfect".

He was found to be 5ft 5in tall, although undoubtedly an inch or two taller in life; on his head was the Cap of Unction, which is used after the anointing part of the Coronation ceremony, and a sword was at his left side. The body had been covered with a crimson damask robe embroidered with Plantagenet leopards, and delicate fragments of this robe are kept at the cathedral.

On display in the cathedral library today is King John's original will – the only surviving medieval royal will in England. There is also a bone from the King's thumb that was stolen while the tomb was open in 1797. Later the culprit owned up and returned it to the cathedral, but by this time the tomb had been resealed and so the bone was put on display instead. It could be the very thumb with which he pressed his seal on to the Magna Carta. Although, as the library now purports to have no fewer than three of King John's thumbs, we shall never know.

So, was King John all bad? He spent more time in England than most of his predecessors since the Norman invasion, travelling widely across the country, often dealing with routine matters of administration or local legal issues that he need not have troubled himself with. He had additional castles built during his reign, which increased England's defenses.

There are many small, almost forgotten acts of generosity that he undertook, such as the many gifts he gave to small clerical houses. He had the Worcester priory gatehouse rebuilt after a serious fire in 1202, ordering that the best quality wood and timber should be used. King John lived in a brutal age, yet he cared particularly about justice for the ordinary working man, declaring that everyone had the right of protection and he even made a proclamation about the welfare of dogs.

In Holy Week 1210 King John gave out clothing, food and gifts to the poor of Knaresborough, Yorkshire, in the first recorded distribution by a sovereign of Maundy alms. Although the Maundy ceremony itself is of ancient origin, our monarch today follows in King John's footsteps when personally distributing the Royal Maundy money each year. Charles Dickens may have described John as a "miserable brute", but maybe the King was not as black as history has painted him.

With King John dead, and the English having forcefully rejected the French Dauphin Louis, it was John's nine-year old son who was handed the crown. Not since Ethelred the Unready, before the Norman Conquest, had England been ruled by a boy king.

Chapter 22

Henry III 1207–1272
Reign: 1216–1272

Throughout England's royal history, only four monarchs have had reigns lasting longer than 55 years. Although Queen Elizabeth II is now in the record books, it is easy to forget that her ancestor, Henry III, was king for over 56 years and for more than five centuries held the record of being our longest-reigning monarch.

Henry was born in England on 1 October, 1207, at Winchester Castle and spent most of his life in England, which was very unusual for a king until this time. He was the eldest son of King John, one of our most unpopular monarchs, and his second wife Isabella of Angoulême. Theirs was an unhappy marriage and Henry was brought up largely in his father's household.

A weak and sickly child, Henry was tutored at home by Philip D'Aubigny – a royal councillor and prominent knight of the Crusades – and was also educated by priests, which encouraged his lifelong faith.

Henry was just nine years of age when his father died on 19 October, 1216, and for the first time in nearly 250 years England had a child on the throne. There was little dispute over the succession as King John had declared Henry as his heir, although some rebellious barons invited Prince Louis, Dauphin of France, to come and take the throne. But with far greater support for the young English king, Prince Louis was defeated and returned to France.

King Henry's Coronation took place at Gloucester Cathedral on 28 October, 1216. He was crowned by Peter des Roches, Bishop of Winchester, with a plain circlet of gold belonging to his mother, as the Crown Jewels had been supposedly lost in the Wash by King John. With concerns from the Pope as to the legality of this Coronation, however, Henry was crowned again on 17 May, 1220, this time by the Archbishop of Canterbury at Westminster. On the same day Henry laid the foundation stone of a new Lady Chapel at Westminster Abbey.

Despite undergoing two Coronations, Henry was still a boy and decisions were made for him until he came of age. William Marshal, 1st Earl of Pembroke, acted as Regent and was given the title Rector Regis et Regni. He died within three years and power moved first to Hubert de Burgh, the Chief Justiciar (the equivalent of our Prime Minister) and later to Peter des Roches, Bishop of Winchester. Des Roches completely controlled the King and denied many courtiers access to him. He was soon dismissed following the threat of civil war if he remained in control and was sent on a Crusade to keep him out of the way.

By the time he reached the age of 18, Henry wanted to be master of his own fate and declared that he was ready to reign. Those acting as regent during his minority had agreed that they would be guided by the terms of Magna Carta, and so the young King was called upon to accept its conditions.

In 1225 Henry completely revised the charter, making it much shorter with only 37 articles, and swore to keep it "as a man, as a Christian, a knight, a king crowned and anointed". Castles and land were surrendered to him and only from this point did the reign of Henry III really begin.

As he approached adulthood, Henry developed physically into a short, stocky man with dark hair and beard, which began to grey prematurely as he matured. It took him time to find a suitable bride, but he eventually married Eleanor La Belle, the 14-year-old daughter of Raymond Berenger IV, Count of Provence, on 14 January, 1236, at Canterbury Cathedral. Eleanor has the dubious reputation of being one of England's most disliked queens. The couple had at least five children, and possibly as many as nine.

Henry was said to be a weak and indecisive character. Some say that he was ruthless and untrustworthy. A contemporary account described him as "changeable, impulsive alike in good and ill, unbridled in temper and tongue, reckless in insult and wit".

All are agreed that he was a spendthrift, and he accumulated huge debts amounting to four times his annual income. He once had to sell off his silver plate just so that he could pay his household's wages, and he even sold items from the Chapel Royal to settle debts.

Although his royal motto was "He who does not give what he has, does not receive what he wants", the King was much more ready to receive than to give. Nobility were invited to entertain the King and Queen, and for the "honour" of having the couple in their home were also expected to give expensive gifts to their royal guests as a token of their appreciation.

Sometimes gifts were unceremoniously returned if they were not considered to be of a high enough value. The hosts then felt obliged to provide a much more valuable gift instead.

Henry loved rich materials for himself and his wife, such as velvet and satin, and he was the first to wear baudekin in England, a material from Baghdad that was a mixture of pure gold thread and silk woven together, decorated with elaborate embroidery so that it sparkled impressively. At the time of his marriage, Henry sumptuously renovated the Palace of Westminster as a luxury royal residence with every comfort of the period, which included glass in the windows. He also gave his bride jewellery worth £30,000. Considering that the average weekly wage was a matter of a few pence, it puts Henry's extravagance into perspective.

Not only did Henry spend his own money beyond his means, but the people of England had to endure high taxation to fund a series of costly, fruitless wars as he attempted to win back territory that his father had lost. There were three disastrous campaigns to France, with Henry and his army unsuccessfully besieging castles.

There was also discontent amongst the English that Henry's court was dominated by Frenchmen. French-born Faukes de Breauté, for example, was sheriff of six counties of England and in control of six castles. His London home was called Faukes's Hall; later changed to Fox Hall, and eventually to Vauxhall. Another Frenchman, Peter de Rivaux, was sheriff of 21 English counties and held the positions of Lord Privy Seal, Treasurer of the King's Household, and Keeper of the King's Wardrobe. Even Henry's jester was French.

Many courtiers were his French wife's relatives, who were given titles and top jobs, and hundreds of their dependents also followed them to England to seek their fortune. The Queen's uncle, Count Peter of Savoy, took the chief place at Henry's council-board. His London house in the Strand was known as the Savoy Palace and was said to be the most magnificent nobleman's house in England. Another of her French uncles, Boniface, was appointed Archbishop of Canterbury. Londoners were outraged and surrounded Lambeth Palace in protest. Boniface, who was "noted for his birth rather than his brains", quickly fled the country. The

13th-century chronicler Matthew Paris wrote during the King's reign:

"At this time the King daily, and not just slowly, lost the affection of his natural subjects. For, like his father, he openly attracted to his side whatever foreigners he could and enriched them, introducing aliens and scorning and despoiling Englishmen."

Henry was also a great supporter of the Pope, which resulted in 300 English benefices becoming Roman Catholic. Italian priests were appointed who spoke no English and invariably did not even visit England. This inevitably led to anti-papal sentiments in England, as the people's spiritual welfare was in the hands of priests that they never saw. Henry did not help the situation by sending thousands of pounds to Italy each year to pay for these absentee clergy.

Many declared indignantly that they were "prepared to die rather than be ruined by the Romans". Eventually the matter came to a head and tithes intended for the Pope were seized and distributed amongst the poor. Although Hubert de Burgh as Judiciar was appointed to investigate, many felt that he had secretly instigated the anti-papal rebellion in the first place.

Hubert de Burgh also tried to reduce the French influence over England and thwarted one of the King's military campaigns to regain French territory. When Henry arrived at Portsmouth, he discovered that there were not enough ships to transport his army. Henry blamed de Burgh, accused him of treason and rushed at him with a sword. Only the intervention of the Earl of Chester prevented his slaughter.

Later, when there were riots over high taxation, the King again blamed his Justiciar and had him arrested. A blacksmith was ordered to shackle de Burgh, but he refused saying, "I will die any death before I put an iron on the man who freed England from the stranger and saved Dover from France." Hubert de Burgh was imprisoned in the Tower of London and, although later released, his power was gone.

In addition to funding Italian priests, the King also financed papal wars in Italy, Pope Innocent IV having promised the crown of Sicily to Henry's son, Edmund, in return for cash. Whilst Henry agreed, it was the English people that actually had to pay for these campaigns with the burden of even heavier taxation. One third of England's wealth went to pay for the wars, plus the Pope took per cent of the church's income, which met with widespread resistance.

Simon de Montfort, Earl of Leicester, tried to curtail Henry's power so that the barons could have a greater say in the running of the kingdom. Frenchman Simon de Montfort was once one of Henry's closest friends, and even married the King's widowed sister, but he eventually became one of the King's foremost opponents.

When Henry was once caught in a thunderstorm whilst rowing on the River Thames, he took refuge at the Bishop of Durham's palace. Simon de Montfort was a guest at the time and reassured the King that the storm was abating and that the thunder would do him no harm. "I fear you more than all the thunder in the world," the King replied.

At de Montfort's instigation, an assembly was called at Oxford in July 1258 – now often referred to as "The Mad Parliament" – which forced Henry to sign a document known as The Provisions of Oxford to limit his power and try to stop him financing the Pope. The Provisions were also intended to reform the Church, negotiate financial aid, and to establish a council of 15 men who would advise the King on the work of government.

It ultimately meant that Henry was the King in name but the barons held the power. "The King himself had nothing but the shadow of a name," wrote chronicler Matthew Paris. Further reforms came a year later with the Provisions of Westminster; one of these provisions was that high offices should be given only to Englishmen.

Within less than three years Henry renounced the Provisions and refused to abide by them. Soon there were riots in London over dissatisfaction with the King. Queen Eleanor was staying at the Tower of London at the time and tried to escape to Windsor in a barge on the River Thames but was spotted by the angry crowd. Rioters stood on London Bridge and pelted the Queen with anything they could lay their hands on, including lumps of wood and stone, shouting "Drown the witch!" due to malicious rumours that she had been dabbling in sorcery. The Queen was quickly rowed back to the Tower of London. Eventually she took refuge in France for her own safety.

With exasperation at Henry's extravagance and autocratic behaviour, matters finally came to a head on 14 May, 1264 at the Battle of Lewes, when forces mustered by Simon de Montfort clashed with the King's army in Sussex. The King was staying at Lewes Priory to celebrate the Feast of St Pancras, while his eldest son, Prince Edward (later King Edward I) was being entertained at Lewes Castle by John de Warenne. Their soldiers were camped in fields just outside the town walls, unaware that Simon de Montfort's men were on nearby Offam Hill looking across the town, waiting to attack at daybreak.

In an area known as Landport Bottom, north of Lewes, de Montfort's soldiers rushed down on the King's army and the ensuing battle began, spilling out on to the streets of Lewes, where there was much bloodshed and slaughter. Although de Montfort had fewer men, the King's soldiers were inexperienced at battle and had been awaiting reinforcements. Eventually the King and Prince Edward were defeated, captured and taken prisoner.

Simon de Montfort now became head of state and forced the King to reaffirm adherence to the Provisions. In January 1265 de Montfort formed an assembly at Westminster, made up of people from the counties, towns, and clergy of England, including two representatives from each Borough and four knights from every Shire.

It was the first time that all classes, other than serfs, had been represented in government. Merchants and traders sat beside knights and bishops. Commoners and Lords together. Although many decades were to pass before we had a House of Commons and a House of Lords, this was the beginning of Parliament in England as we know it.

Whilst there was initially much support for Simon de Montfort as a leader, soon divisions began to occur over his reforms and the barons began to desert him. The King's son, Prince Edward, managed to escape captivity and gathered some 8,000 men of the King's army. They headed towards Worcestershire, where they knew Simon de Montfort was planning a rendezvous with his son, Simon the Younger. Prince Edward lured de Montfort into a trap by having his army carry de Montfort banners.

When Simon de Montfort saw an army bearing his own family's banner, he mistakenly assumed it was his son's army. Prince Edward finally defeated him at the Battle of Evesham on 4 August, 1265, where Simon de Montfort was killed.

King Henry III regained authority, perhaps wiser and humbled by his experiences, and stability returned to England. Certainly, in the closing years of his reign he appears to have been more modest and less extravagant, shunning rich materials for very simple robes, and his Christian faith became more important to him. He attended mass three times a day and was said to be so devout that if he met a priest while travelling, mass had to be said. He was once so late arriving to meet Louis IX that the French king had all priests banned from Henry's route the next time he was travelling to France.

Throughout his life Henry was greatly influenced by an earlier King of England, Edward the Confessor, who had been canonised in 1161. He even named his eldest son and heir Edward. Henry threw his energies into creating a new shrine for the Saint, who he felt deserved a more majestic resting place. Over a 24-year period, from 1245 to 1269, Westminster Abbey was significantly rebuilt, and the bones of Edward the Confessor were transferred to the newly built tomb in 1269.

King Henry III is credited with being a great builder and under his influence the Early English Gothic style of architecture flourished. His reign was the age of the abbey and the cathedral. Norman architecture was remodelled and more elaborate designs were introduced with pointed arches, vaulted roofs, flying buttresses, lancet windows and tall spires. Many English churches of the period reflect this style.

A superb example of Early English Gothic architecture is Salisbury Cathedral, instigated by Henry. Although the building was consecrated in his presence and there is a statue of him on the west front, he did not live to see the magnificent 404-foot-high spire constructed, which was not completed until some 40 years after his death. Westminster Abbey and Salisbury Cathedral are considered to be his legacy to England and for which he is best remembered.

Lesser known is a royal palace known as Cippenham Moat, which Henry had built near Slough. By the 16th century it was a ruin, but the foundations were rediscovered by farmers in Victorian times and can still be seen on the site today, which is now a listed monument.

Henry's love of architecture and design developed because he had a great eye for detail. He could instantly spot an error in a written document and paid great attention to every area of his household, from the kitchens to the stables. He once listed the names of the 250 baronies of England to chronicler Matthew Paris from memory. He also did a great deal to encourage education in England at this time and three Oxford colleges were founded during his reign: University College (1249), Balliol (1263) and Merton (1264).

One of the more unusual establishments of Henry III's reign was the development of a zoo at the Tower of London, with animals that included a lion, a bear, three leopards, buffalo and a camel. Matthew Paris wrote: "About this time, too, an elephant was sent to England by the French king as a present to the King of England. We believe that this was the only elephant ever seen in England, or even in the countries on this side of the Alps; wherefore the people flocked to see the novel sight."

The lion remains a potent emblem of the monarchy, particularly in heraldry, and the earliest written record of a live lion in England was at the King's zoo in 1240.

For the English, King Henry III's reign has one very significant legacy, for in 1222 it was decided that St George's Day would be celebrated on 23 April as a feast day in England. The English royalist forces also wore the red cross of St George on their uniforms during their victorious Battle of Evesham in 1265. This led to it eventually becoming England's national emblem.

Following a period of failing health, King Henry III died peacefully in his sleep at the Palace of Westminster on 16 November, 1272, aged 65. He was buried in Westminster Abbey, which owes its present magnificent appearance to his reconstruction and devotion. While a suitable burial chamber was being built, Henry was temporarily placed in the old tomb of Edward the Confessor, whom he admired so much. The two kings of England now rest within yards of each other in a chapel east of the Sanctuary at the heart of the Abbey.

Chapter 23

Edward I 1239–1307
Reign: 1272–1307

"As the arm of King Edward I was accounted the measure of a yard,
generally in England: so his actions are an excellent model
and a praiseworthy platform for succeeding princes to imitate."
Thomas Fuller, *Church History of Britain*

King Edward I stood, quite literally, head and shoulders above his
contemporaries. Although not quite the tallest King of England (a record
held by King Edward IV), he grew to be 6ft 2in tall at a time when the
average man was only 5ft 7in, earning himself the epithet Longshanks
because of his very long legs. When his tomb was opened in 1774, his body
was found to be well preserved and measurements taken confirmed that he
truly warranted this nickname.

The King was said to be "bodily in proportion" and so also had very long
arms. Whether they were actually a yard long, as recorded by Thomas
Fuller in 1655, is uncertain, but we do know that it was King Edward I who
established that a yard measured 36 inches in length. A statute of his reign
declared:

"And be it remembered that the iron ulna (iron yard) of our Lord the
King containeth three feet and no more, and a foot ought to contain 12
inches by the right measure of this yard measured; to wit, the 36th part of
this yard rightly measured maketh one inch, neither more nor less . . ."

Prior to this, a yard had been the distance from a man's nose to his thumb
when the arm was outstretched, but now it was an official and consistent

length. Even though England now uses metric weights and measures, some people still think in feet and inches 700 years after this statute, and many of the laws and practices that exist today have their origins in Edward I's reign. A great reformer, he is described as being both physically and mentally strong: decisive, powerful and diplomatic.

He established what has become known as the Model Parliament, which was much more democratic than in previous reigns, giving the people a voice. Instead of meeting on an ad hoc basis, Parliament began to meet regularly for the first time, launching a pattern of government which continues to this day.

Some of Edward's administrative reforms were an attempt on his part to reassert royal authority after the weak reign of his father, and to restore crown lands that had been lost. For example, Edward defined "time immemorial" as being "prior to 2 July, 1189, before the accession of Richard I". Many people were therefore able to claim rights of land ownership because their families had been in a property since time immemorial. Any lands granted after 2 July, 1189, now needed proof of possession and rigid investigations were carried out under the direction of the Chancellor.

Like his predecessors, Edward tried to curb the powers of the barons and the Church. With the Statute of Gloucester in 1278 he challenged feudal privileges, forcing barons to present warrants to prove that they had rights of jurisdiction and franchises. In 1279 he set up the Statute of Mortmain which prevented landowners donating property to the church to avoid taxation. Many similar statutes and laws were introduced during his reign.

Edward had only partial success in trying to curb the illegal practice of coin clipping, whereby people clipped pieces of gold and silver from coins, which they later sold when they had sufficient quantity. Sometimes coins could be between 40% and 60% underweight because so much had been clipped from the edges. In Edward's reign people were encouraged not to accept any coin that had been clipped, but it was not until coins were produced with milled edges in the reign of Charles II that the practice ended.

We tend to think of concerns about pollution as being a modern trend, but by the beginning of the 14th century there were many complaints in the east end of London because people were using sea-coal on their fires as it was cheaper, but it had the side effect of producing an unpleasant stench because of the gases contained in the coal. The King made a proclamation that only wood and mined coal should be used for fires.

Although his ancestor Edward the Confessor was said to have begun the practice of "touching for the King's Evil", Edward I is the first king for which there is documentary proof that the practice was actually carried out. In 1276 some 600 people with "the King's Evil" (scrofula) were blessed by Edward in the hope of being cured and towards the end of his reign it amounted to over 2,000 people a year. Those who could not receive the royal touch in person would often obtain coins that had been handled by the King. These "touch pieces" were then worn as amulets or charms in the hope that some of the healing power would be transferred to them. The last royal "healer" was Queen Anne, who touched 200 sufferers in 1712, after which the practice seemed to die out.

When Edward first came to the throne the laws of the land were very inconsistent. He tried to end the confusion that existed by making laws subject to Parliament and to make punishment for offenders much more reasonable and humane. Edward is often known by the epithet "the English Justinian" because of this and towards the end of his reign he said, "No man ever asked mercy of me and was refused". His maxim throughout life was "Keep troth" – troth meaning not just truthfulness, but faith, loyalty and trust – which has become the motto of many a school over the centuries.

Edward was the first son of King Henry III and Eleanor of Provence and was born at the Palace of Westminster on the night of 17/18 June 1239. He was named after King Edward the Confessor, whom his father greatly admired and had canonised. It is reported that Edward had a happy, contented childhood, spent largely at Windsor.

It was something of a charmed life. He was once playing a game similar to chess in a large vaulted room. For no obvious reason he suddenly got up and walked away. Just a second later a massive stone fell from the ceiling and landed on the very spot where he had been sitting. If he had not moved, he would certainly have been killed. Later in his life, while in France during a storm, a bolt of lightning killed two of Edward's attendants who were standing immediately behind him. In battle, arrows pierced his saddle but missed him and on occasions his horses were killed from under him, but the King remained unharmed.

The closeness of the Royal Family can be seen from an account by chronicler Matthew Paris, who tells of Edward as a young boy standing on the shore as his father set out for a visit to France. Waving his father goodbye, Edward wept uncontrollably, and refused to move until the sail of his father's ship had completely gone from the horizon. This was clearly a child that loved his father.

Mindful of Edward's position as heir to the throne, Henry III made his son Lord of Gascony at the age of 15, and the young prince spent a year in France with relatives of his mother in the hope that he would develop a love of Gascony and would therefore become protective of the territory. In 1254 Edward was also made Earl of Chester and became responsible for monitoring the border between England and Wales trying, not always successfully, to repel any insurgents. He also became overlord of Ireland.

Although it may seem a young age to us now to be given such responsibility, within months of his 15th birthday Edward was already a married man. His bride was ten-year-old Eleanor of Castille, and their wedding took place on 1 November, 1254, at the Abbey of Las Huelgas, Burgos in Castille. Initially it was a political union to protect the borders of Gascony but ultimately it became a love match. Edward continually professed his love for Eleanor and, unlike previous Kings of England, there is no record that he ever had a mistress.

When Edward was 16, he and Eleanor were given a home of their own, Savoy Palace in London. Unusually for this period, she travelled nearly everywhere with her husband and their 16 children were born in various parts of the world. Of the children 12 were girls, and three of the boys died young, so Edward's eventual heir to the throne was actually his 14th child, also an Edward.

A 13th-century Benedictine monk named William Rishanger chronicled the times in which he lived and has left us with a physical description of Edward. He was a silver-blond child, although his hair turned very dark in adolescence and in adulthood eventually went snow-white. His hair was worn at shoulder length, his beard was clipped short, and we are told that he had a broad forehead and a left eyelid that drooped. Rishanger wrote, "No man was ever endowed with greater muscular strength for wielding a sword. His breast swelled above his stomach, and the length of his legs ensured that he was never dislodged from his seat by the galloping and jumping of horses."

Often portrayed as a warrior prince, because of his size Edward could be a fearsome foe and even in tournaments and sporting events his opponents could end up losing a limb. At worst, they could lose their lives. During a period of civil unrest in England in 1264, Edward found himself caught up in a conflict between his father, Henry III, and his godfather, Simon de Montfort, which culminated in the Battle of Lewes.

Edward was staying at Lewes Castle in Sussex to celebrate the Feast of St Pancras, while his father was at nearby Lewes Priory. Simon de Montfort and his army launched a surprise attack which culminated in King Henry and Prince Edward being taken prisoner. They were held in various castles around the country, but Edward eventually escaped from Hereford Castle while exercising his horse. He gathered an army and killed de Montfort at the Battle of Evesham on 4 August, 1265. After this, Henry III was King in name only and it was Edward who took control. For England it was a time of peace.

Three years later, following a very elaborate ceremony in June 1268, Edward committed himself to going on the Ninth Crusade to relieve the besieged Christian stronghold of Acre in the Holy Lands. It took a long time to raise the necessary funds, but Edward finally sailed from Dover on 20 August, 1270, taking his wife with him, along with some 1,000 soldiers and knights. While at Acre in 1271, Edward and Eleanor were in their tent when an envoy arrived with letters. As the Prince studied the documents, the envoy reached into his cloak and pulled out a dagger. Edward grabbed the weapon, receiving a wound in the arm in the process, and managed to kill his would-be assassin.

After a few days Edward's wound became septic and the skin blackened. There is a mythical story that Eleanor sucked the poison from the wound and saved her husband's life but in reality the King's surgeon cut away the infection and within two weeks Edward had recovered. Eleanor was not quite the heroine that history paints her, as the surgeon reported that Eleanor was distressed and weeping at the sight of her husband's injury. The surgeon asked her to leave the room, saying it was better that she should weep "than that all of England should mourn".

Edward was eventually forced to abandon the Crusade because of his health and the poor weather conditions, and began the return journey to England. He was in Sicily when news reached him that his father had died on 16 November, 1272. Edward was distraught, saying, "I may get more children, but never another father." Confident of his succession and with no fear that someone else would take the crown, he did not rush home, suppressing a rebellion in Gascony on the way. He finally reached Dover in August 1274.

"England saw in her ruler no stranger, but an Englishman," wrote a contemporary. "The last trace of foreign conquest passed away when the descendants of those who won and those who lost at Senlac (the Battle of Hastings) blended forever into an English people. The national tradition returned in more than the golden hair or the English name which linked him to our earlier Kings. Edward was English to the core."

King Edward I's Coronation was held in Westminster Abbey on 19 August, 1274. Edward took the crown off immediately after he had been crowned, saying he would not wear it again until all his father's lands had been recovered. *Holinshed's Chronicles*, published in the 16th century, tell us that on Coronation Day, Edward was received "with all the joy that might be devised; the streets were hung with rich cloths of silk, arras and tapestry; the aldermen and burgesses of the city threw out of their windows handfuls of gold and silver to signify the great gladness which they conceived of his safe return".

Although England had been a peaceful country when he departed for the Crusade some years earlier, there were now threats from all sides: from France, Scotland and Wales. One of King Edward's ideals was a unified country – a "Great Britain" more than 400 years before it was actually called that. He began by trying to take control of Wales. His aim was to bring in English laws and divide the country into shires, but this led to rebellions. Initially he imposed a trading blockade, but eventually was forced to send in troops.

Edward's enemy there was Llewelyn ap Gruffydd, variously called Lord of Snowdonia, Prince of Wales, and Lord of Most Welsh Chieftans. In 1277 Edward invaded north Wales with a successful campaign that saw Gruffydd's lands taken from him. A further conflict five years later resulted in the death of Llewelyn, who was decapitated, and his head placed on a spike at the Tower of London.

In 1284 Edward finally ended Welsh independence with the Statute of Rhuddlan, which provided the constitutional basis for the government of the Principality of Wales as it became "united and annexed" to the crown of England. Wales was finally divided up into shires and the English common law system was introduced, although was administered from Caernarfon rather than London.

Edward had a network of castles built at Beaumaris, Conway, Caernarfon and Harlech as defenses to make Wales a stronghold of England. His third son, also called Edward, was born at Caernarfon Castle in 1284. Legend has it that baby Edward was presented to the people as "the first English Prince of Wales", although he was not actually invested with the title until he reached the age of 16. There have since been 21 English Princes of Wales. The present holder of the title, Prince Charles, can trace his ancestry through an aunt of Llewelyn ap Gruffydd's right back to Rhodri Mawr, who was King of Gwynedd until his death in 878. From the Welsh, Edward adopted the Welsh longbow. Until the use of gunpowder led to the development of guns and canons, it became the deadliest weapon in England, a longbow arrow being able to penetrate through several inches of solid wood, and Edward introduced it into his army.

Having taken control of Wales, Edward next turned his attention to Scotland. When Alexander III of Scotland died in 1286 his heir was his granddaughter, Margaret, who was just a baby. In 1289 Edward arranged for his five-year-old son to become engaged to Margaret to cement the union between England and Scotland, but Margaret died within a year in a shipwreck, which led to a succession crisis. There were 13 claimants to the throne and from them Edward chose John Balliol to be the next King of Scotland. But Balliol soon came under the control of Scottish barons and was persuaded to wage war against Edward.

John Balliol was therefore seen as a traitor and, in April 1296, Edward invaded Scotland and deposed Balliol and had him sent to the Tower of London. To show that England was now in control of Scotland, Edward removed the ancient Stone of Scone to Westminster. He had a Coronation Throne constructed with the Stone of Scone placed underneath, and all monarchs of England have since been crowned on it. The Stone of Scone was returned to Scotland 700 years later in 1996, but it will be brought back to Westminster for future Coronation ceremonies.

The Scots took exception to being ruled by an English monarch and turned to William Wallace, who had been named Protector of the Kingdom, to fight for them. He and a Scottish army were victorious at the Battle of Stirling Bridge in 1297 but Edward defeated Wallace at Falkirk in 1298. The war carried on until 1305 when Wallace was finally captured, hung, drawn and quartered. Instead of dispiriting Scotland, as Edward had hoped, the country became even more united.

Robert the Bruce replaced Wallace and was crowned King of Scotland at Scone Palace in 1306. Although he was defeated at Methven in 1306, Bruce went into hiding. He had strong support amongst the Scots and lived to fight another day. Although Edward tried his hardest to hammer the Scots, he was unable to conquer them.

It was while he was trying to subdue the Scots that Edward's beloved wife died. In 1290 Eleanor was journeying north to join the King in Scotland, but she was taken ill and died very suddenly on 28 November in the village of Harby, Nottinghamshire, aged around 44. The distraught Edward arranged for her body to be returned to London. "My harp is tuned to mourning," he wrote to a friend of Eleanor's. "I loved her tenderly in her lifetime, I do not cease to love her in death."

Edward had stone crosses erected at each of the 12 places that the cortege stopped on the route to London. They are known as Eleanor Crosses and were at Lincoln, Grantham, Stanford, Geddington, Hardingstone near Northampton, Stony Stratford, Woburn, Dunstable, St Albans, Waltham, Cheapside and Charing. The latter is probably the best known of all and the village near Westminster became known as Charing Cross.

Only three of the original crosses remain today: Geddington, Hardingstone, and Waltham Cross. The impressive Eleanor Cross which now stands in front of Charing Cross station in London is a Victorian copy erected in 1863. The original, which was destroyed by Cromwell's soldiers, stood on a site that today forms the junction of Whitehall and Trafalgar Square, and is occupied by a statue of King Charles I on horseback.

Eleanor's internal organs were buried in a tomb at Lincoln Cathedral, her heart at the abbey church of Blackfriars in London, and her body at Westminster Abbey. Edward ordered that two candles should burn perpetually at her tomb in Westminster Abbey. Candles did in fact burn at the spot for some 250 years until the around time of the Reformation.

In 1299 Edward married for a second time, taking Margaret of France as his wife. She was the daughter of Philip III and sister of Philip IV of France and the union ultimately led to the return of Gascony to England, territory which Edward had long tried to protect. There is no evidence that Margaret was ever crowned Queen Consort. With her, Edward fathered two sons and a daughter.

With the Scottish situation unresolved, Edward set out on a further invasion, but became ill with dysentery on the route north. He died at the age of 68 on 7 July, 1307, at Burgh-on-Sands, Cumbria, and his body lay in the village church until preparations were made to transport him to London. A monument stands on the marshes to mark the exact spot where he died.

Edward had told his son, the Prince of Wales, that he wanted his heart to be taken to the Holy Land with a 100 knights and that he did not wish to be buried until the Scots were finally defeated. He left instructions that his bones should be taken to each battlefield so that he could lead his army to victory, even in death. The new King Edward II ignored his father's wishes.

King Edward I was buried at Westminster Abbey in a very plain tomb, as there was no money in the coffers to pay for an effigy. It bears a simple Latin inscription, which translates as: Here lies Edward I, Hammer of the Scots.

Chapter 24

Edward II 1284–1327
Reign: 1307–1327

"King Edward has now reigned six full years," recorded a biographer in 1313, "and has 'til now achieved nothing praiseworthy or memorable." Some 350 years later, churchman and historian Thomas Fuller wrote in his *History of the Worthies of England* that "No Prince ever ascended the English throne with greater or used it with less advantage to himself."

Other historians over the centuries have referred to Edward II variously as worthless, brainless, feeble, incompetent and idle. He was a man who did not really want to be King, appeared half-hearted about his official duties and had little concern about his reputation. In fact, he seemed to almost deliberately go against the public image of a monarch. Instead of following popular royal pursuits of the day, such as jousting or hunting, he preferred to dig ditches or thatch roofs. In medieval times, the idea of a King enjoying manual labour was frowned upon by all classes.

Tall and good looking, he enjoyed expensive clothes and extravagant jewels, loved good food and wine, and frequently gambled more money than he could afford. Although vain and self-indulgent, he was by no means unintelligent. He loved music and played several instruments; he spoke at least three languages, was a prolific writer of letters and poetry, had a strong faith and was generous to religious establishments. His weakness lay in the fact that he was not a natural born leader. At various periods in his reign, he seemed content to sit back and let others rule.

Edward was born at Caernarfon Castle on 25 April, 1284, and legend has it that as a baby he was presented to the people as "the first English

Prince of Wales". He was the fourth son of King Edward I and his wife Queen Eleanor of Castille and only became heir to the throne through the premature deaths of his three brothers. His mother died when Edward was just six years old and he succeeded her as Count of Ponthieu and Montreuil on 28 November, 1290 and later also became Duke of Aquitaine.

As the son of King Edward I – the Hammer of the Scots – the young Prince Edward was expected to emulate his father's virtues and strengths. Although the King tried to guide his son in leadership, took him to see Parliament in action and had Edward with him during one Scottish military campaign against William Wallace, the seed fell on stony ground. Edward was a romantic, extravagant and frivolous, preferring amusement to business or affairs of state. When he became King he often chose as his ministers younger men of inferior status, rather than the hereditary barons who had become powerful through their wealth and aristocratic background. Edward's own cousin Thomas, the Earl of Lancaster, headed the English baronage at this time and had royal blood as a grandson of King Henry III. The cousins became locked in a power struggle and Thomas became Edward's leading opponent.

Prince Edward was largely brought up by a guardian, Sir Guy Ferre, a courtier who served the Plantagenet family for over 50 years. The Prince had a lonely childhood with very few playmates and so when he reached the age of 14 a companion was deliberately found for him. A French boy called Piers Gaveston, who was to become Edward's favourite at court. The pair were roguish and uncontrollable. King Edward I despaired of his son and once attacked him physically, pulling out handfuls of his auburn hair, when Prince Edward wanted to pass on one of his titles – Count of Ponthieu – to Gaveston. The King became concerned that Gaveston was a bad influence and getting his son into bad ways. Eventually he had him removed from court altogether, but within a month King Edward I was dead and the new King Edward II quickly brought his friend back into the fold.

On becoming King on 8 July, 1307, Edward II gave Gaveston the title 1st Earl of Cornwall (not to be confused with the Duchy of Cornwall which was later reserved for the monarch's eldest son). Bestowing Gaveston with an Earldom did nothing to improve Edward's relationship with the barons and there was much jealousy. Less than six months into his reign he angered them still further when he appointed Gaveston as Regent of England and left him in charge of the country while he went to France to get married. "It was thought remarkable that one who had recently been in exile from the land should now be its keeper," wrote one medieval chronicler.

On 25 January, 1308, Edward wed 12-year-old Isabella, a daughter of Philip IV of France, at Boulogne Cathedral. She was then known as "Isabella the Fair" but later less flatteringly as the "She-Wolf of France". Back in England a month later, the couple were crowned at Westminster Abbey on 25 February, 1308. Isabella's father gave Edward various rings and items of jewellery for his daughter but she very quickly became aware that the same jewels were being worn by Edward's closest companion, Piers Gaveston. She wrote home to her father that she was feeling miserable and wretched, but soon resigned herself to living a life as Queen Consort in the shadow of the King's best friend. Edward and Isabella, nevertheless, went on to have two sons and two daughters: Edward, John, Eleanor and Joan. The King is also known to have had at least one illegitimate son, Adam.

Eventually the barons became exasperated by the way in which Edward indulged Gaveston and forced the King to banish him from the country. Edward did so, but in his own way, for he only sent him as far as Ireland, where Gaveston became the King's representative and with a high income. Within two months Gaveston was back in England, spending Christmas at Windsor and was soon in charge of the King's administration. He recklessly squandered money from the Treasury and seemed incapable of taking his role seriously. As a result, Parliament appointed 21 Lord Ordainers to manage the economy, and the King and Gaveston gradually found their authority reduced.

By 1311 power was almost entirely in the hands of the barons, and Piers Gaveston's days were numbered. In 1312 he was captured in Scarborough where he had taken up residence at the castle. He was held prisoner at Warwick Castle and was later taken a couple of miles away and beheaded on Blacklow Hill at Leek Wootton. Although the execution took place on 19 June, a monument erected in 1821, nearly 500 years after the event, gives the incorrect date of the beheading.

Edward was so devastated by the death of his close friend that he spent seven days a week digging ditches and bricklaying, throwing himself into physical activity to assuage the grief. Gaveston could not receive a Christian burial as he had been excommunicated by the church and the King had to fight for over two years to secure a Papal absolution so that his favourite could be given an elaborate funeral ceremony. Piers Gaveston was finally laid to rest at Langley in Hertfordshire (now known as King's Langley because of its royal associations), where Edward had a palace and also founded a Dominican Priory. Today there is little remaining of the Priory and the site of Gaveston's grave is uncertain.

The six years after Gaveston's death were described by contemporaries as "some of the darkest in England's history". There was a succession of famines, causing terrible suffering. Disagreements between the barons and the King continued, and Edward was humiliated in battles with the Scots.

Robert the Bruce fought hard to free Scotland from English domination. In 1314 Edward was forced to lead an army into Scotland to save Stirling Castle, which was England's only remaining stronghold north of the border. On 24 June at Bannockburn, two miles south of Stirling, Edward's English army of 10,000 faced Bruce's much smaller Scots army of some 6,000. Quantity, however, proved no match for the quality of the strong spirited Scots. Edward's army has been described as "ill-fed and ill-led". The men were exhausted from the long march north, through lack of food and lack of sleep, and the English were completely trounced. Edward fled from the battlefield as far and as fast as his horse would carry him, which was to Dunbar more than 50 miles away. The King's reputation as a leader suffered as a result and his cousin Thomas, Earl of Lancaster, became virtual ruler of England.

By 1318 Edward had cultivated more favourites at court and came to rely on Hugh Despenser, the Earl of Winchester, as his chief advisor. The Despensers were newly enobled and not an old aristocratic family. In later centuries they changed their name to De Spencer, and then to Spencer, and were the ancestors of Lady Diana Spencer. Hugh Despenser's son (also named Hugh) replaced Piers Gaveston as the King's closest friend. Edward gave Hugh Junior the post of Court Chamberlain. Once again, this favouritism sparked jealousy amongst the barons and in August 1321 they banished both father and son into exile. Within a year Edward had overruled this and brought the Despensers back to England, an action that led to civil war. The Earls of Lancaster and Hereford rebelled against the King's royalist army but were defeated at Boroughbridge in March 1322. Hereford was killed in battle and Edward had Thomas, Earl of Lancaster, beheaded.

With the opposition gone, Edward allowed the Despensers to virtually rule England for the next five years. This angered Queen Isabella, who had tired of her husband's partiality and she took up residence in France, refusing to return to England until the Despensers had been stripped of power. She formed an alliance with Roger de Mortimer, Baron of Wigmore, who had been one of Edward's adversaries in the civil war. The Queen gathered an army and came back to England with Mortimer, landing on the

Suffolk coast. They had the Despensers captured and brutally murdered. Hugh the elder was hanged and beheaded in Bristol and his body was fed to dogs. Hugh the younger was hanged from a gibbet 50ft high, then drawn and quartered before being beheaded. In February 2008 what is thought to be his remains were discovered on the site of the former Hulton Abbey in Staffordshire.

Edward fled to Glamorgan, but he had no supporters and was captured on 16 November and imprisoned at Kenilworth, where he was under the control of Henry, Earl of Lancaster, the younger brother of his antagonist Thomas. The King wrote a poem while in prison, now known as *The Lament of Edward II.*

> *In Winter woe befell me,*
> *By cruel Fortune thwarted;*
> *My life now lays a ruin.*
> *Full oft have I experienced,*
> *There's none so fair, so wise,*
> *So courteous nor so highly famed,*
> *But, if Fortune cease to favour,*
> *Will be a fool proclaimed.*

On 20 January, 1327, Parliament forced Edward to renounce the throne in favour of his 14-year-old son, who was crowned King Edward III on 1 February that year. The now ex-King Edward II became known simply as Lord Edward, Sometime King of England.

Edward was moved around the country so that his whereabouts could be kept secret. From Kenilworth he was taken to Corfe, then Bristol, and finally on 3 April to Berkeley Castle in Gloucestershire. He was not given any food in the hope that he would starve to death or succumb to illness. Rotting animal carcasses were thrown into a pit beneath his cell in the belief that the fumes of putrefaction would suffocate him. But he had a strong constitution and managed to survive. He was regularly woken from his sleep, shaved with stagnant water, and was even 'crowned' with hay to humiliate him.

On 21 September, 1327 Edward was murdered on his wife's orders, although it was publicly announced that he had died of natural causes. There was a request of his assassins that no physical mark was to be left on the body and so legend has it that a red-hot poker was inserted into his bowels through a horn. The exact cause of death will never be known, but hideous shrieks rang out through the castle and it was reported that: "Many a one woke and prayed to God for the harmless soul which was passing that night in torture." The next morning Edward's unblemished body was shown to the citizens of Gloucestershire to prove that he had died of natural causes. He lay in state at Berkeley Castle and was later buried in Gloucester Cathedral. The cell where Edward was imprisoned and murdered at the Castle can still be seen to this day.

Some historians feel that Edward may have been murdered earlier in the year and the announcement of his death delayed. There is even a belief that Edward II was not murdered at all. A Genoese priest and papal notary called Manuele de Fieschi wrote a private letter to Edward's son in 1337 in which he claimed that a servant gave the King his clothes so that he could disguise himself and escape. Dressed as a servant, Edward managed to get to the castle door unrecognized. He killed the gatekeeper so that he could get the key and let himself out, and then he fled to Ireland for safety. Nine months later he went to Europe and spent the rest of his life in a monastery near Milan. When his captors, Thomas de Gourney and John de Maltravers, came to murder Edward, they found his cell empty. Fearing the wrath of the Queen, they hurriedly had the body of the dead gatekeeper embalmed and showed it to the people of Gloucestershire, and it is he who was buried in the tomb at Gloucester Cathedral and not the former King Edward II.

Whether there is any truth in the story remains a mystery. Either way, it was an ignominious end for one of England's least successful monarchs.

Chapter 25

Edward III 1312–1377
Reign: 1327–1377

On a Monday afternoon in June each year, sandwiched between Trooping the Colour and Royal Ascot, the monarch dons a medieval-style blue velvet mantle, a black velvet hat with white plumes, and processes with similarly dressed knights to St George's Chapel, Windsor, to commemorate England's oldest Order of Chivalry, founded by King Edward III.

Legend has it that on St George's Day, 1348, the Countess of Salisbury was dancing after a banquet at Windsor when her garter fell off. As the King picked it up, some of his courtiers laughed and jeered. Edward III tied the garter around his own leg, saying, "Honi soit qui mal y pense" – shame on him who thinks ill of it. In this is the origin of the Most Noble Order of the Garter.

The King had recently established a refuge at Windsor for impoverished soldiers who could no longer sustain themselves financially, originally known as Alms Knights. His intention was to set up an Order of the Round Table which would be attached to these poor knights and support them with food, money and shelter. It became instead the Order of the Garter.

There were 24 founder-knights, who wore robes of blue bearing the arms of St George, and to this day there are always 24 Knights of the Order, who ceremonially wear a garter bearing the motto: "Honi soit qui mal y pense". New members are announced on St George's Day in April and are formally invested with their insignia by the sovereign on Garter Day in June.

Although of ancient origin, the current Garter ceremony dates from 1948, having been revived by King George VI to mark the 600th anniversary of the Order, and it is still an important date in the royal calendar. The Alms Knights of Edward Ill's day are now known as the Military Knights of Windsor, retired army officers on a military pension, who are given accommodation at Windsor Castle, and take part in the annual Garter Day procession, weekly services in St George's Chapel and are present at all state occasions at Windsor. There are 24 Military Knights to mirror the 24 Knights of the Garter.

The reign of King Edward III was an age of chivalry and he was very much inspired by the legend of King Arthur and the heroic story of St George. At Windsor Castle he had the Round Tower built to house a round table for his knights, just as King Arthur had done, and the chapel at Windsor Castle was eventually renamed St George's Chapel in the patron saint's honour.

Tall, handsome, of athletic build, and with straight fair hair, King Edward III was the epitome of the gallant warrior. He was a keen sportsman, he loved taking part in tournaments and jousting, and his 50-year reign did much to unify England and create a national identity. Instead of French, which had been commonly spoken since the invasion of the Normans in 1066, English became the predominant language.

English literature began to develop during his reign as French romances went out of fashion. One of Edward's own courtiers was the poet Geoffrey Chaucer, who was Controller of Customs and later Clerk of the Royal Works at the Palace of Westminster. He wrote *The Canterbury Tales*, a masterpiece of storytelling, which gives us the closest indication of the English dialect of this time. Significantly, Chaucer was the first poet to be buried in Poets' Corner in Westminster Abbey.

In 1362 English was ordered to be used in courts of law, and it became widespread in all areas of life from Parliament to the Church. Soon it was recorded that: "in all the Grammar schools of England children leaveth French, and construeth and learneth in English."

Edward III was the eldest son of King Edward II and Queen Isabella of France and was born at Windsor Castle on 13 November, 1312. He was known throughout his early life as Prince Edward of Windsor. Until the age of 13 Edward was tutored by Richard de Bury, an Oxford scholar and an avid bibliophile who encouraged Edward's love of books. De Bury was a Benedictine monk. He became Treasurer and Chancellor of England during Edward's reign, and, finally, Bishop of Durham.

On completing his formal education, Edward joined his mother in France – although very much against his father's wishes. Edward II warned his son to be wary of Queen Isabella's plotting and not to trust her lover, Roger de Mortimer. While in France, Queen Isabella made plans for the teenage Edward to marry Philippa of Hainault. Although it was an arranged marriage to create a bond between England and France, it turned into a love match and they were married for over 40 years. The wedding took place in York Minster on 24 January, 1328, when Edward was aged just 15 and Philippa a year younger.

The couple went on to have eight sons and five daughters, although three of the boys died in infancy. Each of the sons were given English titles, such as Duke of Cornwall, Earl of Chester, Duke of Clarence, Duke of York, Duke of Gloucester, and Earl of Buckingham, many of which still exist within the Royal Family. The eldest son, also christened Edward, later became known as the Black Prince, either because of the colour of his armour or because of his dark temper. It was another son, John of Gaunt, to whom Shakespeare in his play *Richard II* gave the immortal line, "This blessed plot, this earth, this realm, this England."

When Philippa gave birth to Edward the Black Prince, a tournament was held in Cheapside, London, to celebrate the happy event. A raised wooden stand put up for spectators collapsed. Fortunately no-one was badly injured, but the King was furious and threatened to have the carpenters executed. Philippa publicly pleaded for their lives and the men were reprieved, an act which endeared her to the people and secured her popularity. In later years when Edward intended to have six men hanged in Calais, it was Philippa who persuaded her husband to grant a stay of execution.

Just before his marriage to Philippa, Edward unexpectedly became King on 25 January, 1327, when Parliament forced Edward II to renounce the throne in favour of his son. The deposed monarch was later murdered. King Edward III was crowned on 1 February, 1327, at Westminster Abbey, and Queen Philippa a year later.

For the first three years of his reign the young Edward III was controlled by his mother Queen Isabella, known as the She-Wolf, and Roger de Mortimer, his father's murderer. Isabella and Mortimer were taking more than half of the country's revenue for their own use. They were incompetent and ruthless, alienating many courtiers and supporters.

When he reached the age of 18, Edward felt that it was time to take control. Mortimer was with Queen Isabella at Nottingham Castle on the night of 19 October, 1330, when Edward and his men entered through a secret passage in the rock on which the castle stands, taking the couple by surprise. Mortimer was captured and tried before Parliament for being an enemy of the state and for his part in the murder of the King's father. He was thrown into the Tower of London and was later executed at the newly erected gallows at Tyburn on 29 November, 1330.

Isabella disappeared into the background, banished to Castle Rising in Norfolk on a limited income and under virtual house arrest for the remaining 28 years of her life. Only now did Edward's reign truly begin.

The young King was immediately popular with the English people and the monarchy came to be held in high regard. Those who proved trustworthy and loyal were handsomely rewarded with land and titles, and Edward aimed to restore order and stability to the country. He had a magnificent tomb built for his father in Gloucester Cathedral and tried to erase the bad reputation that Edward II had as a monarch.

In everyday life, the woollen trade flourished and agriculture developed with the rise of the tenant farmer and the freeholder. It was during Edward III's reign that Parliament was divided into the House of Lords and the House of Commons. Parliament also gained greater power, regulated civil administration, controlled expenditure and taxation, and debated national security and territorial rights. Treason was defined by statute for the first time, and the Office of Justice of the Peace was created in England.

Although in England life appeared to improve, the question of Scotland remained unresolved for Edward. In 1328 Queen Isabella and Roger de Mortimer had signed a treaty acknowledging Scotland as an independent nation. The treaty was strengthened by the marriage of Edward's sister to King David II, the son of Robert the Bruce. The treaty became known as The Shameful Peace. In 1333 Edward tried to reverse this and bring an end to Scottish independence. He led and won the Battle of Halidon Hill to restore English control and David II was sent into exile. In the battle Edward became the first King to use cannon as a weapon.

Edward Balliol, the son of John Balliol, became King of Scotland, paying homage to the King of England. Most Scottish territory south of the Forth became part of England and it was seen as a great victory, although successive generations fought over ownership. In 1346 David II came out of exile and invaded England. Edward was in France at the time and so Queen Philippa ordered the English army to fight, resulting in another victory. David was captured at Neville's Cross, near Durham, and was held prisoner for 11 years until the Scots offered to pay a ransom for their King's release.

Ten years into his reign, Edward III began to pursue his claim to the French throne. His mother's brother, King Charles IV of France, had died in 1328 without an heir and the crown had passed to his nephew, who became Philip VI. But through his mother's line Edward felt that he also had a legitimate entitlement. He even had French lilies added into his coat of arms to show his French ancestry. In 1337 he made his first attack on France. It was the start of what was to become known as the Hundred Years War – although it actually lasted for 115 years.

The Hundred Years War was not just about Edward's claim to the throne, but also over commercial activities at the time. There was an attempt to take Gascony and control the wine trade of Bordeaux. The cloth weavers of Flanders were dependent on English wool, which gave Edward some bargaining power and he made his Chancellor sit on a woolsack in council as a symbol of the English supremacy in the wool trade.

By reducing the amount of wool being sent to France, Edward had the power to cripple cloth production in Flanders. There was also the matter of an "auld alliance" between Scotland and France for trade and an agreement between them that if England ever invaded Scotland, the French would be on the side of the Scots. Edward could not hope to conquer Scotland unless he had control of France.

Edward led various military campaigns, which bankrupted him, but he managed to destroy the French navy at Sluys in 1340. Around 140 English ships fought against 190 French in the Channel. Although outnumbered, Edward had the advantage of skilled English archers and favourable weather conditions. The French faced the sun and were blinded by it, while quick lime was thrown into the wind straight into the faces of the French archers. The French ships were quickly overtaken, with cries of, "King Edward! Saint George!" Edward earned himself the epithet King of the Sea.

Success continued and in 1346 he won the Battle of Crécy. Edward had an impressive army of 30,000 men. For the first time English archers showed their skills with the longbow, resulting in a decisive victory. A contemporary chronicler wrote that so many English arrows were fired that it looked as if it was snowing. The French lost over 15,000 men in the battle; the English only around 100 men. A major battle in the Hundred Years War took place at Poitiers in September 1356, with the English army again victorious and King John II of France taken prisoner by the Black Prince.

Despite military successes, in 1360 Edward III signed the Treaty of Brétigny, renouncing his claim to the French throne in return for sovereignty over Acquitaine, Gascony, Calais, Poitou and Guienne. King John II of

France agreed to pay three million gold crowns for his release from prison. Edward returned to England for the remainder of his life and gave up the fight with France. But France had not yet given up the fight with England.

When John II died in 1364, the Dauphin came to the French throne as Charles V and was determined to win back all lands lost during the reign of his father. By this time Edward III was ailing and his son, John of Gaunt, lacked the qualities of a great military leader. Soon, all that Edward had fought over was lost, and England was left with the control of Calais and nothing else.

During his reign, Windsor Castle was Edward III's main residence and where he spent the most time. He made many improvements and additions to the castle over a 20-year period, including St George's Hall, designed for meetings with his Knights of the Order of the Garter, the Norman Tower and Gateway, a Chapel of St George to replace Henry I's chapel and the Deanery and Canons' residences. He had various rooms constructed along the south and east walls of the Upper Ward, plus houses for his impoverished Alms Knights. He spent £51,000 turning it into a magnificent castle, the most money any medieval monarch had spent on a single residence. Although his Round Tower no longer exists, other than perhaps in the foundations of the present tower of the same name which was dramatically remodeled in the 19th century, there is an Edward III Tower in the south-west corner in his memory.

Edward III was a popular monarch, but celebrations for his victories in France were to be short lived. The bubonic plague reached England, killing at least a third of the population. The plague was thought to have been spread by fleas carried on black rats. Modern research suggests that it began in China and spread across Europe via the trade routes, resulting in the deaths of 25 million people. It is reputed to have come to England via ships landing at Melcombe Regis — now Weymouth – in 1348. From there it spread to Bristol and London, and soon entire families were completely wiped out. Thought to have been transmitted by the bite of an infected flea, symptoms included black marks all over the body, which led to the disease being dubbed the Black Death. Three of the King's children died in 1348, probably from the plague.

The arrival of the Black Death was a tremendous blow to England at a time when the country was struggling financially due to the high cost of funding military campaigns in France. Wages remained static and the cost of living rose. In the 1350s the labour force became greatly reduced because so many had died of the plague, and those that could work suddenly had the power to ask for more money. A contemporary chronicler tells us, "The shepherd and the cowherd now demand more wages and withsoever we look, whatsoever be the work, labourers are now of such a price that, when we must needs use them, where we were wont to spend two shillings we must now spend five or six." Economic recession and price increases are nothing new.

In August 1369 Queen Philippa died from dropsy at Windsor Castle. Edward then became infatuated with Alice Perrers, a former lady of the bedchamber to the late Queen, who was extremely unpopular with the English people. Alice was manipulative and dominated the court, supported by John of Gaunt. She even sat beside judges in courts so that she could control sentences, and in ecclesiastical courts where she attempted to change the law as she saw fit. On one occasion she had the Speaker of the House of Commons arrested and imprisoned. In 1374 she publicly accompanied the King in a carriage procession from the Tower of London to a tournament in Smithfield. Not only did she act as if she was queen, it was noted that she was wearing Philippa's jewels.

In the latter years of his life, Edward III was less active and gave his two sons, the Black Prince and John of Gaunt, greater responsibility for day-to-day affairs in England. When the Black Prince died from amoebic dysentery on 8 June, 1376, Edward became deeply depressed and sank into a decline.

Edward died at Sheen Palace on 21 June, 1377, and was succeeded by his grandson, Richard II. As he lay dying of a stroke, which took from him the power of speech, Alice Perrers removed his rings and jewels, and fled, as did the King's courtiers. A lone priest remained with Edward to administer the last rites and heard him mutter his final words, "Miserere Jesu".

Edward was laid to rest in a tomb of Purbeck marble in the chapel of St Edward the Confessor at Westminster Abbey. A wooden effigy of the King carried in his funeral procession is still preserved at the Abbey and is said to be a true likeness. Thought to have been based on Edward's death mask, it has formed the basis of portraits of him ever since.

On his tomb is carved a Latin inscription, which translates as: "Here is the glory of the English, the paragon of past kings, the model of future kings, a merciful king, the peace of the peoples, Edward the Third fulfilling the jubilee of his reign, the unconquered leopard, powerful in war like a Maccabee. While he lived prosperously, his realm lived again in honesty. He ruled mighty in arms; now in Heaven let him be a king."

Within a century of his death, Edward's reputation had been so enhanced that he was held up as model of kingship that all monarchs should emulate.

Chapter 26

Richard II 1367–1400
Reign: 1377–1399

The climax of the celebrations to mark the 60th anniversary of her Coronation in 2013 saw Queen Elizabeth II return to Westminster Abbey where she and past Kings and Queens of England had been crowned. In the Abbey nave there is an historic reminder of one of her ancestors – a painting of King Richard II seated in the Coronation chair, holding the orb and sceptre. Still brightly coloured after more than 600 years, it was personally donated to Westminster Abbey by King Richard.

Sumptuously dressed in a crimson robe lined with ermine, a heavily embroidered tunic, vermilion hose and golden shoes, with a magnificent crown on his head, it would be easy to think that this splendour was just for Coronation Day. Yet Richard II was always extravagantly dressed. He loved jewels, silks, brocades and velvets and wore outfits that he felt befitted a king. On a visit to France in October 1396 he spent more than the equivalent of £150,000 on his wardrobe.

"Every day he wore different and more gorgeous clothes," wrote a contemporary chronicler. There is also documentary evidence that the flamboyant monarch invented the handkerchief. From the royal accounts we can see that he used a square of fabric to blow his nose called a handkercher. The first time such an item is recorded.

Richard's extravagance did not just extend to clothes. He also had a passion for baths and had an elaborate Bath House built at Sheen Palace, decorated with 2,000 hand-painted tiles. He lavished gifts and hospitality on his friends and gave each a jewelled badge bearing his emblem of a white hart. He employed over 10,000 people in the royal household. In his kitchens alone there were said to be 300 staff. A contemporary wrote, "He kept the greatest port and maintained the most plentiful house that ever any King of England did."

Richard loved good food and his court cookery book *The Forme of Cury* still survives, containing almost 200 recipes. Unsurprisingly, they are very exotic dishes filled with herbs and spices such as cardamom, nutmeg, cinnamon, caraway, ginger and saffron. It is the oldest known English cookery book, dating from around 1390 and is now preserved in the British Library. Disturbingly to 21st century palates, there are recipes for cooking porpoises, seals, herons and whales.

Richard was born at the Abbey of St Andrew, Bordeaux, in the English principality of Aquitaine, on 6 January, 1367. He was a grandson of King Edward III, who was on the throne at the time of his birth, and a son of Edward the Black Prince and Joan Plantagenet, the Fair Maid of Kent. Richard had a somewhat lonely early childhood and was tutored by Sir Simon Burley. His studies were in both English and French, he was taught theology, read French romances and poetry, and enjoyed composing poems and ballads.

Richard's first visit to England was at the age of four. Just a few years later, as the Black Prince's eldest surviving son, he became heir to the throne in June 1376 when his father died. King Edward III presented the nine-year-old to Parliament as his successor. Richard was created Prince of Wales, Duke of Cornwall and Earl of Chester, and was made a Knight of the Garter. Maybe such adulation at a young age fostered an increasing arrogance in the boy and a feeling of self-importance that would eventually lead to his downfall.

As the new Prince of Wales, Richard was given an elaborate Investiture service at Westminster Abbey in November 1376, which had been preceded by a period of fasting. Hunger took its toll on the boy and Richard collapsed during the ceremony.

After barely 12 months as heir, Richard succeeded his grandfather on 21 June, 1377, when he was just 10 years old. The new King Richard II was crowned at Westminster Abbey on 16 July in an elaborate ceremony organised by his uncle, John of Gaunt. The day before his Coronation, Richard processed through the streets from the Tower of London to Westminster on horseback. During this first ever Coronation procession, the streets were lined with people eager to catch sight of their young king. There were banners, flowers and decorations along the route, while entertainers and musicians amused the crowds. Later monarchs developed this idea and had even more elaborate processions and river pageants to mark their Coronations.

There is an apocryphal story that during the Coronation ceremony itself, Richard lost a shoe, a spur, and his crown fell off – said to foretell that he would lose the support of the House of Commons, his army, and would finally lose his kingdom.

Until the young monarch reached maturity, England was ruled by a council. It was a time of civil unrest in the country. The Black Death had wiped out a third of the population, resulting in a reduction in manpower and, therefore, a demand for higher wages from those that were able to work. This inevitably led to higher prices for goods and services. A Statute of Labourers to try and return wages back to their level before the plague was deeply unpopular. The poll tax of 1381, a charge of one shilling for every adult in England, proved to be the straw that broke the camel's back and led to what has become known as the Peasants' Revolt.

The poll tax was a measure to try and recoup money spent on the Hundred Years War. The uprising began in Brentwood, Essex, where the people refused to pay the tax and attacked and murdered collectors. At Deptford in Kent a tax collector was killed during a heated argument with a roof tiler – named Walter Tyler – when he demanded tax from Tyler's daughter, who was still underage.

News of the man known as Wat Tyler spread, with people supporting his actions against the poll tax. Tyler was elected leader of an insurrection and in June 1381 between 10,000 and 20,000 men from Kent and Essex marched on London. Rochester Castle was seized en route, and the homes of noblemen were set on fire.

King Richard was only 14, but he decided to take the situation into his own hands. He rode out to meet the angry mob at Mile End on 14 June. Calm and majestic for one so young, he promised to sort out their grievances, calmed the men down and many returned home quietly.

However, a small group of militant rebels led by Wat Tyler remained, now with even more demands, and the next day John of Gaunt's impressive Savoy Palace was destroyed by fire, as was the Treasurer's manor house at Highbury. Men took over the Tower of London, ransacking rooms, and they burned Temple Bar. The demonstrators murdered the King's Treasurer and the Archbishop of Canterbury. In retaliation the Mayor of London killed Wat Tyler in front of the Abbey of St Bartholomew at Smithfield.

Richard went out again and met the men at Smithfield, although this time he had a large back up of soldiers. The outraged crowd was preparing to fire arrows at him, when he asked, "Would you kill your King? I am your Captain and your leader. Follow me and you shall have all you asked for."

He rode off out of the city with the mob following. Further trouble was abated and in a quiet spot in Clerkenwell Fields, Richard calmly agreed to all the rebels' demands, saying that the poll tax would be repealed, serfdom would be abolished and rent on land would be fixed at a low rate. The men dispersed. When he returned to the Tower of London, Richard told his anxious mother, "Rejoice and praise God, for I have recovered today my heritage, which was lost, and the realm of England."

Richard did not, however, fulfil any of his promises and many of the rebels were tracked down and, through the summer and autumn of that year, 7,000 men were slaughtered. On 28 June, the King personally defeated a small band of rebels at Billericay in Essex, which brought an end to the Peasants' Revolt once and for all.

The young monarch was growing up and the strong way in which he had taken control of a difficult situation did much to enhance his reputation. But the feeling of power went to his head and he began to resent any kind of opposition. When the Earl of Arundel complained about bad government, Richard took it as a personal insult and flew into a rage, saying, "If it is to my charge that you would lay this and it is supposed to be my fault that there is misgovernment in the kingdom, you lie in your teeth. You can go to the devil!"

On another occasion he threatened the Archbishop of Canterbury with a sword when the Archbishop suggested that Richard should remove his favourites from court. The King screamed that he would not dismiss as much as a kitchen maid.

As the years progressed, the King's promotion of his favourites became a bone of contention. Richard gave his close friend Robert de Vere the title Earl of Oxford and later made him Duke of Ireland. Another favoured member of Richard's circle, Michael de la Pole, was created Earl of Suffolk. Richard formed a team of nine magnates on whose loyalty he could rely.

In return they received titles, land and wealth from the King. Members of the Royal Household became Sheriffs to govern the shires. Others close to the King became judges to administer local laws. This favouritism made him many enemies at court, particularly his uncle Thomas, now Duke of Gloucester, and the Earls of Arundel and Warwick.

In 1387 the Duke of Gloucester, and Richard's cousin, Henry Bolingbroke, opposed the King by establishing a group of five noblemen known as the

Lords Appellant to try and curb Richard's power. The following year Parliament met, in what has become known as the Merciless Parliament, and the Lords Appellant drew up a bill of 39 charges against Richard's ministers and favourites. Robert de Vere was sent into exile and several of Richard's circle, including his old tutor Sir Simon Burley, were imprisoned and condemned to death. Although Richard refused to sign death warrants, beheadings took place without royal authority and there was nothing that the King could do. Heads could not be replaced.

Richard refused to be cowed and simply bided his time, waiting until he was over the age of 21. In 1389 he marched into Parliament and surprised those present by asking them how old he was. When ministers replied that the King was aged 22, Richard took hold of the Great Royal Seal which symbolises the sovereign's power and told them that, as he was now of age, he was going to take control of his kingdom. He immediately dismissed the Lords Appellant and eventually took his revenge. Within a few years the Earl of Arundel had been found guilty of treason and was executed. The Earl of Warwick was sent into exile, while the Duke of Gloucester was imprisoned and murdered. Henry Bolingbroke was banished to France.

Richard established royal authority and began to govern in his own name, entering a period of public popularity. In January 1382 he had married Anne of Bohemia at St Stephen's Chapel in the Palace of Westminster. She was a daughter of Emperor Charles IV and a sister of King Wenceslas. It was Anne who began the fashion amongst younger ladies in England for the horned cap, two feet wide and two feet high, built on a wire frame and covered with a sparkling gauze. Like her husband, the Queen clearly had an interest in clothes.

It was a happy marriage which lasted just 12 years. Anne died suddenly of the plague in June 1394. Richard was completely overcome with grief and had the family home at Sheen Palace razed to the ground and took up permanent residence at Windsor Castle. He found it unbearable visiting any places that he associated with his wife.

In November 1396 he married for the second time but it was very much a marriage of convenience. His new wife, Isabella of France, was only six years old but brought with her a dowry of £50,000 and it meant a good political relationship with the French. Richard signed a 25-year truce agreement with France to ensure peace. Because of her age, the marriage was never consummated. Having no children from either marriage, Richard named his cousin Roger Mortimer, Earl of March, as his successor.

During his 22-year reign, Richard II was a man of contrasts. Acceding to the throne at such a young age, he had no role model as monarch. His grandfather, Edward III, was old and had gone into a decline by the time Richard became heir to the throne and so he had little training for kingship. Instead of being a warrior King, like so many of his predecessors, Richard was much more interested in the courtly knight with a romantic notion of chivalry.

He was himself handsome, with a fair complexion and golden blond hair, and was above average height for his times at six foot tall. In character he was flamboyant, garrulous, ruthless and quick-tempered. Yet at the same time he was sensitive, with a love of beauty and the arts. He also adored animals, particularly dogs and had a greyhound call Math. Unusually, he also had a pelican at court.

Perhaps the most colourful description of Richard II comes from Tobias Smollett in his *History of England*, written in the 18th century: "Richard was a dupe to flattery, a slave to ostentation . . . he was idle, profuse, and profligate, and, though brave by starts, naturally pusillanimous and irresolute. His pride and resentment prompted him to cruelty and breach of faith: while his necessities obliged him to fleece his people, and degrade the dignity of his character and station."

Yet there were many positive achievements during his reign. Richard had Westminster Hall rebuilt to create an impressive 240ft by 70ft wide space, making it the largest hall of this period, now known for its magnificent hammer beam roof and arch ribs. He gave £100 a year towards the completion of the nave of Westminster Abbey, and also made improvements to Canterbury Cathedral and York Minster.

Among his accomplishments was greater protection for England, with paid reservists throughout the country. He also developed a strong personal army for family conflict. Richard had deprived his cousin, Henry Bolingbroke, the only son of John of Gaunt, of his father's estates and so needed protection.

While Richard was on a visit to Ireland in June 1399, Henry Bolingbroke came over from France with an army landing at Ravenspur on the Yorkshire coast (a town now lost due to coastal erosion). Henry and his army marched to Chester, intent on taking his rightful inheritance and deposing Richard. The Earl of Northumberland met him and said that King Richard had agreed to give him John of Gaunt's estates back, as long as he could remain King, but Henry had his sights on the throne.

Richard had been completely taken by surprise, was unprepared and without his army to protect him. He was unable to leave Ireland quickly and did not sail across to Wales until 24 July, by which time Henry had established himself at Flint Castle. The two men met and, realising that his life was in danger, Richard agreed to abdicate if his life was spared. Richard was taken to London as a prisoner and was locked in the Tower of London.

On 30 September, 1399, it was announced that King Richard II had abdicated. That day he had been forced to sign a document:

"I, Richard, by the grace of God, King of England and of France and Lord of Ireland . . . resign all kingly majesty, dignity and crown . . . and with deed and word I leave off and resign them and go from them for evermore, for I know, acknowledge and deem myself to be, and have been, insufficient, unable and unprofitable."

He gave up the Crown, and was formally deposed by Parliament. From the Tower of London he was taken to Leeds Castle in Kent, then to Pickering, Knaresborough and, finally, to Pontefract Castle where he died on 14 February 1400 at the age of 33. There was an official report issued declaring that Richard had starved himself to death, although he was much more likely to have been deliberately starved. His body was put on show to the public, but well covered so that only part of his face could be seen. A more recent examination of the King's skull shows that he met a more violent end.

Although Henry Bolingbroke was chosen to succeed Richard as King Henry IV, it led to a century of conflict known as the Wars of the Roses which was to blight the reigns of the next seven kings of England.

Richard II was buried initially at King's Langley Church in Hertfordshire, but was later removed to Westminster Abbey in 1413 by King Henry V so that the deposed monarch could lie beside his beloved Anne. Even then he was not allowed to rest in peace, as it was possible to reach inside between gaps in the paneling of the tomb. In 1766 a Dean of Canterbury reported that a Westminster schoolboy had helped himself to Richard's lower jawbone.

The tomb was opened for cleaning and inspection in August 1871. Present that day was Sir George Scharf, the first director of London's National Gallery. In 2010 a small box belonging to Scharf was uncovered by an archivist cataloguing his papers. Inside were fragments of wood from Richard II's coffin, leather from his glove and silk taken from inside the tomb and with it were detailed sketches and measurements of the King's skull and bones. An extraordinary discovery, over 600 years after Richard's death.

In the year 1400 there was little mourning in England. Only the men of

Bordeaux, where Richard had been born, were said to shed a tear for him. The popular image of Richard today as a tragic figure is greatly coloured by Shakespeare's play about his life and death, although the playwright took many liberties with the story and used dramatic licence rather than hard facts. Classed as one of Shakespeare's history plays, from its first printing it was known as *The Tragedie of King Richard the Second.*

In the final act, fact and fiction merge for Richard speaks of "the hollow crown that rounds the mortal temples of a king". For all his love of jewels and sumptuous clothes, by the end of his reign the power and the trappings of royalty were all stripped from him and the crown must have seemed very hollow indeed.

Chapter 27

Henry IV c.1366–1413
Reign: 1399–1413

"Uneasy lies the head that wears a crown", lamented Shakespeare's King Henry IV. They are words that could very easily have been uttered in reality, for the man who founded a dynasty as the first monarch of the House of Lancaster spent most of his 13-year reign desperately trying to hold on to his own. It was a period of English history described by Shakespeare as "a scrambling and unquiet time".

From the outset, Henry was considered a usurper. He was not the immediate heir to the throne and there were others who had a better claim. Without universal support in England, Henry continually faced a barrage of rebellions, revolts and even assassination attempts to remove him from power.

Henry claimed the throne "by right of descent vindicated by conquest", but many others were in the same position. The drawback in the line of succession at this time resulted from the fact that King Richard II had no children and therefore no immediate heirs. His predecessor King Edward III, on the other hand, had 13 children, many of whom survived him, with offspring marrying into influential noble families.

This resulted in disagreements about the succession amongst his many descendants. Edmund Mortimer, 3rd Earl of March, actually had a much better claim than Henry but life in 14th-century England was far less cut and dried than today, when our line of succession is established and beyond dispute.

Henry IV was the sixth child and eldest surviving son of John of Gaunt, the Duke of Lancaster, and was born probably in April 1366 or 1367, at Bolingbroke Castle in Lincolnshire. The exact date of his birth has long been the subject of scholarly debate for two reasons. Firstly, there is no contemporary record of his actual birth date. Secondly, it is believed that Henry was born on Maundy Thursday, which is a moveable feast and so he celebrated his birthday on a different date each year, depending upon when Easter fell.

He became known as Henry Bolingbroke because of his birthplace and was the first of our kings since the Norman conquest of 1066 to have been born in England with English parents. His mother was Blanche of Lancaster, formerly Lady Blanche Plantagenet and a direct descendant of Henry III. Blanche died from the bubonic plague when Henry was just two years old.

Henry was brought up by his father's trusted household servants, rather than blood relatives, for the first nine years of his life. His home was Savoy Palace in London, which was later destroyed by fire and looted by Wat Tyler's supporters during the Peasants' Revolt. Henry studied French and Latin, loved literature and was particularly good at music. Despite being short and stocky, Henry had a muscular build, which gave him great physical strength. He excelled in martial arts and was extremely successful in tournaments.

At the age of 14 Henry married Mary de Bohun, co-heiress of the Earl of Hereford, Essex and Northampton. The couple had five sons – one being the future Henry V – and two daughters. Mary died in childbirth in June 1394 at the age of 24 and was buried in Leicester, although there is controversy as to where her remains are today. In April 1402 Henry married Joan of Navarre, sometimes referred to as Joan of Brittany, by proxy at Eltham Palace in Kent and later in person at a ceremony in Winchester Cathedral in February 1403.

In childhood the flame-haired Henry was very close to his cousin Richard and the pair were made Knights of the Garter at Windsor in 1377. Henry was given the title Earl of Derby and within weeks was carrying the Sword of Mercy at his ten-year-old cousin's Coronation as King Richard II. Henry's own public life began in 1386, when he became his father's representative in Lancaster and administered the family estates. By this time, however, the cousins had grown apart and Henry had become disillusioned by Richard II's manner of ruling.

In 1387 Henry became one of five Lords Appellant, a group who were determined to topple the King's closest counsellors. Their ultimate intention was to depose Richard and place either Henry or his uncle Thomas, Duke of Gloucester, on the throne instead. Their plans proved fruitless, as Richard refused to be cowed by the Lords Appellant or to yield to their demands.

Henry's father, John of Gaunt, remained staunchly loyal to the King and so insisted that his son should remain neutral. In line with his father's wishes, Henry reluctantly withdrew for a while and spent several years travelling around Europe. In 1390 he headed a campaign of 300 men to Lithuania and successfully fought at the siege of Vilna. Only one Englishman was killed and just two were taken prisoner.

In 1392 Henry embarked on a year-long Grand Tour, visiting many countries including Austria, Hungary and Crete, staying at various royal courts along the way which fostered good diplomatic relations with a number of European monarchs. He ended his tour with a pilgrimage to Jerusalem, a city where Henry was convinced that he would eventually die.

Although Richard II had most of the Lords Appellant executed for opposing him, he spared the life of his cousin Henry, even elevating him to the Duke of Hereford. But once settled back in England, Henry continued to express his dissatisfaction with the King. His forthright views were overheard by the Duke of Norfolk, who considered the remarks to be treasonable and reported back to King Richard. Consequently, Henry was banished from England for six years and went to live in France.

In February 1399 Henry's father died. Richard II suddenly changed Henry's banishment from six years to life and claimed John of Gaunt's land and possessions for himself. Having stolen Henry's rightful inheritance, Richard made a deadly enemy of his cousin.

While Richard was on a visit to Ireland that summer, Henry sailed over from France with an army of several hundred men, landing at Ravenspur on the Yorkshire coast in July. Henry and his army then marched to Chester, intent on taking his inheritance and deposing Richard. Henry gained increasing support including that of many leading noble families, such as the Nevilles and the Percys, and before long his father's brother the Duke of York, who had once opposed Henry, now swore allegiance to him.

The two cousins met and, realising that he was in mortal danger, Richard agreed to abdicate if his life was spared. Richard was taken to London as a prisoner and was locked in the Tower of London.

Having a rather tenuous claim to the throne, Henry could only become King if it could be proved that Richard had abdicated willingly and had named Henry as his successor. In the end Richard did sign an abdication statement, although almost certainly under pressure. Ultimately Henry was chosen by Parliament to be King of England. This actually put Parliament in a position of strength as it meant that the sovereign was under its control. Like his predecessor, however, Henry refused to accept that he ruled under Parliament's authority. He deluded himself that he was on the throne because of the "will of the people".

The new King Henry IV was crowned in Westminster Abbey on 13 October, 1399. His was the first Coronation since 1066 in which the king made his address in English. During the ceremony Henry was anointed with holy oil, said to have been given by the Virgin Mary to Thomas Becket while he was deep in prayer one evening. It was stored in a receptacle in the shape of a golden eagle, which is known today as the Ampulla and is still used at Coronations to hold the oil for the sacred moment of anointing.

The exact age of the Ampulla is unknown, with some experts believing that the head of the eagle may be older than the body, but the design and primitiveness of the screw, which allows the head to be removed so that it can be filled with oil, is said to date from the 14th century. The Ampulla somehow escaped Oliver Cromwell's destruction of the regalia in 1649, as did the silver gilt spoon used for the anointing, which is the oldest piece of English regalia, dating from King John's coronation in the 12th century.

Just weeks into the reign, the Earls of Huntingdon and Kent (half-brothers of Richard II) and the Earl of Salisbury, together with Lord Despenser, plotted to depose the new King. Henry fled from Windsor to London for his own safety, but the plotters had little support and were quickly beheaded by a mob of the King's supporters. Another 30 were found guilty at a trial and were publicly executed. Such barbarity was intended to deter other rebels from opposing the King.

Henry spent the first Christmas of his reign "quietly and without joy", suffering from a severe stomach upset, thought to be an attempt on the King's life by poisoning. Other attempts followed later, the most daring being the placing of a man-trap device in Henry's bed, described as "an iron trident with three long and sharp points", which would have seriously injured the King, possibly fatally, if he had become caught in the trap.

The deposed King Richard II died in February 1400. But even with Richard out of the way, life did not get any easier for Henry IV. Scotland, Wales and France proved to be thorns in his flesh as long-established enemies of England and civil wars and rebellions dogged him, just as they had his predecessors. In September 1400 a Welsh uprising escalated into a bigger crisis when landowner Owen Glendower (Owain Glyndwr), who claimed descent from ancient Welsh princes, headed a rebellion against English rule with the aim of liberating Wales. In 1401 Glendower's daughter married Edmund Mortimer, Earl of March, who had been the heir to Richard II until Henry usurped him. This added to the ill feeling towards the King.

In 1403 the Earl of Northumberland's son, Henry "Harry" Percy – known as Hotspur – felt that the King had not supported his family in the Welsh conflict and there was animosity when Henry gave land in Cumberland to a rival, when he had promised it to the Percys. Hotspur turned his allegiance to Edmund Mortimer instead. This hostility ultimately led to the Battle at Shrewsbury, which was fought on 21 July, 1403, between Henry IV's army and a rebel army under the leadership of Harry Hotspur. It was the first English battle in which archers on both sides fought against each other using deadly longbows.

It was a fierce battle in which Henry IV's army was victorious and Hotspur lost his life. His body was quartered and the parts were later displayed in London, Bristol, Chester and Newcastle as a warning to others. It is this area of Henry's reign that Shakespeare concentrated on in his play *Henry IV Part I*, although the bard re-wrote history by having Hotspur killed by the Prince of Wales, when he actually died at the hands of an unknown archer. Finding his armour too hot, Hotspur had raised the visor on his helmet to get some air and an arrow fatally struck him in the head.

Hotspur had been told by a fortune teller that he would die at Berwick. He assumed this was Berwick-on-Tweed in the north of England, but he had stationed his troops near Shrewsbury at a Shropshire hamlet called Berwick. Three miles north of Shrewsbury, the village of Battlefield now marks the place where the battle was fought and a church was built on the site. Although called St Mary Magdalene's, it has always been commonly known as Battlefield Church. In a niche above the east window is a statue of Henry IV.

Despite victory at Shrewsbury, Henry continued to face conspiracies and rebellions on all sides. The Percy family and their allies made several attempts to overthrow him. One notable plot in 1405 involved Thomas Mowbray, the Earl Marshal, and Richard Scrope, the Archbishop of Canterbury, who, along with other leading noblemen, accused Henry of murdering Richard II, of usurping the throne and "winning the crown by treachery", of levying high taxes on the English people and many other calumnies. A list of grievances was placarded all over the city of York and some 9,000 men marched from there towards Thirsk, but Henry's supporters soon quashed the revolt and the leaders were executed, including the Archbishop of Canterbury.

On 19 February, 1408, Henry faced his final confrontation with the Percy family at the Battle of Bramham Moor. The long-standing feud between the rivals would later become known as the Wars of the Roses, conflicts that spread across the reigns of seven kings of England, each monarch struggling to retain the crown. At Bramham Moor, south-west of Tadcaster, Henry's forces were under the leadership of Sir Thomas Rokeby, and faced the hastily gathered army of Henry Percy – Hotspur's father – the 1st Earl of Northumberland. The battle is not well documented but Henry IV's longbow archers triumphed once again. Northumberland was killed and Rokeby was rewarded by being given the Percy family estate at Spofforth.

For the first time, Henry IV felt that his throne was secure. Owen Glendower had been worn down and his rebellion was no longer effective. The Percy family had, temporarily, been defeated and insurgences to depose the King abated. But Henry was now plagued by money worries and was forced by Parliament to reform the royal household and reduce his spending. His health had also begun to deteriorate and he was frequently bedridden. Initially he appeared to be suffering with sciatica, but he was soon beset with stomach upsets and skin problems

His eldest son, Prince Henry, should have come to his father's aid, but they had an uneasy relationship with feelings of mistrust on both sides. By 1409 the Prince was taking on more power but was frequently in opposition to his father. Following a major quarrel between them in November 1411, Prince Henry tried to get his father to stand down. At the close of Shakespeare's play, while Henry IV lies ill in bed, Prince Henry (Hal) thinking that his father is dead, takes the crown from his pillow. When King Henry wakes he is distraught to discover what his son has done and dies soon afterwards.

How much of Shakespeare's play is based on fact we shall never know, but by end of 1412 it became clear that Henry IV was gravely ill. Within weeks he had an epileptic fit or possibly a stroke while praying at the tomb of Edward the Confessor in Westminster Abbey and fell into a coma. The exact nature of his illness is not known, but some historians believe he had leprosy, the King's face and body becoming disfigured and wasted, although this has never been confirmed and it could have been psoriasis or a similar condition.

By the end of his reign, many of the King's opponents felt that the ill health which had plagued him was divine retribution for his actions, particularly for having had an Archbishop of Canterbury executed. In 1408 Henry had written a new will, which began, "I, Henry, sinful wretch . . ."

and he asked for the pardon of his people for any ill that he had done in his life.

Henry IV died at Westminster on 20 March, 1413, at the age of 47. He had firmly believed that he would die in Jerusalem and although he passed away in London, the room he died in was the residence of the Abbot of Westminster and was known as the Jerusalem Chamber.

Henry's body was taken by boat down the Thames estuary to Faversham in Kent. At his own request he was buried in Trinity Chapel, Canterbury Cathedral, beside his second wife, and close to the tomb of his uncle, the Black Prince. It was considered to be one of the most hallowed places in the Christian world at that time because of its proximity to the tomb of Saint Thomas Becket. Henry IV remains the only English monarch to be laid to rest in Canterbury Cathedral.

Over the centuries that followed, there were persistent rumours that Henry's body had been ditched into the sea during a storm on his final journey to Canterbury and that his tomb was empty. To disprove this rumour once and for all, on 21 August, 1832, the King's lead coffin was opened. A Dr JH Spry, who was present, wrote an account of the examination: "To the astonishment of all present, the face of the deceased king was seen in complete preservation . . . the jaws were perfect and all the teeth in them, except one fore-tooth, which had probably been lost during the King's life." The russet-coloured beard was as red as it had been in life and confirmed that the cathedral tomb is indeed the final resting place of King Henry IV.

Chapter 28

Henry V c.1387–1422
Reign: 1413–1422

As a warrior king, Henry V is considered to be one of England's heroic monarchs, ranking alongside Alfred the Great and Richard the Lionheart in popular culture. During World War II a film version of Shakespeare's play *Henry V* was made to boost public morale. It starred Laurence Olivier and was partly funded by the British government at the instigation of Winston Churchill. Its release in 1944 coincided with the Allied invasion of Normandy and the film was dedicated to the "Commandos and Airborne Troops of Great Britain, the spirit of whose ancestors it has humbly attempted to recapture". Clips of Olivier's St Crispin's Day speech can still stir the heart, "We few, we happy few, we band of brothers . . ."

The real King Henry V was born in the Queen's Chamber of Monmouth Castle around 1387, the eldest surviving son of Henry Bolingbroke (later King Henry IV) and his first wife, Mary de Bohun. There is a statue of Henry above the entrance to the Shire Hall in Agincourt Square, Monmouth, to mark his birth in the town and to honour his famous victory.

A weak child, he was put in the care of a nurse called Johanna Waring at Courtfield, near Monmouth, who is credited with his survival. His gratitude is shown in the fact that when he eventually became king, Henry granted Johanna an annual income of £20 for life, which was a great deal of money in that period.

Henry was well educated, fluent in French and Latin, and his great loves were music and reading. Between the ages of 8 and 10, the Duchy of Lancaster records show that books, a sword and a harp were purchased for him. For a short time he studied divinity at Queen's College, Oxford, under the guardianship of his uncle, Henry Beaufort, then Chancellor of Oxford. In adult life he was pious to the point of being almost obsessive about religion. He regularly visited shrines and could spend long periods in solitary prayer.

Despite his piety, it is often speculated that Henry had a wild youth but much of what we know comes from Shakespeare's dramatised character of Prince Hal, so it could possibly be the Bard's invention rather than an accurate portrait.

By the age of 13 Henry was on military campaigns with his father, with little opportunity for making merry, although a 15th-century biography reveals: "He was in his youth a diligent follower of idle practices, much given to instruments of music, and fired with the torches of Venus herself."

Henry grew to be very tall, said to be in the region of 6ft 3in, was slim, clean shaven, and with dark hair cropped into a ring in an almost monk-like fashion. Extremely intelligent, he was a man of few words and was very decisive. He considered his options carefully before answering a question and it was said that his replies were "It is impossible," or "It shall be done". Never, "I don't know," or "I'm not sure."

Henry was athletic, a skilful soldier and has become the embodiment of chivalry. He also had a keen sense of justice. The 15th-century French chronicler Georges Chastellain wrote, "He gave support to none out of favour, nor did he suffer wrong to go unpunished out of regard for affinity."

When he became King, he faced the inevitable dilemma of reconciling his compassionate nature with having to be ruthless to enemies in order to protect his country. It was a predicament that led him to seek periods of solitude and quiet reflection.

Henry's royal training began at a very young age and he was forced to grow up quickly. His mother died in 1394, when he was just seven years old, and four years later his father was exiled to France by Richard II for publicly expressing his dissatisfaction with the King. Henry remained in England and was looked after by Richard II's court. The animosity that existed between the King and Henry's father clearly did not extend to Henry himself, and Richard II took the boy under his wing. In 1399 Richard took him Ireland, where Henry showed the first signs that he was going to be a good soldier.

It was during this visit that Henry's father took advantage of the King's absence to return to England and eventually deposed Richard II. The young Henry remained in Ireland for his own protection with the Mortimer family at Trim Castle in County Meath, only coming back to England once his father had been chosen by Parliament as the next sovereign of England, the new King Henry IV.

At his father's Coronation, Henry carried the ceremonial sword Curtana, the Sword of Mercy, and that same month was made Prince of Wales, Duke of Cornwall, Earl of Chester, a Knight of the Bath, a Knight of the Garter, Duke of Acquitaine and Duke of Lancaster. Still barely 12 years old, the weight of obligation and duty was already descending on him.

A year later he accompanied his father on a military campaign to Wales and in October 1400 was given control of Chester, with Harry "Hotspur" Percy as his guardian. Hotspur taught Henry how to develop his military skills. Unfortunately Hotspur soon began to oppose the new King, which eventually led to the Battle of Shrewsbury in July 1403. Henry found himself fighting against his former friend and although he did not actually kill Hotspur, as in Shakespeare's play, Harry Percy did lose his life that day. Henry was himself injured by an arrow, but it was a facial wound, from which he quickly recovered.

The young prince was involved in further skirmishes with Wales and the rebellious Owen Glendower in the years that followed and at the siege of Aberystwyth in 1407 he was able to take control of an impenetrable fortress by starving the occupants into submission. It was a tactic that he was later to use successfully in France.

Energetic and a good organiser, Henry's training continued and from 1406 he sat in on Council meetings dealing with his father's administrative matters. Early in 1409 he was made Warden of the Cinque Ports and Constable of Dover. By this time King Henry IV was in poor health and soon the Prince took his father's place in Council and became monarch in all but name.

On 3rd November, 1410 there was a formal proposal by Parliament urging the King to stand down in favour of his son. Henry's eagerness to rule caused animosity between father and son, so much so that King Henry IV had Prince Henry removed from the Council altogether, leading to a major quarrel. The question of abdication continued to be a bone of contention between them and Henry gained further support from within his own family. The situation was only resolved when the King died in March 1413 and Henry succeeded without having to force the issue further.

At the age of 26, Henry V was crowned the second monarch of the House of Lancaster at Westminster Abbey on Passion Sunday, 9 April, 1413, amid a snow storm. He seemed to transform once King and his goal became one of reconciliation. Thomas Walsingham, a medieval historian, wrote, "As soon as he was crowned, suddenly he was changed into a new man, and all his intent was to live virtuously."

Henry's aim was to put right some of the wrongs of his father's reign. One of the first things he did as King was to have Richard II's body moved from King's Langley to Westminster Abbey, where he was reburied in an elaborate tomb. Some felt that this was to atone for the murder of Richard and it also brought an end to the rumours that Richard might still be alive.

Some noblemen who had become outcasts under Henry IV were returned to the fold. The Percy family received back their estates that had been denied them by Henry IV. Even Edmund Mortimer, the Earl of March, whom Richard II had named as his heir and many felt was the rightful king, had his estates restored. Although there were plots by the Earl's supporters to oust Henry, he quickly suppressed them and treated the Earl of March as if he was one of his own family. The Earl himself seemed to bear no animosity at having been denied the crown and even informed Henry of the plots against him.

Like his father, Henry V faced a rebellion by members of a sect called Lollards over church reform, but he ended it quickly and a gathering in January 1414 was dispersed by royal forces. Magistrates were instructed to arrest all Lollards and 40 prominent supporters were executed. The political activity of the Lollards came to an abrupt end and although it continued as a religious movement, Lollardry seemed to lose its momentum and caused Henry little further trouble.

France rather than England, however, dominated his reign. Henry wanted to take control of the old Angevin Empire, which included Normandy, Maine, Anjou, Touraine, Brittany and Aquitaine that had been lost during the reign of King John. His great-grandfather, Edward III, had unsuccessfully tried to claim the French throne, which started the Hundred Years War. Henry wanted to settle the matter once and for all.

He initially tried diplomatic means but was unsuccessful and decided that a military campaign was the only option. The French Dauphin sent Henry a barrel of tennis balls, with the mocking message that Henry would be better off playing a game of ball than fighting for French land. Henry saw this as an insult to his military prowess, replying, "If God so wills and my life lasts, I will within a few months play such a game of ball in the Frenchmen's streets that they shall lose their jest and gain but grief from this game."

Having failed in negotiations, Henry was determined to take military action, confident that a victory against the French would win him back his family territory and enhance his own reputation in England. In August 1415, his ship *Trinity* headed a fleet across the English Channel.

Shortly after their arrival they captured the port of Harfleur and then in the following months Henry marched with his army towards Calais. After crossing the Somme, he eventually found his way blocked at Agincourt by 20,000 French knights. The English army was outnumbered, and Henry's troops were hungry and weakened through dysentery, but he had no option other than to attack. On 25 October, 1415 — St Crispin's Day – the Battle of Agincourt was fought.

The ground was very wet, which worked to Henry's advantage as it slowed the French horses down and soldiers in heavy armour sank into the mud, which enabled the English to advance. Henry was a dazzling figure, wearing a crown over his helmet and a surcoat emblazoned with the arms of England. The English bowmen were told that, if captured, they would each have three fingers cut off by the French to prevent them ever firing an arrow again. This incentive spurred them on, firing arrows with great vigour from their longbows.

The battle lasted only three hours, but the slaughter was great. Numbers vary in differing eyewitness accounts, but after the battle there were said to be around 10,000 French dead, and only 400 to 500 Englishmen lost.

When Henry returned to England, church bells rang out across the country to celebrate the triumph. Henry typically remained calm and sombre and rode to St Paul's and Westminster Abbey to give thanks, later making a pilgrimage on foot from Shrewsbury to St Winefride's Well in Wales as his way of thanking God for the victory.

The Battle of Agincourt did not resolve the issue with France completely. In August 1416 the English beat the French again, this time showing their naval supremacy at the Battle of the Seine. On 23 July, 1417, Henry returned to France with 50,000 men and 1,600 ships, securing castles and finally taking control of Normandy.

In 1418 the English advanced on Rouen. As in earlier campaigns, Henry had the Norman capital surrounded and waited until hunger eventually caused his enemies to surrender. Soon some 12,000 people were starving. Henry himself said, "War has three handmaidens ever waiting on her: Fire, Blood and Famine, and I have chosen the meekest maid of the three."

A compassionate man, on Christmas Day Henry provided food for the women and children — the innocent victims of his military campaign. When the town finally surrendered on 19 January, 1419, Henry had food sent to all the inhabitants and went to Rouen Cathedral on a black charger to give thanks to God.

Following more campaigns and further attempts at negotiation, on 21 May, 1420, Henry signed the Treaty of Troyes. As a concession, rather than claim the French throne immediately for himself, he agreed to be just heir to the throne so that he would become the next French king. He became known as King of England and Regent of France.

For allowing him to keep his crown, King Charles VI of France agreed to let Henry marry his daughter, Catherine of Valois. Although known as Catherine the Fair, she was not a great beauty and had a very long nose which was said to curl down and almost touch her top lip. The couple married at Troyes on 2 June, 1420, before Henry set off to direct further military operations in France. They eventually returned to England in February 1421, when Catherine was crowned Queen at Westminster Abbey on 23 February.

Henry had been away from England for nearly four years. When in France he had to continue to deal with matters of state back home, with parliamentary reports being forwarded to him. But the people were glad to have their King home and he and Catherine undertook a nationwide royal tour through many towns and cities of England, including Beverley, Bridlington, Bristol, Coventry, Kenilworth, Leicester, Lincoln, Norwich and York.

In June 1421 there was more trouble in France with a siege at Meaux, north of the Loire. The town finally capitulated on 11 May, 1422. It was to be Henry's last military success. While away fighting, Queen Catherine had given birth to their first and only child at Windsor in December, also christened Henry.

Now ill with dysentery and pleurisy, the King had been weakened by war. He had always suffered the same hardships as his soldiers, encouraging by example, and now it was beginning to take its toll physically. Henry V died at Bois de Vincennes in the early hours of 31 August, 1422, aged 35. He had been King of England for just nine years. Had he lived eight weeks longer, he would have achieved his goal of becoming King of France when Charles VI also died.

Fully aware that he was dying, Henry had spent his final days planning the future of his government and making arrangements for his successor's reign, in the knowledge that he was leaving a nine-month-old baby to rule England.

Henry's embalmed corpse was returned to London in a grand procession, leaving Bois de Vincennes at night led by torch bearers dressed in white, accompanied by five hundred soldiers in black armour mounted on jet black horses. He was buried in the Chapel of Edward the Confessor at Westminster Abbey, with a funeral costing £1,052-15s-7d. His shield, helmet and saddle are still kept at the Abbey.

The widowed Queen Catherine later married Owen Tudor, a union which would eventually lead to a new royal dynasty in England. She died in 1437 and, as a very macabre postscript, 222 years later diarist Samuel Pepys paid two pennies and was allowed to see her bones at Westminster, writing, "I had the upper part of her body in my hands and I kissed her on the mouth, reflecting upon it that I did kiss a Queen, and that this was my birthday."

By the time of his death King Henry V was considered a national hero. Chronicler Raphael Holinshed, writing a history of England in 1577, said: "This Henry was a king, of life without spot, a prince whom all men loved, and of none disdained, a captain against whom fortune never frowned, nor mischance once spurned, whose people him so severe a justicer both loved and obeyed (and so humane withal) that he left no offence unpunished, nor friendship unrewarded; a terror to rebels, and a suppressor of sedition, his virtues notable, his qualities most praiseworthy."

When Shakespeare came to write his historical and biographical play around 1599, his main source was Holinshead's *Chronicles*. And it is with the help of Shakespeare's patriotic portrayal that King Henry V remains a national hero to this day. Laurence Olivier's film version has lost none of its passion and transports us back six centuries to the triumphal Battle of Agincourt as if we were there in person.

"Once more unto the breach, dear friends, once more . . ."

Chapter 29

Henry VI 1421–1471
Reign: 1422–1461 and 1470–1471

Kingdoms are but cares,
State is devoid of stay;
Riches are ready snares
And hasten to decay.
Poem written by King Henry VI

With the sudden death of King Henry V in 1422, a baby became King of England. Henry's nine-month-old son entered the history books as the youngest person ever to succeed to the English throne. With England's glorious victory at Agincourt still resonating in people's hearts and minds, coupled with the heroic reputation of his father, the infant King Henry VI had a very hard act to follow.

As he grew older, the weight of his father's crown seemed too much for him to bear and his reign became dominated by power struggles between the Houses of Lancaster and York, in what has become known as the Wars of the Roses.

King Henry VI, from the House of Lancaster, came to throne as a descendant of John of Gaunt – the third son of Edward III. But his cousin Richard, Duke of York, felt that he had a much better claim as a descendant of Edward III's second son. It was this conflict between two rival branches of the Plantagenet family that eventually led to many bloody battles for the crown.

Henry was born in the family fortress of Windsor Castle on 6 December,

1421, blissfully ignorant of the difficult life that lay ahead of him. It is said that every bell in London rang out to celebrate his birth. The first and only child of King Henry V and Queen Catherine of Valois, the infant was christened Henry in honour of his father and immediately became Duke of Cornwall. Before the year was out, his father was dead and not only was Henry the ruler of England, but also Lord of Ireland and King of France.

Although just an infant, he attended many ceremonies and royal events. At the age of three he was taken to Westminster to open Parliament, held in his mother's arms; at four he was driven through London in a state procession with the Duke of Gloucester through streets of cheering crowds.

He was, however, considered too young to be crowned and Henry VI's Coronation was delayed until 6 November, 1429, just one month before his eighth birthday. It was recorded that he "beheld the people sadly and wisely with humility and devotion". He was crowned King of England at Westminster Abbey and underwent another coronation as King of France in Notre Dame Cathedral, Paris, on 16 December, 1431.

By the time of the Coronation, his widowed mother Queen Catherine had formed an attachment to a Welsh soldier and courtier named Owen Tudor, who was Keeper of the Queen's Wardrobe. Whether they married has been the subject of much debate. Although it is believed that they wed secretly in Wales in around 1429, no documentation for the marriage exists.

In 1431 Owen Tudor was granted "the rights of an Englishman" and the couple had at least four children together, one of whom was Edmund Tudor (born at Much Hadham Palace in Hertfordshire), the father of a future king. So, the "only child" Henry VI actually had some siblings. The Queen initially lived with Henry at Windsor and brought him up, but she eventually moved to Wallingford Castle with Owen Tudor when those acting as regents disapproved of their relationship.

With a child on the throne, England was governed by a combination of leading nobles and churchmen, often with conflicting interests and struggles amongst themselves for power. Henry was easily dominated by members of his family, particularly his uncles, John, Duke of Bedford and Humphrey, Duke of Gloucester, who took control until Henry reached the age of 16, protecting his interests in England and France. His cousin Richard, Duke of York, was the heir presumptive.

The young Henry VI undertook many tours across England, staying mainly in monasteries, so that he could get to know his country. In 1428 Henry began a more formal education under a tutor, Richard Beauchamp, 13th Earl of Warwick. His instructions were to teach Henry "to love, worship and dread God . . . to teach him virtue, literature, language and other manner of cunning. To chastise him when he doth amiss, and to remove persons not behoveful or expedient to his presence."

As a monarch from infancy, Henry was a precocious child and fully aware of his position. At the age of 10 he questioned his tutor, saying that, because he was King, he should not be reprimanded for any misbehaviour. He was swiftly reprimanded.

By 1437 Henry was considered old enough to rule. Although King of England and France, Henry's allegiance was always to England and by this time he was seen as virtually powerless in France and leading French aristocrats failed to recognise him as monarch. Although English armies had fought on Henry's behalf, most French territory had been lost until eventually only Calais was left.

Henry had become King of France on the death of his maternal grandfather, under the Treaty of Troyes — but the late Charles VI of France had a son, the Dauphin, who many considered was the rightful heir to the French crown.

In 1424 Joan of Arc began to have visions and the voices of various saints told her to rescue Paris from English domination. She set out to save France and bring the young Dauphin to the throne as Charles VII. Joan led a French army to victory at the Siege of Orleans and Charles was crowned at Reims, although with limited territory. Joan was later betrayed, captured and handed over to the English in exchange for 10,000 livres. She was put on trial for heresy and sorcery. Henry was present at her trial in Rouen in 1430, which must have made a great impression on a boy of nine. Joan of Arc was subsequently burned at the stake in May 1431.

As Henry developed into manhood, he grew tall. His hair was brown and curly. He remained clean shaven as an adult, but was not considered to be handsome. His style of dress never reflected the fashions of his day and he rarely wore the sumptuous robes, materials and jewels often associated with medieval monarchs. Instead he dressed simply, invariably in black, wearing a full-length gown with a rolled hood, and his round-toed shoes and boots were described by contemporaries as being of a style usually worn by farmers. Even when wearing his crown, he wore a hair shirt under his tunic.

The precocious child turned into a humble adult. He had a strong Christian faith, and was more interested in culture and religion than politics. He hated bad language and was almost prudish in his attitude. When visiting Bath he was extremely shocked at seeing men remove their clothes to take the waters. Henry intervened to spare the lives of criminals and abhorred public executions and the practice of having traitors hung, drawn and quartered.

"I will not have any Christian man so cruelly handled for my sake," he once said. Many of his contemporaries felt that he was not really cut out to be king in the ruthless age in which they lived.

At the age of 22 Henry married 14-year-old Margaret of Anjou, first by proxy on 24 May, 1444, at the Cathedral of St Martin, Tours, France, and in person on 23 April, 1445, at Titchfield Abbey in Hampshire. She was a niece of the French Queen and it was hoped that the union would bring peace with France, although this did not happen.

As a diplomatic arrangement rather than a love match, the couple were betrothed before they had even met. Henry had only seen a portrait of his bride-to-be. Although Margaret appeared to be a great beauty, Henry wanted to see for himself if the painting was accurate. When she finally arrived in England, he decided to take a discreet look at his prospective wife and so he dressed as a squire and took her a letter "from the King of England".

Henry delivered the letter, kneeling before her. Margaret read it very carefully, not bothering to look at the man who had brought it to her. When he had gone, the Duke of Suffolk asked her what she had thought of the squire and she had to admit that she had barely glanced at the man. Only then was it revealed to her who Henry really was.

After the wedding, Margaret was crowned in Westminster Abbey on 30 May, 1445. She has often been described as a tigress and he as a pussy cat, so they were ill suited. They were married for over seven years before she became pregnant with their first and only child: a son named Edward, who was born on 13 October, 1453. He was created Prince of Wales at Westminster in March 1454.

Three months before the child was born, Henry suffered a stroke. It affected him mentally and he was said to have "lost his reason and his memory" and was unable to move. When Queen Margaret gave birth to his heir, Henry was unaware that he had a son. Many historians write of Henry's "recurring bouts of madness" during his life, but his mental failings could have been a lasting result of this stroke.

Queen Margaret became more powerful as the King's health deteriorated and Henry was soon completely under the control of his wife. Her main focus was their only son and she did everything to protect the young Prince of Wales's interests. There is a story of the Queen being ambushed by a robber in the woods, who threatened to cut her son's throat. It is said that the Queen threw herself at his feet and pleaded for her son's life to be spared. So eloquent was she that the murderous thief burst into tears and promised to reject his life of crime.

It took Henry some six months to recover. During this time Queen Margaret and the Duke of Somerset effectively ruled England. The heir presumptive, Richard, Duke of York, was appointed Protector and Defender of the Kingdom of England. By Christmas 1454 the King had regained his health. Letters of the day reveal that when Henry's senses returned, he admitted that during his illness he had not known what was said to him or where he had been.

With the King back in control, the Duke of York lost his power and had to relinquish the Protectorate. The birth of the Prince of Wales had also pushed away the Duke's chances of acceding to the throne. Feeling that he had a stronger claim, Yorkist supporters mustered an army of 3,000 men to fight for their cause. Henry took an army of 2,000 soldiers to face them at St Albans in May 1455.

The Wars of the Roses had begun. Supporters of the King, from the royal House of Lancaster, took a red rose as their heraldic emblem, and Yorkists siding with Richard, Duke of York, adopted the white rose of York. The name Wars of the Roses for the civil wars of this period has been credited to Sir Walter Scott, who used it in a book called *Anne of Geierstein or The Maiden of the Mist* in the 19th century.

The Duke of York was victorious at the Battle of St Albans. King Henry received an arrow wound to the neck during the battle and had a mental relapse as a result and withdrew from public life for a while. As a pacifist, he hated fighting and found the stress of civil war too much to cope with.

The Duke of York was declared Constable of England, but not for long. As soon as the King was back in good health, he made a surprise visit to Parliament at Westminster on 24 February, 1456, saying that now he was fully recovered his kingdom did not need a Protector. Over the years that followed Henry tried to resolve the differences between the warring nobles from the houses of York and Lancaster. He had a chantry established at St Albans with masses regularly sung for those who had lost their lives in the battle, and led a procession of opposing Lords to St Paul's Cathedral as a public display that their differences had been laid aside.

The Queen, however, did not share her husband's sentiments and remained very anti-Yorkist. In 1459 Margaret raised an army herself and marched to the Yorkist stronghold at Ludlow where supporters were routed.

By November that year she had encouraged Parliament to proclaim the Duke of York a traitor.

In July 1460 the fortunes of the Yorkists changed with a victory at Northampton. It was only a 30-minute battle, but crucially the King was captured and taken prisoner.

In October Richard, Duke of York, broke into the royal apartments at Westminster and installed himself in the Queen's rooms. Determined to claim the throne for himself, he stormed Parliament to make his intentions known. Eventually it was agreed that Henry should remain King for his lifetime, but the Duke of York would succeed him — thereby cutting out the Prince of Wales. Henry became depressed and withdrawn at the turn of events.

Furious that her son's rights had been renounced, Queen Margaret became determined to fight for the Prince's right of succession. On 29 December, 1460, she and her army headed to Yorkshire, where she met the Duke of York at Wakefield. In the ensuing battle his army was defeated and the Duke was killed. Only weeks before, Richard had been declaring that he was the rightful king; now his head was unceremoniously displayed on a spike at Micklegate Bar in the city of York, wearing a crown of paper. "Hail King, without a kingdom!" mocked the Lancastrians. Despite this triumph, the Wars of the Roses continued.

Richard's 18-year-old son, Edward, became the new Duke of York and fought on, winning a victory at Mortimer's Cross, Herefordshire, on 2 February, 1461. At this battle, Henry's stepfather Owen Tudor was captured and later beheaded at Hereford. On 17 February, 1461, at a second Battle of St Albans, Queen Margaret's army was victorious. It was all too much for Henry, who was found underneath an oak tree at the end of the battle, singing to himself.

One of the principal players in the Wars of the Roses at this period was Richard Neville, Earl of Warwick. He had married Anne Beauchamp, a daughter of Henry's tutor Richard Beauchamp, and was one of the wealthiest landowners and the most powerful noblemen of his age. Initially a staunch Yorkist supporter, he later changed his allegiance. History has nicknamed him "Warwick the King Maker" for having been responsible for bringing two kings to the throne. On 4 March, 1461, Henry VI was deposed by Warwick and Edward, Duke of York, was proclaimed ruler and began calling himself King Edward IV.

Soon there was another battle in the north. On 29 March, 1461, an estimated 30,000 Lancastrians attacked an equal-sized Yorkist army at

Towton, 10 miles from York. It has been called "the largest and bloodiest battle ever fought on English soil". During it a snowstorm swirled up and blew into the faces of the Lancastrians, giving their enemy the advantage. Yorkist archers also had an innovative new arrow with extra feathers, which could be fired a greater distance.

The Lancastrians were defeated because of the dreadful weather conditions and their inferior arrows. Henry did not take part in the battle and remained at York in prayer because it was Palm Sunday. Afterwards Henry and Queen Margaret went into hiding, while Edward headed to London to finally be crowned King. He travelled in a royal procession from St Paul's Cathedral to Westminster Abbey on 28 June, where he sat in the Coronation Chair wearing the regalia and was crowned King Edward IV of England.

Queen Margaret bided her time in Scotland before returning with her army in October 1462, ready to do battle again, taking various castles including Bamborough and Alnwick on their way south. But she finally met her match on 15 May, 1464, when the Lancastrian army was defeated at the Battle of Hexham. Queen Margaret withdrew back to Scotland, going first to Edinburgh and later to France. Henry became a fugitive, staying at the homes of Lancastrian supporters.

A year later Henry was betrayed and captured near Clitheroe in Yorkshire by Edward, Duke of York. He was tied to a horse and taken to London where he was met by the Earl of Warwick in Islington and a jeering crowd. He was then imprisoned in the Tower of London for five years. Although "dirty, ill-dressed and neglected", Henry's Christian faith saw him through the ordeal.

In 1470 the Yorkist Earl of Warwick had a disagreement with King Edward IV and defected to the Lancastrian side. In a conspiracy with Queen Margaret, Warwick set about restoring Henry to the throne. Warwick's daughter, Anne Neville, married the Prince of Wales, which cemented the relationship between the two families.

The plot to overthrow Edward IV was successful. Edward was briefly thrown into prison before being allowed to flee to exile in Burgundy and a rather bewildered King Henry VI came back to the throne on 30 October, 1470, in a period of English history known as The Readeption.

Henry VI had a second Coronation as King of England at St Paul's Cathedral on 13 October, 1470, but after barely six months the former Edward IV returned to England and attacked with an army. The Battle of Barnet took place on Easter Sunday, 14 April, 1471. It was a decisive battle in the Wars of the Roses. The Earl of Warwick led the Lancastrian army but was killed in combat. Henry was taken prisoner once again and was deposed for a second time in favour of Edward IV.

Less than a month later Queen Margaret's army was defeated at the Battle of Tewkesbury. The Prince of Wales, whom she had fought so long to protect, was killed at the age of just 17. With the death of Henry's only son, Margaret's ambitions were destroyed and she had no fight left in her. She was taken prisoner by the Yorkists and held captive for four years until her cousin, King Louis XI of France, paid a ransom for her. She lived out the rest of her days quietly in France.

King Edward IV had kept Henry alive only to prevent the Prince of Wales proclaiming himself as successor. But with the Prince dead, the threat had gone and Henry was no longer needed. On 21 May, 1471, Henry VI was murdered in the Wakefeld Tower at the Tower of London, possibly by Edward IV's brother, Richard, Duke of Gloucester (later Richard III) although this is unproven. It is recorded that Henry was "put to death" between eleven and twelve o'clock at night as he knelt in prayer. In 1911 his body was disinterred and it was found that the back of his head had received a severe blow.

Henry was buried at Chertsey Abbey in Surrey, where his tomb became a place of pilgrimage and some professed that miracles happened there. Later his body was reburied at St George's Chapel, Windsor, in 1484 by Richard III. This was less out of respect for Henry and more so that Richard could control who had access to the tomb, amid fears that Henry could become a saint. Even today there are calls for him to be canonised, some 550 years after his death.

It is easy to look back on the life of Henry VI and consider that he was little more than a puppet king, with a delicate constitution and always being manipulated by others. Although his reign was dominated by civil war, he took a great interest in education, culture and architecture. His lasting legacies to this country are the founding of Eton College and King's College, Cambridge.

His late uncle Henry Beaufort, Bishop of Winchester, had bequeathed Henry £2,000 in his will, an incredibly large amount of money at the time. The pious monarch refused to accept such a huge sum for himself and so used the money instead to build Eton and King's as places of education. Eton was originally a charity school, offering an education to poor students. He laid the foundation stone of King's in 1441 and the college was intended to specifically take students from Eton.

Whenever he met students he would say, "Be you good boys, gentle and teachable, and servants of the Lord." Following his example, in 1448 his wife founded Queen's College in Cambridge. Every year on the anniversary of Henry's death the Provosts and representatives from Eton and King's lay white roses and lilies in the Wakefield Tower on the spot where Henry is traditionally thought to have been killed. At both establishments Henry's birthday is celebrated as Founder's Day.

Many consider Eton and King's to be Henry's only lasting memorials. Whatever Henry's achievements during his reign, he will always be regarded as the catalyst that unwittingly sparked the Wars of the Roses. Wars that would continue throughout the reigns of three more English monarchs.

Chapter 30

Edward IV 1442–1483
Reign: 1461–1470 and 1471–1483

"This Monarch was famous only for his beauty and his courage," wrote Jane Austen in her book *The History of England*, "of which the picture we have here given of him, and his undaunted behaviour in marrying one woman while engaged to another, are sufficient proofs."

Although Miss Austen's account of our Kings and Queens is intended to be satirical, she was not far off the mark when it came to Edward IV. At just over 6ft 3in tall, clean shaven and with long brown hair, Edward was considered to be extremely handsome and was known as the "Rose of Rouen". He loved sumptuous clothing and bought very expensive furs, velvets and cloth of gold.

Towards the end of his life, in an average month he would order five jackets, three pairs of doublets, and four multi-layered cloaks. He favoured long velvet gowns, usually trimmed with ermine and lined with satin, and records show that he had many in green, purple and crimson, so he looked every inch a King. Little wonder that he adopted the Sun in Splendour as his heraldic badge.

Born in the French city of Rouen on 28 April, 1442, Edward was the second surviving son of Richard, Duke of York and Cecily Neville. Cecily was the youngest and 23rd child of Ralph Neville, Earl of Westmorland. Edward was known as the Earl of March from the time of his birth until the death of his father at the Battle of Wakefield in December 1460, when he succeeded to further titles to become Duke of York, Earl of Ulster and Earl of Cambridge.

Shakespeare punningly refers to Edward in the opening lines of his play *Richard III*, when the deformed Richard, Duke of Gloucester, declares:

"Now is the winter of our discontent

Made glorious summer by this sun of York . . ."

In other words, the bad times are over and this "son of the Duke of York", the "Sun in Splendour", is going to bring peace and prosperity.

At the age of five Edward was brought to live in England at Ludlow Castle in Shropshire, but it was not to be a time of peace. In 1448 his father, Richard, assumed the surname Plantagenet to emphasise that his claim to the throne was stronger than that of King Henry VI. A dynastic feud between the descendants of King Edward III led to the Wars of the Roses; wars that would come to dominate Edward's life and reign, with battles between the Houses of York and Lancaster for the crown.

When Edward was born, his third cousin King Henry VI had already been on the throne for 20 years, having acceded as an infant. But Henry's right to the crown was to be challenged by Richard, Duke of York, with increasing vehemence as the years rolled by.

In October 1459 at the Battle of Ludford Bridge, near Ludlow, the Yorkists suffered a setback and the Duke of York escaped to Ireland, having been denounced as a traitor. Edward was a youth of 17 by this time and he and his older cousin Richard Neville, Earl of Warwick, fled to France in a sailing boat. They remained in France for eight months for their own safety.

In 1460 Edward and Warwick set out from Calais for a surprise attack and defeated the Lancastrian army at the Battle of Northampton in July, at which King Henry VI was taken prisoner. In December that year Queen Margaret retaliated with an army at Wakefield. Richard, Duke of York, was killed in the fight.

Edward was in Shrewsbury celebrating Christmas when news reached him of his father's death. As the new Duke of York, Edward immediately fought back, defeating the Lancastrians at the Battle of Mortimer's Cross in Herefordshire in February 1461. Not long after this victory Edward, just a few weeks short of his 19th birthday, was declared King by his cousin, the powerful Earl of Warwick, known as "Warwick the King Maker".

Still a youth, the new King wanted to enjoy life and was content to let the Earl of Warwick have the power. Warwick was 14 years older than Edward. His grandmother was Joan Beaufort, a daughter of John of Gaunt, and through her Warwick was a descendant of King Edward III and so had royal blood.

Through his own marriage he had properties and castles in half the counties of England, making him one of the country's wealthiest landowners. His brother John became Earl of Northumberland and another brother, George, was Archbishop of Canterbury. Warwick had a very powerful and influential family behind him.

Edward was crowned at Westminster Abbey on 28 June. To mark his Coronation, he gave titles to his younger brothers, with 12-year-old Richard being made Duke of Gloucester and nine-year-old George the Duke of Clarence.

A more peaceful period followed in England and it was a time of greater personal happiness for Edward. Just prior to the Battle of Hexham he had married Lady Elizabeth Grey (née Woodville). He was then 22 and she was a widow of 27 with two children.

Tradition places their first meeting in the forest of Whittlebury, Northamptonshire, while he was out hunting. Elizabeth is said to have waylaid the King under an oak tree, where she stood holding her orphaned children and pleaded for the restoration of her inheritance. This he granted and, finding her attractive, made an improper suggestion.

"I know that I am not good enough to be your Queen," Elizabeth responded. "But I am far too good to be your mistress!"

Impressed with her spirit, it was not long before the King married her in a secret ceremony in the Northamptonshire village of Grafton Regis on 1 May, 1464. Elizabeth was crowned Queen Consort at Westminster Abbey on 26 May 1465. Although considered by some "not good enough" to be Queen at the time, Elizabeth is now the ancestor of every English monarch since King Henry VIII (as his maternal grandmother) and every Scottish monarch since King James V of Scotland.

For the first five months the marriage was kept secret, as many princesses were being put forward as potential brides to try and secure an alliance with a European ruler. But Edward married for love. As Elizabeth was only a mid-ranking member of the aristocracy and one of the King's subjects, this offended the Earl of Warwick and eventually caused him to switch his allegiance from the House of York to the Lancastrian side.

Warwick wanted Edward to marry the sister-in-law of King Louis XI, which would have strengthened relations with France. Warwick had worked hard behind the scenes to secure a betrothal and was due to receive lands and titles in France as a reward but Edward shocked Parliament by announcing that he could not possibly marry Louis's sister-in-law, because he was already married.

Warwick was livid and felt further undermined when Edward encouraged his wife's relatives to marry into the nobility, forming a new court. The most outrageous union perhaps was the marriage of Queen Elizabeth's 19-year-old brother John to Warwick's 65-year-old aunt, Katherine Neville, which became known as the maritagium diabolicum!

There was more disharmony when Warwick wanted his elder daughter, Isabella, to marry Edward's brother, George, Duke of Clarence. Even though Edward opposed this, Warwick defied the King and the couple were married anyway. The ensuing bad feeling between the King and his cousin led Warwick to defect to the Lancastrian side and soon he was conspiring with Queen Margaret to restore Henry VI to the throne.

As if to prove that he was still powerful, the Earl of Warwick had Edward taken prisoner during a skirmish at Edgcote Moor on 26 July, 1469, and hoped to have himself accepted as monarch by supposedly ruling "in Edward's name". Neither the nobility nor Parliament would accept this and so Warwick was forced to release the King on 10 September.

In March 1470 there was a rebellion near Stamford, Lincolnshire, with Warwick seizing the opportunity to join forces with the Duke of Clarence against the King. The rebels were defeated and Warwick fled to France, where he joined forces with Queen Margaret and King Louis XI and hatched a plan to restore Henry VI to the throne.

When several leading noblemen suddenly switched their allegiance to the Lancastrian side, Edward realised that he no longer had the support or military capacity to fight off an attack.

Now it was Edward's turn to seek refuge in France, while a triumphant Warwick returned to England and had King Henry VI released from captivity and in October 1470, put back on the throne. From the safety of his retreat in France and with financial support from his brother-in-law, the Duke of Burgundy, Edward carefully planned his return to England to win back the crown.

On 12 March, 1471, Edward landed in Cromer with a small force of men and travelled to Yorkshire to raise an army. He received a favourable welcome and at Doncaster some 600 soldiers joined him. His support gathered momentum as he marched southwards, with some noblemen returning their allegiance to him, including his brother, the Duke of Clarence. Soon Edward's army reached London unopposed, where Henry VI was taken prisoner once again and was deposed for a second time. The crown was back on Edward's head.

The Battle of Barnet swiftly followed on Easter Day 1471 and is considered one of the most decisive battles in the Wars of the Roses. The

Lancastrian army, led by the Earl of Warwick, was defeated and Warwick himself was killed.

With Edward's main adversary dead, Lancastrian morale was severely weakened. Edward IV returned to London on 21 May and that same night Henry VI died in the Tower of London. With Henry out of the way, Lancastrian opposition was virtually extinguished and he faced no further rebellions in England. His reign really began from this point.

With England at peace, in 1472 Edward made the decision to invade France, but Parliament refused to provide the funding. Not to be thwarted, Edward introduced an extraordinary new tax, one in which people could simply give what they wanted! One lady gave him £20, so King Edward kissed her. She immediately doubled it to £40.

He also introduced a new tax for property owners, who had to pay 10% of their net worth. In 1474 Edward summoned the merchants of London and requested from each one a gift or "benevolence" in proportion to his needs, which gave him guaranteed financial security.

Fines also became a good source of income and he clamped down on any misdemeanors of the nobility. In a single "bill of attainment", 12 senior nobles and more than 100 knights and squires were stripped of their estates to swell the royal treasury. This meant that Edward owned one-fifth of the land in England. With an already large hereditary income, this made the King extremely wealthy.

By 1475 he was ready to embark on his last military campaign and in June he landed in Calais with an army, set to invade. But King Louis XI of France was not prepared to fight and offered to buy Edward off. The two monarchs eventually met on a specially constructed bridge across the River Somme, covered over in case of bad weather during their negotiations. Edward accepted 75,000 crowns and an annual income of 20,000 crowns. It was also agreed that Louis's son, the Dauphin, should be engaged to Edward's daughter Elizabeth. What began as a possible battle ended in an amicable agreement, without bloodshed.

Edward IV instigated a new style of monarchy, laying the foundations of an absolute rule. Some have even called him a despot. He introduced a spy system, the use of the rack, and interfered with the course of justice when it suited him.

The way in which Parliament operated changed dramatically under his rule. The number of meetings was reduced, and the two Houses of Parliament ceased to have a prominent role, although this was not particularly detrimental to his kingdom.

With vast amounts of land, Edward owned a lot of sheep and so he built up the wool trade. This was good for England and, although Edward made a fortune himself from wool, he used the money for good, particularly for administration in running the country.

His motto was "modus et ordo", method and order, and he liked to see administration running smoothly and efficiently. He personally wrote threatening letters to any company that owed money to the Exchequer to ensure that payments were received. He stimulated the economy and developed an agreement with the Hanseatic League, which controlled north German ports, encouraging trade with England.

The King's ships, freighted with tin, wool and cloth traded as far as Italy and Greece. As a shrewd businessman, Edward invested in several major companies in the City of London. He also made the Duchy of Lancaster property of the Crown and even today the monarch derives income from the revenue profits.

By the end of his reign England was a much more stable country financially. Edward also brought about a better relationship with Wales than had existed with his predecessors, insisting that it was time to cast aside ancient enmities. His aim was for greater prosperity for the people in the border shires of England and Wales, with Ludlow (where he had spent his early childhood) established as the financial centre.

He also developed a more amicable relationship with Scotland, particularly through the betrothal of his four-year-old daughter, Cecily, to the seven-month-old son and heir of King James III of Scotland. Edward agreed to pay a dowry in yearly instalments until the couple were old enough to marry.

Edward was interested in literature and established a collection of books and historical manuscripts that is now in the British Library in London. One of his most important achievements was to become the patron of William Caxton, who established a printing press at Westminster, which Edward financed. The press had moveable type, which meant that documents could be printed quickly. This revolutionised and transformed the availability of the printed word in England.

Caxton was born in Kent in 1422 and had a career as an English merchant, travelling across to the continent for around 30 years, during which time he was also a copyist to Edward's sister Margaret, Duchess of Burgundy. Finding the process of copying manuscripts tiresome, Caxton wrote, "My pen is worn, my hand weary and not steadfast, mine eyes dimmed with over much looking on the white paper."

He became interested in the process of block printing and took it a stage further by creating his own unique style of printing press, the first of its kind in England. Caxton translated many works into English, printed 108 books, and is credited with standardising the English language through printing. A painting by Victorian artist Daniel Maclise portrays Caxton showing the first specimen of his printing to King Edward IV.

The family life of King Edward was far less ordered than his administrative affairs. He had his own brother George, Duke of Clarence, executed for treason in 1478. George, a widower by this time, wanted to marry Mary, the only daughter and heiress of the Duke of Burgundy. Queen Elizabeth was opposed to this union, as she really wanted her own brother Anthony to marry the girl.

George insulted the Queen for preventing the union and later hurled insults at the King. Edward sentenced his brother to death and had him imprisoned in the Tower of London. Legend has it that he was drowned in a "butt of Malmsey wine" on 18 February, 1478. One account says that this method was chosen as it left no mark on his body; another claims that George was allowed to choose the manner of his own death.

Although Edward IV and Queen Elizabeth had seven daughters and three sons, which included Elizabeth of York (the future Queen Consort of Henry Vll), Edward (later Edward V) and Richard (who was created Duke of York in May 1474, beginning a tradition of the second son of the sovereign always being made Duke of York), it did not stop Edward siring a number of illegitimate children, including Arthur Plantagenet, Lord de Lisle and Elizabeth Lumley.

Edward IV had an eye for the ladies and took many mistresses. A contemporary wrote that Edward pursued women "with no discrimination, the married and the unmarried, the noble and the lowly; however, he took none by force. He overcame all by money and promises and, having conquered them, he dismissed them." There was one, however, that the King was devoted to and that was Elizabeth Shore, the wife of a London merchant. They first met in 1476 and had a relationship that continued until his death. Sir Thomas More (1478-1535) wrote "many he had, but her he loved", adding that she "delighted not men so much in her beauty as in her pleasant behaviour." It is said that she refused to use her influence with the King for her own personal gain, as some of his other mistresses did.

Edward greatly enjoyed his wealth and position. His homes were sumptuous in their decoration to show off his status to visitors, and he dressed as he felt befitted a King. One contemporary commentator recorded,

"The King of England wore a black velvet cap upon his head, with a large fleur de lys made of precious stones upon it; he was a prince of a noble and majestic presence, but a little inclining to corpulence." Edward particularly loved good food and wines, and certainly grew stout with age. When he died suddenly at Westminster on 9 April, 1483, at the age of 40, it was reported that he had died through "overeating".

The actual cause of the King's death remains a mystery, although it is generally agreed that it was a result of gluttony and his having lived a debauched life. Over the centuries it has been variously claimed that he died of typhoid, of a fever or a stroke, although the consensus today is that the King developed pneumonia. He holds the somewhat alarming record of being one of the few male members of his immediate family to die as a result of natural causes!

Within months of his death Edward's marriage to Elizabeth was actually declared invalid by an Act of Parliament, because he supposedly had a pre-existing contract to marry Lady Eleanor Butler and even had children by her. But the marriage to Elizabeth was later validated under the first Parliament of King Henry VII. The purpose of the Act was really to alter the line of succession, because if Edward's marriage to Elizabeth was not legal, then their children were illegitimate and so could not inherit the crown. With the marriage recognised by Parliament, the bloodline of succession continued.

Edward was buried in St George's Chapel, Windsor – a building that is considered to be one of his lasting achievements. The Chapel had originally been built by Henry III, but Edward had it remodelled in a gothic style, said to be one of the finest examples in England. In it he had an elaborate tomb built for himself, which is at the east end of the north aisle. Although impressive, it is less ornate today as the original rich decoration that included pearls, rubies and gold were removed when the Chapel was plundered in 1642. At the end of the 18th century, the tomb was renovated with fragments of stone collected from other parts of the Chapel, and there is now a black marble slab with the King's name in solid brass lettering.

The successor of Edward IV was his 12-year-old son, also called Edward. In a codicil to his will the King had named his brother Richard, Duke of Gloucester, as the boy's protector until he came of age. But, instead of protecting the boy, Richard was determined to claim the throne for himself.

Chapter 31

Edward V 1470–1483

Reign: April 1483–July 1483

Edward V is possibly England's most tragic king, with one of the shortest reigns which lasted barely 75 days. A monarch known more for his death than his life, he will be forever remembered as one of the "Princes in the Tower".

He was the eldest son of King Edward IV and his Queen, Elizabeth Woodville, and was born at the Abbot's House, Westminster around November 1470 during the Wars of the Roses. His mother had taken refuge within the bounds of Westminster Abbey to escape the Lancastrians, while Edward IV was briefly in exile, having lost the throne earlier that year to Henry VI.

When Edward IV was restored to the throne in 1471 he immediately created his son Prince of Wales and Earl of Chester, later also giving him the Earldoms of March and Pembroke and making him a Knight of the Garter. The infant Prince Edward was taken to Ludlow Castle in Shropshire at the age of two and this is where he spent most of his childhood.

The Prince had a solid education carefully arranged for him by his father. It was said of Edward that "his special knowledge of literature enabled him to discourse elegantly, to understand fully and to declaim most excellently from any work whether in verse or prose that came into his hands, unless it were from the more abstruse authors . . ."

His day had a religious framework with Matins before breakfast and Evensong before supper. He was never allowed to be idle and even during his midday meal heroic stories were read to him to feed his mind. In the afternoon he was allowed time for sport and exercise, with a brief period of relaxation in the evenings before bed.

As Prince of Wales and heir to the throne, Edward's future was mapped out for him by his family and beyond his control. In 1480 he was betrothed to four-year-old Anne of Britanny in an alliance with France. It was agreed that the pair would marry when they came of age.

Life was to change suddenly for the Prince on 9 April, 1483, when King Edward IV died unexpectedly at Westminster from pneumonia, and the 12-year-old boy succeeded his father to become King Edward V.

As Edward was still a minor, someone had to be Regent. Before his death, Edward IV had named his brother Richard, Duke of Gloucester, as his son's "protector" should he die prematurely. This led to animosity and soon the young king found himself caught up in the middle of a family struggle for control. Torn between his mother's relatives and his father's, Edward V became a pawn in the game of power.

The Queen's family, the Woodvilles, were unpopular and had many enemies amongst the long-established aristocracy, who resented the favours and titles that Edward IV had bestowed on his wife's relatives. Conscious that Richard, Duke of Gloucester, was ambitious and had his eye on the crown for himself, the Woodvilles attempted to have his protectorship replaced by a Regency Council so that they could have a say in Edward V's future and thwart Richard's aspirations.

On his accession, Edward and his younger brother Prince Richard, Duke of York, were taken from Ludlow Castle straight to London, accompanied by their uncle Anthony Woodville, Earl Rivers, one of the Queen's brothers. The Woodvilles felt it was imperative that the young Edward V should be crowned as quickly as possible to prevent him being usurped by the Duke of Gloucester.

Word, however, was passed to the Duke, who personally intercepted the King's convoy at Stony Stratford in Buckinghamshire on 29 April and took his nephew away from the Woodvilles. The royal party had broken the journey and was staying overnight at the Rose and Crown Inn when the young monarch was taken.

Today the inn is a private house, but a plaque on the wall still records the event. Earl Rivers was arrested and later murdered, while Edward was taken to stay with the Bishop of London before being housed in the royal apartments at the Tower of London. His residence became the Garden Tower, known today as the "Bloody Tower".

Richard, Duke of Gloucester, had arrived in London innocently enough without any opposition. He was, after all, the King's protector, and why should he not have the boy living in royal apartments at the Tower? Especially as previous monarchs had taken up residence at the Tower of London prior to their Coronation. In reality, Edward V's new home became his prison.

Worried that Gloucester was taking complete control of the King, the Queen took Edward's younger brother Prince Richard, Duke of York, and most of her possessions to the sanctuary of Westminster Abbey. Plans were quickly put in place to hold the Coronation on 4 May, but this was later postponed until 22 June. Once the date had been announced, Elizabeth felt that it was safe to let Prince Richard join his brother Edward at the Tower, although some sources say that she was threatened and forced to surrender her younger son.

The ambitious Richard, Duke of Gloucester, was now in a precarious position. Once Edward was crowned, his power would be diminished. All he could do was seize the crown for himself as quickly as possible. He had Edward's Coronation date postponed yet again, with a date set for November.

This gave him breathing space and, with both Edward and his brother safely in the Tower, he put a plan into action. He made a claim at a meeting of the Council that the Queen and her late husband's mistress, Elizabeth Shore, had practised witchcraft on him to disfigure his body. The Bishop of Ely wrote that Richard "plucked up his doublet sleeve to his elbow upon his left arme, where he shewed a withered arme."

A further accusation was made by the Bishop of Bath and Wells that Edward IV's marriage to Elizabeth Woodville was invalid, stating that Edward IV was already engaged to Lady Eleanor Butler (daughter of the Earl of Shrewsbury) when he had married Elizabeth.

At this period, an engagement was considered to be binding and the Bishop even went as far as to hint that Edward IV had actually married Lady Eleanor and had children by her. If this were true then his marriage to Elizabeth Woodville was unlawful, and any children would therefore be considered illegitimate and unable to accede to the throne. As a consequence, Edward V could not be King.

This claim was approved by Parliament on 24 June, which left the path open for Richard of Gloucester to become King as the "true heir". Edward V was deposed and Gloucester was offered the crown. He was crowned King Richard III just eleven days later on 6 July and the Coronation was attended by nearly all the peers in England.

Edward was now a virtual prisoner in the Tower. No longer able to call himself King, he became known once again as Prince Edward. He is one of just four English monarchs since the Norman Conquest not to have been crowned.

English chronicler Raphael Holinshed, writing a century later, recorded that when the young Edward V was told that he could no longer reign "but that his uncle should have the crowne, he was sore abashed and began to sigh and said, 'Alas, I would that my uncle would let me have my life yet though I lose my Kingdom'."

The two young Princes had access to the gardens, but neither was seen outside the Tower in public again. The last sighting of them was in the gardens playing with bows and arrows in September 1483 and by Easter 1484 there was said to be "much whispering among the people that the King had put the children to death." What actually happened to Edward V has been the subject of much conjecture across the centuries, but it is generally agreed that he was murdered, along with his brother, in the Tower of London.

In the reign of King Henry VIII an investigation by Sir Thomas More concluded that they had been killed at the instigation of King Richard III. The deadly deed, Sir Thomas claimed, was devised by knight Sir James Tyrrell, and carried out by groom John Dighton and gaoler Miles Forest, who went to the boys' bedroom at midnight, smothered them in their own bedclothes and suffocated them by stuffing feather pillows into their mouths until "they gave up to God their innocent souls into the joys of heaven."

When Sir James was informed that the boys were dead, the three men buried the children's bodies deep in the ground under a mound of stones at the foot of a staircase in the White Tower. Sir James later confessed to his part in the murder and was executed for treason in 1502, although his confession was made while being tortured.

During building work at the Tower in 1674, two skeletons were discovered some ten feet under a staircase leading to the White Tower. Two earlier skeletons had previously been discovered walled up within the Tower of London, but because the position under the staircase seemed to tally with Sir Thomas More's version, the two newly discovered remains seemed more likely to be those of the Princes.

An anonymous eyewitness account records: "This day I, standing by the opening, saw working men dig out of a stairway in the White Tower the bones of those two Princes who were foully murdered by Richard III. They were small bones, of lads in their teens, and there were pieces of rag and velvet about them . . . Being fully recognised to be the bones of those two Princes, they were carefully put aside in a stone coffin or coffer."

On the orders of Charles II they were buried in Westminster Abbey in the Henry VII Chapel. Sir Christopher Wren was commissioned to design a marble tomb for the boys, which still houses the remains. A plaque at the Tower of London, on a wall near a staircase, marks the site where the bones were discovered.

Edward V's death has been regarded very much as a murder-mystery, with both Richard III and Henry Tudor, the future Henry VII, considered to be suspects. It is now possible for visitors to the Tower of London to vote electronically who they think murdered the Princes – with Richard III consistently receiving the most votes.

In recent years Richard III's involvement has been refuted. Some say that, as Richard had already been approved as King by Parliament and crowned, he had no need to dispose of the Princes and that his reputation was later blackened by Tudor propaganda and the writings of Sir Thomas More.

More was only five years old at the time of the murder, so had no first-hand knowledge of events and worked for an enemy of Richard III, so was inevitably biased in his account. Others blame Shakespeare for further damage to Richard's character. In his play *Richard III*, the Bard has Richard reveal to Tyrrell that he has two enemies in the Princes in the Tower and Tyrrell offers to have them murdered, returning a short time later to say that the "tyrannous and bloody deed is done".

Although Henry Tudor has also been considered a contender for the assassination of the Princes, when he became King he was plagued by an imposter called Perkin Warbeck, who professed to be Richard, Duke of York, the younger of the two Princes. Warbeck's story was that although his brother Edward V was murdered, his own life was spared on the condition that he swore on oath to keep the secret for a number of years.

In 1497 he tried to claim the crown for himself as the "rightful king". It cost Henry some £13,000 that he could ill afford to try and prove that Perkin Warbeck was a fraudster. If Henry had known for certain that the Princes were dead, Warbeck, as a "pretender to the throne", would never have been believed. Warbeck eventually confessed to being an imposter and was hanged at Tyburn.

In 1933 the skeletons were exhumed and re-examined, but other than confirming that they were two youngsters of similar age to Edward and his brother, no cause of death could be established, and they were reinterred. There has been criticism since that time that a more detailed analysis should have been made for a definitive conclusion.

The discovery of Richard III's skeleton in 2012 reignited the demand that the two skeletons should be exhumed once again for DNA testing and carbon-dating but to date no permission has been granted. Both the Church of England and the Queen feel that it could set a precedent and would be followed by a demand for other royal bodies to be exhumed to satisfy historical curiosity.

Although they died more than 538 years ago, there is one poignant image of them that remains enduringly popular and that is the waxwork tableau of the Princes in the Tower that has been on display at Madame Tussaud's in London since the 1860s. Remodelled several times across the decades, the scene continues to offer a startling reminder of innocent lives lost.

In the early 20th century Madame Tussaud's great-grandson, John Theodore Tussaud, recalled watching two young boys staring intently at the scene. "Both boys were a great deal moved as they gazed on the tableau showing the murder of the two little Princes in the Tower of London, a representation over which many impressionable people have been unable to keep dry eyes."

The two young boys were brothers and future Kings of England – Edward VIII and George VI. We can only guess what might have been going through the minds of those two young Princes as they encountered the lifelike figures of their ancestors.

It is perhaps a sign of our times that today Edward V is not featured in the Grand Hall, as in previous generations, but because of his tragic death is the only King of England to be featured in the Chamber of Horrors at Madame Tussaud's.

Chapter 32

Richard III 1452–1485
Reign: 1483–1485

Across the centuries the character of Richard III has been blackened by critics to such an extent that it is now difficult to separate truth from fiction. He has been called the most villainous King of England and many murders have been laid at Richard's door, most notably those of King Henry VI and the Prince of Wales, his own wife, Anne Neville, and his nephews – the Princes in the Tower – with some even maintaining that Richard drowned his brother in a butt of Malmsey wine, although evidence is hard to find.

One of the first unflattering descriptions of the King was written by chronicler John Rous in 1490, who said that Richard had a two-year gestation and was born with shoulder length hair and a full set of teeth! John Morton, Bishop of Ely and later Archbishop of Canterbury, claimed that Richard was a hunchback with a deformed hand, a claim repeated by Sir Thomas More in his *History of King Richard III* and it was this image that was eventually dramatised by Shakespeare.

No contemporary description of Richard III remains, yet a letter written by Thomas Langton, Bishop of St David's, three months after the Coronation in 1483 paints a different picture: "I trust to God soon, by Michaelmas, the King shall be at London. He contents the people wherever he goes . . . for many a poor man that hath suffered wrong many days have been relieved and helped by him and his commands in his progress. And in many great cities and towns were great sums of money given him which he hath refused. On my trouth, I never liked the conditions of any prince so well as his; God has sent him to us for the well-being of us all."

By the 17th century Richard III was seen very much as the villain, with no redeeming features whatsoever, and another century was to pass before historians began to reappraise the monarch and show him in a more favourable light, as a much more rounded figure. In more recent times the Richard III Society, founded in 1924, has fought hard to see that the King is looked upon justly.

Richard was born at Fotheringhay Castle, Northamptonshire, on 2 October, 1452, the fourth and youngest surviving son of Richard, Duke of York, and Cecily Neville. His childhood was dominated by the Wars of the Roses. Following the Battle of Ludlow when he was barely seven years old, Richard and his older brother George were looked after by the Duchess of Buckingham and later the Archbishop of Canterbury. When their father was killed by Lancastrian enemies during the Battle of Wakefield in 1460, Richard and George were taken by their mother to safety in the Netherlands. They remained there until the Yorkist victory at the Battle of Towton a year later, after which their eldest brother became King Edward IV.

On the eve of the Coronation that July, Richard was made a Knight of the Garter and just four months later received the title Duke of Gloucester and was appointed Admiral of the Sea. His brother George was created Duke of Clarence.

For the next four years the young Dukes lived at Middleham Castle in Wensleydale, North Yorkshire, with his mother's relatives, the Earl and Countess of Warwick. Richard undertook military training and became involved in administrative matters and was appointed Constable of England in 1469.

With the ongoing conflict between the Houses of Lancaster and York, the Earl of Warwick suddenly changed his allegiance from King Edward IV of York and sided with the Lancastrian cause instead. Richard did not follow suit and continued to support the King. Richard had adopted the Anglo-Norman motto *Loyaulté me lie*, translated as "loyalty binds me", and he did indeed remain loyal to his brother during his lifetime. Warwick and the Lancastrians eventually deposed Edward IV in October 1470 in favour of Henry VI. Richard and Edward fled across the Channel and sought refuge in France.

When Edward IV was restored to the throne in April 1471, Richard returned to England and proved to be a proficient commander of the Yorkist army in the ensuing Battles of Barnet and Tewksbury, with the Earl of Warwick being slain at Barnet. On 14 July that year Richard was made Sheriff of Yorkshire and was given Middleham Castle, which became his main home. He was also appointed Sheriff of Cumberland and Warden of the West March, and had the use of Penrith Castle in Cumbria when fulfilling his duties and was granted "all the royal manors and revenues in the county of Cumberland".

On 12 July, 1472, he married Anne Neville, younger daughter of the Earl of Warwick, at Westminster Abbey. They had one son, Edward, in December 1473. Richard is also known to have fathered at least three illegitimate children before his marriage, including master-builder Richard Plantagenet, Katherine Herbert and John of Gloucester.

Richard's detractors suggest that he only married Anne Neville because of the great wealth and properties she had inherited from her father, but the two had grown up together at Middleham and Richard remained faithful to her once betrothed and always protected her family. At the time of their marriage, the Warwick estates had been forfeited to the Crown and so Anne had no great fortune and their wedding was a very simple ceremony.

Animosity, however, developed between Richard and his brother George, Duke of Clarence, who had married Anne's elder sister Isabel. The sisters were co-heiresses and George did all within his power to prevent Richard from marrying Anne in the hope that the inheritance would eventually return to the family. He, as heir to the throne, hoped to obtain the lion's share.

Although it is Richard's character that has been blackened, his brother genuinely proved to be motivated by avarice. George was continually disloyal to their brother Edward IV and was eventually tried for high treason and sentenced to death. His gruesome end, supposedly drowned in a butt of Malmsey wine, is often attributed to Richard because of Shakespeare. Contemporary accounts, however, say that Richard was overcome with grief and within three days had obtained a licence to set up two religious foundations to pray for his late brother's soul.

After this Richard seldom visited the King's court and preferred to remain in Yorkshire, where he had a good reputation and was well liked by the people. It is said that he preferred a life of service in the north to a life of luxury in the south and on 12 May, 1480, he was made the King's Lieutenant-General in the north. Contemporary records from the City of York list many of Richard's good works and the city fathers once presented him with six swans and six pikes to show their gratitude to him as an accomplished administrator.

As a skilled soldier, Richard was also responsible for defending the border between Scotland and England and fought several successful campaigns, notably recovering the border town of Berwick in a fight with the Scots in 1482, for which he received public recognition from Parliament.

Everything changed for Richard on 9 April, 1483, with the death of his brother, King Edward IV. Through events that followed over the next two years, his character and reputation were to be defamed for the subsequent 500 years. If Richard truly had a villainous side, it was in the months that followed when it really came to the fore. Clearly ambitious, he had his sights set on becoming King himself, but there were a few obstacles in his path.

Richard had never trusted his sister-in-law, Elizabeth Woodville, now the widowed Queen of Edward IV. He considered that she had abused her position by giving favours and titles to her many relatives. Her 12-year-old son now became King Edward V but because he was under-age Richard was named as his protector.

Richard was fighting in Scotland at this time and it was ten days before he learned of his brother's death. Taking advantage of Richard's absence, Elizabeth and her family had his protectorship overturned and replaced with a Regency Council. The Woodville family also arranged for the young Edward V to be crowned as quickly as possible so that they could be the powers behind the throne, rather than Richard.

News reached Richard in a letter from a confidant, Lord Hastings, and he quickly formed a counterattack. Knowing that Edward IV had already been engaged to Lady Eleanor Butler at the time he married Elizabeth Woodville, Richard fought to have the union declared invalid, an engagement being considered as a binding contract at this time. If the marriage could be annulled, Edward V and his brother the Duke of York would be considered illegitimate and therefore unable to inherit the crown. Only these two children stood between Richard and the throne.

Richard headed south with his ally the Duke of Buckingham and intercepted Edward V's entourage at Stony Stratford. There they arrested the king's guardian, Anthony Woodville, and took the 12-year-old boy under Richard's protection to London. Arriving on 4 May he first presented the young King, dressed in blue velvet, to the crowds lining the streets. Edward V then lodged at the Bishop of London's house before taking up residence at the Tower of London. He was later joined at the Tower by his younger brother, the Duke of York. There seemed nothing sinister about the pair living at this royal fortress.

When Parliament met at the end of June and accepted the petition that Edward IV was unlawfully married, Richard immediately became the successor. At Baynard's Castle in London (a medieval palace near the Thames) Richard received the news he had been waiting for and accepted the crown. Some say he consented with humility, almost showing reluctance to be king; his enemies consider this was all bluff and a mere theatrical display of modesty.

Edward V, having now lost the right to reign, became known simply as Prince Edward. He and his younger brother were last seen at the Tower in September 1483 and by Easter 1484 were said to have been put to death. What actually happened to the Princes in the Tower has been the subject of much conjecture across the centuries, and it seems unlikely that the truth will ever be known, but the most common consensus is that they were killed at Richard's instigation. This unproven act, more than any other, cemented his reputation as a villain.

Richard III was proclaimed King on 26 June, 1483, at the age of 30, followed by a swift Coronation at Westminster Abbey on 6 July, with his wife Anne as Queen Consort, both walking barefoot from Westminster Hall to the Abbey. But within three months Richard III discovered that his friend and collaborator, the Duke of Buckingham, had switched allegiance and had become his enemy. Buckingham now sided with the Woodville family and Henry Tudor, the Earl of Richmond.

Henry was a son of Margaret Beaufort, a descendant of John of Gaunt and considered that he also had a claim to the throne. From the House of Lancaster, Henry Tudor could trace his ancestry back to Edward III, just as Richard III could through the House of York. The Wars of the Roses were far from over.

Having resided in France for 12 years, Henry Tudor now set sail across the English Channel in an attempt to claim the throne for himself. But the navy was too vigilant and he was thwarted and forced to turn back without even reaching the coast of England. Richard was alerted to the threat and was on his guard. On 2 November the Duke of Buckingham was executed for his part in the plot.

Henry Tudor wished to marry Elizabeth of York, eldest daughter of Edward IV and Elizabeth Woodville. To thwart Henry still further, Richard had her guarded at Westminster Abbey so that she could not run off to marry. With his own wife in poor health, there were suggestions that Richard intended to marry Elizabeth of York himself in the event of his wife's death, although this rumour could have been enemy propaganda.

The year 1484 proved to be a difficult one for Richard III. Not only did he have to keep his wits about him for fear of enemy attack, on 9 April his only son, Edward, died at Middleham Castle. It was recorded at the time that Richard and his wife Anne were beside themselves with grief, with one chronicler stating that they were "in a state almost bordering on madness". The sudden death left Richard III with no direct heir and by December he learned from his emissaries in France that Henry Tudor planned another invasion. Then on 16 March, 1485, his wife died from tuberculosis. Despite this further grief, Richard faced gossip that he had poisoned her so that he could marry Elizabeth of York. Whether true or not, Richard was forced to publicly deny the calumny and did not live to remarry.

Although often credited with the murder of King Henry VI in the Tower of London, Richard was known to have been away from London when the deed took place. In 1485 Richard had the body of Henry VI transferred from Chertsey Abbey to the private St George's Chapel at Windsor Castle. Some saw it as a benevolent act, others felt that Richard was more calculating and that he had moved the body because people were making pilgrimages to Chertsey and he wanted to prevent Henry VI being treated as a saint.

The rumours of an invasion proved to be true and Henry Tudor landed at Milford Haven on 7 August, 1485, with an army of some 2,000 to 3,000 French mercenaries, enlarging his army with English supporters as he marched north. Meanwhile, Richard rode on a horse named White Surrey from Lichfield to Leicester in newly burnished armour, a crown placed on his helmet. Although Richard had a much larger army, morale amongst his troops was said to be low.

On the morning of 22 August Henry Tudor met Richard III at Market Bosworth, Leicestershire, in a decisive battle between the Houses of York and Lancaster. In the heat of battle Richard charged towards Henry with a lusty cry of "Treason! Treason!" (Not "A horse, a horse! My kindom for a horse!" as written by Shakespeare.) He managed to strike Henry, but was himself overpowered, fell from his horse and was beaten to death by soldiers. As he fell, his crown caught on a hawthorn bush. Lord Thomas Stanley, Steward of the Royal Household, grabbed the crown and placed it on Henry Tudor's head. He was to become Henry VII, England's first Tudor king, and adopted as his emblem the image of a crown on a hawthorn bush. It began a new era and marked the end of what historians call "medieval England".

Richard III's body was unceremoniously tied across the back of a horse and was ridden to Leicester, where he was buried in Grey Friar's Abbey, without respect or dignity. Until the discovery of his remains in 2012, many historians believed that Richard's body had been later exhumed and tossed into the River Soar in 1538 following the dissolution of the monasteries.

An enormous plaque, now set into a modern wall, near Bow Bridge over the river states "Near this spot lie the remains of Richard III, the last of the Plantagenets, 1485", but it was erected by a local businessman, Benjamin Broadbent, almost 400 years after Richard's death, and is now known to be inaccurate. Richard's body did actually remain at the Franciscan Friary church, Grey Friars.

The bridge itself is a Victorian replacement and bears two other plaques relating to Richard. One on the western side has a quotation from John Speed's 17th-century *History of Great Britain*:

"Upon this bridge (as tradition hath delivered) stood a stone of some height, against which King Richard, as he passed toward Bosworth, by chance struck his spur: and against the same stone, as he was brought back hanging by the horse side, his head was dashed and broken, as a wisewoman (forsooth) had foretold, who before Richard's going to battle, being asked of his success, said that where his spur struck, his head should be broken."

The site of the Battle of Bosworth has long been debated. It was thought to be at Ambion Hill, Sutton Cheney in Leicestershire, and a flag and a memorial stone mark the spot where Richard is said to have died. In 1999 archaeologists discovered a hoard of medieval weapons and armour, and university lecturer Carl Dawson found a silver white boar badge – the livery badge of Richard III, probably worn by one of his knights – on marshy ground at Fen Hole, a mile away from the traditional location of the battle.

A search for the King's remains was initiated by Philippa Langley of the Richard III Society. In August 2012 an archaeological team from the University of Leicester set out to find the exact location of Richard III's grave and began digging up a car park in Leicester in what was described as "the first ever search for the lost grave of an anointed King of England". Although the challenge was regarded as a long shot by some, incredibly a skeleton was unearthed on the first day of the dig. Following extensive tests, which included DNA comparisons with descendants, it proved "beyond reasonable doubt" to be that of Richard III.

In December 2014 it was announced that DNA investigations showed evidence of infidelity somewhere along the male line of the family tree. At a press conference Dr Turi King from Leicester University, who led the study, said, "If you put all the data together, the evidence is overwhelming that these are the remains of Richard III."

Forensic research on the King's skull concluded that there were nine wounds and that he was probably killed by two massive blows to the head from a medieval weapon in an attack at Bosworth. His skeleton revealed many injuries, which could have been sustained after death when his body was slung over his horse en route for Leicester, not forgetting the striking of his head against Bow Bridge.

The skeletal remains show that Richard was of slender build, approximately 5ft 8in tall, and had curvature of the spine (scoliosis), which would have made his right shoulder higher than the left, but he was not a hunchback. There was no sign of a withered arm, unlike Shakespeare's imagined King.

Analysis of Richard's teeth and bones revealed that he ate a lot of freshwater fish, drank large quantities of wine and consumed bird meat such as heron and swan. Two of his teeth had been removed in life through crude dentistry; he had signs of tooth decay and probably ground his teeth through stress. Following an anatomical assessment of Richard's skull, experts were able to build up a three-dimensional portrait to reveal his face to the world, so that today we have a close idea of how he looked when alive.

Over 500 years after the Battle of Bosworth, another battle raged as to where Richard III's final resting place should be. There were calls for him to be laid to rest in Westminster Abbey amongst other Kings of England; there were claims that Richard of York would have wanted to have been buried in York Minster, but, following a High Court review, ultimately it was decided that the King should remain in Leicester.

On 26 March, 2015, King Richard III received the respectful burial that he was denied in 1485 and was given a place of honour in Leicester Cathedral. His remains were laid in a simple tomb carved from pale Swaledale stone from North Yorkshire, resting on a plinth of dark Kilkenny stone carved with Richard III's name, dates, motto and armorial bearings.

A bronze statue of the King, originally donated to the city by the Richard III Society in 1980, had already been given a new home within the Cathedral gardens. A new Richard III Visitor Centre opened nearby in July 2014, ready to cope with the anticipated influx of tourists that would now be drawn to Leicester.

Although Richard III had a very short reign of just 26 months, he has retained a dominant position in English history because of his character and particularly because fact and fiction have intermingled. History, said Winston Churchill, is written by the victors, and today we have to look beyond Tudor vilification. Had he lived longer, he would undoubtedly have accomplished a great deal more and may have been less maligned. Richard III still has several lasting achievements. He introduced the bail system for defendants in court, which exists to this day; he introduced laws to protect buyers of land; he took a great interest in forestry across England and had great areas cleared; he built chantries and churches, such as St Mary of Barking by the Tower of London; established three colleges in the north; gave an annual endowment to Queen's College, Cambridge, and because of his interest in heraldry he founded the College of Arms in London.

Richard III was the last monarch from the House of York and the Plantagenet family, and the last English king to die in battle, yet in our own time he seems destined to be remembered as the "King beneath the car park".

Chapter 33

Henry VII 1457–1509
Reign: 1485–1509

When Richard III's crown was removed from a hawthorn bush after the Battle of Bosworth and placed on the head of Henry, Earl of Richmond, it heralded the beginning of the Tudor dynasty: a royal house that would rule England for the next 118 years, with a succession of formidable characters on the throne that included King Henry VIII and Queen Elizabeth I.

The founding monarch, however, has been described as a dull man, whom the people admired but did not love. It perhaps says something about his personality that Shakespeare chose to write plays about Henry IV, Henry V, Henry VI and Henry VIII, but omitted Henry VII. Some Tudor monarchs acquired robust nicknames, such as Bluff King Hal, Bloody Mary and Good Queen Bess, but the first of them is remembered simply as King Henry the Seventh.

Henry Tudor was a son of Lady Margaret Beaufort, a descendant of John of Gaunt, and through her could trace his ancestry back to Edward III. Although it was the illegitimate side of the family tree, the Beauforts were legitimised by statute during the reign of Richard II.

Henry also had a claim to the throne through his father Edmund Tudor, 1st Earl of Richmond, who was the half-brother of King Henry VI. Of the House of Lancaster, Edmund was captured by Yorkists during the Wars of the Roses and died of the plague at Carmarthen Castle in November 1456. Consequently, Edmund did not live to see his first and only son.

The widowed Margaret was taken by her brother-in-law, Jasper Tudor, Earl of Pembroke, to the safety of Pembroke Castle and it was here that she gave birth to Henry on 28 January, 1457. The boy immediately inherited his father's title, Earl of Richmond.

It was said to be a difficult birth, during which both mother and son almost died. Both survived, although Margaret had no further children and remarried a year later. Henry remained in Wales under the care of his uncle, Jasper Tudor, for four years until the Earl lost his title and castles in a Yorkist victory during the Wars of the Roses.

Jasper fled to France and the young Henry began to lead a rather peripatetic childhood, being moved between various of his father's relatives for the next nine years. Although devoted to his mother, their relationship appears to have been conducted by letters during his childhood rather than in person.

As a result, Henry is reported to have been a withdrawn, reserved, quiet child, with few friends. He was educated by a tutor, Andreas Scotus, who revealed that Henry was a very quick learner. He was passionate about books, loved playing cards, and enjoyed music and dancing. In adulthood he was also keen on hunting.

When King Henry VI was restored to the throne in October 1470 Jasper Tudor returned from France and took his nephew to London to meet the monarch. Although a favourable meeting, it was a short-lived association. Within barely six months both King Henry VI and his immediate heir were dead.

Although young Henry Tudor became head of the House of Lancaster and was its leading claimant to the crown, his life was in danger once the Yorkist King Edward IV was back on the throne. Jasper Tudor took Henry to the independent Duchy of Brittany for safety, where he remained for some 14 years, although little is known about his life in exile.

In 1483 Edward IV died and Richard III took the throne. Henry, however, felt that he had an equal claim and, now aged 26, decided that the time was right to assert himself. With the Duke of Buckingham and the Bishop of Ely both promoting his claim, Henry set sail across the English Channel with some 40 ships in an attempt to oust Richard. But the weather was bad, and the navy was too vigilant, and he was forced to turn back without even reaching the coast of England. Alerted to the fact that Henry was a threat, Richard was on his guard and had Buckingham and the Bishop executed for their part in the scheme.

Less than two years later Henry embarked on a second invasion, setting sail from Harfleur. He reached Milford Haven on 7 August, 1485, with an army of some 2,000 to 3,000 French mercenaries, enlarging his army with

English supporters as he marched north. On the morning of 22 August Henry Tudor met Richard III at Market Bosworth, Leicestershire, in a decisive battle between the Houses of York and Lancaster. With the dead King's crown on his head, Henry became England's first Tudor monarch. Firmly believing that God decided who would win a battle, Henry was convinced that he was King by divine right. It began a new era and marked the end of what historians call "medieval England". Historically, Henry VII was the last monarch to take the English crown by force. Interestingly he dated his accession retrospectively as 21 August, the day before the Battle of Bosworth. This meant that anyone who had fought against him in the battle was guilty of treason.

The King's Coronation took place at Westminster Abbey on 30 October, 1485, and it was not long before he had a Queen at his side. On Christmas Day, 1483, Henry had made a solemn oath in Rennes Cathedral, Brittany, that he intended to marry Princess Elizabeth of York, the sister of Edward V and eldest daughter of Edward IV and Elizabeth Woodville. To thwart Henry, Richard III had kept her guarded at Westminster Abbey so that she could not run off to marry. But Henry was determined to fulfil his promise and the couple were married on 18 January, 1486 at Westminster Abbey. He was 28 and she was 20.

This union was significant in that the joining of the Houses of Lancaster and York finally brought an end to the Wars of the Roses and peace to England at last. The stained glass in the great Rose Window in the South Transept of York Minster commemorates their marriage, showing the combined red and white roses.

Elizabeth was a great beauty, with a fair complexion and long golden blonde hair. Traditionally the image of the Queen featured in the court cards of a standard pack of 52 playing cards is said to be her. If true, her portrait appears eight times in every deck. Gentle by nature and a devout Christian, she proved to be a devoted wife and consort and they were reported to have a settled home life.

The couple eventually had four sons and four daughters, and Henry tried to secure dynastic marriages for them to strengthen his own position. Their first child was born at St Swithun's Priory, Winchester, in September 1486 and was named Arthur, after the legendary king and symbol of English heroism. He was created Prince of Wales and Earl of Chester at the age of three, by which time Henry had already decided that his son would marry Catherine of Aragon to ally England with Spain. In October 1501 Catherine finally set foot on English soil and the couple were married at St Paul's

Cathedral that November, but within months Prince Arthur was stricken with consumption and died on 2 April, 1502.

Henry arranged for the widowed Catherine of Aragon to marry his next son and heir, Prince Henry (later King Henry VIII). She had brought a large dowry and Henry was determined that it should not be lost from the family. Two of Henry's daughters married Kings of Scotland and France, which helped secure peace.

As a monarch, historians have variously referred to Henry VII as being crafty, calculating, autocratic, cold, and a somewhat shadowy, elusive figure. None of his personal papers survive and so he has left little information about himself for future generations. But we can deduce from contemporary reports that he was a very shrewd man, intelligent and scholarly, and was continually making notes which he studied every day.

In his assessment of the King, Francis Bacon wrote in 1621 that Henry VII was "sad, serious, and full of thoughts and secret observations, and full of notes and memorials of his own hand, especially touching persons; as, whom to employ, whom to reward, whom to enquire of, whom to beware of, what were the dependencies, what were the factions, and the like; keeping, as it were, a journal of his thoughts."

For a time he kept a pet monkey that once tore up his notebook. This caused great merriment amongst his courtiers who felt that the King was far too meticulous in the records that he kept. Like many of his predecessors, Henry enjoyed a high standard of living and loved pomp and ceremony, but he was never frivolous with money.

By 1492 royal accounts showed a surplus and the King had no debts. He left around £1,500,000 when he died, which was an extraordinary amount at this time. Although some consider him to be avaricious, he could be exceptionally generous. On one occasion he paid £30 to a dancer at Court, which was a fortune for entertainers, who were then paid just a few pence.

The royal coffers were partly filled through Henry's heavy taxation of the rich. He used a method called Morton's Fork, which worked on the basis that if a nobleman had spent little during the year, then he must have saved a lot and so could afford to pay taxes and if a nobleman had spent a lot during the year, he must have plenty of money and so could afford to pay his taxes! Henry got them either way.

One of Henry's achievements was to weaken the power of the great baronial houses, bringing about an end to feudalism. He abolished the private armies of the nobility and ended the power struggle between barons and the crown that had gone on for centuries.

He also set up the Court of Star Chamber, which dealt with any wrongdoings by the Lords and punished them for any abuse of power. Sometimes the verdicts were harsh. The Duke of Buckingham was fined £2,000 because he did not seek the King's permission for his widowed mother to marry.

Italian chronicler Polydore Vergil in his *Anglia Historia*, tells us that Henry "cherished justice above all things; as a result he vigorously punished violence, manslaughter and every other kind of wickedness whatsoever." Vergil's vivid description of the King is particularly revealing:

"His body was slender but well-built and strong; his height above the average. His appearance was remarkably attractive, and his face was cheerful especially when speaking; his eyes were small and blue, his teeth few, poor and blackish; his hair was thin and white; his complexion sallow. His spirit was distinguished, wise and prudent; his mind was brave and resolute and never, even at moments of the greatest danger, deserted him.

"He had a most pertinacious memory. Withal he was not devoid of scholarship. In government he was shrewd and prudent, so that no one dared to get the better of him through deceit or guile. He was gracious and kind and was as attentive to his visitors as he was easy of access.

"His hospitality was splendidly generous; he was fond of having foreigners at his court and he freely conferred favours on them. But those of his subjects who were indebted to him and who did not pay him due honour or who were generous only with promises, he treated with harsh severity."

Vergil also tells us that Henry was very devout and participated in daily religious services with great piety. He often secretly gave alms to priests in order that they should pray for his salvation. He was particularly fond of Franciscan friars for whom he had many monasteries built so that they might flourish in his kingdom.

Christopher Urswick, the King's Almoner (chaplain), has left us with one telling anecdote about Henry's character. An astrologer once predicted that the King would die within the year. Henry sent for the man and asked him to predict what he would be doing on Christmas Day. The man confessed that he was unable to do this. "Then I am a better astrologer than you," replied Henry, "for I can tell you exactly where you will be – in the Tower of London." He then had the man sent to the Tower. Once the man had admitted that his skills as an astrologer were lacking, Henry had him released unharmed, declaring him to be a "silly fellow".

During his reign, Henry had many achievements. He instituted the

Yeomen of the Guard as his personal bodyguards, now the oldest British military corps. They still wear a distinctive Tudor-style uniform. He encouraged trade with European countries and exploration flourished. Christopher Columbus had recently voyaged to America and Henry financed the exploration of Newfoundland and Nova Scotia.

"Well-beloved John Cabot," wrote the King, granting permission "to seeke out, discover and finde whatsoever isles, countries, regions or provinces . . . which before this time have been unknown to all Christians."

It was hoped that new trade routes would be discovered, and the King gave Cabot a £10 bonus for finding a new island off the coast of China.

Although the English fleet was expanded under Henry, he kept the country largely out of war during his reign, which was not only beneficial for England's morale but saved lives and money. In 1491 he invaded France, but by the Treaty of Etaples he agreed to withdraw troops on the condition that the French King paid cash for any former English possessions. This resulted in a large sum of money for the Treasury.

Closer to home he strengthened England's powers in Ireland through the Poynings Law, which gave the crown authority over the Irish Parliament. Following the theory of keeping your enemies close, he appointed the Earl of Kildare as Lord Deputy of Ireland – a man who had previously stirred up trouble.

This kept Kildare onside and he was virtually the uncrowned King of Ireland, although he was later replaced by Baron Henry Grey as it was felt that "an Englishman can do the job better".

There was great building activity in England during Henry's reign. Many cathedrals were expanded and a chapel was added to Westminster Abbey to house a shrine to Henry VI. It took many years to build and was completed in 1519.

Henry also built a new palace for himself. Previously the Royal Family had enjoyed retreating to a small palace on the River Thames at Sheen in Surrey. Henry and his family were making plans to spend Christmas there in 1489 when the building was destroyed by fire. Henry had a new, much larger residence built in 1501, Gothic in style and with many turrets, which he called Richmond Palace – one of his titles was Earl of Richmond, from the seat at Richmond Castle in Yorkshire. The palace became a great favourite with future generations of his family, particularly Elizabeth I, although not much of the original building remains today. The town that built up in this area south-west of London became known as Richmond.

When Henry acceded in 1485 it was said that some 18 people had a better right to the throne than him, including his wife and mother. Some died young, some in battle, some through execution; others chose not to contest his claim. But throughout his reign he faced problems with his own mother-in-law, Elizabeth Woodville, who plotted with enemies of the Lancastrians against him, and he was beleaguered by challenges for his crown.

Within the first year of Henry VII's reign nobleman Viscount Lovell, an ally of Richard III's, organised an unsuccessful revolt in Yorkshire to try and have the King captured.

A year later Lovell became a supporter of one Lambert Simnel, a pretender to the throne. In 1487 Lambert Simnel claimed to be Edward Plantagenet, Earl of Warwick (the son of George, Duke of Clarence, the brother of Richard III). The 22-year-old Simnel was described as a "comely youth" with "extraordinary dignity and grace of aspect".

A plot had been devised by Richard Simon, a corrupt priest, who presented Simnel to the people of Dublin, and support for him grew. The true Earl of Warwick, a possible contender to the throne, was locked up in the Tower of London to prevent him being a threat to Henry. In an attempt to counteract the Simnel deceit, Henry had the real Earl taken from his prison in the Tower and paraded him through the streets London. But there were many who believed this was a sham and that Simnel was the genuine Earl of Warwick. Such was the support that Lambert Simnel was actually crowned Edward VI in Dublin on 24 May, 1487.

Simnel and his followers then sailed to England, landing near Furness in Lancashire, before moving on towards Nottinghamshire. Following the Battle of Stoke on 16 June, in which up to 3,000 men died, Simnel was taken prisoner. He was eventually released from prison and put to work in Henry's kitchen, doing menial tasks. Priest Richard Simon was imprisoned for life for his part in the plot.

For seven years Henry VII was particularly plagued by another pretender to the throne, Perkin Warbeck, who claimed to be Richard, Duke of York, the younger son of King Edward IV and one of the two Princes presumed murdered in the Tower. So convincing was he that Warbeck met members of European royal houses and satisfied them that he really was the young Prince. In England, Henry had some of Warbeck's prominent supporters tried in a court of law and eventually beheaded, but this threat did nothing to stop others believing in the pretence.

Perkin Warbeck visited Scotland, was accepted warmly by King James IV and was even offered the hand of James's cousin, Catherine Gordon, in marriage. Warbeck planned an invasion of England and, with troops sent over from Ireland, he crossed the border in September 1496. His aim was to win over support from the English but, to his dismay, he found himself shunned and he returned to Scotland with his tail between his legs.

In the following year Warbeck tried a different approach and launched an assault from the opposite end of the country. He landed in Cornwall and headed an army of some 3,000 men at Bodmin, claiming himself to be "the rightful King Richard IV", and marched on towards Exeter. When he heard that larger armies headed by the Earl of Devonshire and Lord Daubeney were approaching, ready to attack, the imposter fled to Hampshire and went into hiding at Beaulieu.

The King's cavalry soon tracked Warbeck down and took him to meet the King. Henry managed to elicit a confession out of the imposter, who clearly realised that his cause was fruitless, and he was sent to the Tower. Surprisingly, considering the trouble he had caused, Henry later had Warbeck released although kept him under close watch. When Warbeck attempted to elude the King's men, he was taken back to the Tower and was eventually hanged at Tyburn in 1499. To save any further claims, Henry had the genuine Earl of Warwick executed, too.

Tragedy struck the King in 1503 when Elizabeth his Queen died in childbirth on 11 February. Although it is reported that Henry considered remarriage after her death, he was very half-hearted about it. One candidate was Joanna, Queen of Castille, until he discovered that she took the embalmed body of her dead first husband everywhere with her. Little wonder that she was known as Joanna the Mad.

Henry then considered the widowed Queen of Naples but had no idea what she looked like. Very extensive enquires were made about her appearance and character, but she obviously did not appeal to him, as he never remarried and turned into a virtual recluse.

Like the widowed Queen Victoria of a future generation, Henry VII's court became one of mourning and he seemed to age prematurely. Elizabeth was buried in Westminster Abbey and each year on the anniversary of her death, bells were tolled, a requiem mass was sung and 100 candles were lit in her honour.

Henry's health deteriorated and he was plagued with pain from gout and rheumatoid arthritis. After contracting pneumonia, he died at Richmond Palace on 21 April, 1509 at the age of 52. He was laid to rest beside his wife in a chapel that is now named after him in Westminster Abbey. In his will he had left instructions that effigies should be made for their tombs. These were carved by the Florentine sculptor, Petro Torrigiano, along with one for the tomb of his mother, Margaret Beaufort, who died in June 1509, just two months after her son.

Henry VII may have been a dull man to many, but as a ruler he left England stable and with far greater prosperity than his predecessors for more than a century. Although you cannot take your money with you, Henry VII left a specified amount so that 10,000 masses could be said for the salvation of his soul. Maybe he hoped that he could buy his way into heaven.

Chapter 34

Henry VIII 1491–1547
Reign: 1509–1547

Probably the most recognisable of all English kings, Henry VIII was truly a larger- than-life character. An imposing figure at over 6ft 2in tall, with a girth that increased with age, the King was a man with a contradictory image. He was considered selfish, despotic and had no qualms about having those who crossed him executed.

"Heads will fly!" was his claim whenever his authority was challenged and Charles Dickens concluded, "The plain truth is that he was a most intolerable ruffian, a disgrace to human nature, and a blot of blood and grease upon the History of England."

Yet Henry was extremely popular with the English people and, after centuries of turbulence, his was a reign that largely brought peace and prosperity to the country.

Henry was born at Greenwich Palace on 28 June, 1491, the second son of King Henry VII and Elizabeth of York. Unlike his restrained father, Henry VIII was a showman. Paintings of him, particularly those by Hans Holbein, portray him as an imposing figure with velvets, furs and jewels aplenty. Even his hats were decorated with pearls and semi-precious stones.

Maybe this enduring image of a powerful and majestic King of England is what endeared him most to his people. Before the reign of Henry VIII, English kings were addressed as "Your Grace" or "Your Highness", but significantly he adopted the term "Your Majesty".

As the second son, Henry was not expected to inherit the throne and the intention was for him to become Archbishop of Canterbury. Kingship may not have been his anticipated path, but Henry was still of royal blood, and honours were heaped upon him from a very young age.

In 1493 he was appointed Constable of Dover Castle and Lord Warden of the Cinque Ports; in 1494 he was created Duke of York; in 1495 he became a Knight of the Garter and by February 1504 had been given the titles Prince of Wales and Earl of Chester. The most significant title of all, however, came on 2 April, 1502, following the premature death of his elder brother, Prince Arthur, when Henry became Heir Apparent. It changed the course of his life.

At the age of just 10 Prince Arthur had married Catherine of Aragon. She was a daughter of King Ferdinand V of Aragon and so the marriage had formed an alliance with the powerful Spanish empire at this time. Following Arthur's death, Henry VII advised his next son and heir to marry Catherine – essentially because he did not want to lose her large dowry – which is how Henry came to be betrothed to his widowed sister-in-law.

Henry VII died on 21 April, 1509, and his son and namesake succeeded him to become King Henry VIII. In compliance with his late father's wishes, the new King quickly married Catherine at Greenwich Palace on 11 June, 1509, and they were crowned jointly on 24 June at Westminster Abbey.

Although we are very used to seeing the masterful, often bloated, image of the mature King Henry VIII, when he first came to the throne he was a tall, slim, handsome youth of 17. Clean-shaven, with reddish brown hair, Henry was clever and spoke several languages, including French and Latin. He was a keen sportsman and excelled at archery, jousting, tilting (a medieval sport in which two mounted knights tried to knock each other off their horses with lances), real tennis, and hunting. At the age of 30 it was said that Henry could still exhaust eight horses a day.

He was a gifted musician and could play the lute and virginals, and was also a good singer. Although he is generally credited with having composed *Greensleeves* for Anne Boleyn when she initially thwarted his advances ("Alas, my love, you do me wrong to cast me off discourteously"), the tune is based on an Italian style melody that did not reach England until Elizabethan times and the first printed version of the lyrics was not produced until some 35 years after Henry's death.

However, Henry was known to compose music and a manuscript dating to around 1518 includes 20 songs and 13 instrumental pieces ascribed to "The Kynge H". One particular song, *Pastyme With Good Companye*, celebrates the joys of princely life such as hunting, singing and dancing.

Unlike many of his predecessors Henry VIII acceded unopposed, so there was no family antagonism or dynastic conflict. His careful father had amassed a fortune of £1,500,000 and so Henry faced no financial worries when he became king. As a young, handsome and sporty youth, he was instantly popular throughout England. One of his first acts was to have two of the most ruthless tax collectors, Richard Empsom and Edmund Dudley, charged with high treason and executed, which added to his popularity. It was a time of peace in England too, so the country was contented with its new monarch.

With great wealth, Henry was able to dress immaculately in the finest clothes, cutting the sort of glamorous figure that the 21st-century media would go wild to feature. One of Henry's outfits was described by a contemporary as being made of white damask encrusted with diamonds and rubies.

In the early part of his reign Henry enjoyed his pleasures and was happy to leave the burden of administration to three people: Thomas Wolsey, Thomas More and Thomas Cromwell, who became the most powerful men in England and exploited their position.

Wolsey, for example, was the son of an Ipswich butcher, but went on to become Lord Chancellor of England and a Cardinal of Rome. He had houses built for himself that were as magnificent as the King's, particularly Hampton Court and York Place in Whitehall. After Wolsey's downfall, Henry took Hampton Court from him and then had York Place transformed into the splendid Whitehall Palace which then covered an area of 24 acres. Today only the Banqueting Hall survives.

Henry built imposing new homes, too, including Nonsuch Palace in Surrey which no longer exists. St James's Palace and Greenwich Palace also became impressive royal residences at this time, During Henry's reign many castles became palaces rather than fortresses. Gunpowder now greatly improved the use of canons, which made England's castles largely redundant as forms of defence, as canons could blast through walls.

For a country that had been blighted by the Wars of the Roses in earlier reigns, Henry's England experienced a period free of hostility or invasion. Henry, nevertheless, was fully prepared for warfare should the situation arise. He was the first monarch to draw a real distinction between the Army and the Navy and developed what would eventually become known as the Royal Navy.

He established Deptford and Woolwich as Royal Dockyards as they were close to Greenwich Palace and he enjoyed being able to go and watch ships being constructed; he also expanded his father's Royal Dockyard at Portsmouth, and increased the English fleet from just five ships at the beginning of his reign to around 60 ships. Henry had the *Great Harry* built, then the largest ship that there had ever been at 1,500 tons, and the 600-ton *Mary Rose*. His warships had a combined might of over 2,000 cannons. Henry also created a great chain of coastal fortresses to defend England against any threat of invasion.

The King was keen to be seen as a military commander. In 1513, some three years into his reign, Henry invaded France as a member of the Holy League – founded by Pope Julius II to defend the Papacy from its enemies with military force. Henry led an English army with Austrian mercenaries and won a cavalry action at the so-called Battle of the Spurs. Taking advantage of Henry's absence, the Scots invaded England but were decisively beaten at Flodden Field. The Earl of Surrey killed King James IV of Scotland at Flodden, and as many as 12,000 Scots were slain. Thereafter, there was peace between England and Scotland for almost three decades.

In Europe, Francis I of France and Charles V, the Habsburg ruler of Germany, Austria, Spain, the Netherlands and parts of Italy, were vying for supremacy. In 1519 Charles was elected Holy Roman Emperor and a year later both he and Francis I tried to form an alliance with England. Henry first met with the Emperor at Canterbury, then crossed the Channel to meet Francis at Guines, a summit that was intended to establish lasting peace in Europe and which subsequently became known as the Field of the Cloth of Gold.

The two monarchs were entertained lavishly at banquets and with jousting competitions over a four-week period, each trying to outdo the other in grandeur. It was a hollow event for Francis, as Henry had already formed an allegiance with Emperor Charles.

Francis I and Charles V were soon at odds and in 1521 France went to war with Italy, a costly conflict that England joined in 1522. Known as The Four Years' War, peace came through diplomatic channels rather than military success. In January 1528 the tables turned and this time England and France declared war on Charles V as part of Henry VIII's quest for greater power in Europe. It proved detrimental to England, as it brought about an end to lucrative trade with Spain and the Netherlands.

Waging war in Europe depleted Henry VIII's coffers and so he decided to debase the coinage in England. As funds diminished, he was forced to lower the percentage of silver in coins to the point where they were mostly copper with a silver coating. They were also smaller than the coinage that people had been used to and were not universally popular. Once in circulation, the silver coating gradually wore away from the relief image of Henry's face, starting with the nose, resulting in the nickname "Coppernose" for the King.

Although Henry VlII had many achievements throughout his reign, there are two major matters with which he will be forever associated: marriage and the church. In many ways the two issues were inextricably linked.

Even if people know very little about Henry VIII, everyone remembers that he married six times. Many schoolchildren learn a simple rhyme to recall the fate of his wives in the correct order:

Divorced, beheaded, died,
Divorced, beheaded, survived.

Unchronological, a less well-known nursery rhyme dating from around 1750 tells us that: *Bluff Henry the Eighth to six spouses was wedded;*
One died, one survived, two divorced, two beheaded.

Because of his six wives, many have regarded him as an inveterate womaniser. Much as he enjoyed the company of women, at the root of it all was Henry desperatation to father a male child, an heir who would secure the Tudor line for future generations. It was this extreme anxiety that led to so many marriages and caused him to break with the Church of Rome in the process.

In accordance with his father's wishes, Henry married his first wife, 24-year-old Catherine of Aragon, within six weeks of becoming King. After several miscarriages and stillbirths, a son was finally born on New Year's Day, 1511. There was great rejoicing and Henry held a tournament to celebrate the arrival of his new heir. Named Henry after his father, the baby Prince died at the age of six weeks. The King was devastated. Some five more years were to pass before Catherine delivered another child that survived – a daughter, who was named Mary.

"By God's grace, boys will follow," Henry optimistically told an ambassador, but none did and the couple eventually separated.

This separation caused Henry's first great conflict with the church and his court, resulting in his break with the Church of Rome. From 1517 the Reformation had begun in Germany. Martin Luther highlighted the abuses of the Roman Catholic Church as a result of what he described as the "spiritual and moral depravity of the Pope and his Cardinals".

Reformers denied the spiritual pre-eminence of the Pope, holding up the Bible as the only guide to follow, and by 1527 Henry VIII had become involved. He wrote a pamphlet against Luther, called *Assertio Septem Sacromentorum – Defence of the Seven Sacraments*. It was a work that Henry later came to regret, particularly because of his declaration that marriage was indissoluble. The booklet did, however, become a best-seller in its day and because of the stance he had taken about the church, Pope Leo X gave him the title "Defender of the Faith" — a title our monarch still bears to this day.

When Henry wanted to divorce Catherine of Aragon because of her failure to provide him with an heir, he began to consider the theological implications. She had been the widow of his brother and Henry's marriage to her was a union condemned by the Bible. In Leviticus, for example, it says, "If a man marries his brother's wife, it is an act of impurity; he has dishonoured his brother. They will be childless."

Henry started to question the legality of his marriage and considered that his lack of an heir may be divine judgement. He asked Cardinal Wolsey to obtain a divorce for him, but he failed in his quest. Henry dismissed Wolsey from court in 1529 and charged him with high treason. The Cardinal died before he could be executed, with his position of power gone and his reputation in ruins.

Thomas Cromwell, Henry's chief adviser, took over the issue and campaigned to secure Henry's supremacy over the Church. When the Pope refused to grant a divorce and excommunicated the King, Henry broke away from the Church of Rome so that England could head in its own direction as a Protestant country. It was a newly appointed Archbishop of Canterbury, Thomas Cranmer, who eventually had Henry's marriage to Catherine of Aragon declared invalid in 1533. Their only living daughter, Mary, was pronounced illegitimate and had her title removed. Catherine of Aragon died of natural causes, possibly cancer, on 7 January, 1536, and was buried in Peterborough Cathedral.

On 25 January, 1533, Henry secretly married Anne Boleyn, a former lady-in-waiting to Catherine of Aragon. Then aged 26, Anne was said to have "almond-shaped eyes and raven hair". Unusually, she had a sixth finger on her left hand. The marriage was made known and declared legal once Henry's marriage to Catherine was officially annulled. In June 1533 Anne was crowned Queen Consort in Westminster Abbey. The Pope denounced the marriage and Henry VIII was excommunicated. Henry's close adviser Thomas More refused to recognise the divorce from Catherine or accept Henry as Head of the Church, and consequently lost his head.

On 15 January, 1534, Henry was recognised by Parliament as the

Supreme Head of the Church of England. He began to exert his authority and in 1536 appointed Thomas Cromwell Vicar General of England and instructed him to dissolve the monasteries as part of a campaign against the Pope for his failure to grant a divorce. Some 800 Roman Catholic monasteries, abbeys and convents were closed down over a four-year period. Money, lands and estates were confiscated. Shrines were demolished. With the closure of Waltham Abbey, in March 1540, there was not a single monastery left in England.

Although Henry Vlll was a dogmatic Head of the Church, for example forcing Parliament to pass an Act of Six Articles which imposed punishments, even the death penalty, on anyone who did not follow the same Christian doctrines as the King, there were positive aspects. He created six new dioceses: Bristol, Chester, Gloucester, Oxford, Peterborough and Westminster, and in 1539 Henry decreed that there should be an English Bible in every church so that it would be accessible to all and could be read easily.

A male heir was still very much on Henry's mind, but in September 1533 Anne Boleyn gave birth to their only living child, a daughter (later Queen Elizabeth I). Henry quickly tired of Anne and within three years she was convicted of high treason, incest and infidelity. She was beheaded at the Tower of London on 19 May, 1536, and was buried in the Royal Chapel of St Peter ad Vincula within the Tower.

Parliament declared Henry's first two marriages invalid. Henry's engagement to Jane Seymour (a maid of honour or lady-in-waiting to both Catherine of Aragon and Anne Boleyn) was announced within 24 hours of Anne's execution. They married less than two weeks later on 30 May, 1536, in the Queen's Chapel, Whitehall. Unlike her predecessors, Jane was never crowned Queen.

Jane Seymour gave birth to Henry's only surviving son, Edward, on 12 October, 1537. She died less than two weeks later at Hampton Court. Henry was completely overcome with grief. She is his only wife to have been buried in St George's Chapel, Windsor, and Henry left instructions that when he himself died, he was to be buried next to her. Jane had given him the one thing he had yearned for: a male heir.

Henry remained a widower for over two years, before marrying Anne of Cleves on 6 January, 1540. It was very much a political alliance with Germany, encouraged by Thomas Cromwell, rather than a love match and Henry had not even met Anne when he agreed to marry her. She spoke no English and he found her unattractive and not at all like the flattering portrait by Holbein that he had been shown. Henry referred to her as the "mare of Flanders" and after just six months he divorced her on the grounds of non-consummation. For bringing about the marriage, Thomas Cromwell went to the scaffold.

Henry's health was poor by this time. He had a painful fistula on one leg and had put on a great deal of weight. His early armour reveals that as a young man he had a waist measurement of 34 to 36in, indicating a weight of about 180 to 200lbs. The final suit of armour made for him shows a waist measurement of 58 to 60in, giving an approximate weight of 300 to 320lbs

On 28 July, 1540, Henry married Catherine Howard, a niece of the Duke of Norfolk, at Oatlands Palace in Surrey. Like Jane Seymour and Anne of Cleves, Catherine was never crowned. Henry's health began to improve and he went on a royal progress as far as York. Although he had referred to Catherine as "a rose without a thorn", on his return he was informed that she had been unfaithful to him. Catherine Howard was found guilty of high treason and was beheaded on 13 February, 1542, for "disloyalty and indiscretion". Henry declared that he had been unlucky in marrying "such ill-conditioned wives".

Henry VIII was 51 when he married his sixth and final bride, Catherine Parr, on 12 July, 1543, at Hampton Court. She was 20 years his junior but had already been widowed twice. In 1544 he made her Regent. By this time Henry had the male heir he wanted and said he was really only looking for someone who could be a mother to his children and care for him in old age.

It was not a love match, but they were intellectual equals and enjoyed one another's company. Catherine was to survive him and within months of Henry's death had married Thomas Seymour. A year later she was dead herself, dying in childbirth.

Proud and relieved to have an heir in Prince Edward, when King James V of Scotland fathered a daughter, Mary, in 1542 Henry VIII decided that she would make an ideal bride for his son, but the Scottish parliament refused to accept the proposal. As a result, Henry went to war with Scotland to try and force the Scots to agree to the marriage.

It was a conflict that was to go on for some eight years, continuing after Henry's death, and became known as the "Rough Wooing" after George Gordon's remark, "We liked not the manner of the wooing, and we could not stoop to being bullied into love." Although Mary succeeded as Queen of Scots as an infant, she never did marry Henry's only son. His desire to subdue the Scots and make them loyal to England was also doomed to failure.

King Henry VIII died at Whitehall Palace on 28 January, 1547, at the age of 56. His doctors had been afraid to tell him that he was dying because the Treason Act forbade anyone from predicting the death of the King. Archbishop Thomas Cranmer came to the royal bedchamber at midnight on 27 January. Finding the King unable to speak, Cranmer asked him to give a sign that he trusted in Jesus Christ. Henry gripped his hand and died shortly afterwards. So corpulent had the King become that, rather gruesomely, his body exploded in the lead coffin prior to the funeral.

In accordance with his wishes, Henry was buried at St George's Chapel, Windsor, with his fourth wife Jane Seymour. It took 16 strong Yeoman of the Guard to carry Henry's coffin into the chapel and lower it into the vault in the choir.

For a flamboyant monarch, Henry Vlll's tomb is remarkably unostentatious and it was not until the early part of the 19th century that he was given a memorial slab. Somewhat surprisingly, just over a century after Henry's death, the body of the beheaded Charles I was deposited in the same vault.

Henry had intended to have an elaborate tomb built for himself, having appropriated the design and materials originally intended for Cardinal Wolsey's. Work on the tomb was never finished and the black marble sarcophagus that was going to be used now forms the base of Nelson's tomb in St Paul's Cathedral.

In 2015 the Victoria and Albert Museum in London acquired four bronze angels that had been made for Cardinal Wolsey's tomb and would have stood at the four corners of Henry's had it ever been completed. Four gilt-bronze candlesticks that would also have formed part of Henry VIII's tomb are now at St Bavo Cathedral in Ghent, Belgium.

Despite the many marriages, his often tyrannical behaviour and the executions of those that displeased him – which according to the English chronicler Raphael Holinshed amounted to some 72,000 – Henry VIII remained a well-liked king with his people and he changed the course of English history by transforming England into a Protestant country. Leaving three children as heirs, he died knowing that the Tudor dynasty was secure.

Chapter 35

Edward VI 1537–1553
Reign: 1547–1553

The only surviving son of Henry VIII, Edward, was born at Hampton Court on 12 October, 1537. From the very moment of his birth Edward was brought up to be the next King of England.

He spent his first weeks in the nursery at Hampton Court under the care of a wet-nurse, Margaret Gigs, known affectionately as "Mother Jak". At the age of five months the baby Prince was taken to the safety of Hunsdon House near Ware in Hertfordshire under the care of governess Lady Margaret Bryan, who was paid an annuity of £20 a year, and it was at Hunsdon that he spent much of his childhood.

In 1546 Edward's portrait was painted and the house can be seen clearly in the background. He also spent time with his half-sister, Elizabeth, but saw little of his other half-sister, Mary, who was an adult by the time he was born.

There is a misconception that Edward was a weak and sickly child but it was only in the last two years of his life that his health deteriorated. Although we know that Queen Elizabeth II keeps a private diary, and Queen Victoria even published extracts from her own extensive diaries during her lifetime, it is less well known that Edward VI kept a diary himself, which he called his chronicle and it is now preserved in the British Library.

It provides a fascinating insight into his life and interestingly there is no mention of illness until 2 April, 1552 when he wrote that he "fell sick of the measles and the smallpox", which was possibly less serious than it sounds considering that he attended the Order of the Garter service on St George's Day just three weeks later. His chronicle shows that he lived a full and active life, far removed from the sickly child that many consider him to have been.

It is recorded that Edward could walk before the age of one and that he danced whenever minstrels played, so vigorously "that he could not stand still" as soon as the music started. It is one of the few images that remain of the boy having fun, for his education began very early and we know much more about the academic side of his life than his recreation. He was certainly musical and could play the flute.

As he grew older he enjoyed riding and archery, and had an interest in astronomy, but in his journal he reproached himself if he spent too much time at leisure and not enough on study. "We forgot ourselves," he wrote.

Edward had an amazing memory and it was said that he could recite the name of every river, pond, stream and bog in the whole of England. He was a serious, some would say precocious, child. One eminent historian, the late Sir Geoffrey Elton, even went so far as to describe Edward as "a cold-hearted prig".

From the age of six Edward had a series of tutors, notably the humanists Richard Cox and John Cheke, who were concerned only with the Prince's scholarly life and took no part in his religious training. An intelligent child, by the age of eight he could write competently in Latin and was soon fluent in spoken French and Italian. Some of his work survives and we can see that he was studying Cicero and Aristotle from a young age.

It is perhaps appropriate that his name is still associated with a number of schools in England, such as those at Birmingham, Bury St Edmunds, Chelmsford, Lichfield, Stafford, Stratford-upon-Avon and Southampton. Edward also established a school for 700 orphans in London's Newgate Street, with a distinctive uniform of blue coats and yellow stockings. In addition to being taught to read and write, the children learned the art of spinning and weaving so that they would have a trade in life.

For one so young, he was a remarkably pious Protestant. It is recorded that when Edward was once trying to reach a book on a high shelf, he refused to stand on a large Bible as a step considering it to be sacrilegious. When one of his tutors, John Cheke, was seriously ill, Edward said, "He will not die at this time, for this morning I begged his life from God in my prayer and obtained it."

Edward attended Mass every day, read Solomon's Proverbs, and wrote that he feared God's commandments and was brought up to "beware of strange and wanton women". He once wrote to his friend Barnaby Fitzpatrick in France, warning him to avoid the company of women "as far forth as ye may". The young Fitzpatrick did not take kindly to the advice and wrote back that Edward was being "more fatherly than friendly".

Unlike some of his predecessors, Edward did not have a lonely childhood and was brought up with children of his own age, including several boys and one girl – Jane Dormer – who became the Prince's dancing partner. One particular friend was Henry Sidney, the son of Edward's tutor, Sir William Sidney. Henry spent much of his childhood at court and was Edward's closest companion. In 1552 Edward gave the magnificent Penshurst Place in Kent to Sir William as a reward for his services as tutor and later Steward to the King's Household, an estate that Henry Sidney eventually inherited.

Edward was made Duke of Cornwall and Earl of Chester on the day of his birth, but never became Prince of Wales. Although he undoubtedly would have been invested, he unexpectedly inherited a higher title in 1547.

He was staying at Hatfield House in Hertfordshire, then considered to be a royal palace, and was taken to Enfield to be with his sister Elizabeth so that they could receive the news together that Henry VIII had died on 28 January, and that Edward was now King. He recorded in his diary that his father's death caused great grief in London but reveals nothing of his own personal feelings.

Edward's Coronation took place at Westminster Abbey some three weeks later on 20 February, after which he dined at Westminster Hall with his crown still on his head. In his sermon that day Archbishop Thomas Cranmer said, "Your Majesty is God's vice-regent and Christ's vicar within your own dominions."

This effectively gave the King great power over the church and the young monarch steered England to adopt a fully Protestant approach to religion. Cranmer's *Book of Common Prayer* became available on Whit Sunday 1549, the earliest form of the Anglican prayer book. During Edward's reign services became much simpler and many churches were stripped of their elaborate decorations and icons.

At a mere nine years old King Edward VI was considered too young to reign and so the Privy Council chose his uncle Edward Seymour (eldest brother of Jane Seymour) as Protector and Governor of the King's Person, with an annual income of £7,400. Seymour was ambitious and effectively ruled England, granting himself the title 1st Duke of Somerset.

He worked from Somerset House, which he built using materials from demolished churches and abbeys, and is said to have been condescending towards the King, treating him as a mere child. Somerset's younger brother, Thomas Seymour, became Lord High Admiral and married Henry VIII's widowed queen, Catherine Parr. For a time, the Seymour family appeared to be in control and the two brothers vied for power. Thomas secretly gave Edward pocket money to try and win his favour.

When Edward was just six years old Henry VIII had attempted to secure a marriage between his heir and Mary, Queen of Scots, (then aged just 7 months) to try to unite the two countries and end centuries of bitterness and warring. But the Scots tore up his treaty.

Now that Edward was King, the Duke of Somerset tried to revive Henry's plan but by military force rather than negotiation. It resulted in the Battle of Pinkie Cleugh, in which the English army defeated the Scots and relations were soured rather than enriched. The infant Mary was quickly taken to France and was soon betrothed to Francis, son of the French King.

The Duke of Somerset's power was not to last. The Privy Council turned against him following his failure over Mary, Queen of Scots, and his relationship with his brother became strained. When Thomas Seymour announced his desire to marry Princess Elizabeth, following the death of his wife, Somerset took the opportunity to have his brother tried for treason, plus embezzlement of the Bristol Mint, and Thomas was executed.

This act added to Somerset's unpopularity and Edward dismissed him from his role as Protector and later wrote matter-of-factly and without emotion in his chronicle: "The Duke of Somerset had his head cut off upon Tower Hill between eight and nine o'clock in the morning."

After Somerset's downfall John Dudley, Earl of Warwick, became Edward's Protector and was created Duke of Northumberland. As power crazed as his predecessor, Northumberland was not a good leader. England's economy suffered under his management, prices rose and rebellions broke out, most notably that led by Robert Kett as a direct result of landowners fencing off common land to make it part of their own property.

Previously peasants could keep their livestock on wasteland to help them survive, but with the economic situation many farmers stopped growing crops and began breeding sheep and cows instead, as there was more profit to be had, and so adopted what had once been common land. This meant that peasants had nowhere to graze their own animals, which inevitably led to loss of livelihood. Many tenant farmers were also forced out of their homes so that owners could convert the arable land into pasture for sheep.

This all came to a head on 8 July, 1549 when a group of rebels began tearing down fences at Wymondham that had been erected by a wealthy yeoman farmer named Robert Kett. Instead of being intimidated, Kett turned the tables, pulled down his own fences and offered to lead the rebels. A meeting place was established under an oak tree (now known as Kett's Oak) on the road from Hethersett to Norwich and within four days 16,000 men had set up camp at Mousehold Heath.

Edward's government sent forces to quell the unrest, led by John Dudley. In a furious battle, in which some 3,000 men were killed, the rebels were defeated and Robert Kett was captured and put on trial at the Tower of London before being hanged for treason at Norwich Castle. Landowners restored common lands to the public, although lost their sheep and cattle to the rebels.

There was further unrest in Devon and Cornwall during Edward's reign, when rebels took against the new prayer book and the imposition of standardised services in English rather than Latin. A new Liturgy was introduced in 1552, uncompromising in its Protestant stance, and commissioners were sent to every parish church in England to make an inventory of the silver and vestments that were no longer considered necessary for a non-Catholic Mass.

As Edward grew older, he began to take a more active role in affairs and a Council for the Estate was formed, with weekly meetings so that the King could hear debates about important issues, and he worked closely with the Privy Council so that he knew exactly what was going on in his kingdom. It was agreed that Edward would be able to rule in his own right when he reached the age of 16.

When Edward's health started to deteriorate in 1552, the Duke of Northumberland began to look to the future and how he might ensure that his family remained at the heart of the monarchy. At court was the King's cousin, Lady Jane Grey, daughter of Henry Grey, the Duke of Suffolk.

Northumberland engineered that his son, Lord Guildford Dudley, should marry Lady Jane. Although the girl abhorred the idea, Northumberland plotted with her parents and the couple were married in haste when Edward became very ill in May 1553.

It was assumed in many quarters that Edward's half-sister Mary, daughter of Catherine of Aragon, would succeed him as stipulated in Henry VIII's will. But Mary followed the Roman Catholic religion and so, at the behest of the Duke of Northumberland, Edward agreed to change the line of succession so that the male heirs of his Protestant cousin Lady Jane Grey would inherit the throne.

When it became clear that the King had consumption, what we now call tuberculosis, physician John Banister wrote on 28 May, "He does not sleep except when he be stuffed with drugs. But the doctors do not exceed 12 grains at a time and then only if the patient be in great pain or racked by violent coughing. The sputum which he brings up is livid, black, fetid and full of carbon; it smells beyond measure. His feet are swollen all over.

"To the doctors these things portend death, and that within three months. Today the Duke called the doctors together and asked them what the King's chances were. They answered that when autumn comes it will end his life."

Conscious that the King would die before Lady Jane could produce a son, the Duke of Northumberland had the document that Edward had signed surreptitiously altered so that it named "Lady Jane and her heirs male" as the successors, rather than just Lady Jane's male heirs.

Although physically weak, Edward's mind was still strong and on his deathbed he composed a prayer, which he dictated to his attendants:

"Lord God, deliver me out of this miserable and wretched life, and take me amongst thy chosen; howbeit, not my will but Thy will be done. Lord, I commit my spirit to Thee. O Lord, Thou knowest how happy it were for me to be with Thee: yet, for Thy Chosen's sake, send me life and health, that I may truly serve Thee. O my Lord God, defend this realm from papistry and maintain Thy true religion, that I and my people may praise Thy holy name, for Thy Son Jesus Christ's sake, Amen."

King Edward VI made his last public appearance in Greenwich on 1 July, 1553, shocking those who saw him by his emaciated appearance. He died at nine o'clock on the evening of 6 July in the arms of his closest friend, Sir Henry Sidney. His last words were, "Lord, have mercy on me and take my spirit." He was 15 years old and his reign had lasted just six and a half years.

The Duke of Northumberland hid Edward's death from the public for several days, until he could decide what to do about announcing the successor. There are even stories that he had Edward's body brought out each day, seated in a chair as if reading a book, so that there would be eyewitnesses to the fact that the King was still alive. When Northumberland told Lady Jane that she was now Queen, she fainted with shock. Edward's body remained at Greenwich Palace for several weeks and his funeral did not take place until 8 August.

On 16 August, 1553, a cloth merchant from Strasburg named John Burcher wrote an account of the King's passing:

"That monster of a man, the Duke of Northumberland, has been committing a horrible and portentous crime . . . our excellent King has been most shamefully taken off by poison. His nails and hair fell off before his death so that, handsome as he was, he entirely lost all his good looks. The perpetrators of the murder were ashamed of allowing the body of the deceased King to lie in state and be seen by the public, as is usual: wherefore they buried him privately in a paddock adjoining the Palace and substituted in his place, to be seen by the people, a youth not very unlike him whom they had murdered. One of the sons of the Duke of Northumberland acknowledged this fact."

Modern historians dispute the notion that Edward was murdered, believing that someone from court in the month between his death and burial would have noticed that the corpse had been substituted. It is, however, possible that Tudor remedies given to the King unintentionally hastened his demise. Remedies that included crushed ants, excreta from a variety of creatures, snakeskin and "moss from the skull of a person who had died violently".

Edward's body, if indeed it is his, was laid to rest in Henry VII's Lady Chapel at Westminster Abbey in an unmarked grave. Not for him the elaborate tomb of an English monarch. More than 400 years were to pass before a simple black paving stone was inscribed to mark the spot:

In Memory of King Edward VI buried in this Chapel. This
Stone was placed here by Christ's Hospital in Thanksgiving
for their Founder, 7 October 1966

Chapter 36

Lady Jane Grey c.1537–1554

Reign: 10–19 July 1553

Known as the Nine-Day Queen, with the shortest reign of any English monarch, the tragedy of Lady Jane Grey is still a great source of fascination. Some chronicles of our Kings and Queens fail even to list her, yet she has inspired numerous biographies across the centuries and even films in recent years.

Although it is recorded that she was a great beauty, Jane is said to be the only English sovereign for more than 500 years for whom there is no surviving contemporary portrait. A painting long believed to be of her in London's National Portrait Gallery was proved 20 years ago to be of Catherine Parr instead.

In 2005 the so-called "Streatham portrait" of Lady Jane Grey was discovered in London. Although painted half-a-century after her death, it is thought to be a copy of an earlier portrait and may be the closest that we will ever come to knowing what she looked like.

Descriptions from those who knew her leave us with an impression of a petite girl with a clear complexion, brown eyes, reddish-brown hair and even at the age of 16 so slight of stature that she occasionally wore platform soles on her shoes to increase her height.

Lady Jane Grey was born at Bradgate House, Bradgate Park, Charnwood Forest, in Leicestershire, around 12 October, 1537, although this date is now disputed and modern historians consider that she may possibly have been born a year earlier than originally recorded. She was the eldest surviving daughter of Sir Henry Grey, Marquis of Dorset and Lady Frances

Brandon, and she had two sisters, Catherine and Mary Grey. In 1551 her parents were created Duke and Duchess of Suffolk.

Through her mother, Lady Jane was a great-granddaughter of King Henry VII; her great-uncle was King Henry VIII, and she was a first cousin once removed of King Edward VI. It was this background that eventually cleared a pathway for her to the throne of England, although it was a journey that she had no desire to take.

A very intelligent child, she was literate from an early age and preferred reading books to participating in sporting activities. One of her teachers, Roger Ascham, reported finding her one day reading Plato's *Phaedo* in the original Greek text when she could have been out hunting with her family.

"I asked her why she would lose such pastime in the park," Ascham wrote. "Smiling, she answered me, 'I wist all their sport in the park is but a shadow to that pleasure I find in Plato'." She continued that books were her greatest source of pleasure and that all other pleasures "are but trifles and troubles unto me."

Although a committed Protestant and taught largely by Bishop John Aylmer, she had a humanist education, starting when she was three years old. She studied French, Italian, Greek, Latin and Hebrew, was good at music and learned how to play the harp, lute and cithern (a pear-shaped, six-stringed instrument resembling a guitar), and in her leisure time did needlework and enjoyed dancing.

She had a very strict upbringing and seems to have had a challenging relationship with her parents. One of her teachers reported her as writing: "When I am in the presence either of father or mother, whether I speak, keep silence, sit, stand or go, eat, drink, be merry or sad, be sewing, playing, dancing, or doing anything else, I must do it as it were in such weight, measure and number, even so perfectly as God made the world, or else I am so sharply taunted, so cruelly threatened, yea presently sometimes with pinches, nips and bobs and other ways . . . that I think myself in hell."

Possibly because of this, by the age of ten she was living at Sudeley Castle in Gloucestershire as part of the household of Queen Catherine Parr, the last wife of Henry VIII, who had married Thomas Seymour, Lord High Admiral of England. Jane remained with them until Catherine's death in September 1548. Thomas became Jane's ward and it was said that he had plans to marry her to his nephew King Edward VI. Had this happened, she would have lived a safe life as Queen Consort rather than the weightier role of Queen.

Thomas Seymour's brother, Edward, was then acting as Lord Protector to the boy King Edward VI and became concerned that Thomas was much more popular with the monarch than he was himself. As a result, Thomas Seymour was soon arrested for High Treason, and was quickly executed. Such was the world at court that Lady Jane found herself growing up in.

Edward Seymour may have rid himself of his brother but he was soon ousted from power as Lord Protector and replaced by John Dudley, the Duke of Northumberland. The 1544 Act of Succession had placed Henry VIII's daughters, Mary and Elizabeth, in direct line to the throne. This meant that Edward VI's half-sister, the Catholic Mary Tudor, would be the next to inherit. If this happened, the Protestant Northumberland knew that he would undoubtedly lose his head as a result. As a matter of self-preservation, it became imperative that he took matters into his own hands.

Through the Act of Succession, if neither Mary nor Elizabeth had any children then the crown would eventually pass to the offspring of King Henry VIII's sister Mary – one of whom was Lady Jane Grey's mother Frances.

In a further attempt to cement his own future, Northumberland had his youngest son, 19-year-old Lord Guildford Dudley, marry Lady Jane Grey at Durham House in the Strand, London, on 21 May, 1553. Lady Jane was an unwilling bride, coerced into marriage through beatings.

Within six weeks of the wedding, King Edward VI died at Greenwich. Lady Jane reluctantly accepted and signed an official proclamation of accession, but it shows something of her strength of character that she adamantly refused to allow her husband to be Consort. It was a bitter blow to Northumberland that his son would never be called King.

Lady Jane was publicly proclaimed Queen on 10 July, 1553. As with previous monarchs awaiting their Coronation, she took up residence in the Tower of London and travelled there in an impressive procession by barge along the River Thames. It was to be the only piece of royal pageantry in her short reign. At the Tower, the Crown Jewels were handed over to her.

Although the Duke of Northumberland had achieved his wish, he did not take into account the fact that Mary Tudor – the daughter of King Henry VIII and Catherine of Aragon – had tremendous support throughout England. After Edward VI's death, Mary wrote to Parliament claiming that she was the rightful heir, but received a reply from Northumberland and 20 councillors to say that the throne was already occupied by Queen Jane.

Mary fled to the medieval market town of Framlingham in Suffolk, to the safety of its castle, to rally her followers. She was quickly pursued by Northumberland and his troops, who hoped to take her prisoner and thereby stem the tide of opinion that was changing in her favour. This was a misjudgement on Northumberland's part, because while he was away from London the Privy Council changed its allegiance from Jane to Mary Tudor. By the time he reached Cambridge, Northumberland's own troops had become supporters of Mary.

Soon, even Jane's father declared that Mary should be Queen. He encouraged his daughter to give up the throne, which she had never sought in the first place. After a reign of just nine days Jane was replaced by Mary, who made a triumphal return to London on 3 August with some 20,000 supporters. Within weeks, the Duke of Northumberland was executed. His plans had all been scuppered and he paid the ultimate price for his scheming.

When Mary became Queen, she immediately had the hapless Lady Jane imprisoned in the Tower of London. What had for a short time been her palace, suddenly became her gaol. In November 1553 Jane and her husband, Lord Guildford Dudley, were tried for high treason at the Guildhall in the City of London. A contemporary chronicler describes her as being calm and entering the chamber dressed in a "black gown of cloth, a French hood, all black; a black velvet book hanging before her and another book in her hand, open." Jane pleaded guilty to having signed documents as Jane the Queen.

Although Lady Jane was sentenced to death, the sentence was suspended. She would have survived had there not been a rebellion by Sir Thomas Wyatt in January 1554 to try and prevent Queen Mary from marrying the Catholic Philip of Spain. Mary intended to make England a Catholic country again and was determined to marry in order to strengthen her position and produce a Catholic heir.

The support that she previously enjoyed from her people quickly began to wane. A delegation from Parliament urged Mary to choose an English husband and Thomas Wyatt headed a rebellion "to prevent us from over-running by strangers". This resulted in what has become known as the Battle of Fleet Street, when the rebellion was quashed by Mary's troops at Ludgate. Thomas Wyatt and more than 100 of his supporters were executed.

When Lady Jane's father and brothers became supporters of Wyatt's rebellion, they unwittingly prompted her demise. In retaliation, the government decided to carry out the execution of Jane and her husband after all. Queen Mary reluctantly signed their death warrants, as her husband-to-be made it a condition of their marriage contract that Jane be permanently removed, so that she could never usurp the throne in the future. The date for the execution was set for 9 February but was delayed for three days so that Jane could convert to the Roman Catholic faith.

On 12 February, 1554 Lord Guildford Dudley was publicly beheaded on Tower Hill and his corpse was cruelly taken by Jane's window so that she could see her husband's fate. She was then herself taken to Tower Green, within the Tower of London, to the scaffold. Before her death, Jane made a speech:

"Good people, I am come hither to die, and by a law I am condemned to the same. The fact, indeed, against the Queen's highness was unlawful, and the consenting thereunto by me: but touching the procurement and desire thereof by me or on my behalf, I do wash my hands thereof in innocency, before God, and the face of you, good Christian people, this day."

It is recorded that she then recited Psalm 51, handed her gloves and handkerchief to her maid, before asking the executioner to "dispatch me quickly". She put a blindfold on herself and had to be helped by the Deputy Lieutenant of the Tower to find the block on which to lay her head. Her final words were, "Lord, into thy hands I commend my spirit." She was just 16 years old.

At the time of her execution, legend has it that the foresters at Bradgate, where she had been born, "beheaded" oak trees in the park as a mark of respect. Pollarded oaks of a great age are still to be seen at Bradgate Park today. The body of Lady Jane Grey and her husband were buried in the Royal Chapel of St Peter ad Vincula at the Tower. She died because of a crown that she never wanted, a victim of other people's ambition and power.

Chapter 37

Mary I 1516–1558
Reign: 1553–1558

If Lady Jane Grey is considered to be England's most tragic queen, Mary Tudor must rank a close second, for hers is very much a story of rejection. Rejected by her father, her brother, her husband and ultimately by her country.

The eldest surviving child of King Henry VIII and Catherine of Aragon, Mary was born at Greenwich Palace on 18 February, 1516, and was baptised at the Friary Church there. Although Henry was pleased to have fathered a child, he was disappointed that it was a girl for he desperately needed a male heir to continue the Tudor dynasty. It was this failure to produce the heir Henry so craved that led to his separation and eventual divorce from Catherine and resulted in an unhappy childhood for Mary.

Possibly because of tensions in her home life, Mary developed into a strong-willed child; some would say precocious. She was initially educated by her mother and Margaret Pole, the Countess of Salisbury, and was later tutored in astronomy, geography, mathematics and science.

She excelled at languages, studied Greek and spoke Latin, French, Italian and Spanish fluently. Like her father, Mary was musical and could play the virginals before her fifth birthday, and learned to play the clavichord and lute. For relaxation, Mary enjoyed needlework and embroidery, and she loved dancing. At the age of eleven she took part in several entertainments at Greenwich Palace for the French ambassador, dancing as an Icelandic maiden and later, richly dressed in a costume of crimson and gold, as an ancient Roman lady.

Almost from birth Mary was a pawn in the game to strengthen relations with other countries. At the age of just two she was engaged to the French Dauphin, although Cardinal Wolsey later changed his mind and the young Mary found herself betrothed to Charles V of France instead. She was five years old, he was 23. With no dowry offered, Charles V backed out of the arrangement. James IV of Scotland was then suggested as a possible husband but the idea was abandoned.

When she was ten, Cardinal Wolsey tried to arrange a marriage between Mary and 32-year-old Francis I of France. Henry of Orleans was also considered before Wolsey turned his attention to England and suggested that Mary marry Henry Fitzroy, the Duke of Richmond. As the Duke was an illegitimate son of Henry VIII with his mistress Elizabeth Blount, the union between a girl and her half-brother proved too much even for the Tudors.

Then the son of the Duke of Norfolk was proposed, but also rejected. Love did not appear to be a requisite and poor Mary seemed to have no say in her choice of future husband. The bargaining that had gone on in her own life and the six marriages of her father must have coloured her feelings towards relationships. Having first been engaged at the age of two, Mary did not actually marry until she was 37.

Caught up in her father's marital problems, Mary found herself rejected by him when he separated from Catherine of Aragon. When the marriage was nullified Mary was declared illegitimate and even had to give up her title of Princess. Henry VIII's second wife, Anne Boleyn, saw Mary as an enemy. When Anne gave birth to a daughter in 1533, Mary was rejected still further.

Instead of being treated royally, Mary was now considered to be nobody. She was given the smallest room at Hatfield House and was almost a servant, acting as a nanny to her baby half-sister, Elizabeth. Anne Boleyn's sister, Lady Skelton, took control of all that Mary did and was instructed to beat her if she disobeyed orders. Not surprisingly, Mary became ill.

"While my father lives I shall be only the Lady Mary," she said, describing herself as "the most unhappy lady in Christendom". So severe was the attitude towards her that if anyone wrote a letter to her addressing her as Princess Mary, they were sent straight to the Tower. Knowing that her own life could be in danger, the young Mary learned to act with humility at this time.

When Catherine of Aragon was dying at Kimbolton in 1535, Mary was forbidden to go and see her. She was not allowed to go to the funeral, or to accept a bequest in her mother's will.

After Anne Boleyn's execution in 1536, Henry married Jane Seymour who was sympathetic to Mary's situation. Mary, then aged 20, tried to initiate a reconciliation with her father, but was told that first she had to agree that his marriage to Catherine of Aragon was illegal and also to accept Henry as Supreme Head of the Church of England.

Mary's religious conviction was essential to her and she was drawn to the old Catholic faith and believed in the supremacy of the Pope, which was completely at odds with her father's position.

Initially Mary refused to accept Henry as Head of the Church, but eventually relented. Many people were being executed at this time for their faith, including some close to Mary, and she feared that she might also lose her head. Strong willed, however, she could not relinquish her Catholic leanings and upset the King when he heard that she had "entertained a group of dispossessed nuns".

The Duke of Norfolk said threateningly that were he Mary's father, he would knock her head against a wall "until it was as soft as a baked apple". Thomas Cromwell told her that she was "the most obstinate and obdurate woman, all things considered, that ever was".

There is a story, no doubt apocryphal, that Mary's first words as a child were, "Priest! Priest!" when she spotted a friar who was Henry VIII's organist. Stubborn and with a horror of appearing weak willed, she maintained her religious convictions. When she was once visited by the Protestant Bishop of London, Nicholas Ridley, she is reputed to have said, "My Lord, for your gentleness to come and see me, I thank you; but for your offering to preach before me, I thank you never a whit."

Mary was to remain something of an outsider within the Royal Family until Henry VIII married for the last time. His sixth wife, Catherine Parr, took pity on Mary, was said to have treated her like a sister and tried to pour oil on troubled waters. As a result, a statute of 1544 put Mary back in line of succession after her brother, Edward, although she still seemed to be considered illegitimate.

After Henry VIII's death in 1547, the new King Edward VI was determined to maintain his father's Protestant stance and the Catholic Mass was outlawed. This caused friction with Mary, who told her brother that her faith would never change. In 1549 she was informed that she could not hold a private mass even in her own home.

Two days after Edward died at the age of 15 on 6 July, 1553, it was revealed that the powerful Duke of Northumberland had persuaded the young King to name his Protestant cousin, Lady Jane Grey, as his successor instead of Mary. Mary had been rejected once again.

Mary was in Suffolk when Jane was proclaimed Queen and sent a letter to Parliament stating that she was the rightful heir to her half-brother King Edward VI. Lady Jane Grey's father-in-law, the Duke of Northumberland, sent a reply signed by 20 councillors confirming that Jane was now Queen of England.

Mary set out for London, staying overnight at Sawston Hall near Cambridge, then owned by the Roman Catholic Huddleston family. She was forced to leave early in the morning disguised as a dairy maid when news reached her that the Duke of Northumberland's soldiers and a group of Protestant supporters were approaching, with the aim of taking her prisoner.

When they discovered that they had been thwarted and Mary had escaped, they set fire to Sawston Hall, destroying a large part of it. "Let it burn," said Mary, "I shall build a finer one there." This she did, granting a licence for stone to be used from Cambridge Castle. It is now a Grade I listed Tudor manor house and, not surprisingly, has one of the finest priest holes in England where the Catholic Mass could be said in secret.

It soon became clear that Lady Jane Grey was not the popular choice of the people and there was much greater support in England for a true daughter of King Henry VIII. On 13 July Mary's supporters proclaimed her Queen and marched towards London, where she was met by the Lord Mayor at Aldgate and received a rapturous welcome from the people.

She went on to the Tower of London to be met by Roman Catholic prisoners who had been incarcerated during the reigns of Henry VIII and Edward VI. Mary immediately ordered their release. Mary officially became Queen on 19 July, 1553, and her reign dates from then.

On 30 September Queen Mary rode to Westminster, a spectacle that is described in the 16th-century *Holinshed Chronicles*. Mary was "in a chariot of cloth of gold, wearing a gown of purple velvet trimmed with ermine, her crown so heavy with jewels that she was faine to beare up her head with her hand".

Her Coronation took place in Westminster Abbey on 1 October, when she became the first crowned Queen to reign over the whole of England. Significantly, the service was conducted by a Roman Catholic Bishop. The Archbishop of Canterbury, Thomas Cranmer, had been arrested, later to be tried for treason.

As monarch, Mary had a number of achievements which included reforming England's financial position and making improvements to the roads, but it is for issues with the church that she is largely remembered.

One of her first acts was to dismiss all the advisers that had surrounded Edward VI and brought in her own supporters. At her first Parliament she rescinded all of Edward VI's laws concerning the Protestant church, restored the mass and made the *Book of Common Prayer* illegal.

The question of her marriage was soon high on the agenda and Mary was given a list of six possible suitors. She was 37 and it seemed as if people had been trying to find her a husband for her entire life.

She eventually settled on Philip, son of her cousin Charles V the Holy Roman Emperor and King of Spain. Philip was heir to the Spanish throne, a widower who was 11 years younger than Mary. He was said to be a zealous Catholic and just what she needed by her side if she was ever to make England a Catholic country again.

Parliament urged her to opt for an English husband, fearing that the union would be a threat to England's independence, but Mary stubbornly refused. She did make one concession with Parliament that if she died childless, Philip and his heirs would not have any claim to the throne and he was refused the title King of England.

Mary's choice of husband did not go down well and there was hostility prior to the marriage to Philip of Spain. Her popularity with the English people plummeted and children even threw snowballs at visiting Spanish envoys that winter. There was a rebellion led by Sir Thomas Wyatt in January 1554, when 15,000 people marched in protest from Kent to Southwark, with Wyatt at the head, to oppose the Queen's marriage.

Mary refused to be cowed and went instead to London's Guildhall, where she made a dramatic speech. "I am come in mine own person to tell you what you already see and know," she said. "I mean the traitorous and seditious assembling of the Kentish rebels against us and you. They pretend to object to the marriage with the Prince of Spain . . . good subjects, pluck up your hearts and like true men stand fast against these rebels and fear them not, for I assure you I fear them nothing at all."

Her advisers urged her to go to the safety of Windsor Castle, but Mary refused and defiantly watched from the gatehouse of St James's Palace as the rebels marched past.

In the ensuing Battle of Fleet Street, the rebellion was quashed and Wyatt and over 100 men were executed. The Queen even had her own sister Elizabeth imprisoned in the Tower of London for fear that she supported the rebellion, but when no evidence could be unearthed Mary had her moved to Woodstock Palace until the fuss died down.

Philip arrived at Southampton ahead of the marriage in a howling gale and torrential rain. Although he told the deputation that greeted him in London that evening that he had come to live in England as an Englishman, he addressed them in Latin as he did not speak any English.

Mary married Philip on 25 July, 1554, in Winchester Cathedral and the couple honeymooned at Hampton Court. On marriage Mary adopted the title Queen of England, France, Naples, Jerusalem and Ireland. When Philip acceded to the Spanish throne in January 1556, Mary also became Queen of Spain.

Although the couple appeared content in public, it was an unhappy relationship and through the marriage she lost the affection of the English people. With an eye for the ladies, there was soon gossip of Philip's liaisons in London with what were described at the time as "females of low condition". A ballad of the day lampooned his dalliances:

The baker's daughter in her russet gown,
Better than Queen Mary without her crown.

One of the reasons for the couple's unpopularity in England was that Philip had a reputation for having Protestants tortured to induce them to give up their beliefs. This is borne out by a letter that he wrote to his own sister saying, "We have made a law, I and the most illustrious Queen, for the punishment of heretics and all enemies of Holy Church; or rather, we have revived old ordinances of the realm, which will serve this purpose very well."

After her marriage, Mary did indeed revive an old law which allowed people to be burned at the stake as punishment for heresy and some 300 Protestants suffered this dreadful fate. Not surprisingly, the Queen became known as Bloody Mary as a result. The first to suffer was John Rogers, a married Prebendary at St Paul's Cathedral. His family were forced to watch the execution in the hope that the priest would see them and renounce his Lutheran faith. He did not. In fact his family supported his martyrdom and cheered him on his way out of this world.

Notably, Mary had three Bishops put to death in Oxford: Thomas Cranmer, Nicholas Ridley and Hugh Latimer, often referred to as the Oxford Martyrs. It was recorded that the flames were so fierce that the heat scorched the doors of nearby Balliol College. A gruesome reminder is a sunken cobbled cross, set into the road at the western end of Broad Street in Oxford, marking the exact spot where the Bishops were executed.

There is also a Martyrs' Memorial in Oxford, a stone monument in the shape of an Eleanor Cross with statues of the Bishops. Uncowed, Latimer had shouted out to Ridley as the flames licked around them, "We shall this day light such a candle in England as, by the grace of God, shall never be put out."

It was not just clergy that suffered during the regime. Long records include weavers, butchers, barbers . . . people from all professions, who lost their lives for refusing to renounce their faith. Four women in Essex were put to death for not knowing what a sacrament was.

Because the Queen was so fanatical about Catholicism, married clergy were now forced to leave their wives if they wanted to stay in the church. Where churches had been stripped bare of ornamentation by her predecessors, Mary now had altars, icons and statues restored, and soon there were Acts of Parliament acknowledging the Pope's supremacy.

In November 1554 it was announced that Queen Mary was expecting her first child and there was public celebration throughout England at the prospect of a new heir to secure the Tudor line. In May 1555, when the birth appeared to be imminent, the waiting game continued and it eventually became apparent that this was a phantom pregnancy and there was no baby to be born.

Fluid retention as a result of dropsy, now known as oedema, had caused her stomach to swell. With Mary and Philip's relationship stormy from the outset, he now packed his bags at the news and set sail for Spain, leaving her alone and rejected. He was to marry twice more after Mary's death and fathered at least 10 children.

Philip returned to England briefly in 1557 simply to muster English troops to join in a war between Spain and France, and some 8,000 soldiers departed with him to fight. On 5 January, 1558, England lost Calais. Its last piece of French territory, won in 1347, had gone and Mary was humiliated.

"When I am dead and opened, you shall find Calais lying on my heart," she said. Centuries later Charles Dickens poured scorn on her sentiment: "I should have thought, if anything were written on her heart, they would have found the words – Jane Grey, Rogers, Ridley, Latimer, Cranmer, and 300 people burnt alive within four years of my wicked reign, including 60 women and 40 little children."

Physically, Mary was never a great beauty. Short, plump, pale-skinned with dark hair, a Spanish gentleman described her at the time of her marriage as "flabby rather than fat . . . and she dresses badly". Venetian Ambassador Giovanni Michieli recorded in 1557 that Mary's "eyes are so piercing that they inspire not only respect but fear in those on whom she fixes them, although she is very short-sighted, being unable to read or do anything unless she has her sight quite close to what she wishes to peruse or to see distinctly. Her voice is rough and loud, almost like a man's, so that when she speaks she is always heard a long way off."

Mary also suffered many dental problems and had periods of depression throughout her life.

In the summer of 1558 Mary suffered with dropsy again, but deluded herself that she was pregnant. She had not seen Philip for over nine months, yet insisted that it was her husband's child. This time the condition proved fatal and modern physicians conclude that she may well have been suffering from ovarian cancer.

On 17 November Mary was anointed and a Mass was said at her bedside at St James's Palace. She died while being blessed by the priest. Few people mourned her passing and there was no great national outflow of grief. Her husband wrote to his half-sister: "The Queen, my wife, is dead . . . I felt a reasonable regret for her death."

When the news was announced in London there was in fact jubilation at Elizabeth's accession rather than Mary's passing. "Did anyone ever see such a time?" said one Londoner. "No one would think that a queen had died since the day began; there has been nothing but bonfires and bell-ringing and feasting and shouting."

Mary's heart and bowels were buried at the Chapel Royal, St James's Palace, and her body at Westminster Abbey. Whilst many of our English monarchs were given elaborate tombs, Mary shares her final resting place with her half-sister and successor, Queen Elizabeth I, in Westminster Abbey.

It is Good Queen Bess's effigy that adorns the tomb and a Victorian inspection of the burial chamber revealed that Elizabeth's better quality coffin had been placed directly on top of Mary's. Even in death, Mary was overshadowed.

Chapter 38

Elizabeth I 1533–1603
Reign: 1558–1603

Good Queen Bess . . . Gloriana . . . The Virgin Queen . . . there have been many nicknames for one of our most illustrious monarchs who reigned over what has been called the Golden Age of England, but for almost 400 years she was officially known simply as Queen Elizabeth. Only in 1952, when a second Elizabeth came to the throne, was there a need for the Tudor monarch to be specified as Elizabeth I.

There are, in fact, many similarities between the two Elizabeths. Both became Queen at the age of 25. Both enjoyed very long reigns, and yet, at the time of their birth, neither Princess Elizabeth was expected to become Queen. Elizabeth I's motto was *Semper Eadem*, which means "Always the same", and one of Elizabeth II's enduring qualities is that she remains steadfastly and reassuringly the same. Both Queens devoted their lives to duty and service to their country, receiving the love and loyalty of their people, and both shared a strong faith in God. And when Elizabeth II opens Parliament each year, from the Imperial State Crown hang pear-shaped pearls reputed to have been worn by Elizabeth I.

Elizabeth Tudor was born at Greenwich Palace on 7 September, 1533, the daughter of King Henry VIII and his second wife Anne Boleyn. She was named after both her grandmothers, Elizabeth of York and Elizabeth Howard. Henry had divorced his first wife through her failure to produce a male heir, and now his second wife had given him a daughter. It was not long before he had his sights set on wife number three, Jane Seymour, and Anne Boleyn's days were numbered.

Elizabeth was not yet three years old when her mother was executed on trumped-up charges of adultery. On the day after Anne Boleyn's death, Henry VIII married Jane Seymour. Elizabeth and her older half-sister Mary were both declared illegitimate. As a young girl, she could not understand why she was suddenly called "Lady" Elizabeth when she had always been Princess Elizabeth. Although her father was distant and cool, Elizabeth remained devoted to him.

Much of her early childhood was divided between Hunsdon House and Hatfield House in Hertfordshire and she was cared for by Lady Margaret Bryan and later a governess called Catherine Champernowne, who began her education. The child was not treated like a member of the Royal Family and was allowed only simple food. Lady Bryan had to write to the King for new clothes for the girl, saying that she had no gowns, petticoats, nightclothes or linen of any kind, and was suffering greatly with her teeth.

When Elizabeth was four years old, Jane Seymour bore Henry VIII the son that he had so craved. Happy that the Tudor line was secure, his attitude appeared to soften towards his daughters, as Mary and Elizabeth were present at the christening in robes of state with long trains and took part in the service, with Elizabeth carrying a golden vessel of chrism for the baby to be anointed.

Elizabeth proved to be an intelligent girl from an early age and was a very quick learner. One courtier remarked that even if the child received no further education, she would still know more than some 40-year-olds. She learned to speak nine languages, including French, Spanish, Italian, Greek, Cornish and Welsh. She read the works of Cicero and the tragedies of Sophocles, was good at music and learned to play the virginals.

When Henry VIII married his sixth and final wife, Catherine Parr, Elizabeth was accepted back at court and lived at Whitehall Palace. She finally began to have a closer relationship with her father and it was probably the first time in her early life that she felt truly settled. Queen Catherine did much to make Elizabeth feel welcome.

At the time of Henry VIII's death in 1547 the direct line of succession was his three surviving children: Edward, Mary and Elizabeth, and so her half-brother became King Edward VI. It was not, however, to be an easy period for Elizabeth. She continued to live with her stepmother, Queen Catherine, who quickly remarried.

Her new husband, Lord Admiral Thomas Seymour, took an unhealthy interest in the teenage Elizabeth. He would come into her room in his nightclothes and her governess once caught him tickling and slapping

Elizabeth in bed. There were later false rumours that Elizabeth had a child by Seymour.

Queen Catherine soon sent Elizabeth to live in Cheshunt, under the care of Sir Anthony Denny, a confidant of Henry VIII, and his wife became Elizabeth's governess. Whether this move was at Elizabeth's request, we do not know. We do know, however, that when Thomas Seymour was eventually executed for treason, Elizabeth said: "This day died a man of much wit, but very little judgement". One of the charges against Seymour at his trial was that he had surreptitiously tried to marry Elizabeth after Catherine Parr's death.

Elizabeth's path to the throne seemed blocked when Edward VI named Lady Jane Grey as his successor. Had Jane been fully accepted as monarch after Edward's death, and gone on to have children of her own to succeed her, then Elizabeth would never have been Queen. But Jane reigned for just nine days before popular opinion turned in favour of Mary Tudor.

When Mary became Queen, Elizabeth rode beside her in the triumphal procession into London. But the relationship between the siblings deteriorated when Mary wanted to marry Philip of Spain. In 1554 there was a rebellion led by Sir Thomas Wyatt to try and prevent the wedding taking place. Mary was convinced that Elizabeth supported Wyatt's Rebellion and had her imprisoned in the Tower of London.

As Elizabeth was taken to Traitor's Gate by boat on Palm Sunday 1554, she said, "Here lands as true a subject, being prisoner, as ever landed at these stairs." With no concrete evidence to link Elizabeth with the rebellion, she was moved from the Tower after two months and put under house arrest at Woodstock in Oxfordshire for the next 10 months, guarded by Sir Henry Bedingfield.

Even out of the Tower of London, Elizabeth feared for her life, convinced that she would be executed, but continued to plead her innocence. On a windowpane at Woodstock Elizabeth scratched with her diamond ring:

"Much suspected by me, Nothing proved can be."

Mary eventually married Philip of Spain but continued to suspect that Elizabeth had plotted against her and so insisted that her sister remain a virtual prisoner at Woodstock. Elizabeth's letters were intercepted and she was even told which books she could and could not read. But the strong-willed Elizabeth played a game of cat and mouse, determined not to be cowed by her sister. She pretended to change her religion to Catholic to keep Mary happy, whilst remaining staunchly Protestant.

When Mary finally had Elizabeth released in April 1555 and allowed her to return to court, she was unhappy that Elizabeth appeared to show no signs of remorse. But Elizabeth felt that she was the injured party and had nothing to apologise for.

Elizabeth moved from court back to Hatfield House for the remainder of Mary's reign, although the icy relationship between the two sisters gradually began to thaw as the months went by. Mary visited her at Hatfield and they celebrated midsummer together at Richmond. The reconciliation was fortunate, as Mary officially named Elizabeth as her heir just as their father had wished.

When Mary died on 17 November, 1558, Elizabeth succeeded her half-sister and became Queen at the age of 25. "This is the Lord's doing; it is marvellous in our eyes," she said, quoting from the Psalms, when she discovered that she was Queen.

Her accession was proclaimed across the land to much rejoicing and at York the people were told that Elizabeth was "of no mingled blood of Spaniard, or stranger, but born mere English here among us." It was a sentiment that Elizabeth herself was proud of, once declaring to Parliament: "Was I not born in this realm? Were my parents born in any foreign country? Is there any cause I should alienate myself from being careful over this country? Is not my kingdom here?"

She was crowned at Westminster Abbey in January the following year. There was no Archbishop of Canterbury at the time, as Archbishop Reginald Pole had died during an influenza epidemic in England in November 1558, within hours of Elizabeth's accession. The Archbishop of York was a Catholic and refused to accept Elizabeth as supreme Head of the Church and so she was actually crowned by the Bishop of Carlisle. The Coronation was organised by Henry, Earl of Arundel, who became her Lord Steward. The Earl of Arundel today is the title of the elder son of the Duke of Norfolk, who lives at Arundel Castle, in West Sussex. The Duke, as Earl Marshal, is responsible for State occasions, including Coronations, and so the family tradition continues.

At Elizabeth's Coronation a blue carpet was woven for Westminster Abbey at a cost of £145. As the Queen walked over it, souvenir hunters cut pieces from it as keepsakes. The Duchess of Norfolk almost tripped on the mutilated cloth. Elizabeth's was the last Coronation to be conducted in Latin, and Bible passages were read in both Latin and English. Traditionally the Coronation ends with mass, but because the Bishop used some Roman Catholic rites that Elizabeth disapproved of, she withdrew in protest for parts of the service to a pew that had been curtained off.

Just as the church had dominated the reigns of Henry VIII, Edward VI and Mary I, so the young Queen Elizabeth faced many challenges. She had inherited a deeply divided church from her Catholic sister. Elizabeth was herself a Protestant, but was tolerant of the Catholic viewpoint, famously saying: "There is only one Christ Jesus, one faith, all else is trifles" and that she had "no desire to make windows into men's souls". Only four men were burned for heresy during her reign, considerably fewer than the hundreds that lost their lives during the reign of Mary I.

Nevertheless, she was determined that England would be a Protestant country as her father had wished. On 15 May, 1559 Bishops were required to take an Oath of Supremacy to their new Queen, but only one agreed. Elizabeth had the rest sent to the Tower to reconsider their position. Some 200 clergymen were also "retired". Mary Tudor's Act of 1554 which had restored the Catholic faith was repealed and Elizabeth appointed new Bishops. She also passed an Act of Uniformity, which allowed King Edward VI's second *Book of Common Prayer* to be used once again and most of his Articles of Religion were restored.

By reinstating her father's form of Protestantism, Elizabeth incurred the wrath of Pope Paul IV who did not accept her as Queen because Henry VIII had declared her to be illegitimate. Elizabeth overcame this by establishing the Anglican Church, with the sovereign as Supreme Governor. In 1563, the Thirty Nine Articles firmly laid out beliefs, doctrines and practices of the Church of England. Article 37 stated pointedly that the Pope had no jurisdiction in the realm of England.

Some opposed Elizabeth's style of worship, which we would now consider to be "Anglo-Catholic". They condemned any form of church ritual, ornamentation or clergy vestments, wanting worship to be restored to its original simplicity. They became known as Puritans. Some Puritans were followers of a French theologian and reformer called John Calvin, eventually adopting his theological views to become Calvinists.

Queen Elizabeth had no time for Puritans or Calvinists and did all she could to suppress them, wanting just one national church. In 1595, the then Archbishop of Canterbury, John Whitgift, drew up the Lambeth Articles – nine doctrinal statements to try and define Calvinism, which accepted a belief in Predestination.

The Articles stated that whether we can look forward to everlasting life or are condemned to eternal damnation is predestined and men can do nothing to change their path. Saving grace was not open to all, and Article Nine stated, "It is not in everyone's will and power to be saved."

The Lambeth Articles did not receive Royal Assent and Elizabeth was furious when she discovered that they had been discussed at a synod without her knowledge or consent. The Archbishop of Canterbury was ordered to withdraw and suppress the articles. Like her father before her, she had extremely strong views on religious practices, and people could actually be fined for not worshipping in the Protestant manner. The power of the Catholics began to fade.

One question that dogged Elizabeth throughout her reign was that of her marriage. Almost as soon as she became Queen, members of Parliament urged her to marry, but she refused, saying, "I have already joined myself in marriage to a husband, namely the Kingdom of England." She felt that she had to put her duty as Queen first, even if it meant sacrificing her personal happiness, and told a Parliamentary delegation, "It would please me best if, at the last, a marble stone shall record that this Queen having lived such and such a time, lived and died a virgin."

Although Elizabeth was known as the Virgin Queen, it does not mean that she was short of suitors. She had a succession of favourites at court throughout her reign, such as Robert Dudley, Earl of Leicester, of whom she once said, "You are like my little dog; when people see you, they know I am nearby."

Dudley's wife Amy Robsart was conveniently found dead at the foot of a stone staircase when he wished to court the Queen. Whether accident, suicide or murder, has never been proved. Dudley was said to be at Windsor with the Queen at the time and so could not be held personally responsible, but the mystery continues to be debated by historians to this day.

The closeness between the Queen and Dudley is shown in her request that he be made Lord Protector of England should she ever become seriously ill or incapacitated.

Christopher Hatton was another who attracted her attention when she watched him dancing at a court masque. She soon appointed him Captain of the Yeomen of the Guard, her personal bodyguards. He wrote passionate love letters to the Queen but, although she dallied with him, she rejected his advances as a possible husband.

She did, however, give him a knighthood, a house and eventually made him Lord Chancellor. When he coveted the London Palace of the Bishop of Ely, Elizabeth had no qualms about taking it way from the Bishop and giving it to Hatton. When the Bishop objected, she wrote to him saying, "Proud Prelate, you know what you were before I made you what you are now. If you do not immediately comply with my request, I will unfrock you, by God." The Bishop gave up the Palace! The former garden is an area of London now known as Hatton Garden.

Elizabeth seemed to enjoy receiving male attention, but always kept them at arm's length. Hatton was clearly one of the Queen's favourites and she visited him in his final illness and fed him with broth just days before his death. In 1583 he had the magnificent Holdenby House built in Northamptonshire, in which to entertain the Queen. He refused to spend a single night at Holdenby until Elizabeth had visited, although there is no record that she ever did. Said to be the largest house in Elizabethan England, the cost of building the house bankrupted him and Hatton died penniless.

Elizabeth had many suitors from overseas, including three Kings, several European Dukes and an Archduke. In 1559 her former brother-in-law Philip II of Spain sent Elizabeth a marriage proposal, but she could see that it was only for political alliance and said that she felt like a fly being drawn into a web, and quickly declined the offer. Yet she often played a diplomatic game when it suited her, looking as if she was on the verge of marriage, but never actually committed herself.

When she wanted to form an alliance with France, she was more than happy to begin a flirtatious courtship with Francis, Duke of Alençon, heir to the French throne. He was more than 20 years younger than her, stunted in height and disfigured as a result of smallpox. She publicly kissed him and gave him a ring. It looked as if he might be successful but at the last minute she told him that she had to put duty first and would have to sacrifice her own personal happiness for the welfare of her people.

It is generally considered that her dalliance with the Duke was simply to tease the Earl of Leicester, after she discovered that while still courting her he had secretly married Lettice Knollys, one of Elizabeth's Maids of the Privy Chamber. The Queen banished the Earl and his new wife from court, referring to Lettice as a "she wolf". Even seven years after the marriage, Leicester wrote that the Queen, "doth take every occasion by my marriage to withdraw any good from me".

The heroic Sir Walter Raleigh was another suitor. She teased him when he discovered tobacco, saying, "I suppose you would even say that you could tell the weight of that smoke of yours. There's no boundary to your impudence!" Raleigh insisted that he could, so she bet him a gold pin that he could not. Raleigh took on the challenge. He weighed out some tobacco, then smoked it in his pipe in front of her. He then weighed the ashes, telling her that the difference was the weight of the smoke. The Queen gave him her pin. "Many a man have I known who has turned his gold into smoke," she laughed, "but you are surely the first who has turned his smoke into gold!"

Uncertain of the Queen's feelings towards him, Raleigh wrote on a glass windowpane, "Fain would I climb, yet fear to fall." Underneath Elizabeth added, "If thy heart fail thee, then climb not at all." When it eventually became clear that the Queen had no intention of marrying him, Raleigh secretly wed her Maid of Honour, Bess Throckmorton instead. Again, Elizabeth was so angered by the slight, especially as Raleigh had continually denied that he was married, that she sent both husband and wife to the Tower and banished them from court on their release.

Finally, when in her late 50s, Elizabeth became infatuated with Robert Devereux, the Earl of Essex, step-son of her beloved Earl of Leicester. Soon he was seen riding beside the Queen as Master of the Horse, and he quickly rose to become a Privy Councillor and then Foreign Secretary. The much younger Essex enjoyed the Queen's favours; they often played cards through the night "until the birds sang in the morning" and he hoped that she would pay off his vast debts, but she refused. Elizabeth and Essex had a tempestuous relationship and once quarrelled over who was to become the new Lord Deputy of Ireland. She struck out, hitting him hard across the ear when he turned his back on her. The Queen soon forgave him and in 1599 Essex was sent across to Ireland with an army, initially to fight against those who opposed the English crown but in the end made a truce with rebel leaders, angering the Queen once again when it was rumoured that he hoped to become King of Ireland himself. When he visited her, they argued once more and he said that her mind was "as crooked as her carcass".

Essex then turned against the Queen and began to spread rumours that the throne was to be occupied by a Spaniard. He then claimed that he was going to seize the Queen and take control of the government himself. In February 1601 he set out up the Strand in London to Ludgate Hill with 100 men brandishing swords, trying to gain support, but was arrested and sent to the Tower of London. He was found guilty of treason and lost his head. Elizabeth was playing the virginals when news reached her that Essex had been executed. She paused briefly, then continued playing.

Whether Elizabeth really loved any of her suitors will remain an eternal mystery, but when Robert Dudley, Earl of Leicester, died in 1588, the Queen locked herself in her room and refused to come out. In the end the door had to be broken down. When she herself died, Dudley's final letter to her was found beside her bed.

Although Elizabeth came to the throne through an Act of Supremacy, because she was unmarried and without children to succeed, her cousin Mary, Queen of Scots, was considered to be her Heir Presumptive. Elizabeth lived with the continual fear that there might be a Catholic plot to put Mary on the throne of England in her place. Mary was a daughter of James IV of Scotland and a descendent of King Henry VII through his daughter Margaret. Mary became Queen of Scots when only a week old, on the death of her father.

She married the Dauphin of France at the age of just 15, eventually becoming Queen of France when her husband became King. She returned to Scotland on the death of her husband in 1560 and then married Henry Stewart, Lord Darnley (another grandchild of Henry VII through his daughter Margaret). Darnley was later murdered in Edinburgh following an explosion in the house where he was staying, although he appeared to have been strangled and his body bore no marks from the explosion.

In 1566 Mary gave birth to a son, who within a year became King James VI of Scotland when she was forced to stand down as Queen. When Elizabeth was informed about the birth, she said regretfully, "Alack, the Queen of Scots is lighter of a bonny son, and I am but of barren stock."

Mary married for a third time, taking the Earl of Bothwell as her next husband. He and Mary were soon implicated in the murder of Lord Darnley. Mary was imprisoned at Loch Leven Castle in 1567, and Parliament urged Elizabeth to have her executed. The Queen's response has been described as a masterpiece of diplomacy: "If I should say unto you that I meant not to grant your petition, by my faith I should say unto you more than perhaps I mean. And if I should say unto you I mean to grant your petition, I should tell you more than it is fit for you to know, and thus I must deliver you an answer answerless."

With the help of loyal supporters, Mary, Queen of Scots, was able to escape in 1568 and sought protection in England from her cousin Elizabeth. But the Queen continued to see her as a threat and Mary was imprisoned for the next 19 years.

During this time there were many unsuccessful plots to remove the "heretical" Queen Elizabeth and place Mary, Queen of Scots, on the English throne. One such was the Northern Rebellion of 1569, led by the Earls of Westmorland and Northumberland, but the rebels were defeated at Hunsdon. Elizabeth's own cousin, Thomas Howard, Duke of Norfolk, was involved with the plot and was executed.

When a conspiracy to have the Queen assassinated, known as Babington's Plot, was unearthed in Mary's household in 1586 Elizabeth reluctantly signed Mary's death warrant. The plot involved the invasion of England by the fleet of Philip II of Spain, its aim to kill the Queen and put Mary on the throne and restore the old Catholic religion to England, just as Elizabeth had long feared.

A complex series of coded letters to and from Mary were intercepted by Sir Francis Walsingham and the Queen of Scots's fate was sealed. Mary was tried and executed at Fotheringhay Castle in 1587. Signing her death warrant was a difficult decision for Elizabeth because she believed that anointed sovereigns, such as Mary, were answerable only to God.

Although the long-standing threat from Mary, Queen of Scots, and her supporters had finally ended, Elizabeth still faced hostility from other quarters. Throughout her reign she was eager to avoid war at all costs, but if England was ever under threat or an ally was in need, then her army and navy were sent into action.

France and Spain were the two great powers that were at odds with England at this time and both wanted supremacy of Europe. When Huguenots were massacred in France, an English army was sent out to protect French Protestants. Elizabeth also assisted the Spanish Netherlands (present-day Belgium) when the country wanted to break away from Spain and become independent.

The threat from the Spanish Armada in 1588 was perhaps Elizabeth's finest hour. She turned to God for help and composed a prayer: "O let Thine enemies know that Thou hast received England . . . into Thine own protection. Set a wall about it, O Lord, and evermore mightily defend it."

An Armada of 130 ships, with an estimated 8,000 sailors and 19,000 men at arms, arrived off the coast of England on 19 July. The English fleet, commanded by Lord Howard and Sir Francis Drake, quickly challenged the attack. England had only some 70 ships available at the time, smaller and less well equipped than the Spanish. Yet they had the advantage of speed and, being smaller, the Spanish galleons fired over them rather than at them. Spanish ships then became trapped in the Channel and could not easily turn round. 77 of them were sunk or set on fire by the English and the Spanish were defeated.

Philip II of Spain sent two further Armadas but both were defeated by the English weather and failed in their attempt to invade. It marked the point where Spanish domination diminished and England became the supreme power.

When the Spanish Armada was first sighted, beacons were lit across England, and Elizabeth rode out at Tilbury to encourage her troops, "I know I have the body of a weak and feeble woman, but I have the heart and stomach of a King, and a King of England too . . . I myself will take up arms; I myself will be your general, judge and recorder of every one of your virtues in the field." Not until Winston Churchill during World War II was England to hear such stirring rhetoric again.

The reign of Queen Elizabeth I is known as The Golden Age because under her rule England prospered. It was an age of adventure. Just as Elizabeth II's reign has seen great advances in technology, Elizabeth I's reign is noted for advances in discovery and colonisation.

Francis Drake circumnavigated the globe. Walter Raleigh founded a colony in America and called it Virginia in honour of the Queen. Trading settlements and colonies were set up around the world and the famous East India Company was formed.

Elizabeth was a great patron of the arts and her reign is noted for its music, paintings and literature. England's foremost playwright of the period was, of course, William Shakespeare, and Elizabeth I was present at performances of *A Midsummer Night's Dream*, *Love's Labour's Lost*, and both parts of *Henry IV*.

It is said that she commissioned him to write *The Merry Wives of Windsor*. The character of Falstaff was originally called Sir John Oldcastle, but as there were descendants of the Oldcastle family still at court, it is said that Elizabeth instructed Shakespeare to change the name.

The poet Edmund Spenser praised Elizabeth in his allegorical poem *The Faerie Queene*, which he dedicated to her, said then to be one of the longest poems ever written in the English language. Elizabeth granted Spenser a pension of £50 a year for life. Many other Elizabethan writers are still known and loved to this day: Christopher Marlowe, Francis Bacon and Ben Jonson, and the music of composers such as William Byrd, Thomas Campion, John Dowland, Orlando Gibbons and Thomas Tallis lives on.

This Sweet and Merry Month of May is a madrigal composed by Byrd in honour of the Queen and she often had as many as 70 musicians at court to entertain her.

Just as Queen Elizabeth II has been credited with initiating the Royal walkabout, Queen Elizabeth I was skilled at making stately progresses across England so that she could be seen by her people. Many a Tudor stately home boasts that "Queen Elizabeth slept here".

She spent several months each year touring the country so that she could be seen by her people and many an aristocrat was almost bankrupted, spending their fortunes on extending their homes, improving the decorations, and buying vast quantities of food and drink in the hope that the Queen would decide to visit. She travelled with a large retinue and would ride slowly through towns, often stopping to speak to the people.

The long list of towns and cities that she visited included St Alban's, Cambridge, Canterbury, Bristol, Norwich, Coventry, Southampton, Chatham, Dartford, Chichester, Gravesend, Hertford, Huntingdon, Bury St Edmunds, Yarmouth, Salisbury, Rochester, Colchester, Ipswich, Lincoln and Oxford to name but a few.

It was pure theatre, showing the magnificence and splendour of the monarchy. And in an age before television, film, photography or the internet, we can only imagine what effect the Queen's glittering arrival had on the ordinary people who crowded the streets to see her for the first time. At each venue she was given gifts, which always included a pair of gloves.

She amassed hundreds of pairs, and several still exist and are on display at locations such as Hatfield House, the Victoria and Albert Museum, Dents Glove Museum, and the Ashmolean Museum in Oxford.

Always ornately dressed and smothered in jewels, Elizabeth was clothed majestically as she felt befitted a Queen of England. Her often over-elaborate dress in adulthood may have been a reaction to her childhood apparel when she was forced to wear simple clothes and had a very limited wardrobe.

When she first became Queen she remarked, "I like silk stockings so well because they are pleasant and fine and delicate, and henceforth I shall wear no more cloth stockings." Records were kept by her dressers recording the Queen's Wardrobe of Robes and at the time of her death she owned some 2,000 dresses. She frequently gave her cast offs to the ladies of her court and a piece of one of these dresses may still exist.

In May 2016 it was reported that the Historic Royal Palaces has concluded that a section of elaborately embroidered silver cloth hanging in a glass case at St Faith's Church, Bacton in Herefordshire, and formerly used as an altar cloth, is a piece of one of Queen Elizabeth I's gowns. It came to the church through Blanche Parry of Bacton, the Queen's Chief Gentlewoman of the Bedchamber who was in royal service for 57 years.

The importance that Elizabeth placed on clothes can be seen in the series of Statutes of Apparel that she introduced, in which she laid down laws as to what people could and could not wear, from the size of ruff around their neck to the colour of garments.

Sumptuous materials such as velvet, satins, damask and embroidered silk could only be worn by certain sections of the nobility to denote rank, and only the monarch could wear purple or cloth of gold. Anyone caught wearing the wrong garments or materials could be fined.

We have a good idea of Elizabeth's appearance from the many paintings of her that survive. In 2016 campaigners prevented one portrait of her being sold abroad. Painted in 1590 to commemorate England's victory over the Spanish Armada, it had been owned by descendants of Sir Frances Drake, but now hangs at the Queen's House in Greenwich where Elizabeth was born.

Early portraits of Elizabeth show her as a fresh-faced girl with auburn hair, but in 1562 she caught smallpox, from which she almost died. Her skin was badly scarred as a result and she afterwards used a make-up made from powdered eggshells, borax, alum, white lead and vinegar.

In old age her teeth blackened and her hair thinned and she took to wearing auburn wigs. It is said that she refused to have mirrors in any of her rooms and when she appeared in public she padded out her mouth with cotton to hide gaps where her teeth were missing and her face had sunk.

In character, Elizabeth was a strong woman who spoke her mind. She frequently swore and cursed when angry, and she would hurl objects across a room at courtiers who displeased her, telling them that they would soon be shorter by a head. One of her godsons, Sir John Harington, revealed, "When she smiled, it was pure sunshine that everyone chose to bask in, if they could. But anon came a storm from a sudden gathering of clouds, and the thunder fell in wondrous manner on all alike."

She could be superior and haughty. When she had a difference of opinion with her advisor William Cecil, Lord Burghley, she chided him with, "I have been strong enough to lift you out of this dirt and I am still able to cast you down again!"

But she remained loyal to courtiers who were faithful to her and Burghley was her Private Secretary and Secretary of State from her accession until his death 40 years later. Any tensions between them quickly disappeared. "My Lord, we make use of you, not for your bad legs, but for your good head," she teased him when he was suffering from gout in old age.

Shortly before her death, Queen Elizabeth I made a final speech to Parliament which tells us much about her character.

"Though God hath raised me high, yet this I count the glory of my Crown, that I have reigned with your loves," she told them. "This makes me that I do not so much rejoice that God hath made me to be a Queen, as to be a Queen over so thankful a people . . . I know the title of a King is a glorious title but assure yourself that the shining glory of princely authority hath not so dazzled the eyes of our understanding, but that we well know and remember that we also are to yield an account of our actions before the great judge. To be a king and wear a crown is a thing more glorious to them that see it than it is pleasant to them that bear it.

"For myself I was never so much enticed with the glorious name of a King or royal authority of a Queen as delighted that God hath made me his instrument to maintain his truth and glory and to defend his kingdom as I said from peril, dishonour, tyranny and oppression. There will never Queen sit in my seat with more zeal to my country, care to my subjects and that will sooner with willingness venture her life for your good and safety than myself.

"For it is my desire to live nor reign no longer than my life and reign shall be for your good. And though you have had, and may have, many princes more mighty and wise sitting in this seat, yet you never had nor shall have, any that will be more careful and loving."

It is a speech that could today just as easily be made by the second Queen Elizabeth.

In January 1603 Elizabeth caught a bad cold, which she found hard to shake off. By February she appeared to be recovering, but then became ill again. It is said that she declined medical intervention and often refused to go to bed. When Robert Cecil, Earl of Salisbury, who had taken over the duties of his father Lord Burghley, told her that she must go to bed, Elizabeth famously retorted, "Must? Is must a word to be used to Princes? Little man, little man, thy father, if he had been alive, durst not have used that word."

Towards the end she stood unaided for 15 hours, determined not to give in, until she was forced into bed through sheer exhaustion.

Elizabeth I, the last of our Tudor monarchs, died at the age of 69 at 3am on 24 March, 1603 at Richmond Palace. It is thought that she died of pneumonia and possibly blood poisoning. Her last words are reputed to be, "All my possessions for one moment in time."

Her funeral took place on 28 April, 1603 and she was buried at Westminster Abbey. An 18th-century copy of the funeral effigy carried on her coffin can be seen there today, complete with its original Elizabethan corset.

Elizabeth had not named a successor and by 24 March she had lost the power of speech through tonsillitis. Surrounded by members of her Council, she silently indicated that her third cousin, James VI of Scotland, was to become the next King of England.

When she died, her coronation ring was taken straight to Scotland to be handed over to the new King. She had worn it for 44 years and only in the final days of her life was it cut from her hand, having become too painful as it dug into her flesh. Deeply superstitious, Elizabeth knew when the ring was removed that her days were over.

Chapter 39

James I 1566–1625
Reign: 1603–1625

When Queen Elizabeth I died in 1603, it not only marked the close of a long reign of some 44 years, but also ended the rule of the House of Tudor on the throne of England. Her successor was the first of our Stuart kings and unusual in that he had been a monarch for 36 years before he became King of England.

James was the only surviving child of Mary, Queen of Scots, who had succeeded her father as Queen of Scotland when she was just six days old and married Francis II of France when she was not quite 16. During her time in France she changed the spelling of the Royal House from "Stewart" to the French "Stuart". Following the death of Francis from an infection after only two and a half years of marriage, Mary married again, taking her cousin Henry Stewart, Lord Darnley, as her second husband in July 1565.

Within less than a year Mary gave birth to a son at Edinburgh Castle on 19 June, 1566. Christened James Charles at Stirling Castle, he was known as the Duke of Rothesay and Prince and Great Steward of Scotland from birth. On the death of his father eight months later, he succeeded as Duke of Albany, Earl of Ross and Baron Ardmannoch.

The young boy faced a troubled childhood. Before he was even born, the marriage of Mary and Darnley had become rocky and quickly foundered. She turned to her Italian private secretary, David Rizzio, for comfort. With Mary six months pregnant, Darnley became jealous by court gossip that the baby was not his and the hapless Italian was soon stabbed to death. Darnley and a group of men led by Patrick, Lord Ruthven, forced their way into

Mary's private dining-room and demanded that she handed over David Rizzio, who was hiding behind the Queen as she attempted to shield him. Rizzio was seized and stabbed 56 times before being thrown downstairs.

Although Darnley swore that he had not inflicted any of the wounds, his dagger was left in Rizzio's side. Mary could not forgive her husband's treachery and within a few months Darnley was himself killed in an explosion at the Provost's House, Kirk o'Field in Edinburgh, where the cellars had been packed with barrels of gunpowder.

Although Mary was likely to have instigated the murder, it remains to this day one of Scotland's unsolved mysteries. Across the centuries many historians believe that Patrick Hepburn, Earl of Bothwell, was the perpetrator and there were rumours that he was seen with a blackened face immediately after the explosion. Two months later Mary, Queen of Scots, married for a third time . . . to the Earl of Bothwell, the man who had probably killed her husband.

It was into this dark world of intrigue, scandal and murder that James was born. Throughout his life he was dogged by persistent rumours that his father was David Rizzio rather than Lord Darnley and he was nicknamed "the British Solomon" as Solomon in the Bible was the son of David.

Mary was forced to abdicate as Queen of Scots in favour of her baby son. She was imprisoned at Loch Leven Castle, eventually escaping with the help of her gaoler and fleeing to England, where she was held prisoner for 19 years. James never saw his mother again.

So it was that the 13-month old boy became King James VI of Scotland on 24 July, 1567. A Coronation ceremony was held at the Church of Holy Rood, Stirling, on 29 July. With a mother in prison and his father murdered, James was brought up by the Earl and Countess of Mar, John Erskine and his wife Annabella, who became his guardians.

The Earl of Mar saw that James's education began early and he had various tutors, notably George Buchanan, a staunch Presbyterian who had no qualms in beating the child to ensure that he worked hard at his lessons. Buchanan believed in the maxim "Spare the rod and spoil the child". But James was diligent in his studies and by the age of 10 had a remarkable grasp of Latin and French, studied the classics and loved literature.

Because of his extreme youth, James had four Regents to rule until he came of age. Firstly, his uncle James Stewart, Earl of Moray, who was assassinated on 23 January, 1570; followed by his grandfather Matthew Stewart, Earl of Lennox, who was killed in 1571 during a scuffle in Parliament with some of Mary's supporters. James's guardian John Erskine,

Earl of Mar, became the third Regent, but died within a year, supposedly poisoned during a dinner party.

Finally, James Douglas, Earl of Morton, became Regent, but he was eventually arrested and executed for having been involved in the murder of Lord Darnley. Morton had himself introduced the "Maiden" to Scotland, an early form of guillotine for executions. Ironically, Morton's own life was brought to a swift end by the same Scottish maiden.

While James's Regents clearly had little luck, the King was not completely immune from danger, either. At the age of 16 he was kidnapped by William Ruthven, 1st Earl of Gowrie, and held prisoner in various houses for 11 months before being rescued by his supporters. Known now as the Ruthven Raid, the aim was to try and influence the way matters were governed in Scotland, to quash any pro-Catholic stance, and prevent the possibility of Mary, Queen of Scots, ever returning to the throne.

Once released, the now 17-year-old King decided to take control and rule the country himself, as Regencies had clearly been unsuccessful. But the Gowrie family were not prepared to give up and five years later they plotted to kill James.

The King and his retinue were out hunting in August 1600 when they were approached by Alexander Ruthven, brother of the 3rd Earl of Gowrie. He said that a stranger with a large quantity of gold had been detained at Gowrie House in Perth and urged the King to go and interrogate the man himself to discover who he was and where then money had come from.

Although James was suspicious, he eventually agreed to make his way to Perth with a few of his entourage. When he arrived, he soon realised that he had fallen into a trap and his life was threatened. The King was rescued by his bodyguards and John Ruthven, 3rd Earl of Gowrie, and his brother Alexander, were killed in the ensuing fight. The Gowrie family later gave a different version of events, but James always maintained that it had been a deliberate assassination attempt.

In the year that James reached the age of 21, Queen Elizabeth I consented to the execution of Mary, Queen of Scots, after the Babington Plot was uncovered. Despite this, James remained on good terms with the English Queen, who was also his godmother. In 1586 she had granted him an annual income of £4,000 and perhaps he feared she might stop payments if he reacted badly to the execution of his mother.

When England was threatened by the Spanish Armada in 1588, James wrote to Elizabeth offering his support and, in 1603, as she was dying, she eventually indicated that she wanted him as her successor.

Although Scottish by birth, James was a great-grandson of Margaret Tudor, the English wife of James IV of Scotland and eldest sister of Henry VIII of England. Margaret Tudor was the grandmother of both Mary, Queen of Scots and Lord Darnley, and through her James was an heir to the English throne. Darnley's mother was a granddaughter of Henry VII; Mary, Queen of Scots, was a niece of Henry VIII and a cousin to Elizabeth I, and so James had strong family ties to England.

When Queen Elizabeth I died a messenger rode on horseback for three days, a journey of some 400 miles, from London to Edinburgh with Elizabeth's Coronation ring to tell James that he was now also King of England.

Although a monarch already, James had very little money because of his extravagant lifestyle. He eventually crossed the Border and headed south, but by the time he reached York his funds had run out and he wrote to the Privy Council for money so that he could make his entry into London with all the pomp and ceremony that people would expect of their new King.

On the way south he visited many country houses, notably Theobalds House in Hertfordshire which belonged to Sir Robert Cecil. James liked it so much that he bought it! He also bestowed some 300 new knighthoods during his progress. His granting of favours, and sometimes the sale of titles, frequently caused him trouble amid claims of corruption.

James finally arrived in London on 7 May and received an enthusiastic welcome from the people, who were pleased to have him in the capital at last and relieved that it had been a smooth transition from one monarch to another. It was not a novice ascending the throne either, but a man who had been a king since infancy, and so he came with experience. He was crowned King James I of England on 25 July, 1603, at Westminster Abbey, with a Coronation that cost over £20,000.

The early optimism felt by courtiers and government ministers soon began to wane when they discovered the contrast between the grand, imperious Queen Elizabeth I and the somewhat vulgar behaviour of the new King, who drank excessively and thought nothing of speaking his mind in a crude and earthy manner. Because he was so outspoken he became known as "the wisest fool in Christendom" and a clergyman once referred to the King in a sermon as "God's silly vassal".

As James matured, he had become self-centred and pedantic. He was brought up with the firm belief that kings were chosen by God and had a divine right to rule. He refused to consider himself a constitutional monarch, a servant of the people. Unlike our Parliament, with a House of Commons and a House of Lords, the Scottish Parliament of James's time had only one chamber and he was in total control.

On 21 March, 1609, he made a speech to the English Parliament declaring: "The state of monarchy is the supremest thing upon earth; for Kings are not only God's lieutenants and sit upon a throne, but even by God himself they are called gods; as to dispute what God may do is blasphemy, so it is sedition in subjects to dispute what a King may do in the height of his power."

This inflammatory statement helps us to understand James's character and behaviour, as he clearly thought he was on a par with God. On another occasion he told Parliament: "If you consider the attributes of God, you shall see how they agree in the person of a King. God hath power to create or destroy; make or unmake at his pleasure; to give life or send death; to judge all and be judged not accountable to none; to raise low things and to make high things low at his pleasure. And the like power have Kings."

By the time he became King of England at the age of 36 James was described as "portly", of medium height, balding, with a brown beard and piercing blue eyes. His tongue was said to be "too large for his mouth, which ever made him speak full in the mouth, and made him drink very uncomely" and his Scottish accent proved difficult for some of the English courtiers to comprehend.

His physician, Sir Theodore Mayerne, recorded that "King James's legs were slender, scarcely strong enough to carry his body." Adding that the King was "very clumsy in his riding and hunting, and frequently met with accidents." Sir Anthony Weldon, Clerk of the Green Cloth (responsible for royal household accounts and organisation of the King's travel), wrote: "He was of middle stature, more corpulent through his clothes than his body, yet fat enough; his clothes ever being made large and easy, the doublets quilted for stiletto proof, his breeches in great pleats and well-stuffed."

As King of Scotland and England, James was the first monarch to rule both countries. He tried to smooth over antagonistic attitudes of the past and nurture a friendship between the two nations. James really wanted to unify the country into one Britain with a single Parliament, but the Commons refused to grant the Scots equal rights and so they continued to have their own separate Parliament and judiciary. Ireland was also part of his realm and James styled himself "King of Great Britain and Ireland", even though he was told by Sir Francis Bacon that it was not an acceptable title in law.

As a result of his belief in the divine right of kings, James always had a difficult relationship with his government. His first Parliament sat from 1604 to 1611, overseen by Elizabeth I's chief minister Sir Robert Cecil, Lord Salisbury. But a second Parliament sat for just six weeks in 1614 and is known as the Addled Parliament, as virtually nothing happened.

Dissolving Parliament that year James said, "I am surprised that my ancestors should have permitted such an institution to come into existence", telling his son, the future Charles I, that he would live to have his "bellyful of Parliament". From 1612 until his death, James virtually ruled alone, making Parliament increasingly insignificant. Parliament at the time took a very staunch anti-Catholic and anti-Spanish stance due to long wars with Spain, so when James wanted his son and heir, Charles, to marry the Spanish Infanta it did not go down well and the plan was rejected by the Commons.

Parliament also rejected the King's notion that he had a right to imprison any MPs who disagreed with him. James immediately had some MPs arrested.

England was not a rich country at this time and when James came to the throne the exchequer had debts of over £400,000 due to costly wars of the past. James himself was extravagant with money and wanted Parliament to grant him a regular fixed income. Sir Robert Cecil, tried to push various schemes before Parliament to reduce the annual deficit and also increase royal revenue, but was continually thwarted.

In 1610 the Great Contract was proposed, in which the King would surrender his feudal rights in exchange for having all his debts paid off and receive an annual income of £200,000. This idea was not accepted by Parliament. He was told in no uncertain terms that he could not "draw honey out of gall".

Nearly a century was to pass before James's scheme came into being, by which time it was called the Civil List, in which the monarch gave to the Treasury all the income from the extensive Crown Estates in return for a fixed income to cover the cost of the Sovereign's official duties, travel, staff wages and upkeep of properties connected with public engagements and ceremonies.

Without such a scheme in his lifetime, James had to resort to other measures to cover his expenses, which is why he began to sell titles. In 1611 he created the new rank of Baronet purely to raise money.

Despite enmity with the English Parliament, James had a successful foreign policy and encouraged his chief ministers to negotiate a peace treaty with Spain in August 1604, bringing an end to the Anglo-Spanish War, an intermittent conflict that had gone on between England and Spain since 1585.

James's plan to marry his son Charles, the Prince of Wales, to the Spanish Infanta, Maria Anna, was for two reasons. It would not only secure a friendly relationship between the two countries, but the Infanta would bring with her money in the form of a large dowry. Talks went on for years but came to nothing as the English government was opposed to the union.

By 1621 there was a demand from Parliament for Charles to marry a Protestant, which would then make the Catholic Infanta ineligible. When Spain invaded the Rhineland territory of James's son-in-law, Frederick V, Elector Palatine, there was a petition for England to go to war with Spain. James told ministers not to interfere and promptly dissolved Parliament.

James was himself a Protestant and, just as his predecessors had reigns dominated by religious matters, he faced equal turmoil. The Puritan movement wanted to simplify all Church of England services and remove anything ceremonial that appeared to be too Catholic. Any kind of ornamentation was frowned upon, even down to wedding rings. Puritans wanted to do away with the episcopacy altogether, famously causing James to say, "No Bishop, no King".

In Scotland he introduced the Five Articles of Perth, which enforced Anglican practices north of the border. In England there were three Catholic plots to remove him from the throne in the first years of his reign. The Bye Plot in 1603 was a conspiracy between some Catholic priests and Puritans to kidnap the King. The Main Plot that same year aimed to remove the King altogether and put his cousin Lady Arbella Stuart (sometimes known as Arabella) on the throne. She was a great-great granddaughter of Henry VII and in the line of succession, but she exposed the plot herself to James, as she had no ambition to be Queen.

The most famous of all, of course, was the Gunpowder Plot of 1605. Planned by Robert Catesby and a group of Catholic conspirators, a Yorkshire soldier named Guy Fawkes was sent to blow up the House of Lords during the State Opening of Parliament on 5 November. If it had been successful, the results would have been catastrophic. Sir Edward Hoby, a Gentleman of the Bedchamber, wrote: "The plot was to have blown up the King at such a time as he should have been sat in his royal throne, accompanied by his children, Nobility and Commons and with all Bishops, Judges and Doctors at one instant and the blast to have ruined the whole estate and Kingdom of England."

The elaborate plan involved the conspirators renting a house opposite the Houses of Parliament, from which they secretly built a tunnel into the cellars and deposited over "30 barrels of gunpowder, with a great store of wood, faggots and bars of iron", which would have caused a devastating explosion if ignited.

The plot was thwarted when one of the conspirators, Francis Tresham, sent a letter to his brother-in-law Baron Monteagle to warn him not to attend the State Opening of Parliament. Monteagle showed the unsigned letter to Sir Robert Cecil. As a result, guards searched the cellars and discovered the barrels being guarded by Guy Fawkes. The conspirators were tracked down and Catesby was killed in a subsequent siege. Guy Fawkes was arrested, tried, found guilty and executed.

Although the Gunpowder Plot was unsuccessful, it shook James's confidence and he feared for his life. A Venetian Ambassador observed, "The King . . . does not appear, nor does he take his meals in public as usual. He lives in the innermost rooms with only Scotsmen about him." It is highly likely that James dwelled on the fact that his own father had been deliberately killed by gunpowder.

With all the divisions that existed within the church, one lasting benefit came during the reign when in 1604 James authorised a new translation of the Bible into English, as people had come to challenge some of the translations in Henry VIII's Great Bible of 1535. Now known as the Authorised Version or the King James Bible, the mammoth task was undertaken by 47 scholars, who each produced their own translation.

All the translations were compared to produce one single draft. This was then revised by the Bishops and the King's Council, before the final edition was passed on to the King himself for approval. It was published in 1611 and, although it has been further revised across the centuries, it remains a much-loved translation of the Bible to this day and is said to be one of the most influential books ever published in the English language. The book was printed by Robert Barker, whose father had been Elizabeth I's official printer.

The first printings contained many mistakes and were said to be in poor quality ink, but Barker had to cover all the financial costs of production himself, which may explain the reason. He later received unexpected notoriety in 1631 when a glaring error was spotted in the Ten Commandments. Barker had unwittingly omitted the word "not" from the Commandment "Thou shalt not commit adultery"! This edition has become known as "The Wicked Bible" and although all copies were ordered to be burned, eleven are rumoured to survive. Barker was fined £300, many thousands of pounds in today's money, and was later imprisoned.

James had a turbulent reign in both Scotland and England and he had an equally tempestuous private life. Because it was essential that he produced heirs to continue the Stuart line he married Anne, daughter of King Frederick II of Denmark and Norway. They were married by proxy in August 1589 at Kronberg Castle, Copenhagen, and then in person on 23 November at Oslo and in a final ceremony at Kronberg Castle on 21 January, 1590. She was 15 and he was 23.

It was said to be a marriage of convenience and they were soon living separate lives. Queen Anne had a home of her own at Somerset House in The Strand, which was renamed Denmark House during her occupancy and her main interests seemed to be clothes and jewellery. She was a Lutheran when they wed, but converted to Catholicism after the marriage, which was something of a snub to her Protestant husband.

"Yet they did love as well as man and wife could do, not conversing together," wrote Godfrey Goodman.

Queen Anne became seriously ill in 1617, but James only visited her three times in the last two years of her life and not at all as she lay dying. Neither did he attend her funeral in 1619, although was said to be "overcome with melancholy" after her death.

The couple had three sons and four daughters. Queen Anne also suffered several miscarriages and had two stillborn children. The eldest son, Henry, Prince of Wales, died of typhoid at the age of 18. The second surviving son, Charles, Duke of York, later succeeded his father as King Charles I. Their only daughter to survive into adulthood, Elizabeth, married Frederick V, Elector Palatine, eventually becoming King and Queen of Bohemia, considered to be the most glamorous couple of their time. Elizabeth is known as the "Winter Queen" and her grandson became George I of England, our first Hanover monarch.

Away from his wife, King James I had a number of favourites at court and formed strong emotional attachments to several men. Two principal favourites were Robert Carr and George Villiers.

Carr was first spotted by the King at a tilting match – mock combat between two armoured knights on horseback – when Carr broke his leg.

Thomas Howard, 1st Earl of Suffolk, recorded that James took an instant liking to the young man and nursed him during his injury. The King soon gave Carr a knighthood and Sherborne Castle, which had been built by Sir Walter Raleigh. In 1611 James made him Viscount Rochester and later a

Privy Councillor, and on the death of Sir Robert Cecil in the following year, Carr took over the position as the King's chief minister. He was not considered suited to the role and proved to be corrupt. Yet in 1613 James created him 1st Earl of Somerset and made him Treasurer of Scotland.

Three years later Carr was tried and found guilty of the murder of Sir Thomas Overbury, his secretary and adviser, although it was originally reported that Overbury had died of natural causes. Carr had decided to marry Frances Howard, wife of the Earl of Essex, and arranged for mutual friend Overbury to try and obtain her a divorce.

Overbury, however, concluded that Frances was suitable "as a mistress but not as a wife". In the end she managed to obtain a divorce herself and Overbury was mysteriously poisoned. When rumours of the murder became widespread Frances pleaded guilty, yet both she and Carr were imprisoned for the crime.

By this time Carr and the King had fallen out, so James had no interest in supporting his former favourite. Carr remained imprisoned in the Tower of London until 1622, although was eventually pardoned.

The King now had a new favourite, George Villiers. Born in Brooksby, Leicestershire, where his family had lived since the 13th century and were described as "minor gentry of Norman stock". His father was a prosperous sheep farmer. George first came to the King's attention when he was a handsome 21-year-old taking part in a hunt at Apethorpe Palace, Northamptonshire, which was then a royal residence.

Many in the King's circle were critical of the influence that Robert Carr had over the monarch and saw Villiers as a possible distraction. He was appointed Royal Cupbearer, serving drinks to the royal table, which was then a very trusted position within the household because it was essential that no-one tried to poison the King.

Clergyman Godfrey Goodman, who eventually became Bishop of Gloucester, described Villiers as, "the handsomest-bodied man in all of England, his limbs so well compacted", and soon he became a dancer in masques to entertain the King. In 1615 Villiers was knighted as a Gentleman of the Bedchamber and by 1616 had become the favoured one. He was soon given peerages to become Baron Whaddon and Viscount Villiers, and was eventually made Earl of Buckingham.

"Never any man in any age, nor, I believe, in any country," wrote Edward Hyde, 1st Earl of Clarendon, "rose in so short a time to so much greatness of honour, power, or fortune, upon no other advantage or recommendation than of the beauty or gracefulness of his person."

More competent than Carr, Villiers greatly influenced the King, such as in forming a Spanish alliance and raising taxes in England to increase revenue. But he took advantage of his position and was unpopular with Parliament. He took a particular interest in Irish affairs, which included the sale of Irish titles, and with the money he bought land and properties for himself.

It was said that he made the King laugh and James referred to Villiers as "my sweet child and wife", writing that he wore his portrait "in a blue ribbon under my waistcoat, next to my heart." His nickname for Villiers was "Steenie" after St Stephen who was described as having "the face of an angel".

Villiers continued to be honoured and was elevated to Marquis in 1618, and finally Duke of Buckingham in 1623. He was also a Knight of the Garter, Master of the King's Horses, and Lord Admiral of the Fleet. The fact that Villiers was a Catholic seemed not to bother the Protestant monarch, although it antagonised Parliament.

Despite the discord that seemed to dog the life and reign of James I, the period had its positive side. It was a time when the first British colonies were founded in America at Jamestown, Virginia, in 1607; Newfoundland in 1610 and in 1620 the Pilgrim Fathers departed from Plymouth, Devon, for a new start in America where they set up the colony of Plymouth, Massachusetts. It was soon thriving economically and today Plymouth is known historically as America's Hometown and is the oldest municipality in New England. Although the Pilgrims left England because of divisions within the church, good eventually came from it.

Just as the arts had flourished under Elizabeth I, so James I was a great patron. Shakespeare continued to write during the reign, notably *King Lear*, *Macbeth* and *The Tempest*, and his sonnets were published for the first time. England's greatest playwright died in 1616 and that same year George Chapman completed his translations of Homer's *Iliad* and *Odyssey* into English, making them available and accessible to all.

There were many notable poets who were prominent during the reign, particularly John Donne, although James was less appreciative of his works than some. Of the poetry of John Donne, then Dean of St Paul's, James said, "Dr Donne's verses are like the peace of God; they pass all understanding!"

James was himself an author, writing poems and works expounding his views on politics and religion, which included *Basilikon Doron* on the art of Kingship and *Daemonologie* about witchcraft and devil worship, which he considered to be a form of religion. In his younger days he had taken a particular interest in witchcraft and attended the North Berwick witch trials, when women were first persecuted in Scotland for being witches. As he grew older, he became very anti black magic, particularly after people were convicted of sending storms to sink one of his ships.

Intriguingly, he hated smoking and in 1604 wrote *A Counterblast to Tobacco*, in which he condemned the practice as "A custom loathsome to the eye, hateful to the nose, harmful to the brain, dangerous to the lungs and in the black, stinking fume thereof, resembling the horrible Stygian smoke of the pit that is bottomless."

Like his predecessors James appreciated art and added to the royal collection. He also founded the Mortlake Tapestry Works in Surrey, where Flemish workers from Brussels and Belgium were brought over to weave tapestries. James was particularly fond of the style of Dutch painters. Flemish Paul Van Somer was commissioned to paint a full-length portrait of the King in his Coronation robes which now hangs in the Queen's drawing-room at Windsor Castle. A less ostentatious re-interpretation of this portrait was later painted by Anthony Van Dyck and hangs in St George's Hall. He not only appreciated Dutch art, but brought in experts in dykes and ditches from Holland to start draining parts of East Anglia to create arable land.

James's reign today is referred to as the Jacobean era, a name given to the arts, literature and architecture of the period. Jacobean furniture is particularly identifiable, with its rich, deep colours and intricate designs, often containing other materials that had now become more easily available, such as mother-of-pearl inlays.

Architecture became increasingly classical in style and England's most prominent architect of the day was Inigo Jones, who designed such buildings as the Banqueting House in Whitehall, the Queen's House in Greenwich, St Paul's Covent Garden, and Wilton House in Salisbury. He also remodelled the front of the old St Paul's Cathedral, later destroyed during the Great Fire of London.

In the final years of his life James showed signs of dementia, and suffered from kidney disease and arthritis. His son and heir Charles effectively ruled for the last year, assisted by the Duke of Buckingham. The pair went to Madrid to continue the long negotiations for securing the Spanish Infanta as a bride for Charles, but failed spectacularly. The Spanish ambassador actually asked for Buckingham to be executed as a result, while Buckingham demanded that England declare war on Spain!

Just weeks before James's death a marriage treaty with the French was drawn up instead, agreeing that Charles could marry Henrietta Maria, daughter of King Henry IV of France. Although this solved the Spanish situation, the fact that she was a Catholic was to lead to more problems in the future.

After suffering a stroke two days earlier, James died "in the distressing throes of dysentery" at his favourite country home Theobalds House, near Hatfield, Hertfordshire, on 27 March, 1625, at the age of 58. The Duke of Buckingham was at his bedside. He was buried in Westminster Abbey. His reign of Scotland had lasted 57 years and he had been King of England for 22 years.

There is one little known reminder of King James I today in the garden of Buckingham Palace. A lover of silk, James ordered thousands of mulberry trees from France for silkworms to feast on in the hope of having the monopoly on silk production in England.

He had them planted on land that now forms the garden of Buckingham Palace and the surrounding areas, and a street in Chelsea is still called Mulberry Walk because of this. Unfortunately, he ordered the wrong variety, with tough leaves that did not appeal to the silkworms and so the project failed. But a centuries-old descendant of one of his original trees is said to remain in the garden. In the year 2000 our present Queen had 29 different species of mulberry tree planted throughout the garden and is now holder of the National Collection. Her Majesty has had greater horticultural success than her ancestor, although complains that the birds eat most of her mulberries!

Chapter 40

Charles I 1600–1649
Reign: 1625–1649

As crowds jostle daily along London's Whitehall, going about their business, few people probably glance up to see the small bust of an English monarch above the entrance to the Banqueting House, all that now remains of a former Royal Palace. But on 30 January every year King Charles I, whose bust gazes down, is remembered with a service at the building from which he was led out on to a temporary wooden scaffold to become the only King of England to be publicly executed.

During the mass, which is organised by the Society of King Charles the Martyr, relics of the King are laid on the altar for veneration and a choir, usually from King's College, Cambridge, sings in his honour. The English Civil War Society also mounts a parade on the Sunday nearest to the anniversary of his death, following the route of Charles's final journey from St James's Palace, across Horse Guards Parade to Whitehall, where a wreath is laid and a service takes place at the site of his execution. Similar commemorative events and observances of his Feast Day are held across the country.

For his firm resolve to keep the Church of England part of the One Holy Catholic and Apostolic church, so that its ancient traditions could be retained and not reformed into the Puritan or Presbyterian style of worship, King Charles I was, after the Restoration in 1660, considered a martyr from the moment of his death.

In 1895 Bishop Creighton, later Bishop of London, wrote, "Had Charles been willing to abandon the Church and give up Episcopacy, he might have saved the throne and his life. But on this point he stood firm; for this he died and, by dying, saved it for the future." Victorian Prime Minister William Gladstone concurred, "It was for the Church that King Charles shed his blood upon the scaffold."

Charles had himself written, "Let my condition be never so low, I resolve by the grace of God, never to yield up the Church. By God's grace, no misery shall make me change Episcopal government into Presbyterian. God is my witness, my chiefest end in regaining my power is to do the Church service".

Today there are at least five churches in England dedicated to King Charles the Martyr, including those in Tunbridge Wells (Kent), Potters Bar (Hertfordshire), Falmouth (Cornwall), Shelland (Suffolk) and Newtown (Shropshire).

Fortunately the King, who is particularly remembered for his death, also has his birthday celebrated at services to mark his nativity. The second son of King James I and Anne of Denmark, Charles Stuart was born on 19 November, 1600 at Dunfermline Palace, Fife. Not until the birth of Princess Margaret at Glamis Castle in 1930 was another heir so close to the English throne born in Scotland.

Charles was created Duke of Albany at his baptism and became Duke of York and a Knight of the Bath at the age of four; he was made a Knight of the Garter by the age of ten, and became Duke of Cornwall and heir apparent on the death of his elder brother, Henry, in 1612. Just days before his 16th birthday, Charles was invested as Prince of Wales and Earl of Chester. His other titles included Marquess of Ormond, Earl of Carrick, Earl of Ross, Baron Renfrew, Lord Ardmannoch, Lord of the Isles, Prince and Great Steward of Scotland.

A weak and sickly child, Charles was very shy, partly because his elder brother was so extrovert. Even as an adult, it was said that Charles blushed if anyone used bad language in his presence. He was smaller than average height and never grew to be more that 5ft 4in, possibly because he had a very spartan diet. He also suffered with weak ankles as a result of rickets and had to wear reinforced boots, made for him by one Edward Stuteville, to enable him to begin walking.

In addition, he had a speech defect and did not actually start to speak until the age of three. Throughout his life he had a slight stammer, although worked hard to control it by speaking in a careful, deliberate way.

Although shy, the boy was wilful, difficult to control and did not accept discipline. But as he matured into adulthood, it is recorded that he had a polite, kind, gentle manner and preferred to avoid confrontation. Somewhat lonely, particularly after the death of his brother, Henry, and the departure of his sister, Elizabeth, to Germany when she married in 1613, Charles struck up a friendship with his father's favourite courtier George Villiers, the Duke of Buckingham.

Some historians credit him for giving Charles attention and helping him to blossom and gain in confidence. James I referred to Charles and George as "my sweet boys".

Charles had a formal education, which included studying languages such as Greek and Latin, mathematics, architecture and the arts. He was extremely musical and could play the viola to a very high standard. Literature was very important to him, too, he loved poetry, and he was particularly fond of the plays of Shakespeare. Poet John Milton commented that Charles's only vice was "reading too much Shakespeare".

For relaxation Charles enjoyed playing tennis and bowls as he grew older, and loved riding and hunting. He was artistic, acted in masques, and was good at painting, although none of his own works are thought to have survived. In adulthood he collected a large number of pictures and was very knowledgeable about the artists. During his reign he employed Rubens to paint the ceiling of the Banqueting House in Whitehall.

Following the death of Queen Elizabeth I, Charles's father became King James I and the family moved to England in July 1604. Although Charles resided in England for the rest of his life, he never completely lost all traces of a Scottish accent.

As Prince of Wales and heir to the throne, the question of Charles's marriage became an increasingly important issue as he grew older. In 1623 Charles went with Buckingham to Madrid in an unsuccessful attempt to woo the Spanish Infanta, Maria Anna, daughter of Philip III of Spain.

Philip would only allow the relationship to proceed on the condition that Charles converted to the Roman Catholic faith, and so he returned to England still a bachelor. As the Infanta ran away as soon as she saw Charles, any relationship seemed doomed from the start. To overcome the humiliation of rejection, Charles demanded that his father declare war on Spain. Parliament wanted Charles to marry a Protestant, but ultimately he went against their wishes and married the staunchly Catholic Princess Henrietta Maria, daughter of King Henry IV of France. As the French and Spanish were sworn enemies at the time, the union may have been another way of rebuffing Spain.

At their first meeting, the 15-year-old Henrietta Maria was keen to make

Charles aware of her height and was adamant that she was not wearing high heels. "Sire, I stand on my own two feet!" she exclaimed in her native tongue. "I have no help by art; this high am I, neither higher nor lower!" As Charles was small himself, it is strange that she felt a need to draw attention to her height.

Charles succeeded his father on 27 March, 1625, when he was aged 24. He was crowned at Westminster Abbey on 2 February, 1626, and again in June 1633 at Holyrood Abbey when he became King of Scotland. Going against tradition, Charles wore white at his Coronation and so became known as The White King.

A few weeks after his accession, Charles and Henrietta Maria were married on 1 May, 1625, by proxy at Notre Dame Cathedral in Paris, then in person at Canterbury Cathedral on 13 June, 1625, spending their wedding night in the state bed-chamber of St Augustine's Abbey in Canterbury.

It was not initially a happy marriage, particularly as Henrietta Maria was unable to speak English when she first came to England, but they eventually grew to love each other. They spent the first two years living apart, meeting only for official duties and state occasions.

Almost five years of marriage were to pass before Henrietta Maria produced an heir, the future Charles II, but the couple went on to have four sons and five daughters, including the future James II. By the terms of the marriage contract, Henrietta Maria was responsible for bringing up their children until they were 13.

When Henrietta Maria arrived in England ahead of their marriage, she had an enormous retinue, numbering several hundred, which shocked the King's courtiers. Within a year Charles had dispensed with the services of more than 400 of them, including 30 clergy. Henrietta Maria was looked upon as virtually a missionary for the Roman Catholic faith and she refused to participate in a Church of England Coronation ceremony, so was not crowned Queen Consort.

She took little interest in England or English affairs and was not sympathetic to the Church of England, either. Yet the Church was to have a profound effect on Charles's life and reign.

Being High Anglican and enjoying ritual, Charles easily accepted his wife's Catholic style of worship, even if she did not accept his. But Parliament was increasingly Puritan (Low Church) at this time, which immediately put the King at odds with his ministers.

King Charles I was a very different character to his predecessors. Perhaps because of his innate shyness, he was said to be aloof from his people. Not for him the royal progresses across England so that he could be seen by his subjects and walk amongst them, as Elizabeth I had done. His progresses tended to involve travelling between royal residences or to hunting lodges for his own amusement. Although he did make speeches in public when required, these were a trial for him and not something that he enjoyed doing.

Through the numerous portraits painted of Charles I in his lifetime, notably the famous triptych painting by Sir Anthony Van Dyck, we have a very clear idea of how the King looked, with long chestnut brown hair and pointed goatee beard. Paintings up to the early 1620s show him wearing a ruff and with collar-length hair, but by the time he came to the throne this had been replaced by a much longer, shoulder-length hairstyle and an ornate lace collar.

From an early age Charles wore a gold earring in his left ear, and a grander pearl earring once he became King. Portraits of Charles all have one thing in common: an air of dignity.

As King, Charles continued to be greatly influenced by George Villiers. The Duke of Buckingham had been unpopular during the reign of James I and was no more welcomed in Charles's time. Spurred on by Buckingham, the King engaged in wars against Spain and France that were disasters for England. Buckingham was described at the time as "the great author of our misfortunes". Parliament refused to grant supplies needed to pursue military campaigns and the pair resorted to selling off royal properties to raise money.

Parliament was particularly suspicious of Buckingham and tried to have him impeached in June 1626 because of his poor leadership in war. Charles was angered and immediately dissolved Parliament. Two years later in August 1628, Buckingham was murdered by a grudge-fuelled infantry lieutenant named John Felton. Felton was owed £80 in back pay and had twice been passed over for promotion. Filled with anger, he plunged a knife into Buckingham's heart at the Greyhound Inn in Portsmouth.

Buckingham, who was about to lead an expedition for the relief of La Rochelle in France, died almost instantly. Felton fled through the kitchen, but eventually gave himself up. Although many felt that he had done the world a service by removing Buckingham, Felton was tried, found guilty, and hanged at Tyburn. His body was taken back to Portsmouth, where it was venerated by the public. The dagger used to kill the Duke was put on display and the cross-guard style actually became known as the Buckingham Dagger.

For the King, Buckingham's murder was a tragedy. He withdrew from public view, grief-stricken. At Charles's insistence, Buckingham was buried in Westminster Abbey in an elaborate tomb in Henry VII's chapel, a place that had previously been reserved for royalty.

Friction with Parliament dominated Charles I's reign from beginning to end. Between 1625-29 he called three Parliaments and each time he ended up dissolving them because of their differing viewpoints. From 1629-1640 he tried to rule without Parliament at all, a period that is now known as the Eleven Years Tyranny. With no Parliament, there was no financial backing for the monarch. Charles therefore increased taxes to raise money, which made him unpopular.

In 1634 he revived the Anglo-Saxon Ship Tax to finance the navy, but faced stiff opposition including at least one attempt through the courts to suppress it. He also brought an end to the costly wars with France and Spain, merely to save money, and attempted to recover church lands that had been lost during the reign of Henry VIII.

The King had two main advisors at this period: Thomas Wentworth, 1st Earl of Strafford (known as 'Black Tom') and William Laud, who was appointed Archbishop of Canterbury in 1633. The latter was a particularly severe man and anti-Puritan. Any clergy who disobeyed his rules could be flogged, branded, imprisoned or have their ears cut off.

Even parishioners faced heavy fines for the least misdeed and people were persecuted in the infamous Star Chamber and Court of High Commission. Puritans sought religious freedom by fleeing to American colonies in Massachusetts and New England.

In 1637 William Laud tried to anglicise the Scottish church and forced a new prayer book on them so that England and Scotland should be uniform in their worship. This was deeply unpopular and thousands of Scots signed a National Covenant, registering their opposition to the new prayer book and also to bishops, as Presbyterians had no time for them. This resulted in two skirmishes known as the Bishops' Wars, when Charles tried to forcibly impose his will on the Scottish church. This created a dilemma for him, because only Parliament could grant funds to finance a war.

Suddenly Charles needed the Parliament that he so detested, and so a "Short Parliament" met in April 1640, but ministers wanted the Scottish crisis settled through negotiation rather than battle. The King was forced to give in to the Scots and promptly dissolved Parliament.

Charles reluctantly agreed to sign the Treaty of Ripon, which was designed to keep the encroaching Scots north of Yorkshire until the situation was fully resolved. By its terms, Northumberland and County Durham were ceded to the Scots, and Charles had to pay them £850 a day to keep their armies there. In light of his financial problems, this did not go down well.

In November 1640 Parliament resumed and is now known as the Long Parliament, as it actually lasted for 20 years. Once again, Charles was forced to concede and accept the terms that Parliament should meet at least once every three years and could no longer be dissolved by the King without consent.

Parliament gained total control over taxes and military matters, and abolished Charles's unpopular Ship Tax. Parliament issued the Grand Remonstrance in 1641, listing all their grievances against the King since the start of his reign.

Parliament also wanted to rid itself of his closest advisors. In 1641 Strafford was tried and executed for being a corrupting influence on the King. Charles was forced to sign a Bill of Attainder, which in essence meant that Strafford could be put to death for any reason.

When Strafford heard that Charles had signed the Bill, he quoted Psalm 146: "Put not your trust in Princes, nor in the son of man, in whom there is no help." Strafford was executed at Tower Hill and Charles's other adviser, Archbishop Laud, lost his head in 1645.

The power of the Crown diminished and Parliament now had control. The Star Chamber and Court of High Commission were abolished. Puritan John Pym was Leader of the Commons, but there was one matter in which Charles adamantly refused to bow to pressure and that was in not allowing any reform of the Church of England. The Commons felt that Charles's Roman Catholic Queen had too much influence and that the Church of England was becoming Anglo-Catholic in style.

On 4 January, 1642, Parliament tried to impeach the Queen. Charles went straight to the Commons himself to arrest five MPs for high treason, but the men had gone. "I see all the birds are flown," he told the Speaker. "I do expect that you shall send them unto me as they return hither. If not, I will seek them myself, for their treason is foul and such a one as you will thank me to discover."

To which the Speaker, William Lenthall, famously replied, "May it please Your Majesty, I have neither eyes to see nor tongue to speak in this place but as this House is pleased to direct me, whose servant I am."

With Royalists and Parliamentarians now at odds over many matters, civil war loomed. In August 1642 the King mustered an army at Nottingham with his nephew Prince Rupert. To raise sufficient funds, Queen Henrietta Maria pawned the Crown Jewels in Holland. A contemporary report states that she received 1,265,300 guilders from the sale and pawning of personal, Crown and State treasures.

Although some pieces were lost forever, a few items were recovered and other medieval objects had remained in England anyway. After Charles I's death, the Crown Jewels were further depleted when the regalia was stripped of precious jewels and the gold melted down to turn into coins.

So, with money available, the Civil War began, with the King and members of the nobility on one side (Cavaliers) and the Parliamentarians with townspeople and yeomen on the other (Roundheads), although it was much more a war of religion – Anglicans versus Puritans – than a class war.

There was a geographical boundary, with a dividing line down the length of England from Southampton in the south up to the River Humber in the north. Royalists were west of this line, Parliamentarians to the east. London, roughly in the centre, became the key stronghold to take. Charles was successful at the Battle of Edgehill, Warwickshire, in October 1642, but was thwarted by nearly 25,000 Londoners at Turnham Green a month later. A series of battles were fought across England over the next two years, with neither side having any great victories.

A defining moment came in July 1644 with the Battle of Marston Moor, when a cavalry general by the name of Oliver Cromwell came to the fore with his New Model Army. The Royalists were defeated and Charles lost control of the north of England.

At the Battle of Naseby in June 1645, Charles suffered further huge losses, including many of his best officers, at least half his cavalry, and all his artillery and infantry. His sons, Charles and James fled abroad for safety.

In September 1645 in a battle at Philiphaugh near Selkirk in Scotland, the King's representative, the Marquis of Montrose, was defeated by the Scottish Presbyterian Covenanters.

In May 1646 Charles surrendered to the Scots and was taken prisoner. Oxford fell a month later and the war ended. The Scots sold the King to the English Parliament.

Cromwell wanted to negotiate with the King but Charles's advisers felt that too much power was being taken away from the monarch. Charles was kept in "honourable captivity" at various locations including Hampton Court but, in November 1647 he escaped and fled to the Isle of Wight, where he tried unsuccessfully to bargain from afar. He sought refuge at

Carisbrooke Castle, where he thought the Governor would be sympathetic towards him, but found himself a virtual prisoner.

He tried to make peace with the Scots over church issues in the hope that they could restore him to the throne but, when the Scottish army crossed over into England in July 1648, they were defeated at Preston by Cromwell's forces. The so-called second Civil War was over and Charles's last hopes were dashed.

On 6 December, 1648, having purged Parliament of those who did not believe the King should be punished, Colonel Thomas Pride set up a court to try the King. The following month Charles was brought to Westminster Hall in London to be tried for waging war against "Parliament and the Kingdom of England". The charge described him as "a Tyrant, Traitor and Murderer". With his belief in the divine right of kings, Charles refused to accept the legality of the court and so did not defend himself or make a plea. This was taken to be an admission of guilt.

On 27 January, 1649, King Charles was found guilty of treason against the state and condemned to death. When he tried to speak out after the sentence had been pronounced, he was told that he was too late and he was led away by force. Colonel Pride's coat of arms was stamped on the King's death warrant.

On the eve of his execution Charles said farewell to his two youngest children, telling eight-year-old Henry, Duke of Gloucester: "They will cut off my head and perhaps make thee King, but mark what I say, you must not be King so long as your brothers Charles and James do live – for they will cut off your brothers' heads if they catch them, and cut off thy head too, at last, and therefore I charge you: do not be made King by them!" A startling thing to say to such a young child. Remarkably the boy replied that he would be torn in pieces before he would be King. To his daughter, Elizabeth, Charles said that he was dying for the laws and liberties of this land, and for maintaining the true Protestant religion.

On 30 January, 1649, Charles rose early, saying that he had much to do and that, by nightfall, "I hope to be espoused to my blessed Jesus." After Morning Prayer and receiving Holy Communion he was led from St James's Palace at 10am for the journey to Whitehall. As the procession reached Horse Guards Parade, Charles felt that the soldiers were walking too slowly and shouted for them to hurry up.

A temporary scaffold had been placed outside the Banqueting House in Whitehall, but neither an executioner or a block could be found, as the original executioner refused to behead his King. Eventually another man agreed to do the deed, on the proviso that he could wear a mask to hide his face from the crowds. Because of this delay, the King was kept waiting for several hours in the bitter cold of that January day. Even the River Thames had frozen over. He put on two shirts as he didn't want to be seen shivering and have people think that it was through fear. The overshirt that he wore on that day is now preserved at Windsor Castle.

Shortly before 2 pm, Charles was led through a window and out on to the scaffold, where a very low block of only around a foot high had been placed. To the masked executioner he asked, "Does my hair trouble you?" Consequently, it was tucked out of the way under a cap. Turning to Bishop Juxon, the then Bishop of London, he said, "I have a good cause, and a gracious God on my side."

To which the Bishop replied, "There is but one stage more, which, though turbulent and troublesome, yet it is a very short one; it will soon carry you a very great way. It will carry you from earth to heaven; and there you will find, to your great joy, the prize you hasten to. A crown of glory."

The King added, "Death is not terrible to me. I bless God that I am prepared. I go from a corruptible to an incorruptible crown, where no disturbance is, no disturbance in the world." Handing the Bishop his St George's Emblem from the Order of the Garter, Charles urged him, "Remember."

After saying that he wished the block was a little higher, for it meant he had to lie almost flat to place his head upon it, the King said a few words of private prayer and then stretched out his hands to indicate that he was ready. The axe fell. Eyewitnesses recorded that there were shrieks, groans and sobs from the crowds in Whitehall. The English people were horrified by the King's death and very soon many came to look upon him as a martyr.

Due to the swiftness of events, no tomb had been prepared for the King and so Charles I was laid to rest alongside Henry VIII in a vault at St George's Chapel, Windsor. In April 1813 this tomb was opened while work was being undertaken to enlarge a passage under the choir stalls and the vault was searched to ascertain that the royal coffins were still there and had not been destroyed by Cromwell's men in earlier times.

King George III's physician, Sir Henry Halford, was present and has left a very detailed account of the opening of Charles I's coffin, revealing that the face, pointed beard and the fact that the head was detached from the body left witnesses, which included the Prince Regent, in no doubt that it was indeed the remains of the Stuart monarch.

The fourth cervical vertebra was loose, as a result of the executioner's axe, and Halford kept this for himself along with other "relics". There is a myth that he used the vertebra as a salt cellar, but a contemporary physician of his wrote that Sir Henry simply passed it around to guests as an "after dinner curiosity".

In 1888 a grandson of Sir Henry Halford returned these relics to the Prince of Wales, later King Edward VII, in an ebony box. Queen Victoria gave permission for the vault to be opened once again and at 7 pm on 13 December the Prince laid the box on Charles I's coffin. One unusual artefact is still retained in the Royal Collection, however, and that is a gold and enamel locket which contains some of Charles's hair that was removed in 1813.

Following the execution of King Charles I his eldest surviving son, Charles II, was declared king in name only. For the first and only time in history England became a Republic, with Oliver Cromwell as Lord Protector.

Chapter 41

Oliver Cromwell 1599–1658
and the Interregnum: 1649–1660

Following the execution of King Charles I in 1649, England entered its most uncertain period in the whole history of the monarchy. Charles I's son and heir was hiding in France for his own safety, and soon Oliver Cromwell took control of the country as Lord General of the Commonwealth and later, Lord Protector. England became a Republic.

Although the man who should have been king, Charles II, tried to return home to England, Cromwell's fleet intercepted him in the Channel and he was forced to seek refuge in the Netherlands. Almost 18 months were to pass before Charles managed to land on our shores, and then in Scotland rather than England. He was eventually crowned King of Scotland at Scone, but when he tried to make his way across the border to England later that year with 10,000 soldiers, he was confronted by Cromwell's forces of almost 40,000 men and really had no hope of success. Charles was forced back in to exile, first to France, then Germany, and later the Low Countries, what we now know as Belgium.

During the Interregnum, when England was without a ruling monarch, Oliver Cromwell and Parliament took control of the country. Initially as the Commonwealth (1649-1653) and later as the Protectorate (1653-1659).

Cromwell, one of ten children, was born in Huntingdon on 25 April, 1599, to a landed family: the Cromwells of Hinchinbrooke. They were descendants of Katherine Cromwell, a sister of Henry VIII's adviser Thomas Cromwell. Katherine was Oliver's great-great-grandmother and had continued to use the Cromwell surname for her family after her marriage.

In a speech to Parliament Cromwell once said that he was "by birth a gentleman, living neither in any considerable height, nor yet in obscurity." He was educated at Huntingdon Grammar School, then at Sidney Sussex College in Cambridge, but dropped out when his father became ill and so never graduated. He also studied law in London for a time.

When his father died in 1617, Cromwell took over the family estate and later began farming in St Ives (then Huntingdonshire, now Cambridgeshire). There is a statue of him on Market Hill, St Ives, to commemorate his association with the town. He married Elizabeth Bourchier, the daughter of a wealthy London merchant, in August 1620 and the couple went on to have nine children.

As well as owning property in Huntingdonshire, Cromwell was left the lease of a house in St Mary's Street, Ely, in an uncle's will in 1636 and this became the family home for more than ten years. The house is now open to the public. Cromwell also inherited the role of tithe collector for Ely Cathedral from his uncle, which greatly increased his income. Stories that Cromwell and his soldiers decapitated statues at the cathedral, however, are untrue. Nearly 150 carved figures in the cathedral lost their heads a century earlier during Henry VIII's reign.

Oliver Cromwell's father and three of his uncles had sat in the Parliaments of Elizabeth I. He followed in their footsteps and became Member of Parliament for Huntingdon in 1628, and later for Cambridge. Courtier Sir Philip Warwick has left us with an image of Cromwell at this time, writing: "I came into the House one morning and perceived a gentleman speaking whom I knew not, very ordinarily apparelled, for it was a plain cloth suit, which seemed to have been made by an ill country tailor. His linen was plain and not very clean; and I remember a speck or two of blood upon his little band, which was not much larger than his collar. His hat was without a hatband. His stature was of good size; his sword stuck close to his side; his countenance swollen and reddish; his voice sharp and untuneable, and his eloquence full of fervour."

Cromwell adopted Puritanism in the 1630s, some would say in an extremist way, and it is recorded that he was a melancholy man. He once revealed that he lived in "blackness", always convinced that his death was imminent. When Sir Peter Lely painted his portrait in 1653, Cromwell famously told him, "I desire you would use all your skill to paint my picture truly like me, and not flatter me at all; but remark all these roughnesses, pimples, warts and everything as you see me, otherwise I never will pay a farthing for it." From this, we have the saying, "warts and all."

Cromwell became particularly prominent in the Commons during the period of Charles I's clash with the Long Parliament in the 1640s, when he was fiercely critical of the King. Although a formidable Parliamentarian, it became clear early on that Cromwell was foremost a soldier and a supporter of the Roundheads. When the Civil War began, Cromwell was captain of a horse troop and showed his strength of character by going against tradition. He promoted men on their ability, rather than their social status.

"I would rather have a plain russet-coated captain that knows what he fights for and loves what he knows," Cromwell wrote to Parliamentarian Sir William Spring in 1643, "than that which you call a gentleman and is nothing else." He continued, "A few honest men are better than numbers."

As a military man, he was soon to prove that quality was better than quantity when it came to fighting and his soldiers were often able to defeat armies that outnumbered his own. Oliver's Mount in Scarborough, an area of high ground above the town, is named after Cromwell and is where his men are supposed to have sited their guns to fire at the castle.

Some historians consider this unlikely because of the distance and believe that the graveyard of St Mary's Church beneath the castle was a more likely position for the guns, because of the damage that the church sustained during a siege of the castle. There is no evidence to suggest that Oliver Cromwell ever visited Scarborough himself during the Civil War.

As a Puritan, Cromwell chose men with religious fervour for his army, considering this to be the best quality of all. A regiment of 1,000 soldiers was made entirely of "men of religion" and Cromwell would allow no blasphemy, drunkenness or impious behaviour in the ranks. Anyone who transgressed was fined. "Not a man swears but he pays his twelve pence," Cromwell insisted. During the Battle of Winceby in Lincolnshire during the Civil War, it is said that Cromwell's Roundheads sang psalms as they charged at the Cavaliers.

Cromwell had success at the Battle of Marston Moor in 1644 and secured victory for the Roundheads. Afterwards, he was described as a military genius. He helped create the New Model Army under commander-in-chief Sir Thomas Fairfax. The aim was to get 20,000 "honest" men into it.

"Be careful what captains of horse you choose, what men be mounted," wrote Cromwell. "If you choose godly honest men to be captains of horse, honest men will follow them." Revolts in Sussex, Kent and Wales were soon quashed by the new army and it helped secure victory at the Battle of

Naseby in 1645. Other military successes followed across England.

By this time, Cromwell was considered to be the foremost cavalry leader of his day and it was he who tried to reach a settlement with Charles I, but ended up condemning the King as "so great a dissembler and so false a man that he is not to be trusted". After another battle at Newbury, Cromwell said bluntly, "If I met the King in battle, I would fire my pistol as at another."

In December 1648 Colonel Thomas Pride's regiment took control of London and the army council, under the orders of Lord General Fairfax, expelled all Royalist elements from the House of Commons. Charles I's Long Parliament was greatly reduced by Colonel Pride to only men who supported putting the King on trial for high treason. Over 230 of the King's supporters were refused admittance to the House. The remaining MPs made up what became known as the "Rump Parliament" – in other words, the little bit of Parliament that was left. Charles I was unwilling to accept the authority of the court set up to try him and as a result was found guilty through his refusal to plead.

Oliver Cromwell was one of the signatories of the death warrant and called the King's beheading "a cruel necessity". After the death of Charles I, a Council of State made up of 41 members of the Commons began to rule, with Cromwell as Chairman. The monarchy and House of Lords were formally abolished. The Church of England was disestablished. In May that year the English government became known as the Commonwealth and England as a Free State. Cromwell was styled Lord Governor.

In September 1649 Cromwell headed to Ireland to quash Royalist campaigns at Drogheda and Wexford in a terrible massacre that saw several thousand slaughtered. It brought an end to the Irish Confederate Wars. The following year his attention turned to Scotland where Charles Stuart (Charles II) was in hiding. In the Battle of Dunbar, Cromwell's army beat the Scots, even though he had fewer soldiers.

There was Scottish opposition to the Interregnum, as Royalists, known as Engagers in Scotland, felt that the King had been executed without their consent. They wanted to restore Charles Stuart to his rightful place on the throne. On 1 January, 1651 Charles was crowned King of Scotland at Scone Abbey. Later that year Charles and his army moved southwards into England, but Cromwell's larger and more powerful army defeated him at Worcester, and the newly crowned King fled. A £1,000 reward was offered to anyone who could capture him but with the help of Richard Penderel, a farmer who supported the Royalist cause, Charles managed to escape detection and eventually found refuge in France.

On one occasion Charles hid in an oak tree near Boscobel House in Shropshire, undiscovered by Cromwell's men. Many inns across England later adopted the name Royal Oak. Although it is still possible to see the "royal oak" at Boscobel, the tree that stands today is a descendant of the original. Nearby is another oak tree, planted as a sapling by the present Prince of Wales in 2011, grown from an acorn of the descendant tree, to mark the 350th anniversary of the royal hiding place.

Meanwhile, in England, the Rump Parliament was hated because it tried to stifle the liberty of the people. On 20 April, 1653, Cromwell became infuriated himself with Parliament for its failure to produce a viable constitution. After listening to a series of speeches, Cromwell horrified Members as he suddenly stood up and shouted, "We have had enough of this. I will put an end to your prating! It is not fit that you should sit here any longer. You should give place to better men. You are no Parliament."

He then marched a troop of 30 musketeers into the House of Commons, took hold of the mace, the symbol of Parliament's authority, called it a "fool's bauble" and ordered his men to take it away. The Speaker was forced out of his chair, some Members of Parliament were insulted and called drunkards and cheats. When the Commons had been completely cleared, Cromwell locked the door and walked off towards Whitehall.

With the dismissal of MPs, England now appeared to have no government at all, but Cromwell said later that, "We did not hear a dog bark at their going." On 4 July a nominated assembly known as the "Barebones Parliament" or "Little Parliament" was formed from men chosen by Cromwell and his army officers in an attempt to stabilise the way in which England was governed.

It was the first Parliament in our history where Members from Scotland and Ireland sat side by side with those from England. It lasted less than six months, due to internal conflict and backbiting, and was dissolved on 12 December 1653.

It was then decided that Parliament should be reformed with a single chamber, a House that would consist of 400 Members from England, 30 from Scotland and 30 from Ireland. A fresh Council of State issued an Instrument of Government – a new constitution – and England became a Protectorate instead of a Commonwealth. Oliver Cromwell was given the position of Lord Protector and was sworn in on 16 December. It was considered a job for life and he received £100,000 a year. Thereafter he signed himself as Oliver P and was addressed as "Your Highness".

Whilst seeming to have the highest position in the land, Cromwell was dismayed to discover that his powers as Lord Protector were limited. Under the new constitution, he could choose members of the Council of State, but he did not actually have the power to remove them without the consent of all the other members. The Council could make new laws and impose taxes, even if the Lord Protector did not give his assent. He did, however, have the power to dissolve Parliament.

Cromwell saw his position as a call from God and considered that his power was a divine right. He wanted Parliament to approve his proposals without questioning his authority. He insisted that his rule as Lord General had been accepted by the people, Parliament, and the army and that they should similarly accept his position as Lord Protector.

Cromwell proposed that there should be joint government between "a single person (himself) and a Parliament" as the only way of ensuring that Parliaments did not become perpetual. Although 100 MPs refused to accept this, 300 Members signed their agreement.

Cromwell was now becoming virtually a dictator, but he faced opposition from some MPs who wished to push forward more reforms and amend the constitution. Instead of opposing this, Cromwell simply dissolved Parliament in January 1655 and introduced military rule instead.

England and Wales were divided into 11 districts, with each being ruled by a Major-General. This system of government was generally unpopular with the people as the Major-Generals became despots, and it was brought to an end in January 1657.

In an ironic twist, the staunchly republican Oliver Cromwell, who lived in many palaces, including Hampton Court, was offered the crown in March 1657 as part of a revised constitution. There was a belief in some quarters that maybe the monarchy was the best system after all. Whilst he was extremely tempted by the idea of becoming King Oliver, and took six weeks to make a decision, Cromwell knew that many leading figures would oppose the move and so in the end he declined. Instead, he was reinstated as Lord Protector in a ceremony at Westminster Hall in June 1657. Although not officially a monarch, Cromwell was seated on King Edward's Chair on which monarchs had been crowned since the 14th century. In the style of an hereditary monarchy, Cromwell named his son Richard as his successor.

With Cromwell at the helm, the Puritan Parliament introduced strict laws for the people of England. Theatres closed. Sporting events were not allowed. Fines were imposed for swearing or travelling on a Sunday. Immoral behaviour became a civil crime. Bishops and the Book of Common Prayer were abolished.

Christian festivities and pagan events, such as May Day celebrations, were stopped. It became illegal even to erect a typically English May Pole. Although the theatres had closed, opera was considered "virtuous" and could still be performed.

As a result, Cromwell and his harsh, restrictive laws were widely disliked. His narrow Puritan religious views were unpopular. His attitude has been described as joyless because of the austere lifestyle that Puritanism imposed. Christmas, for example, was meant to be a time of fasting rather than feasting; shops remained open and Parliament even met on 25 December.

Decorating rooms with festive greenery was not allowed, although some people continued to celebrate the "Old Christmas" in the privacy of their homes. John Evelyn recorded in his diary on Christmas Day 1657 that he had attended a service in a private chapel and everyone present had been arrested by Parliamentarian soldiers and questioned:

"I went to London with my wife, to celebrate Christmas Day, Mr Gunning preaching . . . as he was giving us the Holy Sacrament, the chapel was surrounded with soldiers, and all the communicants and assembly surprised and kept prisoner by them. In the afternoon came Colonel Whalley, Goffe, and others . . . to examine us one by one; some they committed to the marshal, some to prison.

"When I came before them, they took my name and abode, examined me why, contrary to the ordinance made, that none should any longer observe the superstitious time of the nativity (so esteemed by them), I durst offend and pray for Charles Stuart. I told them we did not pray for Charles Stuart, but for all kings, princes, and governors.

"They replied with other frivolous and ensnaring questions, and much threatening; and, finding no color to detain me, they dismissed me with much pity of my ignorance. These men spoke spiteful things of our Lord's nativity."

When Charles Stuart was eventually restored to the throne, Christmas celebrations resumed. Poor Robin's Almanack of 1660 included the following sentiment:

Now thanks to God for Charles's return
Whose absence made old Christmas mourn:
For then we scarcely did it know,
Whether it Christmas were or no.

Yet, despite many draconian measures, Cromwell did appear to have England's best interests at heart when it came to foreign policy. He had control of the army and navy and did much to strengthen them through various ways such as the introduction of pay scales, which encouraged more men to choose a naval career.

In 1651 he had passed a Navigation Act to keep English trade in her own ships, so that England had the monopoly. This led to wars with Holland, rivals when it came to trade and commerce, but he successfully fought the Dutch in 1652 and 1653. His demand for trade rights in the West Indies was opposed by the Spanish and so he formed an alliance with France against Spain. Together they beat the Spaniards at the Battle of the Dunes at Dunkirk in June 1658. He also reopened the Baltic to shipping.

By 1658 Oliver Cromwell was a weakened man. "God knows, I would have been glad to have lived under my woodside, and to have kept a flock of sheep, rather than to have undertaken this government," he told Parliament unexpectedly.

The death of his favourite daughter, Elizabeth Claypole, in August upset him greatly and he began to deteriorate physically. He suffered from frequent bouts of ill health, with what is thought to be a form of malaria which was quite common in the fenlands of East Anglia at that time.

His health was complicated further by a kidney complaint. "I would be willing to live to be further serviceable to God and His people," he told his physician, "but my work is done."

He deteriorated rapidly, probably due to septicemia, and died on 3 September, aged 59. Three days earlier a major storm had blown roofs from houses and felled huge trees across England. It was described as a fitting prelude to the death of a man who, at his height, had been like a tornado across the country.

Oliver Cromwell was buried in Westminster Abbey with all the pomp and ceremony of a King, having first lain in state at Somerset House so that the public could file past and pay their respects. A realistic wooden effigy of Cromwell was placed beside the coffin, dressed in rich velvet decorated with gold lace and ermine.

This figure of the republican who had abolished the monarchy also wore a purple velvet robe trimmed with ermine, and on a chair nearby was a jeweled crown on a velvet cushion. A king in all but name.

Cromwell's son, Richard, took over his father's role as Lord Protector but, lacking the necessary strength, was soon deposed and the Protectorate was abolished. He had no solution to resolve the financial problems that the country faced. There was also constant friction between the army and the government and in May 1659 the Rump Parliament was re-established, but by October this had been overthrown by the Army. Richard Cromwell was placed under house arrest and consequently agreed to resign as Lord Protector. He went to live in France using the pseudonym John Clarke and faded into obscurity. The Protectorate was abolished. Although royalists rejoiced at Richard Cromwell's downfall, referring to him as "Tumbledown Dick", England seemed in turmoil once again.

The time now seemed right for Charles II to come out of exile from Breda in the Netherlands, where he had been residing. General George Monck, English Military Governor of Scotland, acted as go-between and marched his army to London and set the wheels in motion for the restoration of the monarchy. The Long Parliament resumed, as it had been in the reign of Charles I before Colonel Pride's purge.

Charles II issued a declaration, promising an amnesty, religious toleration and Parliamentary rule, known as the Declaration of Breda. It was agreed that England's government should now be "by King, Lords, and Commons" and a temporary Convention Parliament was set up, one that could be assembled "without being summoned by the Sovereign, when the Crown is in abeyance".

On 25 May, 1660 King Charles II landed at Dover, arriving in London four days later in time to celebrate his 30th birthday and restoration to the throne. There was relief across England that the Interregnum was at an end.

Although a statue of Oliver Cromwell now stands outside the Houses of Parliament, one of four statues of him in England, the former Lord Protector was not allowed to rest in peace, being unceremoniously removed from his tomb after the Restoration. Parliament then ordered the "postumous execution" of Cromwell for treason. His body was gibbeted at Tyburn and his head put on a pole outside Westminster Hall.

He was later reinterred at Tyburn, although his actual final resting place is not firmly established, but his head remained on a pole for many years before being blown down during a gale. It later became privately owned as a curiosity. The skull changed hands many times and was occasionally put on public display. On 25 March, 1960 it was finally buried beneath the ante-chapel at Sidney Sussex College, Cambridge, where he had been a student for a short time.

Opinion about Oliver Cromwell, whether an English hero or a tyrant, still remains divided to this day. He has been variously called a devil, a monster, a hypocrite . . . much maligned, he also been called a great leader, a defender of faith, "the raiser and maintainer of the Empire of England".

Archbishop of York John Williams, the last bishop to hold the position of Lord Chancellor, declared, "Every beast hath some evil properties, but Cromwell hath the properties of all evil beasts."

Yet, Samuel Pepys wrote in his diary on 8 February 1667: "At dinner we talked much of Cromwell, all saying he was a brave fellow and did owe his crown he got to himself, as much as any man that ever got one."

Over 350 years later, the debate continues.

Chapter 42

Charles II 1630–1685
Reign: 1660–1685

The contrast between the austerity of Oliver Cromwell's England during the Interregnum and the restoration of the monarchy under King Charles II could not have been greater. As theatres re-opened, a stage comedy of the day had a courtier being advised that a gentleman "must dress well, dance well, fence well, have a talent for love-letters, an agreeable voice, be amorous and discreet – but not too constant." To the Puritan, such sentiments would have been an anathema.

But of the reign of Merry Monarch Charles II, one Victorian historian wrote, "Duelling and raking became the marks of a fine gentleman; honest fellows fought, gambled, swore, drank, and ended a day of debauchery by a night in the gutter". Stressing, however, that such behaviour seemed confined to "the capital and the court. The mass of Englishmen were satisfied with getting their maypoles and mince pies back".

Having been supressed during the first 30 years of his life, Charles was determined to enjoy himself once he became King, saying that he did not believe "God would make a man miserable just for taking a little pleasure."

Charles Stuart was born on 29 May, 1630, at St James's Palace, London, the second son and eldest surviving child of Charles I and Henrietta Maria of France. He was created Duke of Cornwall and Rothesay at birth, and at the age of eight was styled Prince of Wales and Earl of Chester, although no formal investiture ceremony ever took place.

He had an idyllic early childhood, spent at Greenwich Palace, Hampton Court and Windsor Castle. Surviving Van Dyck portraits of the family show Charles as a young Prince of Wales, dressed immaculately in silk and lace, often with a pet dog. Although the paintings are undoubtedly regal, they depict scenes of domesticity that had not been evident in earlier royal portraits.

In a picture from around 1635 by Van Dyck, Charles is with his brother the Duke of York (later James II) and sister Princess Mary (who became the mother of William III) as small children, with Charles leaning very casually against a column, his legs crossed and a spaniel by his side. Another painting of the same period by Dutch artist Gerrit Houckgeest shows the family dining, with servants dashing back and forth with dishes and wine.

Charles's governor was William Cavendish, Marquess of Newcastle (later 1st Duke of Newcastle), renowned for his abilities as a soldier, an athlete and a scholar. The Marquess surrounded himself with poets, playwrights, authors and musicians, known as the Cavendish Circle, and encouraged Charles to take an interest in the arts. He was an extremely skilled equestrian and taught the Prince how to ride, having his own large riding school at Bolsover Castle. William Cavendish reported that he once hit the Prince on his head with a stick because Charles was laughing during a church service and chatting to girls in a nearby pew.

His main tutor was Dr Brian Duppa, the King's Chaplain and later a Bishop. Charles was not a particularly good scholar, and had only a limited grasp of languages, but became very interested in science and the discoveries of his day. His interest in chemistry was to eventually lead to the foundation of the Royal Society for scientific research.

The Royal Observatory at Greenwich was also instigated by Charles when, as King, he established a Royal Commission to look into astronomy. He was also skilled at naval architecture and it is said that he would have been able to build a ship if the need had ever arisen.

Charles's secure world was shaken with the onset of the Civil War, which came to dominate his life. At the age of just 12 he was at the Battle of Edgehill. He accompanied his father on campaigns and was appointed a Commander-in-Chief of Royalist forces in the West Country at Bristol two months before his 15th birthday. Eventually he left England for his own safety, travelling with a small team of advisers, going via the Isles of Scilly and Jersey to eventually settle at St Germain near Paris with his mother. He remained there for two years.

As King Charles I's relationship with Parliament deteriorated and he was put on trial for treason, the Prince tried unsuccessfully to save his father's life and wrote many letters. Once sending a blank, signed letter to

Parliament giving them carte blanche to fill in their own demands. He was in the Netherlands when news reached him of his father's execution on 30 January, 1649.

Charles became King in name only at the age of 18. Within a few days of the execution, the Rump Parliament abolished the monarchy. Six days later Charles was proclaimed King in Scotland, but not in England.

The new King took refuge in France and later the Netherlands, where he began negotiations with Scottish Covenanters, Presbyterians who held power, about establishing an army to attack Oliver Cromwell, who had become a virtual dictator.

In June 1650 Charles sailed to Scotland. He was crowned King of Scots at Scone on 1 January, 1651, and agreed to rule England and Scotland equally. Although his life was protected there, he found his time in Scotland dull and wrote that Presbyterianism was "not a religion for gentlemen", as the clergy frowned upon any attempts he made to have fun.

The Covenanters formed him a Scots-Royalist army and in July 1651 he headed south with some 10,000 men but they were largely unskilled and were soundly defeated by Cromwell's army at Worcester. Charles now became a fugitive with £1,000 offered by the Roundheads for anyone who could take him prisoner.

Charles sheltered at White Ladies Priory in the parish of Boscobel in Shropshire, owned by the Giffard family. After an unsuccessful attempt to cross the River Severn, Charles was taken to Boscobel House, home of the Penderel family, tenants of the Giffards. There he met Colonel William Careless, a Royalist officer in the Civil War and also a fugitive, who offered to help the King escape.

In September 1651 the pair went to a nearby forest and hid in a great oak tree for a whole day in an attempt to avoid capture. Diarist Samuel Pepys recorded that the King had later told him about hiding in the oak, saying, "While we were in this tree we see soldiers going up and down, in the thicket of the wood, searching for persons escaped; we see them now and then peeping out of the wood."

Eventually the King fell into a deep sleep, his head on Careless's arm, which after a time became numb. The Colonel knew that if he spoke to the King, he could be heard and they would be discovered. In the end, he gently pinched the King to wake him up.

Having successfully thwarted the Roundheads, Charles and the Colonel climbed out of the tree and spent the night hiding in priest holes at Boscobel. To celebrate their freedom, the next day Careless killed a sheep, which the

King cooked on an open fire, and with full bellies they went their separate ways. When news of the King's hiding place eventually became public knowledge, many inns in England were later called Royal Oak and over 400 still bear the name today. It is currently the third most popular pub name in England, after Red Lion and The Crown.

Before moving on, Charles had his long hair cut with William Penderel's shears and darkened his skin with soot. He was helped further in his escape by a priest, Fr John Huddleston, who wrote that the King's "shoes were old, all slasht for the ease of his feet and full of gravell, with little rowlls of paper between his toes; which he said he was advised to, to keep them from galling." As he continued his escape through the West Country, Charles darkened his skin more permanently with boiled walnut juice.

On reaching Sussex some weeks later, Charles boarded a coal brig at Shoreham harbour and crossed the Channel. Once in France, he lived in exile at Fécamp. For the next nine years he travelled across Europe, staying at the homes of distant family members, living for a time with his mother in France and in Germany with his widowed sister, Mary.

He had moved on to Brussels when news reached him of the death of Oliver Cromwell. The weakness of Cromwell's successor, his son Richard, opened up a path for Charles to re-take his place on the throne of England.

Charles was in the Dutch city of Breda when negotiations came to a successful conclusion between Sir John Grenville, one of his representatives in England, and General George Monck, Lord-General of the English army who was now effectively running the country. On 4 April, 1660, a Declaration was sent from Breda promising religious tolerance and an amnesty for all in England who had committed crimes during the Civil War and the Interregnum just as long as they accepted Charles as their King.

Parliament approved the Declaration, agreeing that government should be by "King, Lords and Commons" and on 8th May Charles was officially restored to the throne as King of England, Scotland and Ireland. This period of English history has become known as The Restoration. Many official documents were backdated to 1649, as if Charles II's reign had followed straight on from that of Charles I and the Interregnum had never happened.

On 29 May, 1660, his 30th birthday, Charles II made a joyous return to London. Church bells rang out, flowers were strewn across the streets, bonfires were lit, and the wraith of Oliver Cromwell seemed finally to have been banished. After years of puritanical austerity, England now had hope and rejoiced that a King was back on the throne.

May 29 became a public holiday, known as Oak Apple Day, and although it is still celebrated in some parts of England, it ceased officially to be a holiday in 1859.

Charles was crowned at Westminster Abbey on 23 April, 1661 – St George's Day – the last Coronation where the procession set off from the Tower of London. The event was delayed, as Cromwell had destroyed or broken up most of the Crown Jewels. New regalia costing £21,978-9s-11d was created by the royal goldsmith, Sir Robert Vyner, including two crowns, two sceptres, an orb, staff, armills and the ampulla, based on designs of those used by Edward the Confessor, recreated where possible from ancient manuscripts.

Many of today's Crown Jewels date from Charles II's time, although some have been slightly remodelled and added to across the centuries. Only three swords and the Coronation Spoon pre-date him. St Edward's Crown, used for the crowning of Queen Elizabeth II in 1953, is basically the same crown used for Charles II's coronation in 1661, although the jewels have changed.

A setting of *Zadok the Priest* was written especially for Charles II's Coronation by English composer Henry Lawes. "But so great a noise," complained Samuel Pepys, "that I could make but little of the musique." A very impressive coronation portrait painted by John Michael Wright in 1661 presents a majestic image of Charles in sumptuous velvet and ermine robes, crown on his head, and orb and sceptre in his hands. It says more clearly than any words that the monarchy has been restored.

Although he was on the throne, there remained many issues to be resolved with Parliament. England was in a poor financial state after the Commonwealth; there was religious disharmony, and an ongoing war with Spain. Charles wanted to give the country stability.

Parliament granted him a fixed revenue of £1,200,000 for life, but there was insufficient income from taxes to cover this. Charles agreed to a grant of £100,000 a year instead. He had learned from his father's mistakes and was determined not to lose the crown, or his head, by antagonising Parliament too much at the outset of his reign.

Determined to avoid further costly military conflict, he contrived to make peace with Spain. The Army had suffered under the Commonwealth regime and many men had not received their salary. Charles saw that every soldier was paid his due and gave each a financial bonus of an extra week's wages out of his own money.

Although Charles had promised a pardon for past crimes in the Declaration of Breda, this did not include regicide and men involved in the execution of Charles I were tried and sentenced to death. Between 13-19 October, 1660, some who had signed the death warrant were publicly hanged, drawn and quartered. But Charles II was not a vengeful monarch and requested that the hangings stopped. At least 18 lives were spared as a result.

Charles was also much more tolerant in his stance towards religion than either Cromwell or his father, although he had a secret bias towards the Catholics which did not go down well with Parliament. In 1662 Parliament passed an Act of Uniformity to ensure that England abided by Anglican doctrine and accepted the revised Book of Common Prayer.

A Corporation Act stated that only people who received Anglican Holy Communion could serve on the council. This meant that Catholics, Puritans and Nonconformists could not be part of local government. Charles's brother, James, Duke of York, failed to conform by converting to Catholicism. This created great concern for the future, as James was Charles's heir.

In 1672 Charles introduced a Declaration of Indulgence to negate any unfair laws passed by Parliament against Catholics, ordering, "that all manner of penal laws on matters ecclesiastical against whatever sort of Nonconformists or recusants should be from this day suspended."

This gave freedom for people of all denominations to worship as they wanted. Churches and chapels reopened, priests returned to their flocks, and people imprisoned because of their faith were set free. John Bunyan left his prison in Bedford after 12 years.

The Declaration of Indulgence proved unpopular with Parliament, however, as it insisted that "penal statutes in matters ecclesiastical cannot be suspended but by consent of Parliament". In retaliation, the government passed the Test Act of 1673 which excluded from all offices of State anyone who refused to take Anglican Communion.

This meant that no Roman Catholic could be a Member of Parliament or sit in the House of Lords, which affected many of Charles's ministers. The Lord Treasurer was forced to resign for being a Catholic and the King's own brother, James, Duke of York, gave up his position as Lord High Admiral.

The following year Parliament tried to pass an Exclusion Bill in an attempt to remove the Duke of York from the line of succession. Somewhat ironically, Charles II fathered at least 16 illegitimate children by seven mistresses, but had no legitimate offspring who could succeed him. As a result, his brother was next in line. The Whigs wanted the Duke of Monmouth, Charles's eldest natural son, to succeed instead.

Charles fought this Exclusion Bill with a Bill of his own and eventually dissolved Parliament in 1680, saying he would rather see the Duke of Monmouth hanged than legitimised. A year later he called Parliament to Oxford, where military pressure was exerted to prove that the King had power and that he was not going to be defeated like his father. It was an astute political move that worked.

In 1683 republicans amongst the recently-formed Whig faction in Parliament engineered the Rye House Plot, with the intention of assassinating the King and the Duke of York on their way home from the Newmarket races. The plot was thwarted when the King happened to leave Newmarket earlier than expected due to a fire at his lodgings. News of the plot had the effect of making the Whigs unpopular and the people of England became even more loyal to Charles and his brother. An earlier assassination plot by Catholics to kill the King, supposedly unearthed by Titus Oates, turned out to be a fabrication fuelled by anti-Catholic hysteria.

Although Charles took an interest in politics as Monarch, he had a greater interest in horse racing and women. By the time he was 18, Charles had already been seduced by the charms of various ladies. His first love affair was with a Mrs Windham, wife of the Governor of Bridgewater in Somerset. In 1649 a Lucy Walter gave birth to his son and the following year he fathered a daughter with Lady Shannon. Later in life he had liaisons with Lady Byron, the widowed Duchesse de Chatillon, Barbara Villiers, and actress Moll Davies, to name but a few.

His most notable mistress was Nell Gwynn, who went from orange seller in Covent Garden to comedienne at the Theatre Royal, Drury Lane. When she was once mistaken for the King's Catholic mistress, the Duchess of Portsmouth, Nell shouted out of her carriage window, "I am the Protestant whore!" As a result of his liaisons, in court circles Charles was nicknamed Old Rowley, the name of a stallion in the royal stud.

Despite his many love affairs and resulting illegitimate children, once he was monarch, Charles needed to marry and produce a legitimate heir to the throne. When the coronation was out of the way, he began to woo Catherine of Braganza, daughter of the King of Portugal. They were married on 21 May, 1662, at the Church of St Thomas à Becket in Portsmouth and honeymooned at Hampton Court.

Because she was a Roman Catholic, Catherine was never crowned Queen. She did, however, bring with her a substantial dowry, plus Bombay and Tangier, which boosted English trade. By the end of his reign, trading routes with India had been established.

Perhaps because he had already bedded so many beauties, Charles found Catherine physically unattractive and the marriage was childless. He continued to turn to other ladies of the court, notably Barbara, Lady Castlemaine, with whom he had at least four children. Prince William, Duke of Cambridge, can today trace his bloodline directly back to Charles II, through his mother Diana, Princess of Wales, who had two of the King's illegitimate sons in her ancestry.

Shortly after his marriage to Catherine of Braganza, a beautiful fair-haired girl arrived at court. Frances Stuart was a distant cousin and was appointed lady-in-waiting to Catherine. Described as being "a great beauty with very little brain", Charles was instantly attracted to her. So infatuated did he become that he even contemplated divorce, but to his dismay she eventually married the Duke of Richmond.

When Charles was designing a military medal for his forces, the face of Frances Stuart was used as the face of Britannia. This image was also used for the reverse side of coins and appeared on our pennies and halfpennies until 1971, when Britain adopted decimal currency. When Britannia was revived for the 2006 50p piece, she retained the original face. Sadly, in 1669 Frances Stuart contracted smallpox and the renowned beauty became permanently disfigured.

Life was not all pleasure for the King and there were times when he had to face reality. In 1665, war was declared with the Dutch, reigniting an old feud over commercial rights. On 4 June, 1665, the English navy sank eight Dutch battleships in the Battle of Lowestoft off the Norfolk coast. A Dutch colony in North America was captured and eventually became the English colonies of New York, New Jersey and Delaware.

In June 1667 a Dutch fleet took command of the Thames estuary and sailed up to Gravesend, destroyed 13 English ships which protected the Medway near Chatham, and towed away *HMS Unity* and the flagship *HMS Royal Charles*.

War with the Dutch finally ended on 19 February, 1674, with the Peace of Westminster, drawn up by Parliament which felt that no more money could be wasted on war. The Treaty stated, "That whatsoever countries, islands, towns, ports, castles, or forts have or shall be taken on both sides, since the time the late unhappy war broke out, either in Europe or elsewhere, shall be restored to the former lord or proprietor, in the same condition they shall be in when the peace itself shall be proclaimed."

Relations with the Dutch were further improved when Charles's niece, Mary, was married to Prince William of Orange. Relations with the French also improved when Charles sold Dunkirk to his cousin Louis XIV for £400,000. A group of the King's ministers – Sir Thomas Clifford, Lord Arlington, the Duke of Buckingham, Lord Ashley and Lord Lauderdale, whose initials spelt CABAL – devised a Treaty of Dover in 1670, which allied England and France in any future Dutch war.

The Treaty divided up Holland between England and France, bringing Charles an annuity from Louis which finally made him independent from Parliament, something that he had long wanted to achieve. He could now rule without being constrained by his ministers. When poet John Wilmot, 2nd Earl of Rochester and an old friend of the monarch, wrote that Charles II "never said a foolish thing, nor never did a wise one", the King replied, "This is very true, for my words are my own and my actions are my ministers'."

Whilst foreign relationships were better than in previous reigns, life in England improved too during Charles's reign. Public entertainment thrived again and not only were theatres re-opened, but some new ones were built. Charles loved the theatre and one of his first acts on returning to London from exile was to license two new theatres – one at Lincoln's Inn and another in Drury Lane, where the present Theatre Royal now stands. Theatre licences stated that female characters should be played by women, rather than boys or young men.

A new Habeas Corpus Act of 1679 gave personal freedom to every Englishman. No free man could be held in prison except on a charge or conviction of a crime, or for debt, and every prisoner on a charge could demand the issue of a writ of habeas corpus enabling a court to judge whether he had been lawfully imprisoned. There was also greater freedom for the press. From the time printing had enabled public and personal opinions to be widely distributed, there were legal licences to censor them. After 1679, this censorship ended.

With an interest in architecture, Charles personally oversaw the restoration of buildings, such as the Palace of Whitehall, that had been stripped of their grandeur by Cromwell. Splendour returned. Windsor Castle was also extensively modernised during his reign. A series of paintings by Sir Peter Lely, known as The Windsor Beauties, portraits of the most beautiful women at court, were commissioned to hang in the private apartments of the castle, something that would have been unthinkable during Oliver Cromwell's time.

London, however, was hit by two devastating events during Charles's reign. First came the Great Plague in 1664-65, when an estimated 70,000 to 100,000 people died in a six-month period. Charles and his court moved out of the capital to the safety of Salisbury.

Then on 2 September, 1666, a fire began at the premises of the King's baker, Thomas Farriner, in Fish Yard off Pudding Lane and spread westwards, destroying some 13,000 closely-packed timber houses and shops. Fortunately, only six lives were lost because the fire moved slowly, and most people had time to escape, though 461 acres of medieval London were razed to the ground in four days.

The old St Paul's Cathedral on Ludgate Hill was destroyed, as were 87 parish churches and 57 guild halls. Some architects have called it a blessing in disguise, as many unhealthy slum dwellings were removed and some magnificent new buildings arose in their place, including Christopher Wren's glorious new St Paul's Cathedral.

In 1677 a monument to the Great Fire was erected in Pudding Lane. Originally an inscription on the monument included the words 'But Popish frenzy which wrought such horrors is not yet quenched', highlighting the animosity towards the Catholic church that existed. The wording was removed 150 years later.

Diarists Samuel Pepys and John Evelyn both recorded that the King and his brother, James, personally helped put out fires in the City of London and that Charles's face and clothes were blackened with soot and soaked with water. The King later distributed 100 guineas amongst groups of fire-fighters. "It is not indeed imaginable how extraordinary the vigilance and activity of the King and Duke was, even labouring in person, and being present to command, order and encourage workmen; by which he [the King] showed his affection to his people and gained theirs," wrote Evelyn.

Indeed, affection for the King grew as his reign progressed. He was more carefree in his attitude than his father had been. Unlike his father, Charles did not believe in the Divine Right of Kings and so displayed more human qualities.

He was described by his contemporaries as a pleasant gentleman, playing with his spaniels, drawing caricatures of his ministers, throwing bread and cakes to wildfowl in the park. One of his courtiers said that Charles "delighted in a bewitching kind of pleasure called sauntering." Samuel Pepys, an administrator in the Royal Navy, added that "the King do mind nothing but pleasures and hates the very sight or thought of business." He was what today we would call laid back – he tended to take the easiest option.

"Whenever there was any strong opposition, he gave way," wrote one chronicler. "If popular feeling demanded the dismissal of his ministers, he dismissed them."

Charles II was a great conversationalist and raconteur, always telling witty stories, and was known for his sense of humour. When his brother warned him that there were plots against his life, Charles simply laughed it off saying, "They will never kill me, James, to make you king!"

Gilbert Burnet, Bishop of Salisbury at the end of the 17th century, wrote in his *History of My Own Time* that Charles II "loved to talk over all the stories of his life to every new man that came about him. He went over these in a very graceful manner; but so often, and so copiously, that all those who had been long accustomed to them grew weary of them: And when he entered on those stories, they usually withdrew: So that he often began them with a full audience, and before he had done there were not four or five left about him. Which drew a severe jest from Wilmot, Earl of Rochester. He said, he wondered to see a man have so good a memory as to repeat the same story without losing the least circumstance, and yet not remember that he had told it to the same persons the very day before."

Tall, handsome, with black eyes, black hair and a pencil-thin moustache, Charles adopted a black periwig which gave him an air of theatricality. It was a fashion that he had seen in France and he made popular in England once he became King.

One reason for wearing a wig at this period is believed to be because head lice were rife and it was much easier to remove them from a wig than from natural hair. Many people overcame the problem by having their heads shaved and wore a wig instead. Samuel Pepys, however, was less convinced and wrote in his diaries about the drawback of wigs:

9th May, 1663 . . . to Westminster, where at Mr Jervas's, my old barber, I did try two or three borders and periwiggs, meaning to wear one; and yet I have no stomach [for it] but that the pains of keeping my hair clean is so great. He trimmed me, and at last I parted, but my mind was almost altered from my first purpose, from the trouble that I foresee will be in wearing them also.

18th July, 1664 . . . to Westminster to my barber's, to have my periwigg he lately made me cleansed of its nits, which vexed me cruelly that he should put such a thing into my hands.

3rd September, 1665 (Lord's Day). Up, and put on my coloured silk suit very fine, and my new periwigg, bought a good while since, but durst not wear, because the plague was in Westminster when I bought it; and it is a wonder what will be the fashion after the plague is done, as to periwiggs, for nobody will dare to buy any haire, for fear of the infection, that it had been cut off of the heads of people dead of the plague.

4th April 1667 Up, and going down found Jervas the barber with a periwigg which I had the other day cheapened at Westminster, but it being full of nits, as heretofore his work used to be, I did now refuse it, having bought elsewhere.

In the Middle Ages it was believed in England that Kings had healing powers and that a touch from royalty could cure the skin disease scrofula, known as the "King's Evil". Scrofula was usually a swelling of the lymph nodes in the neck caused by tuberculosis. The practice began with King Edward the Confessor in 1058. Belief in the Divine Right of Kings was very strong by the time of the Stuarts and increasingly people wanted to be touched by the King. It is said that Charles II touched over 9,000 people during his reign, the touching usually happening during a religious service. But philosopher and writer John Aubrey recorded the story of a man called Evans: "Arise Evans had a fungous nose, and said it was revealed to him that the King's hand would cure him: and at the first coming of King Charles II into St James's Park, he kiss'd the King's hand, and rubbed his nose with it; which disturbed the King, but cured him."

In 1682, Charles laid the foundation stone for a new hospital for sick and elderly soldiers in Chelsea. The Royal Hospital became home to Chelsea Pensioners in 1692 – old soldiers "of good character" in time of need. It was based on a system the King had seen at the Hôpital des Invalides in Paris, instigated by Louis XIV. Founder's Day is still celebrated every year at the Royal Hospital Chelsea on a date close to Charles's birthday, Oak Apple Day, when a gold statue of him is adorned with oak leaves. A member of the current Royal Family usually attends.

The final years of Charles's life were relatively uneventful. He was financially secure and had a loyal army and navy, with his brother at the helm as Lord High Admiral. He appeared to have the upper hand with Parliament and continued to live a life of pleasure in private.

It was while dining with one of his mistresses, the Duchess of Portsmouth, in February 1685 that the King suffered an apoplectic fit. His condition worsened over the next three days and he was given the Last Rites by Father John Hudleston, who had helped him escape after the Battle of Worcester 34 years earlier. His last act was to be received into the Roman Catholic church and he made his confession and received the Sacrament.

Some of the children of his mistresses gathered around the death bed at Whitehall Palace, London, and Charles blessed each one and pulled them on to the bed to be close to him. Witty to the end, he apologised for taking "an unconscionable time a-dying". His last thought was of his favourite mistress, whispering to his brother and successor, "Do not let poor Nelly starve."

His final recorded words were, "Open the curtains that I may once more see day." He then went on to ask that one of his favourite clocks should be wound, otherwise it would stop. He died at 11.45 am on the morning of 6 February at the age of 54.

After lying in state at the Palace of Westminster, a simple funeral was held on the evening of 14 February before he was laid to rest in the south aisle of Henry VII's Chapel in Westminster Abbey. A life size wax effigy of the King, some 6ft 2in tall, dressed in robes of the Order of the Garter complete with plumed hat, stood beside the grave for over a century. Taken from a life cast of the King's face, it is said to be a remarkable likeness and has been on display in a new museum and gallery at Westminster Abbey since 2018.

Chapter 43

James II 1633–1701
Reign: 1685–1688

Opinions about King James II were mixed in his lifetime and have remained divided ever since. One of his friends and supporters, Thomas Bruce, 2nd Earl of Ailesbury, wrote in his memoirs, "I do affirm that he was the most honest and sincere man I ever knew: a great and good Englishman, and a high protector of trade, and had nothing so much at heart as the glory and strength of the fleet and navy."

Yet the Victorian historian Henry Buckle, in his *History of Civilisation in England* (1857), wrote, "It makes one's flesh creep to think that such a man should have been the ruler of millions," calling James II both "a disgrace" and "a slur on the age." Others concur that he would have made an excellent King of France or Spain but did not quite suit the England in which he lived.

Some historians consider him to have been a very weak man, and the diarist Samuel Pepys wrote of him, "The Duke of York, in all things but his amours, is led by the nose of his wife." But above all he appears to have been a man of considerable contrasts. If an ineffectual King, he was nevertheless a brave soldier. He was married twice and had many mistresses, yet was a religious zealot. He believed firmly in the Divine Right of Kings but too easily gave up his crown.

James II was born at St James's Palace in London at midnight on 14 October, 1633, the second surviving son of Charles I and Henrietta Maria, and the brother of King Charles II. He was called Duke of York from birth, and in 1642 was made a Knight of the Garter. He later became Earl of

Ulster and Duke of Normandy. Unusually, he was appointed Lord High Admiral at the age of three. It was an honorary title, although he did take on the role in a practical way as an adult.

He was educated by private tutors but, as he grew older, it was said that he was not hugely intelligent or witty, and lacked the charm of his brother Charles. He had a fair complexion as a youth and grew to be very tall, once described as being "two yards high". Paintings show him regally dressed and with an elaborately curled periwig as an adult. Even if depicted wearing armour, he would still be swathed with sashes and cloaks.

Armour made for him in 1686 can be seen today at the Royal Armoury in the Tower of London. It is highly decorative and bears his initials IR (Iacabus Rex). It was the only finely embellished royal armour ever made by a member of the London Armourers Company and the last suit of armour made for a King of England.

James's education was curtailed by the Civil War, which came to dominate his childhood. He was with his father at the Battle of Edgehill, and was almost killed when a cannon ball missed him by inches. For his own safety James was sent to live in Oxford, which was a Royalist stronghold, but following a siege there in 1646 he was moved back to St James's Palace.

Instead of being a home, however, his birthplace became a prison. James managed to escape in 1648 with the help of an Irish colonel called Joseph Bampfield. In preparation James started playing hide-and-seek with his brother and sister, and his captors grew used to him disappearing for up to half-an-hour at a time. One evening James was able to slip out of a side door and his absence went unnoticed for long enough that he could run away. Colonel Bampfield was waiting for him at the garden gate and took the 15-year-old straight to the home of a local doctor. He was eventually smuggled out of the country and taken to The Hague disguised as a young girl to avoid detection.

Colonel Bampfield had measured the Duke with a tape and Anne Murray, later Lady Halkett, had a suitable outfit made. In her autobiography which is now in the British Library, Lady Halkett wrote: "When I gave the measure to my tailor to enquire how much mohair would serve to make a petticoat and waistcoat for a young gentlewoman of that bigness and stature, he considered for a long time, and said he had made many gowns and suits, but he had never made any to such a person in his life . . .

"His meaning was, he had never seen any woman of so low a stature have so big a waist. However, he made it fit as exactly as if he had taken the measure himself. It was a mixed mohair colour of light hair and black, with a scarlet petticoat."

Lady Halkett added that when the time came for the young Duke to escape, "His Highness called, 'Quickly, quickly, dress me,' and putting off his clothes, I dressed him in the woman's habit that was prepared, which fitted His Highness very well. He was very pretty in it."

As James set off just before midnight, Lady Halkett gave him a Wood Street cake – a lightly yeasted fruit cake with rose water icing – "which I knew he loved", to sustain him on the journey. James's disguise was effective, even when he rested his feet on a table in an unladylike manner, and he eventually reached Paris, where he was able to stay with his mother.

By the age of 19 he had begun to serve in the French army and became a Lieutenant-General. He was given his own Regiment of York, and experienced military combat in the War of Fronde, a French civil war, receiving praise for his apparent lack of fear. He later said that being part of the French army was the happiest of times for him.

Following the execution of Charles I in 1649, and with England under the control of Oliver Cromwell, James's elder brother Charles attempted to claim the throne that was rightfully his. When Charles turned to Spain for help, the brothers were suddenly at odds. Spain was an enemy of France and James felt strongly that their loyalty should be to France. When it became known that Charles had allied himself with Spain, James was expelled from the French army.

With his younger brother, Henry, James travelled to Bruges, and eventually joined the Spanish army. In a twist of fate, he then found himself fighting unwillingly against French soldiers at the Battle of Dunes, soldiers who had once been his friends. In 1659 there was a truce between France and Spain but by this time James had developed a closer bond with the Spanish and was even offered the post of Admiral in their navy. But everything was to change for the Stuarts when his brother was restored to the throne as King Charles II in 1660.

James was now the heir presumptive, although it seemed unlikely that he would ever inherit the throne. Charles was married and it was assumed that he would father heirs of his own to succeed. As it happened, Charles had numerous children with a variety of mistresses but no legitimate heir.

In the year that the monarchy was restored James married Anne Hyde, who was the daughter of the King's chief minister, Edward Hyde. She and James had been little more than a dalliance in the previous year but when she revealed that she was expecting a child, James offered to marry her.

This did not go down well with King Charles or his court. As a commoner, Anne was not considered to be a suitable bride for a royal Duke.

James refused to acquiesce and married Anne secretly at Breda, Holland. Once the deed was done and there was no going back, James informed his family. Consequently, James and Anne were given a second, more public wedding on 3 September, 1660, at Worcester House in The Strand, London. A son was born two months later but died within weeks. A further five children also died in infancy but two daughters survived: Mary, born 1662, and Anne, born 1665. Both were destined to become Queens of England.

On his brother's accession, James was given the Scottish title Duke of Albany and was eventually made Lord High Commissioner for Scotland, with Holyrood House in Edinburgh as his official residence. The office of Lord High Admiral, that was originally granted to him as a child, now became an official role and he commanded the navy during subsequent wars with the Dutch.

A particular success was his defeat of a Dutch fleet off the coast of Lowestoft in June 1665. He was also appointed Governor of Portsmouth and Lord Warden of the Cinque Ports, and he oversaw the refortification of the South Coast of England.

In 1664 Charles II gave his brother territory in America between the Delaware and Connecticut rivers. The former Dutch territory – surrendered to England without a fight – was renamed in his honour. The port of New Amsterdam became known as New York after James's title, Duke of York.

When London was hit by the Great Plague, James and Anne sought refuge in Salisbury and later Oxford in the summer of 1665 to avoid being infected. They returned to the capital once the plague had subsided but London was soon hit by another disaster: the Great Fire of London in September 1666. James was put in charge of bringing the fire under control.

In his private life, James remained devoted to Anne until her death from breast cancer in 1671, although he was regularly unfaithful. Samuel Pepys wrote in his diary about how at a service in the Chapel Royal "the Duke and Mrs Palmer did talk to one another wantonly through the hangings."

James kept various mistresses including Arabella Churchill (an ancestor of Winston), with whom he fathered four children. He made no secret of the liaison and the offspring were given the surname FitzJames. Another mistress was Catherine Sedley, whom he later created Countess of Dorchester. It became a family joke that James was attracted to plain women rather than great beauties and Charles II teased his brother saying that the women were imposed upon him as a penance.

Even Catherine Sedley wondered why James had selected her as a mistress. "It cannot be my beauty for he must see that I have none," she remarked.

Catherine worked for an Italian princess, Mary of Modena, whom the widowed James married in 1673, first by proxy at the Ducal Palace in Modena on 30 September and then in person on 21 November with a wedding ceremony in Dover, Kent. The fact that Mary, the new Duchess of York, was a Roman Catholic made her unpopular in England and on her arrival, Londoners burned an effigy of the Pope in protest. James fathered twelve children with Mary, most dying in infancy or early childhood, although two survived in to adulthood.

Towards the end of Charles II's reign, there was a republican plot to assassinate both the King and James, as his immediate heir, because of their Roman Catholic leanings. It was known as the Rye House Plot, named after a house at Hoddesdon, Hertfordshire, which the brothers were supposed to pass on their way home from the Newmarket races and outside which they were to be killed. It was their good fortune to leave the races early and the plot was foiled. When it became common knowledge, there was a huge wave of public support and affection for the King and the Duke. The Rye House Plot was instigated by the Earl of Essex, who committed suicide, and the Duke of Monmouth, who fled abroad for his own safety – although Monmouth later returned with a vengeance.

When Charles II died on 6 February, 1685, his brother came to the throne as King James II of England and Ireland, and also James VII of Scotland. He was privately crowned at Whitehall Palace with Catholic rites on 22 April, and the following day, St George's Day, with full ceremony at Westminster Abbey, along with his wife, Mary, although they refused the Anglican sacrament.

It was a time of rejoicing for the people of England and there was no opposition from Parliament at the start of the reign. When Members assembled in May 1685, they became known as the Loyal Parliament. Nearly all officers kept their positions and the new King forgave those who had opposed him in the past and had wanted him removed from the line of succession. So it was a smooth transition.

Parliament also granted the King a very generous financial settlement with a Revenue Bill that assured him an income for life. It is interesting that his speech of thanks was as much a plea that Parliament should also help others, saying that the navy's stores were exhausted; there were great burdens on the Revenue; the late King's debts to his family and servants deserved compassion; and a rebellion in Scotland was proving extremely expensive to bring under control.

"I would not call upon you unnecessarily for an extraordinary supply," he said, "But I am sure such considerations will move you to give me an aid, to provide for those things, wherein the security, the ease, and the happiness of my Government, are so much concerned. But, above all, I must recommend to you the care of the Navy, the strength and glory of this Nation, that you will put it into such a condition, as may make us considered and respected abroad.

"I cannot express my concern upon this occasion more suitable to my own thoughts of it, than by assuring you I have a true English Heart, as jealous of the honour of the Nation as you can be. And I please myself with the hopes, that, by God's blessing and your assistance, I may carry the reputation of it yet higher in the world, than ever it has been in the time of any of my ancestors. And as I will not call upon you for supplies but when they are of public use and advantage; so I promise you, that what you give me upon such occasions shall be managed with good husbandry, and I will take care it shall be employed to the uses for which I ask them."

Although the reign had begun smoothly, it was not long before trouble started brewing and James faced rebellions in both England and Scotland. The most serious was led by his nephew the Duke of Monmouth, an illegitimate son of Charles II by his mistress Lucy Walters. Monmouth felt that, as Charles's son, he should have been the next monarch. He firmly believed that, because he was a Protestant, the whole of England would support him.

He landed at Lyme Regis on 11 June and was proclaimed King by his supporters at Taunton in Somerset. Monmouth stayed at the George Inn at Norton St Philip, which became his headquarters while planning his rebellion. The inn still exists and is one of England's oldest taverns, having first been granted a licence to sell alcohol in 1397.

On 6 July, 1685, Monmouth's army of some 4,000 men mounted a surprise nighttime attack on James II's royalist forces at Westonzoyland, a village near Bridgewater in Somerset. In what has become known as the Battle of Sedgemoor, Monmouth was easily defeated. His army was made up of farmers and local workers that he had gathered, rather than trained soldiers, and he had weapons for only a quarter of the men.

Consequently, they were forced to fight with pitchforks and any improvised weapon that came to hand, which were no match against James's infantrymen and dragoons, led by the Earl of Faversham and

General John Churchill, the future Duke of Marlborough. Around 1,300 of Monmouth's supporters were killed and he was later found hiding in a ditch. He was captured and sentenced to death.

The Duke of Monmouth was executed at the Tower of London on 15 July. More than 300 of his followers were hanged, others were flogged or fined, and around 800 were deported and sold into slavery following the "Bloody Assizes" of Judge Jeffreys. It was not an auspicious start to James II's reign. There were also rumours that the Queen and courtiers had made a shameless profit out of the sale of pardons and that the King had sanctioned acts of cruelty.

"This marble," said General Churchill, tapping on a chimneypiece, "is not harder than the King's heart." James increased the size of his army to 10,000 men to give England greater protection, which he hoped would act as a deterrent to any future insurgents.

Across the border, there was also a small rebellion in Scotland when the Earl of Argyll sailed from Holland, where he had been hiding following a conviction for treason. Accompanied by 300 men, he tried to raise an army of the Campbell clan, but it came to nothing and Argyll was taken prisoner in Edinburgh on 18 June, 1685, and was sentenced to death as a traitor.

As with so many of his predecessors, the matter of religion came to dominate much of James II's reign. He was England's last Roman Catholic monarch and some Protestant MPs fought against him as he tried to obtain acceptance for Catholics and non-conformists to worship, as his brother had done before him.

It was while living in France that James had been drawn to the Catholic faith and secretly converted to Catholicism in around 1668. He applied for a papal dispensation which would enable him to continue worshipping in the Church of England for the sake of appearances, but Pope Clement IX refused to grant it. During the reign of Charles II, Parliament introduced the Test Act of 1673 which required anyone holding civil or military office to denounce Catholic practices and to receive the eucharist only in the Anglican church. James refused to accept this and relinquished his position as Lord High Admiral.

In doing so, he effectively revealed his Catholic conversion and Parliament tried unsuccessfully to have him removed from the line of succession. Whilst remaining a Catholic, James agreed that his daughters, Mary and Anne, should be brought up as Protestants so that their place in the line was secure.

When, as King, he wanted to allow Roman Catholics to command regiments he faced opposition from his once loyal Parliament. The Tories were the dominant power and were staunchly Anglican. The Whigs tolerated non-conformists. Both parties were anti-Catholic. Not to be undermined, James discontinued the Parliamentary session and it never sat again for the rest of his reign.

He placed Catholics in high offices, including important positions at Oxford colleges, and in 1687 issued a Declaration of Indulgence, which effectively ended all laws that were unfavourable to Catholics. In it he said, "We cannot but heartily wish all the people of our dominion were members of the Catholic Church." Later that year the King made a tour of the West of England, giving speeches to encourage greater toleration for Catholicism. In a speech at Chester he made an impassioned and enlightened observation.

"Suppose," he said, "there should be a law that all black men should be imprisoned; it would be unreasonable. And we had as little reason to quarrel with other men for being of different opinions as for being of different complexions."

The following year, at his instigation, it was proposed that a revised version of the Declaration should be read out in every Anglican church in England on two successive Sundays. Most vicars in England refused and, where they did, congregations walked out of church. The Archbishop of Canterbury, William Sancroft, and six Bishops, fiercely opposed the Declaration. They were arrested, imprisoned in the Tower of London, and put on trial for seditious libel, but were later acquitted.

James was at Hounslow when news came of the acquittal and heard a great shout from the army camp. When he asked what the commotion was about, he was told, "It is nothing, only the soldiers are glad that the Bishops are acquitted." The King was annoyed. "Do you call that nothing?" he shouted. He had the camp at Hounslow closed down and the troops were dispersed to distant garrisons.

He also requested the names of every clergyman who had disobeyed him by not reading out his Declaration, although no names were forthcoming. James seemed thwarted on every side. "Are you not aware that I am above the law?" he once asked the Duke of Somerset. "I am the King. I will be obeyed!" he told Fellows of Magdalen College, Oxford. But it was a constant battle to have his religious stance accepted.

On 10 June, 1688, James became a father again when Queen Mary gave birth to a son, christened James Francis Edward and immediately titled Prince of Wales. As a male he superseded James's Protestant daughters and became a Roman Catholic heir to the throne. To discredit this new Prince,

James's Protestant enemies invented the warming pan story, spreading rumours that the baby had been smuggled into the Queen's bedchamber. As a result, there was always doubt that he was actually a son of James II and the Prince became known eventually as The Old Pretender.

On 22 October, 1688, James made a declaration to Parliament that the Prince of Wales was genuinely his son and heir, but it was rejected. In the era before DNA testing, parentage was hard to prove. The young Prince was barred from the line of succession by an Act of Settlement and subsequently had to forfeit his British titles. Although royal births had witnesses, none appeared to be impartial at Queen Mary's confinement.

James's daughter Anne should have been present at the birth but had been persuaded to visit Bath instead. "I should be unfortunate to be out of town when the Queen was brought to bed," said Anne, "for I should never now be satisfied whether the child be true or false. Maybe it is our brother, but God only knows."

Within weeks the Bishop of London and a group of six prominent politicians invited the Dutch William of Orange, who was James's nephew and son-in-law, to come to England to "save the Protestant religion".

William of Orange landed at Brixham, Devon, on 5 November, 1688. A statue at the harbour now commemorates his arrival. An army of some 13,000 men followed and marched through Exeter and on to Bristol and Salisbury. It was the beginning of what is now called the Glorious Revolution, with James's supporters becoming known as Jacobites after the Latin version of James. The King was taken by surprise, expecting William to land in Kent rather than Devon.

His army prepared to confront William's men at Warminster, but the King was stricken with a serious nosebleed on 19 November and withdrew, eventually going back home to Whitehall Palace in London, where he discovered that even his daughter Anne had fled to Nottingham. The army and navy lost confidence in their monarch and soon the whole English navy became supporters of William.

James decided to run rather than fight for his position, first destroying as many government papers as he could lay his hands on. With the Queen and the baby Prince of Wales escaping in advance to France, James set off to join them, leaving London in the early hours of 11 December. At Vauxhall he threw the Great Seal of the Realm into the River Thames, which symbolically marked the end of his reign. He had been on the throne for just three years and many historians consider that he gave up the crown far too easily.

"He had all the weakness of his father without his strength," wrote 17th-century politician John Maitland, 5th Earl of Lauderdale.

James was preparing to set sail from Sheerness when he was recognised, captured, and returned to London. William of Orange, placed in a difficult position with James being his father-in-law, decided that the King should be set free. On 23 December James crossed the English Channel, arriving at Ambleteuse, near Boulogne on Christmas Day. He went directly to his cousin, King Louis XIV of France, who gave him a home at St Germain and a pension.

Jacobite sympathizers in England began to drink a secret toast to "the King over the water" as a sign of their allegiance to him, holding their glasses over finger-bowls of water on the table. Fellow supporters instantly recognised the sign.

The news that James had thrown the Great Seal into the River Thames was taken by Parliament to mean that the King had voluntarily given up the crown. It was agreed that William of Orange would become King of England and rule jointly with his wife, James's eldest daughter, Mary.

A Bill of Rights brought an official end to James II's reign and included clauses that still affected the Monarchy into the 21st century: stating that no Roman Catholic could be King or Queen, and no-one in the line of succession could marry a Catholic. In 1978 Prince Michael of Kent gave up his place in the line of succession to marry the Roman Catholic Marie Christine von Reibnitz.

The Duke of Kent's eldest son, the Earl of St Andrews, also lost his place in 1988 on marrying the Catholic Sylvana Tomaselli. Following a new Succession to the Crown Act, which came into force in 2015, anyone marrying a Catholic is no longer disqualified. Consequently, Prince Michael and the Earl of St Andrews was reinstated in the line of succession.

James II was deemed to have abdicated on 11 December, 1688, when he fled the country. Coincidentally, when Edward VIII abdicated in 1936 it was also on 11 December. James was formally deposed on 23 December and, after a short interregnum, was succeeded in February 1689 by his Protestant son-in-law, and the reign of King William III and Queen Mary II began.

On 11 April, 1689, Scotland also decided that James had given up the crown and was no longer their King.

Although James appeared to cast off the mantle of sovereignty without a fight, he did make attempts to reclaim his crown. In March 1689 he sailed to Ireland, where an Act of Liberty and Conscience had been passed by the

Irish Parliament, which granted religious freedom to all Catholics and Protestants. Basing himself in Dublin, he formed an army and on 1 July 1690 attacked the forces of William of Orange 30 miles away on the River Boyne.

William personally led his army, the last time two Kings of England faced each other in battle, and had a decisive victory at the Battle of the Boyne. It marked a turning point in the Protestant history of Ireland and is commemorated every July with a public holiday and a march of Orangemen through the streets of Northern Ireland.

James returned to France and never visited England again. He did send an invasion fleet from Normandy in May 1692 in one final attempt to regain the throne, but lost in the resulting naval battles of Barfleur and La Hougue. It marked the point where he finally resigned himself to the fact that he would never be King of England again.

In 1697 Louis XIV signed the Treaty of Ryswick, which brought to an end a nine-year French conflict with England, Spain and the Holy Roman Empire, and also stripped James of his independent army. In the Treaty, Louis finally recognised William III as King of England and promised to give James no further military support.

Louis XIV continued to support James on a personal level as his cousin and gave him the magnificent Chateau de Saint-Germain-en-Laye, where he lived with his wife and some English Jacobite supporters, and which became his home for the rest of his life. In 1692 he became a father again with the birth of a daughter, Louise, whom he called "his solace".

A shadow of his former self, James spent his time quietly, composing religious treatises. He was given one last opportunity to wear a crown when Louis offered him the throne of Poland. Being a firm believer in hereditary monarchy, James refused to be king of a country that was not his by right of birth.

James died at the Chateau on 16 September, 1701, at the age of 68 after suffering a brain haemorrhage. Unusually, the former King was not buried but his coffin rested in the Chapel of St Edmund at the Church of English Benedictines in Paris, guarded by monks. They believed that someone from England would make arrangements to transport the body to London to be buried amongst his royal predecessors in Westminster Abbey, but nobody did.

Rather gruesomely, his remains were eventually divided up by the monks, possibly in the belief that he would one day be canonised and the parts would become holy relics. His heart, brain and entrails were given to various religious institutions; even flesh from his right arm was presented to a group of English Augustinian nuns.

The rest of his body was kept at the Church of English Benedictines until the French Revolution, when the building was looted and destroyed. James's remains were rediscovered in 1824 and were reburied, along with those of his second wife, Mary of Modena. In 1855 Queen Victoria visited St Germain and personally paid for a memorial to James in the church to mark his final resting place.

Chapter 44

William III
1650–1702
Reign: 1689–1702

Mary II
1662–1694
Reign: 1689–1694

The "Glorious Revolution" that led to the deposition of King James II saw the Catholic monarch flee to France in December 1688 leaving the throne of England vacant. His successor was his eldest daughter, Mary, who had married Prince William III of Orange. At the instigation of the Bishop of London and several government ministers, the Dutch Prince William was invited to England to try and give the country stability and restore the Protestant faith, although Parliament never actually intended to give him the Crown.

A month before James II's departure, Prince William of Orange landed at Brixham harbour, Torbay, on 5 November, 1688 with an army of some 13,000 men, declaring, "The Liberties of England and the Protestant religion I will maintain." He was soon joined by English soldiers and sailors who had deserted James II. Parliament initially saw William's role as that of Regent but he did not want a Regency and insisted on being King. He told a "Convention Parliament" at the beginning of 1689, "I have not come to establish a Republic or be a Duke of Venice," adding that neither would he be his "wife's gentleman usher".

Equally Mary, the rightful heir, was not content with reigning on her own or simply being a Consort, declaring that she did not want "a divided interest" coming between husband and wife. Parliament reluctantly accepted them as a couple, to rule jointly as King and Queen.

The only time this had happened in England's long royal history was when Mary I married Philip of Spain in 1554. Under the Marriage Act of the time, he was styled King of England to rule alongside her, but only because of his wife's position. He was never actually crowned in England and the marriage was short-lived.

William and Mary officially acceded to the throne on 13 February, 1689, and were crowned King William III and Queen Mary II two months later at Westminster Abbey by the Bishop of London. The then Archbishop of Canterbury, William Sancroft, was a Jacobite, supporting James II and refused to recognise William and Mary as sovereigns.

Over the centuries there had been countless struggles between the monarch and Parliament but this ended with the reign of William and Mary, as they were considered to be constitutional monarchs – chosen to rule by Parliament rather than as heirs under the Divine Right of Kings. In December 1689 a new Bill of Rights was passed, said to be one of the most significant documents in England's constitutional history. It decreed that no Catholic could be King or Queen of England. This was to prevent another James II situation, where a Protestant monarch had converted to Catholicism after being crowned.

The new monarchs had their powers curtailed by the Bill and could not, for example, use the royal prerogative to suspend laws, increase taxes or raise an army without Parliament's approval. Parliament now had the upper hand. The Bill of Rights also established the royal line of succession, with Queen Mary's sister, Princess Anne, being named as the next in line to the throne after any children that William and Mary might have. A later Civil List Act gave Parliament control over royal expenditure and granted William and Mary £700,000 a year for their official duties and the running of the royal household. This figure remained unchanged until the reign of George III.

Within a few months of being crowned, William and Mary bought a property in the Kensington area of London called Nottingham House. The Surveyor of the King's Works, Sir Christopher Wren, enlarged the house, building three-storey extensions at each corner of the original building, an entrance archway and clock tower. William and Mary's court took up residence in time for Christmas 1689 and their new home was renamed Kensington Palace.

Within the grounds is a small property, still known as Nottingham Cottage. In this century it was briefly the home of the Duke and Duchess of Cambridge before they moved into the Palace, and more recently Prince Harry before his marriage. William and Mary had not been residents for long when a fire broke out one night at the Palace. William helped remove furniture and paintings, dressed in his nightshirt.

Although Dutch born, William was a nephew and son-in-law of James II, and a grandson of Charles I, so had some Stuart blood in his veins. He was born at the Binnenhof Palace in The Hague on 14 November, 1650, the posthumous son of William II of Orange (who had died just eight days earlier) and his wife Mary the Princess Royal, eldest daughter of Charles I and sister of Charles II and James II. William had no siblings.

He was baptised Willem Hendrik and from birth was William III, Prince of Orange, and Stadtholder of Holland, although was not allowed to use the title until adulthood. Stadtholder was leader or the "first noble", and throughout his childhood and youth the Dutch people lived through what is known as The Stadtholderless Period. The young Prince William was given an English honour in 1645, being made a Knight of the Garter.

With his father having died, William's guardians became his mother, paternal grandmother and an uncle, although he saw very little of his mother, who appeared to have no real interest in him. He was educated by a succession of governesses and a male tutor, and received religious instruction from a Calvinist minister. He began a more formal education from the age of nine at the University of Leiden, founded in 1575 and now the oldest university in the Netherlands. He studied there until he was 16 and learned to speak French, German, Latin and Spanish.

It was never kept from him that he would one day be head of the House of Orange, an aristocratic dynasty that had long played a central role in politics and government of the Netherlands. By the time William was 16, his mother had died and he was made a Child of the State. It is said that all pro-English supporters were removed from the royal court and William's focus was very much on Dutch affairs. As his 18th birthday approached, champions of the House of Orange pressed for him to become legally Stadtholder and Captain-General.

In a somewhat complicated system the Netherlands at the time was broken into seven provinces, known as the Dutch Republic, with Holland being the wealthiest and most powerful province. Stadtholders governed the country together with the States General (consisting of a Senate and a House of Representatives). William was appointed First Noble of Zeeland, one of the seven provinces, although Holland then abolished the position of Stadtholder altogether. William wrote unsuccessfully to his uncle, King Charles II, asking him to make him Stadtholder in return for an alliance with England.

In 1672 the Netherlands was invaded by France, along with its allies. This caused panic within the country and in July that year Holland relented and made William Stadtholder. As the war went on into a second year, William increased his power as a military leader and became Stadtholder of more provinces.

Throughout his adult life William saw King Louis XIV of France as his staunch enemy. In 1674 he was encouraged by his uncle King Charles II of England to marry Mary, elder daughter of his brother James, Duke of York. It was felt that marriage would unite William and the Dutch with England and make them stronger in their fight against France. But William was unenthusiastic.

"I cannot leave the battlefield," he said, "nor believe it would be agreeable for a lady to be where the battlefield is." He prevaricated for three more years before finally agreeing to marry his cousin Mary.

Mary had been born at St James's Palace on 30 April, 1662, the eldest daughter and heir of James, Duke of York (later James II) and his first wife Anne Hyde. The Duke was disappointed that she was not a boy. Although her parents converted to Catholicism, Mary was raised as a Protestant and remained so throughout her life. She was eventually disowned by her father when she accepted the English crown that he had abandoned.

Her childhood was spent largely at Richmond Palace the home of her grandfather, where she was brought up with her sister, Anne, under a governess called Lady Frances Villiers. The girls rarely saw their parents. Mary had a succession of tutors and proved to be particularly good at drawing and dancing. She also studied music, French, and religious education. At the age of 15, Mary found herself engaged to Prince William of Orange. When told that she was to marry, her chaplain reported that Mary, "wept all that afternoon and all the following day."

The couple married on 4 November, 1677, at St James's Palace in London. It was initially a joyless marriage, and the couple failed to produce an heir, although Mary grew to love her husband, once writing in a letter to him that it was "a passion that cannot end but with my life." Unlike many of his predecessors, William is only known to have had one mistress during his marriage: Elizabeth Villiers, later Countess of Orkney, one of the Queen's ladies-in-waiting and a daughter of Mary's former governess, Lady Frances Villiers.

William and Mary spent the first decade of their married life in Holland and a great deal of time apart. "What can be more cruel in the world than parting with what one loves," she wrote to a close friend. "And not only common parting, but parting so as one may be never to meet again, to be perpetually in fear, for God knows when I may see him, or whether he is not now, at this instant, in battle."

When they moved to England, William was invariably involved in peace negotiations and put his work before his wife, while Mary spent a lot of time at St James's Palace nursing her sick sister, Anne. Mary had a strong faith and it is said that she lived as if she were a nun. She had her dining room turned into a chapel because her husband never ate with her. Short in stature, but buxom, Mary was known for her warm heart and bright smiles. Being English born, she was always more popular than her husband, although William did absolutely nothing to court popularity once he was King of England.

William was also short in height, some 4½ inches less than his wife, and thin. He had contracted smallpox as a child, which had left him asthmatic and with a deep cough throughout his life, exacerbated by the London fog. Described as taciturn, William had a cold manner, few friends and certainly no English ones. It is said that he never loved the English and they never loved him. His greatest passion was hunting, as on horseback he was alone and did not need to speak to anyone.

An example of his remoteness was when he once ate the greatly coveted first peas of the season in front of his sister-in-law, Anne, without offering her a single one. She said later that she "had so much a mind to the peas that she was afraid to look at them, and yet could hardly keep her eyes off them!"

Gilbert Burnet, Bishop of Salisbury, in his *History of His Own Time*, has left us with a first-hand portrait of William's character, writing that he was, "much neglected in his education; for all his life long he hated constraint. He spoke little. He put on some appearance of application, but he hated business of all sorts. Yet, he hated talking, and all house games, more.

"This put him on a perpetual course of hunting, to which he seemed to give himself up, beyond any man I ever knew: but I looked on that as a flying from company and business. He had a way that was affable and obliging to the Dutch. But he could not bring himself to comply enough with the temper of the English, his coldness and slowness being very contrary to the genius of the nation."

Thomas Macaulay in his *History of England* (1848) reveals more of the King's manner, writing: "He was in truth far better qualified to save a nation than adorn a court. He seldom came forth out of his closet, and when he appeared in the public rooms, he stood among the crowd of courtiers and ladies, stern and abstracted, making no jest, and smiling at none. His freezing look, his silence, the dry and concise answers which he uttered when he could keep silence no longer, disgusted noblemen and gentlemen who had been accustomed to being slapped on the back by their royal masters. He spoke our language, but not well. His accent was foreign; his diction was inelegant, and his vocabulary seems to have been no larger than was necessary for the transaction of business."

One of the reasons that William was not particularly liked by the English people during his reign is because it quickly became clear that he primarily considered himself to be Dutch. Through England he was able to save Holland from the grasp of Louis XIV of France, and that was where his main interest in the country lay.

Within months of becoming joint sovereigns of England, William and Mary were also offered the crown of Scotland. There were many Jacobite uprisings to try to prevent this, including the Battles of Killiecrankie and Dunkeld, and the Massacre of Glencoe, which made William unpopular in Scotland as well as England. He had an equally tough fight in Ireland, which was predominantly Catholic and very anti-England. But he did eventually become William I of Ireland, William II of Scotland, William III of England and William IV of Normandy.

England became involved in seven wars during their reign, which kept William out of the country for long periods. Mary was left at the helm during his absence. Although she had more right to the throne than her husband, as the daughter of a King, she did not enjoy these periods of solo rule.

"I found myself at Whitehall as in a new world," she wrote, "deprived of all that was dear to me in the person of my husband, left among those that were perfect strangers to me. My sister of a humour so reversed that I could have little comfort from her; the Great Council of a strange composition, the Cabinet not much better and the Treasury was in a bad condition, there was no money."

The wars with France were very costly, which put a financial strain on England's coffers. Louis XIV wanted to extend his territory, which meant seizing the Spanish Netherlands and neighbouring Holland. Consequently, William joined forces with Spain and Austria against the French. In 1697 the Treaty of Ryswick was signed, finally bringing peace to the Netherlands, and Louis XIV was forced to recognise William as King of England.

Although William appeared cold and remote, he did have some positive achievements and is credited with establishing the Bank of England, to which he gave a Royal Charter, and a style of banking that we would still recognise today with credits and loans. He also set up the National Debt to help ease England's financial situation and help pay for future conflicts. The East India Company, set up in Elizabeth I's reign, was also further developed; a company that was responsible for 50% of the world's trade at its height, employing 25% of the country's population. In 1698 it officially became the English Company trading to the East Indies and was soon in a position to loan the Treasury over £3,000,000.

Being Dutch, William was able to attract his countrymen to England and many Dutchmen worked in East Anglia, digging ditches to drain the fens so that the land became suitable for agriculture. There was also a Dutch influence on architecture and furniture. Houses built during the reign have a distinct Flemish look and there is a definite "William and Mary" style of furniture, with elaborately turned legs, heavily lacquered and painted finishes, marquetry inlays, with dark walnut being a popular wood.

Chairs became more comfortable with upholstery and shaped backs to fit the human frame. China cabinets were introduced, reflecting Mary's love of displaying Delft china and oriental porcelain. Blue and white china started to become a feature in people's homes. Tallboys and lowboys also became practical pieces of furniture.

Hampton Court Palace was extended, replacing half of Henry VIII's Tudor rooms and private apartments with new wings, and William commissioned a new Hospital for Seamen at Greenwich, designed by Sir Christopher Wren.

In the year 1700, King Charles II of Spain died. Being childless, he had named Louis XIV's grandson as his successor. This would inevitably form a strong French and Spanish alliance. There were concerns as to who would now rule this vast empire, which included territories in Spain, the Netherlands, the Americas and parts of Italy. With Louis XIV of France and the Holy Roman Emperor, Leopold I, being the late King's close relatives, William intervened to prevent either becoming a super-power that could dominate Europe. This led to a conflict known as The War of Spanish Succession, with the English army under the command of John Churchill, Duke of Marlborough.

Within months James II, the former King of England died. Louis XIV saw this as the perfect opportunity to remove William from the throne. He pushed to have James II's last child, James Francis Edward Stuart, recognised as King James III of England. He was nicknamed "The Old Pretender", and many believed that he was not truly the son of James II and had been smuggled into the bedchamber as a baby in a warming pan.

The last act of William's reign was an Act of Settlement so that the line of succession did not revert to The Old Pretender. As William and Mary were childless and had no immediate heirs, and the Heir Presumptive, Mary's sister Anne, had no surviving children either, it was agreed that, after Anne, the Electress Sophia of Hanover, a Protestant granddaughter of James I, and her heirs would inherit the throne of England.

Mary died from hemorrhagic smallpox on 28 December, 1694, at Kensington Palace, aged just 32. The records of the Kensington Palace carpenter show a charge for "mending the steps of the grt stairs that was broken in carrying the Queen's body down." Mary was laid to rest in Westminster Abbey amid great public sorrow. Funeral music was composed by Henry Purcell.

William had slept on a camp bed in Mary's room during her final days and was grief-stricken at her death. He wrote to Gilbert Burnet, Bishop of Salisbury, "During the course of our marriage I have never known one single fault with her." Knowing that she was dying, Mary kept people away from her for fear that they might also catch smallpox.

She wrote a letter to William, to be opened only after her death. In it she begged him to give up his mistress, Elizabeth Villiers. He did as she had wished and for the rest of his life he wore a black ribbon on his left arm containing a lock of Mary's hair and her wedding ring.

William reigned alone after her death but spent half the year abroad. He died on 8 March, 1702, aged 52, after his horse, Sorrel, slipped on a mole hill while he was out riding near Hampton Court. The King broke his collar bone, which was badly reset. He went into a decline and died of pneumonia at Kensington Palace. There was no great public show of mourning, other than from his Jacobite enemies who made a toast to the mole that had inadvertently killed the King, raising their glasses "to the little gentleman in black velvet".

William was buried in Westminster Abbey next to Mary. In a touching tribute to the late King, author Daniel Defoe revealed that "Dutch Billy" never came to terms with the fact that he was not fully welcomed by the English people, writing that it, "absolutely broke his heart; for which reason I think him as much murdered as his predecessor was, whose head was cut off by his subjects." Defoe defended the King in a satirical poem, which he called *The True-Born Englishman*. Had William known of these sentiments during his lifetime, he might have felt accepted finally.

Chapter 45

Anne 1665–1714
Reign: 1702–1714

Amongst England's queens, three reigns particularly stand out – those of Elizabeth I, Victoria and Elizabeth II. One English queen often seems to get sidelined in comparison: Anne. Today if people think of Queen Anne, they invariably connect her with the decorative taste in furnishings of the period, elegantly proportioned furniture with cabriole legs, known as the Queen Anne style.

Described by the Victorian constitutional expert Walter Bagehot as "one of the smallest people ever set in a great place", Anne was fiercely patriotic and declared on her accession, "I know my own heart to be entirely English. I can very sincerely assure you there is not anything you can expect or desire from me, which I shall not be ready to do for the happiness and prosperity of England." Words that could easily have been uttered by Elizabeth I.

Anne was born at St James's Palace in London on 6 February, 1665, the second daughter of James II and his first wife, Anne Hyde, and she was named after her mother. As with England's other queens, at the time of her birth Anne was not expected to succeed to the throne. She received only a basic education and had little interest in art, literature or music when young. She also suffered from poor health and was treated in Paris at the age of five for weepy eyes, a condition known as defluxion.

When Anne was aged six her mother died. Her father married again two years later. Although he and his new wife had a strong Catholic faith. Anne and her sister, Mary, were raised as Protestants by Colonel Edward Villiers and his wife Lady Frances at Richmond. The Villiers had six daughters, so Anne was brought up in a very feminine household. Anne's best friend at this time was Frances Apsley, who was 12 years older. Always fond of nicknames, Anne called Frances "Semandra" and herself "Ziphares". Cicely Cornwallis was another great friend, to whom Anne wrote over a thousand letters.

At the age of 17 Anne became the subject of a scandal following rumours of a liaison with John Sheffield (Lord Mulgrave), when letters between them were discovered. He was then aged 35 and was banished from court and sent to Tangiers, although he insisted that his crime was "only ogling". Princess Mary wrote of Anne's predicament in a letter but added, tellingly "not but that I believe my sister very innocent."

The two sisters were very close in their youth but grew apart as the years went by. When Mary became engaged to William of Orange, Anne was distraught at the thought of losing her sister. She was comforted by a new-found friend, Sarah Jennings, who was to play a major part in Anne's life. Anne hated her brother-in-law, William, and in letters to Sarah called him "the Dutch Monster", and often referred to him as Mr Caliban, after Shakespeare's half-man, half-monster character in *The Tempest*.

Following the Lord Mulgrave scandal, it was decided that Anne should marry quickly and settle down. Her cousin, George of Hanover (later George I of England) was considered a possible husband but was rejected. Anne eventually married George of Denmark on 28 July, 1683, at the Chapel Royal, St James's Palace. He became a naturalised English subject in September and the following year was made a Knight of the Garter.

He was generally considered to be extremely dull and his main interest was making model ships. Charles II wrote, "I have tried him drunk and tried him sober, and there is nothing to him." George suffered from asthma, although it was joked that his asthmatic attacks were deliberate so that he should "not be taken for dead and taken away and buried".

Despite negative opinions about her husband, Anne and George were happy together, preferring a simpler way of life rather than attending glittering social functions. Anne enjoyed playing cards, visiting gardens, and drinking copious amounts of tea. Unusually for the society in which they lived, Prince George remained faithful to his wife throughout their 25-year marriage. He was over-fond of the bottle and it was said of them at the time, "Prince George drinks all and Princess Anne eats all." Certainly Anne grew plumper as the years went by and she was described by contemporaries as plain and homely.

On getting married, Anne appointed her friend Sarah Jennings as her Lady of the Bedchamber. Soon afterwards, Sarah married John Churchill, a great military leader. The two couples became close and Anne wrote, "We four must never part til death mows us down with his impartial hand." Sarah Churchill and Anne behaved as social equals and referred to each other in letters as "Mrs Freeman" and "Mrs Morley".

Anne and George had at least 18 children, including male twins, but none of them survived to adulthood. Thirteen were miscarried, stillborn, or died soon after birth. A son and three daughters died in infancy. Only one child lived longer, William Henry, the Duke of Gloucester who died at the age of 10 from hydrocephalus in 1700. The many pregnancies did not help Anne's relationship with her sister, as Mary remained childless and, despite all, envious.

Anne had a convoluted path to the throne. When her uncle, Charles II, died in 1685, her father succeeded as James II. His was a difficult reign with rebellions from Charles's illegitimate son the Duke of Monmouth, who felt that he was the rightful heir. The rebellions were quashed by John Churchill and his soldiers, and Monmouth was eventually captured and executed at the Tower of London

In 1688 Anne's stepmother, Mary of Modena, gave birth to a son, a possible heir to the throne, but Anne did not believe that the baby was legitimate. When King James II fled to France and was deemed to have abdicated, Anne's brother-in-law, William of Orange, took the throne. John Churchill defected his allegiance from James II to the new King William III. The Churchills persuaded Anne to accept William and her sister Mary as joint rulers. As a reward, the new monarchs gave John Churchill the title Earl of Marlborough. The ambitious Sarah Churchill delighted in her elevated position in society as Countess of Marlborough.

Anne did not take a great interest in affairs of state and was quite happy to let her sister reign jointly with William. Anne and her husband George lived comfortably on an income of £50,000 a year in a palace known as The Cockpit in London. The building stood on what is now the Cabinet Office at 70 Whitehall.

During the reign of William and Mary a Bill of Rights established the royal line of succession, naming Anne as Heir Presumptive and next in line to the throne after any children that William and Mary might have, but they remained childless.

William and Mary grew increasingly suspicious of the power that Sarah Churchill seemed to wield over Anne, and when correspondence came to light in 1692 that John Churchill had been communicating with the deposed James II in France, Churchill was dismissed from all his posts, civil and military, and was temporarily imprisoned in the Tower of London. Anne was implicated by association and was forced to move out of the royal palaces. She and George went to live with friends at Syon House in Middlesex.

Two years later Queen Mary died. William III allowed Anne and her husband back to London, where they took up residence at St James's Palace. When William himself died in 1702, following a fall from his horse at Hampton Court, Anne succeeded him as Queen of England, Scotland and Ireland.

She was crowned on St George's Day that year in Westminster Abbey. It was a unique Coronation in England in that Queen Anne was carried into the Abbey in a sedan chair by Yeomen of the Guard because she was suffering very badly from gout at the time. Her six-yard train was threaded out of the back of the chair and carried in procession by her Maids of Honour.

Two weeks after the Coronation, England declared war on France. "It means I am getting old," joked King Louis XIV, "when ladies declare war on me." But the English army, commanded by John Churchill, proved to be invincible.

John Churchill was now back in favour and became Commander-in-Chief of the English forces three days after Anne's accession. With the leading members of her family now dead, Anne in her grief turned increasingly to the Churchills, heaping more honours on John – including the Order of the Garter – and giving Sarah more roles at court, making her Mistress of the Robes and Keeper of the Privy Purse.

Within months the new Queen elevated the couple to Duke and Duchess of Marlborough and gave them a gift of £2,000 a year out of the Privy Purse. As the years went by the Marlboroughs' income increased dramatically from the public purse.

During the War of Spanish Succession John Churchill won some decisive battles which made England a force to be reckoned with. In 1702 battles commenced in the Netherlands and in 1703 England had one victory after another. Churchill was rewarded for his military triumphs, particularly at the Battle of Blenheim in 1704 and the defeat of the French at the Battle of Ramillies in 1706 and the Battle of Malplaquet in 1709.

On her accession, Anne gave the Marlboroughs her former London home, The Cockpit, and later further rewarded John Churchill for his military prowess by presenting him with an estate in the Royal Manor of Woodstock in Oxfordshire. She agreed to build him a house with a grant from Parliament of £240,000. The building, designed by Vanbrugh and Hawksmoor, was begun in 1705 and was called Blenheim Palace. Today there is an impressive statue of Queen Anne in the library by Johannes Michel Rysbrack in memory of the Churchills' benefactress.

Although Queen Anne reigned for just 12 years, it was a time when literature flourished, with Swift, Congreve and Pope at their peak. George Frideric Handel was the great composer of the day and received £200 a year from the royal coffers. He composed *Utrecht Te Deum and Jubilate* for the Queen. In April 1705 Anne personally knighted scientist Isaac Newton for his work while she was on a visit to Trinity College, Cambridge. The first daily newspaper, *The Daily Courant*, went on sale, and the building of Sir Christopher Wren's magnificent St Paul's Cathedral was finally completed. Anne was the last English monarch to touch for the King's Evil and she had something in common with our present monarch in that she enjoyed horse racing. She established the Ascot Racecourse in 1711 and the first race was "Her Majesty's Plate" with a prize of 100 guineas which she presented to the winning owner. The Queen Anne Stakes is still run as the first race on the first day of Royal Ascot and there is an enclosure named after her.

There were some significant achievements politically during Anne's reign. Remarkably for a woman who had taken little interest in affairs of state prior to her accession, Anne presided over Cabinet meetings, the last English monarch to do so, and regularly attended debates in the House of Lords, sitting on the throne or beside a fire in winter.

A two-party system emerged, with Whigs and Tories as great rivals. At heart Anne favoured the Tories over the Whigs, saying that she did not trust a Whig government. She was unhappy that the Whigs won a majority in the House of Commons in 1708. When the Queen celebrated her 46th birthday, the event was attended almost exclusively by Tories. It was reported that the ladies present wore so many jewels that they were barely able to move and that such splendour had not been seen at court for half a century.

Anne considered Parliament to be a necessary evil. "I have changed my Ministers," she told a new Tory cabinet in 1710 after they had been returned to power, "but I have not changed my measures. I am still for moderation and will govern by it."

Jonathan Swift wrote that Anne was obstinate and very difficult to advise, concluding that, "The Queen was by no means inclined to make many changes in employments, she was positive in her nature, and extremely given to delay."

The most significant achievement of Queen Anne's reign was when she presided over the Act of Union with Scotland in 1707, which finally brought England and Scotland together after centuries of conflict. The country subsequently became known as Great Britain. The Scottish parliament was abolished and was represented at Westminster instead, but Scotland kept its own laws and retained the Presbyterian creed.

"I desire," the Queen declared, "and expect from my subjects of both nations that from henceforth they will act with all possible respect and kindness to one another, that so it may appear to all the world they have hearts disposed to become one people."

England no longer feared the threat of invasion from Scotland. The Scots benefited from new avenues of trade and wealth that union with England opened up. Anne attended a thanksgiving service in St Paul's Cathedral to show how important the union was to her.

When Anne opened Parliament in 1713 she revealed that the Treaty of Utrecht had been signed. It was in fact a series of treaties that ended the War of Spanish Succession, brought peace in Europe and prevented the French from dominating the continent. Amongst other benefits, Gibraltar, Minorca, Hudson Bay, Nova Scotia and Newfoundland became British territory. From Anne's point of view, the Treaty officially recognised her as the legitimate sovereign of England and ended the threat of any further Jacobite claim to the throne. Throughout her life Anne maintained a staunch Protestant faith. At the age of just 15 she wrote on the subject of the Roman Catholic church, "The more I see of these fooleries and the more I hear of that religion, the more I dislike it." In 1687 James II had tried to exclude his daughter Mary from the throne on the condition that Anne converted to the Catholic faith, but she refused.

When she eventually succeeded to the throne herself, Anne did what she could to help the church. Queen Anne's Bounty Act was created to increase the incomes of poorer clergy by restoring money to churches that Henry VIII had diverted into royal coffers. Horace Walpole referred to the Queen as "Goody Anne – The Church's wet nurse". Although some of the Act has been repealed, much is still in force today.

To maintain the Protestant succession it had been agreed that, after Anne, the throne would pass to her Aunt Sophia, Electress of Hanover (daughter of Charles II's sister) who was 71 at the time. Anne hated discussing the issue of her successor and refused to allow her Aunt to visit England. There was some ferocious correspondence between the two women in 1714 and Sophia died shortly afterwards. It was said that a savage letter from Anne had upset her so much that it led to her death, although Sophia was 83, which was quite an age in the 18th century.

During her reign the long friendship between Sarah Churchill and the Queen became increasingly fraught as the Duchess tried to wield more power. Sarah was a great Whig supporter, a political stance that the Queen came to resent. It was Sarah who had persuaded Anne to side with William III and Mary against her own father during the Glorious Revolution, something Anne later regretted and felt guilty about.

The two had a violent quarrel in August 1708 at a thanksgiving service at St Paul's Cathedral to mark Marlborough's victory at Oudenarde. On the way to the Cathedral Sarah noticed that the Queen was not wearing the jewels that she had laid out for her. As Mistress of the Robes, Sarah thought this would reflect badly on her at such a public event. The two bickered in their seats at the Cathedral and a vitriolic correspondence continued afterwards.

Sarah Churchill had a notoriously violent and malignant temper and has variously been described as a "whirlwind" and a "volcano". She had four healthy children, which made Anne feel inferior. When they quarrelled, Jonathan Swift wrote that "three furies" reigned in Sarah Churchill's heart: "sordid Avarice, disdainful Pride, and ungovernable Rage". The Churchill family motto, *Fiel Pero Desdichado* – faithful though joyless – seemed appropriate at times.

As Sarah began to fall out of favour, Anne turned increasingly to Abigail Masham (married to the Queen's page Samuel Masham), a Woman of the Bedchamber and royal confidante. Ironically, Abigail was Sarah Churchill's cousin and spent two hours daily with the Queen, which must have put Sarah's nose out of joint.

After Anne was widowed in 1708, Sarah wrote that she had visited the Queen at St James's Palace. "I found her at table, where she had been eating, and Mrs Masham close by her. Mrs Masham went out of the room as soon as I came in, not in the humble manner she had sometimes affected as bedchamber woman, but with an air of insolence and anger." Adding that she never visited the Queen without Mrs Masham having just left the room, "which at last tired me and I went to her seldomer."

Anne finally fell out with Sarah Churchill altogether after a quarrel in 1710 over an issue with the Queen's laundress. Anne turned her back on the Duchess and attempted to leave the room, but Sarah "clapped her back against the door", determined to have the last word. Trenchant correspondence followed about the shoddiness of the laundress's work.

The pair met only once more, after which Sarah threatened to blackmail the Queen, saying that she would publish all the private correspondence between "Mrs Freeman" and "Mrs Morley" over the years. The Queen's counterattack was a threat to take back the Marlborough properties that she had given them. The letters remained unprinted in Anne's lifetime.

Sarah lost her position as Mistress of the Robes and her role as Keeper of the Privy Purse was given to Abigail Masham. The Duke of Marlborough was dismissed as Captain-General of the Army and the Marlboroughs fled abroad, where Sarah continued to upset the Queen by saying that she could now publish their intimate correspondence in Europe, where the Queen would have no power to stop her.

Sarah Churchill wrote copious accounts about her experiences at court, which have formed the basis of many biographies of Anne across the centuries. This has inevitably resulted in Sarah's biased opinion being propagated and might not necessarily reflect the true character of the Queen. She wrote, for example, that Anne "meant well and was not a fool; but nobody can maintain that she was wise, nor entertaining in conversation. She was ignorant in everything but what the parsons had taught her as a child."

Describing her character, Sarah wrote, "Queen Anne had a person and appearance not at all ungraceful, till she grew exceeding gross and corpulent. There was something of Majesty in her look, but mixed with a sullen, constant frown, that plainly betrayed a gloominess of soul and a cloudiness of disposition within." Hardly a flattering portrait.

In a strange repeat of the Sarah Churchill situation, Abigail Masham had an increasing influence over the Queen and subtly intervened in political matters but then felt slighted when Anne became closer to Elizabeth, Duchess of Somerset, known affectionately by her as Carrots. Anne seemed to be capable of only having one close female confidante at a time.

Throughout her life Anne suffered from poor health. She had smallpox in childhood, her eyesight was poor, her many pregnancies weakened her, and she suffered with gout from an early age. As it became more severe, she often had to be carried around and lifted from her bed by pulleys. In 1707 Lord Godolphin, a friend of the Marlboroughs and Lord Treasurer, wrote of witnessing the Queen "under a fit of gout, in extreme pain and agony, and on this occasion everything about her was much in the same disorder as the meanest of her subjects. Her face, which was red and spotted, was rendered something frightful by her negligent dress, and the foot affected was tied with a poultice and some nasty bandages. I was much affected by the sight."

Alcohol could have been a contributory factor in the Queen's worsening gout and she was nicknamed Brandy Nan after scurrilous reports that she drank gin out of a tea pot! When a statue of her was placed outside St Paul's Cathedral, facing towards Ludgate Hill, a popular rhyme at the time was:

Brandy Nan, Brandy Nan,
You're left in the lurch.
Your face to the gin shop,
Your back to the church.

Anne also suffered from erysipelas, an acute skin infection, for which she received painful and undignified treatments from her physician Dr John Arbuthnot. After a heated Council meeting in July 1714 that went on until 2am, Anne collapsed. She died a few days later at the age of 49 on 1 August at Kensington Palace, said to be exhausted by affairs of state which weighed heavily on her mind. When Dr Arbuthnot asked her how she was, she had replied, "Never worse. I am going." He later told Jonathan Swift, "I believe sleep was never more welcome to a weary traveller than death was to her."

Queen Anne was buried in Westminster Abbey with her husband and children. Eye witnesses said that her coffin was as wide as it was long. With no surviving children, she became England's last Stuart monarch and was succeeded by her nearest living Protestant relative, her cousin Prince George of Hanover, son of Anne's recently deceased Aunt Sophia. England now had a German King on the throne who spoke not one word of English.

Chapter 46

George I 1660–1727
Reign: 1714–1727

George the First was always reckoned
Vile, but viler George the Second;
And what mortal ever heard
Any good of George the Third?
When from earth the Fourth descended
God be praised, the Georges ended.

Walter Savage Landor

When Queen Anne died at Kensington Palace in 1714 the reign of the Stuarts came to a close in England after more than a century. It was her German cousin, George, who arrived at Greenwich in a thick London fog to become our first monarch from the House of Hanover, and the Royal Family's surname changed to Guelph. He was the first of four Georges in succession to sit on the English throne; reigns that saw the power of the monarchy diminish, along with public affection.

One of only nine monarchs since William the Conqueror to have been born outside the British Isles, George was a great-grandson of James I of England. Christened Georg Ludwig (George Louis), he was born on 28 May, 1660, at Leineschloss, Osnabrück in Lower Saxony. His mother was Sophia, a daughter of Elizabeth of Bohemia, the Winter Queen and his father was Ernest Augustus, Elector of Hanover. George succeeded his father as Elector at the age of eight. He was made a Knight of the Garter in 1703 and became a naturalised British subject in 1705.

A diligent child, he was brought up with his brother Frederick and the pair were known by the family nicknames of Görgen and Gustchen. Their parents later had four more sons and a daughter, but he was always closest to Frederick. George was trained as a soldier and was present at a campaign during the French-Dutch War, and fought at the Battle of Vienna in September 1683, one of a series of conflicts known as "The Great Turkish War" between the Ottoman Empire and various European allies.

George made a visit to England when he was aged 20 as a potential husband for the 15-year-old Princess Anne (later Queen Anne), but she found him dull and he did not consider her to be attractive, and so he sailed back home to Germany. Two years later he married his first cousin, Sophia Dorothea of Celle, on 21 November, 1682 at Celle Castle Chapel in Germany. Although she was considered very attractive, it was an unhappy match and was arranged mainly for the financial advantages it brought by uniting the territories of Celle and Hanover. There was also the matter of a large dowry that George was allowed to keep for himself. "He did not like it," wrote his mother, "but the money tempted him as it would anyone else."

The couple had two children: a son, George, who later became King George II of England, and a daughter, Sophia, who was to marry the King of Prussia and became the mother of Frederick the Great.

With an eye for the ladies, George kept mistresses during his marriage and had four illegitimate children, although did not approve of his wife seeking male company. Sophia Dorothea, however, was attracted to a young Swedish army officer, Count Philip von Königsmark. When letters came to light in which the Count had written, "Adorable one, I will love you to the tomb!" Sophia admitted her passion for him.

Königsmark disappeared and it was rumoured that he had been murdered and buried under the floorboards of a bedroom in George's palace in Hanover. Sophia Dorothea was accused of adultery and was imprisoned at Ahlden Castle, aged 28. She never saw her husband or children again. George divorced her in December 1694 and Sophia Dorothea died at the castle after being held captive for 32 years. It was said that George kept his wife in prison "because he believed that she was no better than he was."

The nursery rhyme "Georgie Porgie, pudding and pie, kissed the girls and made them cry" is thought by some historians to refer to George I. An earlier version, "Rowley Powley, pudding and pie", has been linked to Charles II, whose nickname was Old Rowley.

Although George was a long way down the line of succession to the

English throne, the pathway opened up for him following the terms of the 1701 Act of Settlement, which stipulated that no Roman Catholic could succeed. As many as 50 heirs preceding him were Catholic, but it was George's mother, Sophia, (a grand-daughter of James I) who suddenly found herself first in line, on the basis that she was Queen Anne's nearest Protestant relative, despite the fact that so many others had a much better claim.

Sophia was 71 at the time of the Act and died 13 years later, barely two months before Queen Anne. Consequently, George, as Sophia's eldest son, succeeded to the crown and became King George I of England. He was aged 54 and then the oldest sovereign to ascend the throne. He also adopted the style King of Hanover, which was significant, because George had a much greater affection for Hanover than he ever did for England.

George was in no hurry to travel to England and it was some six weeks after Queen Anne's death before he set foot in his new kingdom, arriving by barge along the River Thames. When the King and his entourage disembarked, Lord Mahon wrote that they were "like so many famished vultures . . . with keen eyes and bended talons on the fruitful soil of England."

One of George's ladies was later jeered at as she was driven through the streets of London in a carriage. She queried the reaction, but with English not being her first language, instead of pleading that they had come for the good of England, she shouted out, "We come here for your goods!" "Yes, and for our chattels as well!" came the response from the crowd.

The new King took up residence at St James's Palace in London and wrote:

"The first morning after my arrival at St James's, I looked out of the window and saw a park with walls and a canal and was told they were mine. The next day, the ranger of my park sent me a brace of fine carp out of my canal, and I was told I must give five guineas to the man for bringing me my own carp out of my own canal in my own park."

His entourage included 18 German cooks, one laundress, and two mistresses. He gave the mistresses English titles, making them Duchess of Kendal and Countess of Darlington. The Countess was nicknamed "the Elephant and Castle" by courtiers due to her large size and the Duchess "the Maypole" because of her great height.

Of the Countess, Horace Walpole wrote, "I remember being terrified by her enormous figure. Two fierce black eyes, large and rolling beneath two lofty arched eyebrows, two acres of cheeks spread with crimson, an ocean of neck that overflowed and was not distinguished from the lower parts of her body, and no part restrained by stays."

Lord Chesterfield concurred that, "No woman came amiss to him, if she were only willing and very fat." The German mistresses were unpopular because they were easily bribed by anyone seeking a favour from the King and made themselves very rich as a result. Eventually George took an English mistress, Anne Brett. She had black hair and a dark complexion, becoming known as "The Sultana" because of her exotic appearance.

She had a difficult relationship with one of George's granddaughters. Anne Brett was given an apartment at St James's Palace and, when the King went on a visit to Hanover, ordered a door to be knocked through to the royal gardens. Not wishing to walk through the gardens at the same time as her grandfather's mistress, the Princess had Anne Brett's garden door bricked up!

The Coronation of King George I took place on 20 October, 1714, at Westminster Abbey, with the customary glitter and ceremony, but the streets were not lined with enthusiastic crowds. Riots took place in more than 20 towns and cities, notably in Bedford, Canterbury, Norwich, Bristol, Taunton, Birmingham, Dorchester, Nuneaton, Shrewsbury and Tewksbury.

"No Hanover!" shouted the demonstrators, declaring that the new King had not a drop of English blood in his veins.

Soon after the Coronation, George made a return visit to his home in Hanover leaving his son, the Prince of Wales, as Guardian of the Realm in his absence. Father and son had a very poor relationship. When the Prince's wife, Caroline of Ansbach, gave birth to a son in 1717, he and George argued bitterly over the choice of godparents at the christening. The King insisted that his Lord Chamberlain, the Duke of Newcastle, should be a godfather.

After the ceremony, the Prince of Wales still simmered with anger and shouted vengefully at the Duke, "Rascal, I shall find you out!" The Duke misheard and thought the Prince had threatened, "Rascal, I shall fight you out!" and went to the King in fear of his life. As a result, the King had his son and daughter-in-law placed under house arrest for over three years.

The Prince and Princess of Wales eventually left St James's Palace and were allowed to set up their own home at Leicester House, on the site of what is now Leicester Square. Their circle became known as The Leicester House Set and opposed the King wherever possible. Sir Robert Walpole eventually brought about a reconciliation between the King and the Prince of Wales, but their relationship was always cool.

Unlike many of his predecessors, George I did not have a dynamic personality and the English considered their monarch to be cold and uninspiring. Lady Mary Wortley Montagu, who introduced the smallpox inoculation to England in the 1720s, described George as "an honest blockhead . . . more properly dull than lazy". She wrote that he would have been "so well contented to have remained in his little town of Hanover that, if the ambition of those about him had not been greater than his own, we should never have seen him in England."

In Hanover George was autocratic and had great power, but in England was happy to leave affairs of state in the hands of others. This was partly due to communication problems. Although he did eventually learn some of the language, his command of the English vocabulary remained poor and he tended to speak in French.

George took little interest in politics, which led to a change in how the country was governed. Whereas public affairs had once been controlled by the monarch with advice from the Privy Council, George was content to let Parliament have greater power. Sir Robert Walpole became England's first Prime Minister, or First Lord of the Treasury as he would then have been known.

Walpole stood in for the King at meetings as, not only did George have little interest, he could not understand what was being said and his own speeches were read out by the Lord Chancellor. Ministerial meetings without the monarch eventually led to the formation of a formal Cabinet. A new law was passed during George's reign that allowed General Elections to take place in England every seven years. The balance of power shifted.

"Though a despot in Hanover, he was a moderate ruler in England," wrote William Makepeace Thackeray, "His aim was to leave it to itself as much as possible, and to live out of it as much as he could. His heart was in Hanover. We laughed at his uncouth German ways and sneered at him."

George personally designed a new uniform for his guards, but they refused to wear it because the cloth was too coarse, and he was mocked when he came up with a scheme to plant turnips in St James's Park. A plan that never came to fruition and led to him being dubbed "The Turnip King".

Although he was crowned King of England and Scotland, George was not universally accepted in either country. He had been on the throne barely a year when he encountered problems with the Jacobite supporters of James II's son, "The Old Pretender". James Francis Edward Stuart was a Roman Catholic and had therefore been barred from the English line of succession, but Jacobites considered him to be the rightful King James III.

In 1715 some of James's followers took up arms to try and gain him the crown at the Battle of Sherriffmuir in Scotland but the Jacobites had very little support and were quickly defeated. It was to be the last rebellion in the Old Pretender's lifetime and three decades were to pass before his son, Bonnie Prince Charlie, attempted to uphold the Jacobite claims and tried to restore the throne to the Stuarts. He was equally unsuccessful and the Battle of Culloden was the final Jacobite insurrection.

In the comfort of his palace, George banished finger bowls from the royal table because it was known that Jacobites had used them to toast "The King Over The Water" since James II's exile to France. It was Edward VII who revived the use of finger bowls in the early 20th century, believing that the throne was secure enough from Jacobite threats by that time.

Five years into the reign came a notorious debacle known as the South Sea Bubble. When George succeeded to the throne, the national debt stood at up to £54 million, with an astronomical amount of interest added to it annually. The South Sea Company, a British company trading in the American South Seas, convinced the government that a number of financial ventures could help reduce this vast debt.

Although Robert Walpole was dubious about the scheme and advised against any involvement, many investors including the King put money into enterprises which brought a little return in the first year, and thereafter none at all. Inevitably the bubble burst and many, including some prominent people, went bankrupt as a result. Most had bought shares in the South Sea Company at prices between £100 and £1,000, but when they came to sell them, there were no takers. In 1721 an investigation exposed a web of deceit and corruption, with the perpetrators being prosecuted. Some investors never recovered from the debts they had incurred.

It was typical of King George's reserved personality that he lived in just two rooms at St James's Palace, looked after by two Turkish servants, Mustapha and Mohammed. He did not like being seen in public and seldom used the Royal Box if he went to the opera, preferring to remain incognito. In his youth he enjoyed stag hunting, but as he grew older he was more likely to be found cutting out paper patterns in his room.

Up until the time of George I's reign there had been a practice in England of touching for the King's Evil, in the belief that the skin condition scrofula could be cured by the touch of a royal hand. Queen Anne had continued the tradition, but it was discontinued by George, possibly because it brought him in too close a contact with the public. Soon after his accession a man applied to have his son touched by the King, but George refused. The man took his son to France where he was touched by "The Old Pretender" and was supposedly cured.

George was not a great patron of the arts, famously saying in his poor English, "I hate all boets and bainters." But he loved music and employed George Frideric Handel as Kappelmeister at his summer home, Herrenhausen, while he was still Elector of Hanover.

Handel moved to London during the reign of Queen Anne in 1712 and concerts at St James's Palace led to his popularity. It was during George I's reign that Handel wrote the opera *Scipio* from which the slow march became the regimental march of the Grenadier Guards and is still regularly played at Trooping the Colour today.

George also enjoyed architecture and gardening, and developed a garden at Herrenhausen to try and rival that at Versailles.

Although it was his Protestant faith that brought George I to the English throne, he lacked the religious fanaticism and fervour of many of his royal predecessors. He went quietly to services at St Martin-in-the-Fields Church in London and was even a churchwarden there. He also gave £1,500 to the church to purchase an organ, although this has long since been replaced. His royal pew is still to the left of the main altar and the royal coat of arms can be seen on the ceiling.

There was one extraordinary encounter towards the end of the King's life. When George was out hunting in Hertswold Forest, near Hamelin, he came across a naked wild boy who had the agility of a squirrel, walked on his hands and feet, and survived by eating berries, nuts and plants. He was uncivilised and had no language. Perhaps realising that their child was disabled, his parents had abandoned him in the forest and miraculously he had survived. George decided to adopt the boy and he was brought back to England with the royal party and given the name Peter.

The King's daughter-in-law Caroline, Princess of Wales, took a particular interest in Peter and attempts were made to teach him to speak, read and write, but these failed. He was only ever capable of saying "Peter" and "King George", and could hum a few tunes. The fascination and affection that the Royal Family had for the boy is shown in the fact that the painter William Kent included Peter in a painting of King George I's courtiers on the staircase at Kensington Palace, where "Peter the Wild Boy" can still be seen dressed in green, holding a bunch of acorns in his hand.

Peter long outlived the King, spending his last years on a farm in Berkhamsted and he died at around 70 years of age. He is buried in the churchyard of St Mary's, Northchurch in Hertfordshire, where his gravestone can still be seen and flowers are regularly placed there in his memory.

Horace Walpole, the son of Sir Robert, was presented to King George I in 1724 and described him as, "an elderly man, rather pale, and exactly like his pictures and coins; not tall; of an aspect rather good than august; with a dark tie-wig, a plain coat, waistcoat and breeches of snuff-coloured cloth, and stockings of the same colour, and a blue riband over all."

By this time, George was not a well man and suffering badly from gout. He was also troubled by a prophecy that he would die shortly after his wife. So when Sophia Dorothea died in November 1726, the King became concerned and refused to bury her body for a long time.

Six months later he was in Holland, on his way to his palace at Osnabrück, when he was taken ill after eating an enormous dinner and a "surfeit of melons". Desperate to get home, he travelled in a carriage shouting, "Osnabrück! Osnabrück!" out of the window. He was taken to his palace but died in there on 11 June, 1727, in the same room that he had been born. He was 67 and had reigned for less than 13 years.

Instead of being buried in England, as so many of our monarchs have been, it is not surprising that George I was laid to rest in his beloved Hanover at Leineschloss. The palace was destroyed by bombs during World War II and the King's remains, along with those of his parents, were moved in 1957 to the Guelph mausoleum of his former summer palace at Herrenhausen, where George had spent a lot of time developing the gardens and was really at his happiest.

"George the First knew nothing and desired to know nothing; did nothing and desired to do nothing," wrote Samuel Johnson, "and the only good thing that is told of him is that he wished to restore the crown to its hereditary successor."

Chapter 47

George II 1683–1760
Reign: 1727–1760

Various assessments of King George II across the centuries have described him as dull, arrogant, pompous, impatient and obstinate. He hated to be proved wrong and many of his contemporaries described him as a colossal bore.

"No mill horse ever went on a more constant track or a more unchanging circle," said one who had experienced the King's conversation.

George II's behaviour might suggest signs of what today we would call Asperger's syndrome. A stickler for routine and punctuality, he found it difficult to build a rapport with people and had repetitive patterns of behaviour. Being precise in his habits, George visited his mistress Henrietta Howard at nine o'clock each evening, never a minute before or a minute after, but as the clock chimed nine. George had few male friends and preferred the company of woman, although Lord Chesterfield observed that he "sauntered away" his time with them rather than enjoyed their company.

Some of George's reserved manner may have stemmed from a difficult childhood in Germany. The only son of George of Hanover (later King George I) and Sophia Dorothea, he was born at the royal palace of Herrenhausen on November 10, 1683, and was christened George Augustus.

While he was still young, his mother was imprisoned due to an illicit love affair with a Swedish soldier, Count Philip von Königsmarck. Accused of adultery, she was imprisoned at Ahlden Castle, aged just 28, and never saw her husband or children again. She was held captive for 32 years and died at the castle. This separation from his mother blighted George's childhood and affected him for life. It led to many disagreements with his father, who had ordered the incarceration, and they had a very poor relationship as a result.

George went to live with his grandmother, Electress Sophia of Hanover, who was a granddaughter of King James I of England. She made sure that George was taught to speak English, although he was never able to lose his German accent, and he also studied French and Latin.

It has been said that George had a soldier's brain and he found that the military life suited him well. Being very precise, he knew every single detail of a uniform. As a young soldier in 1708 he fought under the command of the Duke of Marlborough at the Battle of Oudenarde during the War of Spanish Succession. George led the Dragoons and had his horse shot from beneath him, but he survived.

When George was 17 his grandmother became direct heir to the English throne, as Queen Anne had no living children. George became a naturalised English citizen in 1705, and Queen Anne gave him the titles Duke of Cambridge, Earl of Milford Haven, Viscount Northallerton and Baron Tewkesbury on his birthday in 1706.

He was also made a Knight of the Garter in April that year. This was in preparation for his family moving to England on the eventual death of Queen Anne, which happened on 1 August, 1714. As Electress Sophia had died less than two months before Queen Anne, it was his father who succeeded to the throne as King of England. George then received further titles to become Prince of Wales, Earl of Chester, and Duke of Cornwall and Rothesay.

The new Prince of Wales became a popular figure in England at this time – some would say because he could speak English. His popularity increased further following a failed assassination attempt in 1716 at the Drury Lane Theatre in London.

Despite their new life in England, the difficult relationship between George and his father did not improve. When King George I returned to Hanover quite soon after the Coronation, he left George, as Prince of Wales, in control as "Guardian of the Kingdom".

The Prince and his wife immediately moved to Hampton Court, where they lived in great splendour. This did not go down well with his father and the next time the King paid a visit to Hanover he left a Regency Council in charge of the country instead of his son.

George had married Wilhelmina Charlotte Caroline of Brandenburg-

Ansbach at Herrenhausen on 2 September, 1705, when he was 23 and they went on to have three sons and five daughters. She was known by her last Christian name, Caroline, and was now Princess of Wales. She was a strong, determined woman and had an equally poor relationship with King George I, who called her a "she-devil".

Sir Robert Walpole intervened to bring about a reconciliation between father and son, but as George was a staunch Tory supporter and Walpole was in power as a Whig, there was inevitably friction. The Prince and Princess of Wales had homes in Richmond Park and Leicester House, on the site of what is now Leicester Square. Their circle became known as "The Leicester House Set" and opposed the King wherever possible.

George I died in Hanover following a stroke in 1727 and George II's Coronation took place at Westminster Abbey four months later. As soon as George was on the throne he attempted to get rid of Sir Robert Walpole. He planned to replace him with Sir Spencer Compton, who was Speaker of the House of Commons and had been George's faithful treasurer for many years. But the Queen came to Walpole's rescue and he kept his position.

During George II's reign Walpole presided over a period of great prosperity. He increased trade and staved off war. The absence of military conflict was of particular benefit, as wars were costly in terms of money and lives. The subtle change during this period was a transference of power from the monarch to the government. It has been said that George II reigned but Parliament ruled. In addition to this, the Queen was very much the power behind the throne.

Sir Robert Walpole's view of George never softened. "The King is – for all his personal bravery – as great a political coward as ever wore a crown."

The two remained at odds and whilst Walpole strove for peace, the soldier King would have been happy to go to war. He soon got his wish. In 1739, England became involved in a conflict with Spain in what is now known as the War of Jenkins' Ear. Although fighting was largely over by 1742, the war dragged on until the Treaty of Aix-la-Chapelle in 1748 returned colonial land to previous owners.

In the meantime, England had also become involved in the War of Austrian Succession, when Maria Theresa of Austria was in conflict with Prussia over who should rule the Hapsburg Empire. The English and the Dutch joined the Austrians and Hanovarians against the French and Prussians. At the Battle of Dettingen in 1743, King George II became the last English monarch to lead troops into battle.

His battle cry was, "Now, boys, now, for the honour of England! Fire and behave bravely and the French will soon run." When his horse bolted, George continued on foot. Although it was the War of Austrian Succession, George's keenness at Dettingen was really to preserve the independence of his homeland of Hanover, where he was still Elector.

When the War of Austrian Succession ended, George commissioned Handel to compose *Music for the Royal Fireworks* for a celebratory firework display in London's Green Park on 27 April, 1749, to mark the end of the war and the signing of the Treaty of Aix-la-Chapelle in 1748.

As a patron of Handel, it was George who began the custom of standing during the Hallelujah Chorus of the *Messiah*.

Although the War of Austrian Succession had ended when the Treaty of Aix-la-Chapelle was signed, tensions remained. By the mid-1750s there were two major causes for concern. There were ongoing maritime and colonial disputes between England, Spain and France. In Europe, Frederick the Great of Prussia invaded Austria, which led to the Seven Years' War.

Britain emerged as the world's dominant naval power, expanded its territories and would soon play a dominant role in the history of Canada and India. But George did not live to see the end of the war or the increase in Britain's rule.

For the last years of his reign George II seemed to take a back seat. Walpole lost power in 1742 and had been replaced by Sir Spencer Compton. Although he had been King of England for over 30 years, courtiers felt that George had become increasingly German in outlook. He eventually came to dislike English traditions and ceremony.

"I am sick to death of all this foolish stuff," he once ranted, "and wish with all my heart that the devil may take all your Bishops, and the devil take your Ministers, and the devil take your Parliament, and the devil take the whole island, provided I can get out of it and go to Hanover."

Such an outburst did nothing to endear him to the English.

During George II's reign, witchcraft was abolished as a crime in England, John and Charles Wesley started the Methodist movement and the first botanical gardens were laid out at Kew. The path was laid for the advent of the Industrial Revolution when Jethro Tull published his book *The New Horse Hoeing Husbandry*, detailing how mechanisation could improve farming. Soon manufacturing would be transformed by machinery.

In his private life, George II had many similarities with his father; notably, he kept mistresses and disliked his eldest son. George had a number of mistresses, including the Duchess of Kendal, Lady Deloraine and Countess von Wallmoden.

To some he bestowed titles, making the German Amalie Wallmoden the Countess of Yarmouth, and one of his wife's ladies-in-waiting, Henrietta Howard, became the Countess of Suffolk and had her own suite of rooms at St James's Palace. Despite the mistresses, George II appeared to remain devoted to his wife, and she even seemed to condone his adultery as part and parcel of the 18th-century court.

Both George and Caroline hated their eldest son, Frederick, Prince of Wales. The Queen told courtier Lord Hervey, "You know as well as I that he is the lowest stinking coward in the world and that there is no way of gaining anything of him but by working on his fear."

George was equally damning, saying Frederick was "the greatest beast, the greatest liar and the greatest fool in the world."

George and Caroline took the "spare the rod and spoil the child" approach with all of their offspring. Perhaps because of his strict upbringing, their eldest son Frederick turned into a rebel and opposed his parents at every turn. In adulthood, he was known as a spendthrift whose chief interests were gambling, drinking and womanising. George kept a very tight rein on the purse strings and continually reduced Frederick's allowance to try to keep him in check, but it was a constant battle.

The situation was further exacerbated by the fact that George knew his expenses would rise when the Prince married, and as heir apparent it was essential to find Frederick a suitable bride to become the next Princess of Wales.

Sarah, Duchess of Marlborough, offered her granddaughter, Lady Diana Spencer (later Duchess of Bedford) to Frederick with an incredible dowry of some £100,000. This arrangement suited them both, as Frederick needed the money and Lady Diana would give the Marlboroughs the ultimate in social status when she eventually became Queen. A date was arranged for a secret marriage, but as soon as Sir Robert Walpole heard the news, he scuppered the plans.

Eventually Frederick married 17-year-old Princess Augusta of Saxe-Gotha. She was an immature girl who arrived in England holding her favourite doll for comfort. The King and Queen took an instant dislike to her. When Augusta was due to give birth to their first child, Frederick told his parents that the baby was due in October, when in fact it was due in July. This was to prevent the King and Queen being present at the birth, as was traditional at that time. As soon as Augusta went into labour, she was taken from Hampton Court to St James's Palace to give birth there in a further attempt to thwart his parents.

When Caroline heard the news she rushed to St James's Palace, but a baby girl had already been born. This opened up a further rift between mother and son that was never bridged.

Caroline had felt unwell since the birth of her last child and was actually suffering with an umbilical hernia, which she kept to herself until her condition deteriorated perilously. Despite his mistresses, George seemed inconsolable when the Queen died on 20 November, 1737, declaring that of all the women he had known there was not "one fit to buckle her shoe".

Frederick, his troublesome heir, died in 1751 from a lung abscess, said to be the result of being hit by a cricket ball. In recent years, historians have come to the conclusion that he more likely died from a pulmonary embolism – a blood clot on the lungs.

George himself died at Kensington Palace on 25 October, 1760, while on the toilet – a victim of severe constipation. He left instructions that he was to be buried next to Caroline and that the sides of their coffins should be removed where they touched. They now lie side by side in Henry VII's Chapel. He was the last King of England to be buried at Westminster Abbey. After his death, there were few glowing tributes to the late King.

Horace Walpole wrote that George II had "the haughtiness of Henry VIII without his spirit; the avarice of Henry VII without his exactions; the indignities of Charles I without his bigotry for his prerogative; the vexation of King William III, with as little skill in the management of parties, and the gross gallantry of his father, without his good nature or his honesty."

Victorian author and politician Justin McCarthy was slightly more gracious, concluding, "The best, perhaps, that can be said of him is that on the whole, all things considered, he might have been worse."

Chapter 48

George III 1738–1820
Reign: 1760–1820

It is unfortunate that when we think of George III today, his name conjures up an image of an old, mad King, bearded and disturbed. Shakespeare's King Lear come to life, muttering "Who is it that can tell me who I am?" It is an impression that was reinforced by the award-winning 1994 film *The Madness of King George*, with actor Nigel Hawthorne's excellent performance as a vulnerable monarch.

We tend to forget that George was a young man of only 22 when he succeeded to the throne. He was extremely health conscious, with a very 21st-century attitude towards diet and exercise, and was over 70 before his mind deteriorated; an illness that was most likely of physical origin rather than mental.

He was our first Hanoverian monarch to have an English accent. "Born and educated in this country, I glory in the name of Briton!" he declared to Parliament on his accession. When George was just 10 years old his father gave him written instructions about how to behave as a Prince, writing, "Convince this nation that you are not only an Englishman, born and bred, but that you are also this by inclination."

It was advice that George took to heart. He indeed gloried in being an Englishman and whilst he travelled widely across England, he never went abroad. Unlike his immediate predecessors, he did not set foot in Hanover.

Prince George William Frederick was born two months prematurely at Norfolk House, St James's Square, London on 4 June, 1738. He was the eldest son of Frederick, Prince of Wales, and his wife Augusta. They were living in temporary accommodation at Norfolk House because the Prince of Wales had been evicted from Kensington Palace, following a dispute with his father.

George became Prince of Wales himself at the age of 12 following the sudden death of his father, who had been hit on the head by a cricket ball. He was raised by his mother and her friend John Stuart, the 3rd Earl of Bute. One of his playmates was the future Prime Minister, Lord North. George had a sense of royal duty instilled in to him by his mother, who regularly told him, "George, be a king!"

George became King unexpectedly when he succeeded his grandfather on 25 October, 1760. George wrote that he was out riding near Kew when a messenger brought him the news that George II had died. Still a young man, it took time for him to absorb the enormity of his role as monarch, but then he decided to breathe fresh air in to the court.

Horace Walpole wrote in a letter that the new King "seems all good nature and wishing to satisfy everybody; I saw him again yesterday and was surprised to find the levee room had lost so entirely the air of the lion's den. This Sovereign don't stand in one spot, with his eyes fixed royally on the ground . . . he walks about and speaks to everybody. I saw him afterwards on the throne, where he is graceful and genteel, sits with dignity, and reads his answers to addresses well." Walpole later described the new King George III as "tall, his countenance florid, and good natured; his manner graceful and obliging."

Once on the throne, the matter of marriage became more pressing and George was keen to find a suitable bride before the Coronation. Before his accession, George had a dalliance with Hannah Lightfoot, a cobbler's daughter, and fell in love with Lady Sarah Lennox, but it was considered important that he married someone of royal birth. He eventually married Princess Sophia Charlotte of Mecklenburg-Strelitz (known as Charlotte) on 8 September, 1761, at the Chapel Royal, St James's Palace.

The couple had not actually met before she came to England for the wedding. Charlotte was not a great beauty, with an upturned nose, pallid complexion and thin figure. As she was driven through the crowds of onlookers, people started shouting insults about her appearance. When she asked the Duchess of Ancaster what the crowds were chanting, the Duchess tactfully told her that the words meant, "God Bless Your Royal Highness!"

Although Charlotte's grasp of the English language was poor when she arrived, her surviving letters and notes show that within a year she had mastered the language. Despite being strangers, the couple got on well and remained devoted to each other. Whereas earlier monarchs had notoriously kept mistresses, George III was very much the family man and enjoyed simple pleasures. George and Charlotte loved dancing with a small group of a dozen friends, and would often dance non-stop for three hours at a time.

The Coronation of the King and Queen was held at Westminster Abbey two weeks after their wedding. George was crowned using the State Crown of George I, the frame of which can be seen today at the Tower of London. On entering Westminster Hall for the Coronation banquet, a large diamond fell from the crown. It was not considered to be a good omen.

The King and Queen lived at Windsor Castle, with the White House in Kew Gardens as a private retreat. As with Queen Elizabeth II, London was very much a place of business and Windsor was home. Even in his sixties George would ride on horseback from the Queen's House (Buckingham Palace) to Windsor Castle after dinner so that he could sleep in his own bed.

George and Charlotte had 15 children between 1762 and 1783. Nine sons and six daughters and 13 survived, which was unusual for the 18th century. They were loving parents and Charlotte instructed their governess to treat the children as if they were her own whenever they were in her care.

In the royal archives there is a height chart that George compiled, with very precise measurements of his children as they grew. In adulthood some of the children became troublesome and the Duke of Wellington described the sons as, "the damnedest millstones about the necks of any government that can be imagined!"

Once on the throne, George tried to regain the power of the crown that had been lost by his predecessors. Feeling that the Whigs were much too powerful, he aimed to put his Tory friends in senior positions and the government became known jokingly as "the King's Party".

But George was not one to sit back and let others take the lead. He was actively involved in all aspects of England's domestic policy, although there was antagonism between him and his first Prime Minister, William Pitt the Elder. Pitt was soon replaced with George's friend and former tutor, the Earl of Bute. This resulted in further discontent that the King's friends were being given political power.

Bute proved to be extremely unpopular and with little experience of politics was not up to the job. Within a year he had resigned. Some half a dozen more Prime Ministers followed in the first decade of the reign, with varying degrees of success, until the King appointed his childhood friend

Lord North, who remained in power for 12 years. Although the King and his First Minister got on well, they have been jointly blamed for England's loss of America.

At the start of the reign England was a leading colonial power but soon began to impose duties on imports to the colonies to help recover some of the costs incurred during the Seven Years War. This caused unrest and by 1770 all duties had been repealed, except on tea. George refused to budge on the "tea tax" and was supported by Parliament.

Discontent was exacerbated by the Tea Act of 1773, which allowed the British East India Company to sell tea to America without paying 25% tax on it, giving them the monopoly on tea sales. This led to a revolt on 16 December, now known as the Boston Tea Party, when demonstrators threw a whole cargo of tea from the British East India Company into Boston harbour: 342 crates valued at £18,000. This act of rebellion was the spark that led to the American Revolution.

The British Government took action and ceased sea trade from Boston until the cost of the destroyed tea had been paid for. The spark turned into flames and by 1775 the American War of Independence had begun. British soldiers were sent out, believing that it would be a short skirmish. They had not bargained for the strength and passion of the 13 original British colonies in fighting for their cause.

In America, George III was considered to be a despot and a tyrant. A huge gilded, lead statue of him on horseback was unceremoniously pulled down and the lead was melted to make 42,088 musket balls, which were fired at British troops. After the decisive Battle of Yorktown in 1781, led by George Washington against Lord Cornwallis, the British surrendered. When Lord North received the news, he exclaimed, "Oh God! It is all over!" The King wrote, "America is lost!"

The war officially ended in 1783 when the Treaty of Paris brought about the separation of the 13 British colonies, which were formed into a United States of America. Consequently, George III is considered to be the last King of America. On the other hand, he was the first King of Australia.

Although he never left England himself, George had a passionate interest in exploration and discovery, and encouraged the voyages of Captain James Cook. In 1770 the east coast of Australia was explored by Cook and the colony of New South Wales was founded in the name of the British sovereign in 1788. Five more colonies were formed in the years that followed. Cook also founded the penal colony of Botany Bay. In India, British rule expanded and the first Governors General were sent out.

Despite the gain in territory, George seriously considered abdication after the loss of America and drafted a letter to this effect, although ultimately decided to remain on the throne. He had begun to feel that he was a virtual slave, surrounded by ministers that he could not trust. His personal power had diminished, and he handed over control of the government to William Pitt the Younger, who was 24. Pitt remained England's Prime Minister for nearly 25 years, with only one term out of office, and is the man responsible for introducing income tax.

Across the channel, many were losing their heads during the French Revolution, and Pitt needed extra income in case of a war with France or Spain. The French were unpopular in England at this time, as they had supported the American colonists rather than their British neighbours. Conflicts eventually came, the greatest of all threats being Napoleon Bonaparte, but the Duke of Wellington and Lord Nelson steered England successfully through. The Battle of Trafalgar was won in 1805 and Waterloo ended the French threat in 1815.

There were many other successes during George III's reign. Great Britain and Ireland united with a single Parliament, so that Irish ministers sat at Westminster following the 1801 Act of Union. George III became officially King of the United Kingdom of Britain and Ireland. In 1807 the slave trade was abolished in areas under British control, although it would be another quarter of a century before slavery was abolished altogether.

Financially, interest rates remained stable throughout the reign. Although the national debt had risen considerably due to overseas conflicts, Pitt's introduction of income tax and a huge increase in foreign trade kept England financially secure and the start of the industrial revolution changed the face of the country for ever.

The textile industry was transformed by mechanical inventions such as the Spinning Jenny, the water frame, the flying shuttle and the power loom. The steam engine was developed under inventor and engineer James Watt and George Stephenson built his first locomotive, Blucher, in 1814. The iron and steel industry flourished, too, with improved smelting processes and cheaper methods of production, which in turn led to the construction of wrought-iron bridges, steel ships and eventually the railways. Across England, transport improved. New roads were laid and canals were constructed.

The industrial revolution created jobs in many manufacturing towns and cities, although led to unemployment in areas where machinery began to do the work that humans had once done manually. Factory owners also exploited workers with low wages and long hours. A need for reform was simmering.

Farming also underwent a revolution, as scientific research led to better feed and, therefore, the improved health of cattle and sheep. Farms grew in size and so productivity increased. George had a particular interest in agriculture and was nicknamed "The Farmer King". He created model farms at Windsor and in the 1780s wrote a series of essays about agricultural improvements, crop rotation and animal husbandry under the pseudonym Ralph Robinson. He made notes about everything from grasses to cabbages.

George was an avid writer and kept almost every piece of correspondence, note and essay that he ever wrote and received, which he carefully collated so that he could easily lay his hands on a particular document for reference. In 2015 it was announced that the Queen was going to allow thousands of George III's private papers to be available for all to see online. It is an ongoing mammoth task, but in recent years the digitised versions reveal how legible the King's handwriting was and his intelligence and attention to detail shine through.

George wanted improvements in education and particularly literacy, so that children could read the Bible. His long reign saw some great figures emerge in art and literature, including Thomas Gainsborough and Jane Austen, along with poets such as Byron, Keats, Shelley, Wordsworth and Coleridge. George set up the Royal Academy of Arts to promote art and design through education and exhibitions across Britain. Painter Joshua Reynolds was appointed its first president.

The *Encyclopaedia Britannica* was published for the first time and George was an avid collector of books. His library of some 65,000 works is now housed at the British Museum in a specially built area known as the Enlightenment Gallery. He also collected maps and works of art.

George was a champion of science and loved scientific instruments. His own private collection of some 2,000 items is now housed in London's Science Museum, one of the most comprehensive assemblies of 18th-century instruments and apparatus to survive. He had received lessons in physics and chemistry when a child, and also astronomy. He had the King's Observatory built at Richmond Park.

From there, George and Charlotte watched the planet Venus pass between the sun and the earth on 3 June, 1769. Fascinatingly, George wrote that the transit of Venus would not be seen again until 1874 and 2004. On 8 June, 2004, Venus once again passed between the sun and earth. Showing the Archbishop of Canterbury around the Observatory one day while the telescope was being constructed, George took his hand teasingly and said, "Come, my Lord Bishop, I will show you the way to heaven!"

George was a very devout Christian and prayed quietly on his own for many hours each day. His prayer book still exists and it is noteworthy in that he has crossed out "our gracious King" in the prayer for him and replaced it with the words "a most miserable sinner".

The King was very musical and loved playing the harpsichord. He took a keen interest in furniture and many pieces that he collected now adorn rooms at Windsor Castle and Buckingham Palace, including a great many clocks. He loved clocks and was skilled at watch repair. He also used a lathe to make ivory buttons.

One of the most impressive clocks that George purchased was made for him by Eardley Norton in 1762. It has a 24-hour dial, records the day and month, shows the position of the sun and planets, phases of the moon, and high and low tides at 32 named sea ports. It cost the King £1,042 and is still working perfectly today.

In his private life, George enjoyed going to the theatre but nothing too highbrow. He did not see the attraction of Shakespeare's plays, although admitted "One dare not say so". He loved comedy, particularly clowns, and positively relished it if humorous references were made about him from the stage. He posed for many painters in all his royal finery to show the majesty and splendour of his position, yet in private was happy to walk around Windsor in simple clothes, chatting to the public, often about farming issues. The royal walkabout is perhaps not such a modern invention after all. People recorded that he spoke very fast and often ended his questions with "Hey? Hey?" or "What? What?" to encourage a speedy response.

To mark his Golden Jubilee, Madame Tussaud made a wax figure of George III from life. A wax cast from her original mould can today be seen at Kew Palace, so we can see exactly what he looked like, with vivid blue eyes and a kindly face.

Three particular items from George III's reign particularly stand out for the people of England. Firstly, he purchased Buckingham House in 1761 as a London home for the Queen, renaming it The Queen's House. It became known as Buckingham Palace 30 years later and 14 of George and Charlotte's children were born there.

He also had the magnificent Gold State Coach built in 1762. Now usually referred to as the Coronation Coach, it weighs four tons and cost £7,562 to construct. Notoriously uncomfortable for its passengers, it was built to impress and show Britain's powerful position. It has now taken every monarch since George IV to their Coronation. Finally, the Union Flag, popularly known as the "Union Jack", in its present design was created in 1801 to mark the Act of Union between Great Britain and Ireland, and was approved by the King. The palace, the coach and the flag are three instantly recognisable English icons.

For a monarch that is now primarily associated with madness, George III was remarkably productive. His strength of character is shown by the way in which he handled two serious assassination attempts. In 1786 a woman named Margaret Nicholson presented a petition to the King outside St James's Palace, but had a knife concealed in the document. As the King leant forward to take it, she removed the knife and aimed it twice at his heart. As his bodyguards attempted to restrain the woman, he shouted, "The poor creature is mad. Do not hurt her. She has not hurt me." He later realised how lucky he had been, saying, "There was nothing for her to go through but a thin linen, and fat."

Nicholson was later found to be insane and was committed to the Bethlem Royal Hospital (Bedlam). George's popularity increased as a result of the way he had conducted himself so calmly during the attack and he received congratulatory messages from all over England. His security subsequently increased to 11 bodyguards instead of four.

In 1800 the King was at the Drury Lane Theatre in London for a performance of *The Marriage of Figaro* when James Hadfield aimed a gun directly at the Royal Box and fired twice. The King did not flinch and the bullets missed him by a couple of inches. Once again he remained completely calm, sitting down to watch the performance as planned. When the National Anthem was sung at the end of the play, the lead singer Michael Kelly sang an additional verse that had quickly been written by Sheridan:

> *From every latent foe,*
> *From the assassin's blow,*
> *God save the King!*

King George's first bout of "madness" was in 1765 but he recovered within four months. Today doctors identify the King's condition as possibly being porphyria, a genetic disease caused by an enzyme deficiency. Symptoms include abdominal pain, seizures, red or purple urine, hallucinations, anxiety, confusion, paranoia, and skin problems, all of which George III suffered from at various times.

His first major breakdown came at the age of 50 in 1788. During a dinner at Windsor Castle that November he attacked his eldest son and was said to be foaming at the mouth. In the days that followed, his health deteriorated and he occasionally became violent and was forcibly restrained by the use of a straitjacket. An analysis of some of the King's hair in 2004 showed that there were traces of arsenic in his system, probably from one of the medicines used to treat him; a treatment that would undoubtedly have made his condition worse.

In December 1788 Francis Willis, a doctor specialising in mental health, treated the King with what would now seem to be cruel and barbaric methods which included strapping him into an iron chair. Another doctor had the King's body covered in mustard and Spanish Fly which resulted in agonising blisters. But George appeared to recover by New Year and recently released correspondence shows him to have been extremely rational and his writings are certainly not those of a mad man. At his own request, George visited an asylum to speak to people suffering from mental illness, almost a form of counselling for him.

On St George's Day 1789 the King attended a thanksgiving service at St Paul's Cathedral to give thanks for his recovery. The following summer he did a tour of southern England where delighted crowds turned out to see him.

To benefit his health, for 14 years the King and his family went to Weymouth every summer, where he bathed in the sea and took long walks through the Dorset countryside. Whilst he loved the holiday in Weymouth, his wife and daughters found it dull. In 1792 he purchased Frogmore House in Windsor as a private retreat for Queen Charlotte, which she called "paradise".

Whilst Frogmore was intended to improve the family's quality of life, one incident added to the mental stress for the King. Their youngest child, Princess Amelia, became infatuated with Charles Fitzroy, an equerry to the King. She wrote passionate love letters to Fitzroy and left him all her jewellery and possessions in her will. When Amelia died prematurely from tuberculosis in 1810 at the age of 27, Fitzroy was forced to forgo the contents of the will to avoid a public scandal.

After his daughter's untimely death George, now aged 72, had a major mental breakdown brought on by grief, and it became clear that he could no longer continue to fulfil his royal duties. He was kept a virtual prisoner at the White House, Kew. For the next 10 years his son, also called George, ruled as Prince Regent.

George III was last seen in public on 21 May, 1811, and retired to Windsor

Castle. From then onwards he descended into a world of his own. Dishevelled and with a long beard, he regularly wore a purple dressing gown with the star of the Order of the Garter pinned to it. His eyesight and hearing deteriorated. On one occasion he got out of his carriage in Windsor Great Park and greeted an oak tree, believing that it was Frederick the Great of Prussia. At Christmas 1819 he began to speak total nonsense for hours on end.

He died at Windsor on 29 January, 1820. At the time, he was England's longest-reigning monarch, having been on the throne for 59 years and 96 days. This record was to be beaten by Queen Victoria in 1901 and Queen Elizabeth II in 2015 but George III still remains the longest-reigning King of England.

"It was consoling," wrote political hostess Harriet Arburthnot after the funeral at St George's Chapel, Windsor, "that such a sovereign was followed to his last home by countless thousands of affectionate subjects, drawn to the spot by no idle curiosity to view the pageant, but to pay a last tribute of respect and to shed a tear of affection and gratitude over the grave of him who, for 60 long years, has been the Father of his people."

Chapter 49

George IV 1762–1830
Reign: 1820–1830

Flamboyant, extravagant and hedonistic, King George IV surpassed all his predecessors with the lavishness of his lifestyle. No building in England defines a monarch more than the magnificent Royal Pavilion in Brighton, a breath-taking palace with every colourful ornamentation possible, which remains today as a glorious gilded symbol of the King who wanted to impress. Walk through the doors of the exotic pleasure dome and you immediately enter this Regency monarch's world.

It is a world that George created for himself, for he found the court of his father, King George III, stifling. In adulthood, he and his brother Frederick became rebels and the Duke of Wellington once described them as "the damnedest millstones about the necks of any government that can be imagined".

It was an accurate observation. Whereas their father was very much the quiet family man, George and Frederick wanted to be stylish men of fashion, craving "wine, women and song".

Prince George was born at St James's Palace on 12 August, 1762, the eldest of 15 children. His father was initially told that the child was a girl and went into the bedchamber to see his daughter, only to discover that the baby was in fact a "strong, large, pretty boy". The infant prince, baptised George Augustus Frederick, was created Prince of Wales and Earl of Chester when less than a week old.

His education included studying languages and he was fluent in French, Italian and German. He particularly enjoyed the arts, learned to play the cello, was a good dancer and a bass singer, and to please his father he also studied agriculture. He was not, however, a model student and at times could be idle and a great practical joker. When George was 15, his tutor remarked, "He will either be the most polished gentleman, or the most accomplished blackguard in Europe, possibly both."

George was witty and a good mimic, and his social circle increased as a young man. Soon alcohol and gambling became features of his life and his behaviour became increasingly immoral. His friends included opposition politicians such as Charles James Fox, whom the King considered to be a bad influence on his son. Fox taught the prince how to swear in three languages.

George soon became a spendthrift, buying what he wanted without any thought to the financial consequences, spending £10,000 a year on clothes. He would spend over £20 a week on perfumes, powders and face creams, and once spent £130,000 at a silversmith. On another occasion, when he wanted a walking stick, he ended up buying 32 rather than one.

Although his father warned the Prince continually about his reckless behaviour, constant partying and extravagance, his mother, Queen Charlotte, was probably a greater influence. She loved fine clothes and enjoyed dressing George up in theatrical-style costumes when he was a boy. Her London home, the Queen's House (now Buckingham Palace), was elegantly and extravagantly decorated, and she loved the Oriental style. His love of rich fabrics and objets d'art certainly came from her.

At the age of 21, George was given Carlton House in London's Pall Mall, next to St James's Park, as his official residence, and £60,000 to refurbish it. Typically, the Prince had the property extended and lavishly decorated at a cost of over £160,000. Some of the decoration at Carlton House was to be recreated later in the Royal Pavilion. By this time, his debts were so great that they had to be settled by Parliament to avoid a public embarrassment.

In his early twenties, George made the seaside town of Brighton fashionable when he rented a home there, a then modest farmhouse in the Old Steine. His health was already beginning to suffer due to overindulgence, and his physician had suggested that some sea air would be of benefit. As fashionable society followed the Prince down to the Sussex coast, Brighton was nicknamed "London by the Sea".

On his first visit, the Prince attended a ball. It was noted that he was tall and good looking with "high colour and powdered hair", and he wore "an exquisitely cut embroidered silk coat, ablaze with French paste buttons, and carried a laced cocked hat, lavishly ornamented with steel beads".

By 1787 the Prince had commissioned architect Henry Holland to enlarge the farmhouse, originally calling it Marine Pavilion. Over the next 35 years, with additional designs by John Nash, the Pavilion was further extended, decorated and furnished in a mix of Chinese and Indian styles, the exterior topped with domes and minarets.

George was probably at his happiest in Brighton, where he could ride on the South Downs, go to the races, walk without being troubled by people and go dipping in the sea from a bathing machine. In 1784 he was famously introduced to Mrs Maria Fitzherbert, who was to become the love of his life. She had her own home, Steine House, built in Brighton in 1804 and it reputedly had a secret tunnel through to the Royal Pavilion, although one has never been uncovered.

Twice widowed and six years older than George, Maria Fitzherbert became concerned about her reputation. She was not prepared to be simply a mistress. For her, it was marriage or nothing. As this seemed impossible, she planned to leave the country to escape from the situation. The infatuated Prince faked a suicide attempt to demonstrate the depth of his love and Maria was so shocked that she relented and agreed to marry him.

On 15 December, 1785 George and Maria secretly married in the drawing room of her house in London's Park Street. The marriage was subsequently declared invalid by the Church of England as it was without the King's consent which was required by the Royal Marriages Act. Plus Maria was a Roman Catholic, which under the Act of Settlement would have removed the Prince from the line of succession. Although they knew their marriage was unrecognised, they lived openly together.

By this time, George's debts had spiralled out of control and were in the region of a £250,000. Having learned of his son's illegal marriage, the King refused to settle the debts and it was left to Prime Minister William Pitt the Younger to sort out the mess. He tried to avoid a scandal by, once again, getting Parliament to pay the debts if the King agreed to contribute, but it was impossible to stop George spending money. Within 10 years his debts totalled nearly £650,000.

In 1788 King George III suffered his first major mental breakdown. During a dinner at Windsor Castle that November he attacked Prince George and tried to throttle him. Although we now know that George III's condition was more likely of physical origin than mental, his eldest son's behaviour cannot have helped his state of mind. It is said that the Prince sat for two nights beside his father's bed, hoping that he would die, but in the New Year the King fully recovered.

Public opinion was that Prince George had behaved badly towards his father and his popularity plummeted. It is largely down to the Prince maligning his father that many came to believe that King George III was permanently insane, rather than having episodic periods of ill health.

As George's debts mounted, the King eventually said that he would pay them if the Prince agreed to settle down and marry a royal bride. George was left with no option and, in 1795, agreed to marry his cousin, the German princess Caroline of Brunswick-Wolfenbüttell, on the understanding his debts would be cleared on their wedding day. George and Caroline became engaged without ever having met.

When they were finally introduced, it was hate at first sight. "I am not well," said George on seeing his future bride for the first time, "pray, get me a glass of brandy." She was equally unimpressed, feeling that the portraits she had seen of him beforehand were over flattering. It is said that Caroline dressed badly and her personal hygiene left something to be desired. Still, they duly married at the Chapel Royal, St James's Palace on the evening of 8 April, 1795. George became inebriated before the ceremony. It was reported that he was eventually so drunk that on his wedding night he collapsed with his head in a fireplace and fell asleep.

In the years that followed, George had dalliances with various society ladies including Lady Jersey, Lady Conyngham and Lady Hertford but his heart remained with Maria. Theirs was a tempestuous relationship. For a period he turned against Mrs Fitzherbert, telling friends that he thought of her with "feelings of disgust and horror". She in turn tried to blackmail him, threatening to release private documents to the public unless George continued to pay her an annuity. Yet, by the end of his life, their close affection appeared undimmed and some historians believe that she and the King had at least one child together.

George and Caroline also had a child: Princess Charlotte, born nine months after their wedding. Charlotte became extremely popular with the British public. At the age of 20 she married Prince Leopold of Saxe-Coburg-Saalfield, later King of the Belgians, but died during childbirth in November 1817 following a 50-hour labour.

The nation mourned her loss. Poet Lord Byron wrote from Venice, "The death of the Princess Charlotte has been a shock even here, and must have been an earthquake at home."

Haberdashers ran out of black cloth in England as so many people went into mourning. Many businesses closed for a fortnight as a mark of respect, and large quantities of memorial souvenirs were produced to mark the passing of "the pride and hope of England". George was grief-stricken and he withdrew from public life for several months.

Charlotte's rooms can still be seen at the Royal Pavilion in Brighton. Her wedding dress was cherished and is today owned by Queen Elizabeth II and is the oldest surviving wedding gown in British royal history.

George and Caroline's marriage was a disaster and he tried unsuccessfully to divorce her, accusing her of adultery and issuing a Bill of Pains and Penalties to try and bring the marriage to an end. During a debate on this in the House of Lords, Caroline declared that she had only committed adultery once, when she went to bed with "Mrs Fitzherbert's husband"!

By 1811 King George III's health had deteriorated further and it became clear that he no longer had the mental capacity to reign. George, as the eldest son and heir, became Prince Regent in order to reign on his father's behalf. With a poor reputation by this time, his elevated position did nothing to improve his popularity and we have been left with an image of a derided figure, generally known as "Prinny", who was constantly lampooned by the cartoonists and satirists of his day.

As Prince Regent, George undid much of the good work achieved by his father and it would be up to future kings and queens to restore the respectable image of the monarchy. In the early 18th century, England was suffering financially through costly wars with France, and many people were experiencing poverty as machinery developed during the Industrial Revolution led to unemployment, particularly in manufacturing. Prinny's extravagant lifestyle did nothing to endear him to the public. As he rode through the streets of London, people would jeer at his carriage and throw rotten vegetables and stones.

He finally succeeded his father on 28 January, 1820, to become King George IV. One of his first acts as monarch was to have Caroline's name excluded from prayer books in prayers for the King, Queen and Royal Family. When Napoleon Bonaparte died in May 1821, a courtier went immediately to the King declaring, "I have, Sir, to congratulate you. Your greatest enemy is dead." Wrongly assuming that he meant Caroline, George replied, "Is she, by God?"

The Coronation took place at Westminster Abbey in July 1821 and he wanted it to be as spectacular as possible, spending £24,000 on robes and a further £54,000 on his crown. Caroline tried to gatecrash the ceremony, but was forbidden entry because she did not have an invitation. By this time she had been living in Italy with her lover, Bartolomeo Pergami, since 1814 and was not regarded by the British people as Queen.

Neither had she smartened up her appearance in the intervening years, as a popular rhyme at the time went:

> Queen, Queen Caroline,
> Dipped her hair in turpentine;
> Combed her hair
> With the leg of a chair,
> And stuck a toothpick in her ear.

Caroline could have proved a thorn in the new King's side, but she died just 19 days after the Coronation. She was buried in her native Brunswick, but her wish that the plate on her coffin be inscribed with "Caroline of Brunswick, the injured Queen of England" was refused by the King.

As monarch, George proved difficult for his government to deal with, as he was extremely single-minded and became belligerent if he did not get his own way. Parliament was nevertheless productive during his reign, promoting free trade and reducing the cost of living. Trade unions were legalised. The Emancipation Act of 1829 saw a repeal of religious discrimination in 1829 which enabled Catholics to become Members of Parliament.

One remarkable development during George IV's reign was the railways. In 1825 the Stockton and Darlington railway opened, the start of a network that would soon transform travel across England. Improved transport in turn benefited trade and industry.

As well as building the Royal Pavilion, George also made changes to Windsor Castle to give it a gothic style to appear more imposing. He also virtually rebuilt what is now Buckingham Palace, turning it into a U-shaped building with a forecourt and triumphal arch, at a cost of over £496,000.

Areas of London were built in his name as Prince Regent, and the architect John Nash was responsible for Regent Street and Regent's Park. Today we refer to styles of architecture and furniture that became popular at this period as "Regency".

Whilst we tend to think of stately homes being open to the public as a modern practice, in June 1811 George actually allowed people to view his Carlton House home in London. Every half an hour, from 11am to 3pm, they let in 200 at a time, with 30,000 people queuing to see the royal splendour. So great were the crowds that many got injured in the crush.

In 1823 he donated his father's vast collection of books to the nation, which became the British Library. George himself loved the novels of Jane Austen. He was the first to buy *Sense and Sensibility* before it was advertised to the public, and Austen dedicated her novel *Emma* to him. George also encouraged his government to purchase the old master paintings collected by philanthropist John Julius Angerstein, from which London's National Gallery developed.

By the time he was in his sixties, George had ballooned in weight and his health suffered as a result. A dinner at the Royal Pavilion reputedly had 121 dishes, created by his chef Carême, including two of George's favourites: meringue and syllabub. Diarist Thomas Creevey recorded that George's belly "now reaches his knees", and years of over-indulgence left the King with agonising gout. A corset made for him in 1824 had a 50-inch waist. In 1830 it was recorded that he weighed 20 stone. He was now blind in one eye due to a cataract and suffered badly with gallstones, dropsy and bladder problems but his appetite remained undiminished.

"I heard of the King this morning," the Duke of Wellington wrote in a letter. "What do you think of his breakfast yesterday morning for an invalid? A pigeon and beef steak pye, of which he eat two pigeons and three beef steaks. Three parts of a bottle of Mozelle, a glass of dry Champagne, two glasses of port and a glass of brandy!"

A letter from Mrs Fitzherbert, wishing him well during this period of ill health, seemed to cheer him and he slept with it under his pillow. He died at Windsor in the early hours of 26 June, 1830, from a burst blood vessel, having raised his hand to his chest, saying, "Good God, what do I feel? This must be death!" Pinned to his nightshirt was a miniature of Maria Fitzherbert. He had requested that this portrait be placed in his coffin and it was hung around his neck before the funeral at St George's Chapel, Windsor.

George's immediate heirs were his brother, William, who now became King, and his niece, Victoria. Queen Victoria later recalled meeting George IV when she was a young girl and having to kiss him. She described the incident as "too disgusting, because his face was covered in greasepaint."

It was found after his death that George IV had been a hoarder, keeping most of his clothes from the age of 18 and many bundles of love letters and locks of hair from his paramours. Alas, much of this was consigned to the fire and is gone for ever. Fortunately, a few choice items remain, such as a pair of breeches, a nightshirt, a colourful floral dressing-gown known as a banyan, and his 16ft-long Coronation robe, which give us just a tantalising glimpse of this extraordinary monarch.

More than anything else, the Royal Pavilion is a glittering memorial to his colourful style and extravagant tastes.

Chapter 50

William IV 1765–1837
Reign: 1830–1837

The reign of King William IV marked the beginning of the modernisation of the monarchy. After the extravagant years, when his flamboyant brother, George, as both Prince Regent and later King, wanted the best of everything with no expense spared, William was more down to earth.

He preferred a simpler life, hated pomp and ceremony, mixed freely with the public, and ensured the survival of the English monarchy when crowned heads of other countries were struggling. French kings had lost their heads, but England's throne remained in safe hands. William's niece and successor, Queen Victoria, was later to build on her uncle's foundation by creating a family image emphasising public duty rather than private pleasure.

That is not to say that William was always public-spirited. In his younger days he was as much a womanising pleasure-seeker and as profligate as his older brothers. But with marriage and maturity there was a sense of settling down. At the age of 64 he was the oldest monarch to accede to the English throne, and contemporary reports describe him as an eccentric, uncle-like figure.

"He was not a man of talent or of much refinement," his obituary in *The Times* said, "but he had a warm heart, and it was an English heart."

Prince William Henry was born at Buckingham House (now Palace) on 21 August, 1765. He was the third son of King George III and Queen Charlotte and, with brothers the Prince of Wales and Duke of York ahead of him in the line of succession, he was never expected to become King.

William spent much of his childhood at Kew Palace, Richmond. He was educated by private tutors, but he was not particularly intelligent or a great academic. He could be volatile at times, but was self-disciplined and orderly. He joined the Royal Navy as a midshipman at the age of 13 and wanted to be treated as any ordinary sailor. He was enlisted as HRH Prince William Henry but insisted that this be amended to William Guelph, his family surname. Unlike most sailors, though, his private tutor accompanied him so that his education could continue.

"I went to every part of the ship and was received with universal joy," he said on joining the navy. He loved life at sea and served in Gibraltar and America, and experienced a naval battle at Cape St Vincent off the coast of Portugal in 1780.

With an increasing fondness for female company as he grew older, it was said that he had a girl in every port. He was once arrested for being drunk and disorderly, although quickly released once his royal status was revealed. When in Halifax, Nova Scotia, a young officer named William Dyatt confided in his diary about William's behaviour, writing, "He would go into any house where he saw a pretty girl, and was perfectly acquainted with every house of a certain description in the town."

In 1785 he became a Lieutenant and later Captain of *HMS Pegasus*. By this time he was writing home: "I am sorry to say that I have been living a terrible debauched life of which I am heartily ashamed and tired. I must in the West Indies turn over a new leaf or else I shall be irreversibly ruined."

It was while stationed in the West Indies that he became friendly with Horatio Nelson, and the two grew very close. William even gave the bride away at Nelson's wedding. They remained friends until Nelson's death at the Battle of Trafalgar and William thereafter kept a piece of *HMS Victory*'s main mast at Windsor Castle, although it has since been returned to the ship at Portsmouth. William also later commissioned a three-foot-high marble bust of Nelson, weighing three quarters of a ton, for the Guard Room at Windsor, which can be seen by visitors to the Castle today.

Why William left the navy that he loved is a mystery and he seemed destined for an undemanding life of princely duty. As his two brothers had been given dukedoms, William felt that he should be equally honoured, but his father was reluctant. Annoyed at the snub, William declared that he was going to stand for Parliament and he put himself forward as the Whig candidate for Totnes in Devon. This did the trick – the King gave him the titles of Duke of Clarence and St Andrews, and Earl of Munster.

In 1793 England declared war on France. Because of his experience in the navy, William expected to be given command of a ship, but it was denied him by the Admiralty. This was probably because he had made an anti-war speech to the House of Lords and some felt that he was not clever enough to command a ship in battle.

William made repeated requests to take part in the French Revolutionary Wars without success. He got his own back when he became King and those who had refused him promotion in the navy had to kneel in front of him. "Who's a silly Billy now?" he smiled.

William was later granted honorary titles Admiral of the Fleet in 1811 and Lord High Admiral in 1827, but they had no particular function. He tried to carve out a role for himself as Lord High Admiral by visiting dockyards and taking squadrons out to sea, but he was considered to be a nuisance and after 15 months the title was taken away from him. During his short time in the role, William abolished the punishment of cat-o'-nine-tails (a whip with nine knotted lashes) for offences other than mutiny, and improved conditions for sailors, so it was not a completely wasted appointment.

In 1797 he was made Ranger of Bushy Park near Hampton Court and Bushy House became his main home, with Clarence House as his London residence. Clarence House, just off The Mall, went on to become the home of Queen Elizabeth the Queen Mother, and is currently the home of the Prince of Wales and the Duchess of Cornwall.

As a young man, William lived with a courtesan called Polly Finch and reputedly had an illegitimate son with Caroline von Linsingen in 1784. From 1790 until 1811 he lived openly with actress Dorothea Bland, known professionally as Mrs Jordan. The couple had 10 children, each given the surname FitzClarence. "Fitz" originally meant "son of", but later came to imply illegitimacy for offspring of the nobility.

Dorothea was a great beauty and continued her stage career throughout their relationship. She had a higher income than William, frequently bailing him out whenever he got into debt. A rhyme of the day lampooned the Prince's situation:

> As Jordan's high and mighty squire
> Her playhouse profits deigns to skim,
> Some folks anxiously enquire
> If he keeps her or she keeps him!

Ironically, when their relationship ended, William asked her to give back any allowance that she had received from him. Mrs Jordan's response was curt. She sent him just one sentence on a theatre playbill: "Positively no money refunded after the curtain has arisen."

After Mrs Jordan, William pursued socialite Catherine Tylney-Long, as she had an income of £40,000 a year, and fell madly in love with Miss Wykeham, a wealthy heiress, but his family persuaded him to find a royal bride as changing family circumstances were bringing William closer to the throne.

He finally married Princess Adelaide of Saxe-Meiningen at Kew Palace on 11 July, 1818, after which he settled into the life of a faithful husband and had no mistresses. The marriage helped him financially and he hoped the union would bring a legitimate heir. William and Adelaide had two daughters – one lived for only a few hours and the other died at the age of three months – plus four stillborn babies.

King George III died in 1820 following years of ill health and William's brother was crowned as King George IV. George's only legitimate heir, Princess Charlotte, had died in 1817, pushing William up a place in the line of succession. When his next elder brother Frederick, Duke of York, died unexpectedly in 1827, William became Heir Presumptive. He seemed surprisingly merry at his brother's funeral, telling people he would be better treated now that he was heir to the throne.

Now over 60 years of age, it was generally said that William had a head shaped like a pineapple and his behaviour was considered eccentric.

"If he doesn't go mad he may make a very decent king," wrote diarist Charles Greville, "but he exhibits oddities."

William and Adelaide awoke to the news, on 26 June, 1830, that George IV had died and he was now King. William immediately went back to bed so that he could "enjoy the novelty of sleeping with a Queen".

Rather than considering the crown a burden, William appeared to relish the idea of being monarch and greeted members of the public cheerily. He walked behind the late King's coffin at the funeral, waving to people in the congregation and shaking hands with friends as the cortège processed up the aisle as if it were a jolly social event.

William IV was crowned at Westminster Abbey on 8 September, 1831, some 14 months after he acceded to the throne. Never enjoying ceremonial occasions, he tried to avoid a Coronation altogether. He called the ceremony "a useless and ill-timed expense" and saw to it that it cost as little as possible. In the end William's cost £210,000 less than his brother's. The lavish Coronation banquet was dispensed with; any unnecessary pageantry was omitted, and the event became known as William IV's "half crown-ation". Yet, when the new King and Queen departed from Westminster Abbey it is recorded that the cheering from the crowds was louder than had been heard for decades. Not only did William shun a lavish Coronation, he had no desire to live at Buckingham Palace, and twice tried to give it away! He was very different from his predecessor, and news of his simplicity endeared him to his people. He would often offer members of the public a lift in his carriage if he happened to be driving by and saw somebody walking. He dismissed the fact that he might be in any danger from the public. "Oh, never mind all this," he said, "when I have walked about a few times they will get used to it and take no notice."

The new King lacked social graces, and the Duke of Wellington once said that William had "insulted two-thirds of the gentlemen in England." When Captain Sir Charles Napier was praised by the President of the Royal Academy as "one of our naval heroes", William vehemently disagreed.

"Captain Napier may be damned, sir," he shouted, "and you may be damned, sir, and if the Queen were not here I would kick you downstairs, sir!"

William loved entertaining and invariably had between 30 and 100 guests to dinner. He enjoyed good English food and the French chefs employed by George IV were quickly replaced with British ones. The wine flowed freely for his guests, too. "I never allow anyone to drink water at my table!" he stated when the King of the Belgians refused a glass of wine at Windsor Castle.

On coming to the throne, William gave all his FitzClarence children titles, which elevated their position in society, though it gave them no rights and did not make them legitimate. The eldest son, George Augustus FitzClarence, Earl of Munster, was so aggrieved that he was not heir to his father's throne that he committed suicide in 1842.

Not just King of England, William IV was also King of Hanover, but he had no fondness for his ancestral territory.

"This damnable country," he had written to his brother George during a visit in 1785, "smoking, playing at twopenny whist and wearing great thick boots. Oh for England and the pretty girls of Westminster!"

Although William's was to be a short reign of less than seven years, it was productive. The Prime Minister, the Duke of Wellington, commented that he could achieve more in ten minutes with William IV than in ten days with George IV. George had been very lax in dealing with mundane paperwork and William signed a backlog of nearly 50,000 documents.

The Liverpool and Manchester Railway opened during his reign, becoming the first public railway in the world. This helped trade and industry by reducing transport costs and so England's economy flourished.

William never actually travelled by train himself, with passenger travel becoming more popular in his successor's reign.

Slavery was abolished in the colonies and in England the Factory Act of 1833 prohibited employment of children under the age of nine and limited the hours those under 13 could work. Before, children as young as seven years of age were employed in factories for 12 hours at a time. The first steps were also taken that would eventually lead to free state education for children in England.

The Poor Law was reformed in August 1834 to try to cut the cost of poor relief and curb the activities of those who abused the system. Workhouses became the last resort for many who had no income, and life in them was made deliberately harsh to encourage people to find employment elsewhere. Agricultural workers in particular suffered because of industrialisation. The introduction of the threshing machine, for example, which could work 12 times faster than a man, put many out of a job and on the brink of starvation.

Six Dorset men formed the Friendly Society of Agricultural Labourers to protest against the lowering of wages, with members swearing a secret oath. The founder members were arrested under the Unlawful Oaths Act and sentenced to seven years penal transportation to Australia. They became known as the Tolpuddle Martyrs and 800,000 people signed a petition for their release. There was a protest march, and the men became heroes in England. They were pardoned by the Home Secretary and eventually returned home. Their stand led to the formation of more trade unions.

Local government was reformed with the Municipal Reform Act which established a system of municipal boroughs to be governed by town councils, the councillors being elected by ratepayers. This made the councils more accountable to the public. The following year a law was passed in England that required all births, deaths and marriages to be formally registered. On the other side of the world, Queen Adelaide was honoured with an Australian city named after her.

The greatest political challenge William faced was the matter of reform. When the Tories lost the General Election of 1830, Whig Prime Minister Lord Grey wanted Parliamentary reform and a reduction in the monarch's power. He introduced a Reform Bill that was rejected by the Lords in 1831.

This led to discontent in parliament. MPs resigned, there were riots on the streets and a stone was thrown through William's carriage window. Reluctantly, William created a sufficient number of peers to allow the Bill to go through. The resulting Great Reform Act of 1832 curbed the powers of wealthy hereditary landowners and helped the property-owning middle classes, although it did nothing to improve the lot of the working classes.

One significant change that the Act brought about was to parliamentary constituencies. Prior to 1832 there was a marked difference between county areas and towns. Constituencies each elected two MPs regardless of how many voters they had. So a huge town could have two MPs, and "rotten boroughs" with maybe only two or three voters also had two MPs. Some new towns that had evolved after the Industrial Revolution had no MPs at all. The Reform Act made the government more democratic and extended the franchise to 300,000 more people. It was no longer just wealthy landowners who could vote.

Following heated debates over reform, ironically it was not long before the Houses of Parliament burned down. From the Middle Ages up until 1826, the Exchequer had used tally sticks for accounting: pieces of wood with various notches to record debts, taxes, and transactions. A tally stick could be split in half, so that one half with identical notches acted as a form of receipt and the other half was kept by the Exchequer.

By 1834 Parliament had six centuries worth of old tally sticks and the Clerk of Works was ordered to burn them. On 16 October he instructed workmen to set fire to them in the basement furnaces. That afternoon the deputy housekeeper, Mrs Wright, noticed the floor of the House of Lords was hot. Soon smoke was coming up between floorboards. By 6pm the chamber had burst into flames and the fire quickly spread, destroying both Houses of Parliament. It was a scene that artist Turner recorded in paintings. The ancient Westminster Hall was saved due to the heroic actions of firefighters and the good fortune that the wind direction changed during the evening.

A Royal Commission was set up to design a replacement building and in 1836 a public competition was held. A total of 97 entries were received, the favourite being a Gothic design submitted by Charles Barry. This eventually became the present building with its much-loved clock tower, designed for Barry by Augustus Pugin, that we all know as Big Ben. It was estimated that the new Houses of Parliament would take six years to build. It actually took over 30 and William never lived to see the project completed.

A pencil portrait of William by his eldest FitzClarence daughter, Sophia, in the Spring of 1837 shows him to be a stooped old man with a walking stick. His health continued to deteriorate that year and he became ill with pneumonia just days before Waterloo Day (18 June). He pleaded with his doctor, "I know that I am going, but I should like to see another anniversary of the Battle of Waterloo. Try if you can to tinker me up to last out that day." The King got his wish and died in the early hours of 20 June, aged 71. He was laid to rest at St George's Chapel, Windsor.

With no legitimate heirs, William had known that the throne would pass to the daughter of his late brother Edward, the Duke of Kent. Were she to be under 18 at the time of her accession, then her mother would act as Regent. As William hated the Duchess of Kent, it was not a situation he wanted. His niece Princess Alexandrina Victoria of Kent celebrated her 18th birthday in May 1837, and William died less than a month later.

Now often referred to as the "Sailor King", William IV may have left his beloved Royal Navy an unusual tradition. It is the custom in the navy to remain seated for the loyal toast. One of the stories to explain this practice stems back to the occasion when William got up from his seat to toast his father and banged his head on a deck beam. Thereafter, he sat for the toast and the practice continues, although officers stand if the National Anthem is played during the toast, whether there are deck beams or not!

Chapter 51

Victoria 1819–1901
Reign: 1837–1901

For more than a century Queen Victoria held two records: as England's longest-lived monarch, reaching the age of 81 years, seven months, 29 days; and the country's longest-reigning monarch, on the throne for 63 years, seven months, two days. She has been superseded by her great-great-granddaughter, Queen Elizabeth II, who became our oldest monarch in 2007 and attained an even longer reign in 2015.

Our image of Queen Victoria has changed in recent years. She was once thought of as the Widow of Windsor. Reclusive, sombre, autocratic and humourless, her name became synonymous with the phrase "We are not amused!" The late Princess Alice, Countess of Athlone, however, said, "Oh, but my grandmother was amused. She was amused by so many things. She loved to be entertained and she did laugh. I remember her rocking with laughter."

Another grandchild, the notorious Kaiser Wilhelm, recalled a particular incident. At dinner one evening, Queen Victoria was seated beside a very deaf admiral, who began telling her about the sinking of his ship, the *Eurydice*. After a while the Queen changed the subject and asked the admiral about his sister, who was a friend of hers.

Believing that she was still talking about his ship, the admiral said in a loud voice, "Well, ma'am, I'm going to have her turned over and take a good look at her bottom and have it well scraped."

"The effect of this answer was stupendous," the Kaiser wrote. "My grandmother put down her knife and fork, hid her face in her handkerchief and shook and heaved with laughter until the tears rolled down her face."

When a Dr Macgregor at Crathie Church, Balmoral, prayed for the Government and asked that God would "send His wisdom to the Queen's ministers, who sorely need it", Private Secretary Sir Henry Ponsonby noted that "Her Majesty turned purple in the face, trying not to laugh." There is little wonder that her diaries frequently contain the phrase "I was very much amused!"

As Victoria withdrew from public view during her 40-year widowhood, there is a mistaken belief that she lived a secluded life behind palace walls, doing little but meddle in affairs of state. In 1983, when I was researching a book about life at the court of Queen Victoria, the memorabilia of her Master of the Household, Lord Edward Pelham-Clinton, offered a revealing insight into the monarch's life. The day-to-day diaries showed that she entertained on a grand scale and needed constant amusement. She may not have visited theatres or concert halls but companies of actors, orchestras, choirs and musical societies were constantly called upon to put on private shows.

From the D'Oyly Carte Opera Company doing Gilbert and Sullivan operettas to the Royal Opera presenting *Romeo and Juliet*, many leading actors, singers and musicians of the day, ranging from Sarah Bernhardt to Paderewski, entertained wherever the Queen was staying. The Queen's own staff and family staged plays for her, and in her seventies she continued to enjoy dancing.

Following afternoon tea during the winter of 1896, the Queen wrote that "so-called animated pictures were shown off, including the group taken in September at Balmoral. It is a very wonderful process, representing people, their movements and actions, as if they were alive."

These were the earliest royal home movies. Victoria was the first monarch to be photographed and these pictures, taken in an age when the sitter had to hold their pose for several minutes, have done much to create the enduringly unamused image of the Queen. Yet, 200 years after her birth, we have now come to see her in a different light. It has been helped by the ITV television series *Victoria* which dramatised her early life; Dame Judi Dench's captivatingly witty portrayals in the films *Mrs Brown* (1997) and *Victoria & Abdul* (2017) as the older Queen; and recently rediscovered archive footage of Victoria on her last visit to Ireland wearing sunglasses and smiling as she received gifts of flowers.

The only child of the then Duke and Duchess of Kent, Victoria was born on 24 May, 1819, and was given the names Alexandrina Victoria. It was not an easy childhood for the girl known as "Drina". When she was just seven months old a boy shooting at sparrows accidentally fired his gun at the Duke while he was holding his daughter. The bullet missed the baby by a fraction of an inch, leaving a hole in her sleeve. One month later the Duke died of pneumonia at Sidmouth in Devon, and the Princess was then brought up by her mother.

Finances were tight and the young child was taught to be thrifty. When she came to the throne, she declared that she never wanted to eat mutton again, as she had eaten so much of it as a child. The Duchess of Kent was determined that her English-born daughter should receive a thoroughly English education. "How well she kept her promise," wrote a contemporary, "and what a debt of gratitude England owes to her."

No mention, however, was made to the girl of her proximity to the throne until she was 12. One day, Victoria, as she now preferred to be called, discovered that a genealogical table had been added to her history book that had not been there before. It revealed to her that she was the direct heir. Her lessons now included English Constitution, drawing and horsemanship. At mealtimes she was made to wear a sprig of holly at her throat, which encouraged her to keep her head up in a dignified manner while she ate.

She was kept largely out of the public eye but undertook private visits to cathedrals and buildings of historical interest. From 1831 to 1834 the Princess and her mother made public tours of England, giving her first-hand experience of the country. As training for royal duty, she received many loyal toasts, listened to speeches and attended receptions.

Throughout her life she was generous to the poor and needy, making private visits each year to families that were suffering through illness or hardship, and made lifelong commitments to people that she found were in trouble. There are many recorded incidents of her sitting at the bedside of the dying and comforting the bereaved, and her financial donations were extensive.

When aged 15 she heard of an actress in Tunbridge Wells who had been widowed, was expecting a baby and was in great financial difficulty. Victoria immediately visited the woman and gave her £20, and later arranged to send the actress £40 a year for the rest of her life.

Three months after Victoria's birth, her cousin Prince Albert was born in Coburg. From their infancy the family discussed the possibility of the Princess marrying Prince Albert one day. When he was three years old his nurse used to tell him about his "bride in England, the sweet May-flower."

In May 1836 the couple met for the first time. Albert enjoyed his visit to

London but frequently fell asleep throughout his four-week stay, being unused to the long social hours that Victoria kept. Although the couple promised to write to each other, soon Victoria was faced with more demanding thoughts than marriage.

On 24 May, 1837, the Princess came of age, a day that was celebrated as a national holiday. In less than a month, however, King William IV died, and in the early hours of 20 June Victoria was informed that she was Queen.

The following day she was publicly proclaimed as sovereign and "wept without restraint", a sight which moved everyone present and prompted Elizabeth Barrett Browning to record the moment in her poem *Victoria's Tears*.

In July the new Queen took up residence at Buckingham Palace, the first sovereign to make it their official home. She instigated many structural improvements and commissioned Edward Blore to build a private chapel. Originally the palace was U-shaped with three wings, but Victoria had a fourth built, turning it into a square, complete with balcony. Despite her youth, she kept a very strict routine and diligently attended to affairs of state, although she drew the line at working on a Sunday.

Queen Victoria's Coronation was held in Westminster Abbey on 28 June, 1838, which she described as "a never-to-be-forgotten day." St Edward's Crown, made for Charles II and used at successive coronations, was considered too heavy for the diminutive Queen, so a new Imperial State Crown was made using historic jewels.

Victoria ordered a smaller Coronation ring, which the Archbishop of Canterbury forced on to the wrong finger during the ceremony. Before leaving the Abbey Victoria had to have her hand bathed in iced water to remove it.

After the Coronation her uncle Leopold, King of Belgium, told her to consider marrying Prince Albert quickly, but she insisted that she was too young. She remained resolute, writing to her uncle in July 1839: "I may like him as a friend, and as a cousin, and as a brother, but not more." That autumn, however, Prince Albert visited and Victoria found him changed. "He is perfection in every way – in beauty, in everything," she later wrote. "Oh, how I adore and love him!"

She proposed to the Prince and the couple married on 10 February, 1840, at the Chapel Royal, St James's Palace. Theirs was undoubtedly a love match rather than a political alliance, although they encountered early problems because the Prince had no official position or duties. "In my home life I am very happy and contented," he wrote to his family in Coburg, "but the difficulty in filling my place with proper dignity is that I am only the husband and not the Master of the house."

Eventually he found a niche as a patron of the arts, reorganising the royal households to run efficiently and, undoubtedly, advising the Queen. He designed and had built Osborne House on the Isle of Wight and Balmoral Castle in Scotland. One of his greatest achievements was the Great Exhibition at the Crystal Palace in Hyde Park in 1851.

Victoria and Albert had nine children and their marriage lasted for more than 21 years. Although Victoria fought with successive governments to improve her husband's status and rank, it was not until 1857 that he was actually created Prince Consort.

In private, she relied upon Albert for everything and would not even buy a hat without first seeking his opinion. When he died in December 1861 she was inconsolable and suffered what today would be considered a nervous breakdown.

For her remaining 40 years she dressed almost entirely in black and kept Albert's rooms as they were on the day he died, to the extent that hot water and a towel were taken to his bedroom each evening. She came to hate change, and too much hustle and bustle could make her hysterical. I discovered a note amongst her papers that she wrote to the driver of the royal train, telling him to slow down because he was "going like the clappers". She became reclusive and anxious about appearing or speaking in public for fear of bursting into tears. There were even rumours she had gone insane.

Despite many personal tragedies in her life, including the premature deaths of two of her children and 10 of her grandchildren, Queen Victoria nevertheless triumphed through adversity. She turned mourning into an art form and became a stronger person through grief. For a woman whose name has come to symbolise prudery, she found strength in a number of men. Lord Melbourne, her first Prime Minister, became a father figure; Benjamin Disraeli flirted with her (I found amongst her papers a tiny envelope with the words "Secret – The Queen" on it, and inside was a pin-up portrait photograph of Disraeli), and her ghillie John Brown became her "strong arm" after the death of Albert.

Her private secretary wrote that Brown was the "only person who could make the Queen do what she did not wish." Throughout her life she disliked tea but would drink a cup if John Brown made it. Once she told him that his was the best tea that she had ever drunk. "Well, it should be, ma'am," he replied. "I put a grand nip o' whisky in it."

When she died, at her request a photo of Brown was placed inside her coffin, along with a lock of his hair and a wedding ring. It had belonged to John Brown's mother, but has since fuelled rumours that he and the Queen might secretly have married.

Following Brown's death in 1883, in old age she came to rely heavily on a young Indian servant, Abdul Karim, "the Munshi". He was 24, slim and clever, and it is said that the Queen "bubbled with enthusiasm" about him. She soon promoted him from waiting at table to the position of her secretary or clerk – the Indian word for clerk is Munshi.

She arranged for him to have an English tutor and she started to learn Urdu and Hindustani and began eating curries. She had his portrait painted by one of the top artists of the day and became preoccupied with India. Cottages were built for Abdul Karim on her various estates and soon he had his own office, with staff. Like John Brown before him, he was hated by the Queen's family and staff. After her death, King Edward VII had a bonfire at Frogmore and burned all Abdul Karim's papers. The Munshi was sent back to India and died there in 1909.

During Queen Victoria's long reign, technological and sociological advances were immense. When she ascended the throne, railway travel was considered a novelty and electricity an "amusing puzzle of physics". By the time of her death the motor car had been invented and two telephones had been installed at Buckingham Palace. Education, medicine, domestic comforts and the general standard of living dramatically improved. Inventions and political changes are almost too numerous to chronicle, more than in any previous period of history. The British Empire expanded and in 1877 she was proclaimed Empress of India.

Although Queen Victoria lived a far less public life than our present Royal Family, she was powerful and ruled her country, family and household with a rod of iron, staying active into her eighties. She was a prolific letter writer, expressing her opinions forcefully. She kept a diary for almost 70 years until just nine days before her death, and published extracts from her journals during her lifetime. She was a skilled artist and pianist. She loved playing cards for money. All who lost to her were required to pay in newly minted coins, so her ladies-in-waiting had to keep a large supply, in case they were asked to play. She loved dogs and owned many in her lifetime of various breeds, particularly Pomeranians. Her kennels at Windsor were luxurious and could house 80 dogs. In 1891 she exhibited seven of her dogs at a show organised by Charles Cruft and became the first Patron of the Battersea Dogs Home.

Her favourite tipple was claret fortified with Scotch whisky, and after Prince Albert died she drank a glass of whisky every night to help her sleep. She loved food, particularly chocolate cake. If there was a choice of puddings, she tried them all. When her doctor tried to put her on a lighter diet and recommended a milky cereal called Benger's Food, she had it in addition to her normal diet.

Queen Victoria also had her dislikes, which included babies, hot rooms, the telephone, the music of Handel, her Prime Minster, William Gladstone, and tobacco smoke. She also never took to the motor car. "I am told that they smell exceedingly nasty," she once wrote, "and are very shaky and disagreeable conveyances altogether".

She took a keen interest in the social welfare of her subjects and tried to keep in tune with the public's wishes. When Sir Robert Peel introduced an income tax for those who earned more than £150 per annum, the Queen paid her sevenpence in the pound like her wealthier subjects. Troubled by the many conflicts during her reign, she instituted the Victoria Cross as the highest award for the most valiant.

Celebrations for her Golden and Diamond Jubilees coaxed Victoria to make more public appearances. "No one ever, I believe, has met with such an ovation as was given to me," the Queen wrote in June 1897. "The crowds were quite indescribable, and their enthusiasm truly marvellous and deeply touching. The cheering was quite deafening, and every face seemed to be filled with real joy."

By her Diamond Jubilee, the Queen had outlived all members of the Privy Council alive at the time of her accession, all but two of the Peers who held their titles in 1837 and all but five members of the House of Commons. She'd seen ten Prime Ministers and five Archbishops of Canterbury.

In her final years the Boer Wars caused her anguish. Despite failing eyesight, rheumatism and sciatica, she visited wounded soldiers and reviewed troops with zest. When Ladysmith was relieved in 1900, the Queen made triumphal drives through the streets of London. Mafeking was liberated days before her final birthday. Although lacking in mobility and suffering from insomnia, Victoria maintained a full diary in 1900, even interrupting her holiday at Balmoral to visit the victims of a train crash.

Queen Victoria attended her last official engagement on 18 December, 1900 when she toured an industrial exhibition before sailing to the Isle of Wight for a subdued Christmas at Osborne House. On 17 January, 1901, she suffered a slight stroke and gradually faded away.

Queen Victoria died at 6.30pm on 22 January, 1901, surrounded by her surviving children and grandchildren. Undertakers were forbidden to attend to her body and it was family members who lifted her into her coffin. The very last person allowed to see her was Abdul Karim, the Munshi.

The Queen's final journey was across the Solent to Portsmouth on the royal yacht *Alberta*, then by train to Victoria Station at a speed she would have hated. Hundreds of thousands of people lined the streets as the cortege made its way to Paddington, from where her coffin travelled by train to Windsor. It is said that people knelt in the fields as it passed by. She, who had been so associated with black, had asked for a white funeral. There was a white pall over her coffin and London was festooned with purple and white.

She was laid to rest in the Royal Mausoleum at Frogmore, near Windsor Castle. When the family came out after the service, it began to snow. Sir Henry Ponsonby once said that there was nobody like Victoria for arranging the minute details and as they looked at the snowflakes all around they felt that she had achieved her wish for a white funeral.

The effigy for her tomb had been carved almost 40 years earlier in 1862, at the same time as Prince Albert's, and so it is the image of a young Queen that now gazes adoringly at her beloved husband for all eternity.

Chapter 52

Edward VII 1841–1910
Reign: 1901–1910

The very phrase "Edwardian England" conjures up an image of potted palms, hansom cabs and country-house parties; of an elegant, if somewhat decadent, age. For the upper classes at least, these were the halcyon days that ended with the outbreak of World War I.

King Edward VII, from whom this era took its name, was a man of contrasts – a stickler for royal protocol and good manners, yet happy to take a score of mistresses and preferring pleasure to politics.

Whilst enjoying the good things of life in private, he earned himself a public reputation as a diplomat, promoting British foreign policy throughout Europe and forming military alliances against the increasing power of Kaiser Wilhelm.

The eldest son and second child of Queen Victoria and Prince Albert was born on 9 November, 1841. It was a difficult labour for the Queen. She had post-natal depression and blamed her son for the rest of her life for the pain he had caused her. The baby immediately became heir to the throne and was created Prince of Wales one month after his birth.

On 25 January, 1842, he was baptised at St George's Chapel, Windsor, and given the names Albert Edward. He was known by his family and friends simply as Bertie. Soon after his birth, the magazine Punch predicted, "The time of the Prince will be glorified by cooking and good cheer. His drum stick will be the drumsticks of turkeys, his cannon the popping of corks."

For a man who was a bon viveur and almost a glutton, it was an accurate forecast, although the Prince had an unpromising start in life.

Because he would one day be King, a taxing educational regime was devised for him. Henry Birch, a strict master from Eton, became the child's principal tutor. Bertie was always compared to his very intellectual older sister, Vicky, the Princess Royal. Birch considered him "disobedient, impertinent and unwilling to submit to discipline", although he did admit that the Prince had "a very amiable and affectionate disposition".

Soon Birch was replaced by an even stricter master, Frederick Gibbs, who forced Bertie to study for six hours a day, seven days a week. Highlights of his childhood were visits to the theatre, opera and the circus – entertainment that he enjoyed for the rest of his life.

Bertie's personality was stifled at home. His mother seemed remote, his father too strict and the boy felt unloved. This may account for his many dalliances in adult life. During an official visit to France when he was 13, the Prince asked the Emperor Napoleon III and Princess Eugenie if he could remain in Paris.

"I think your mother and father might miss you," the Emperor said.

"Oh, no," Bertie replied, "there are plenty more of us at home."

At the age of 16 he begged to be allowed to join the army but his parents refused. When Bertie visited his sister Vicky in Berlin, Prince Albert wrote to her beforehand.

"Do not miss an opportunity of urging him to hard work. Unfortunately he takes no interest in anything but clothes, and again clothes. Even when out shooting, he is more occupied with his trousers than with the game!"

After a period of overseas travel to broaden his education, the Prince was sent to study history and law at Christ Church, Oxford, for four terms. He sat specially prepared exams, was not allowed to live at the college and was treated only as a member of the Royal Family. His fellow students, for example, had to stand whenever he entered a room. Bertie left Oxford having gained little more than weight and a love of rich food.

In 1860 he was sent on an official tour of Canada and America, becoming the first heir to the throne to cross the Atlantic. On his own and unstifled, the Prince blossomed and the tour proved highly successful.

Visiting Niagara Falls he had to be restrained from accepting an invitation to be wheeled across in a barrow by the tightrope-walker Charles Blondin. In New York, 5,000 people crowded into a ballroom intended for half that number, just to catch a glimpse of him. As he arrived the dance floor collapsed. On his return home Queen Victoria noted that her son had become "extremely talkative" and complained that he always had a cigar in his mouth. She detested smoking.

In January 1861 the Prince began studying at Trinity College, Cambridge. He made many new friends and began to enjoy socialising. That June he was sent for ten weeks' infantry training at Curragh Camp near Dublin, attached to the 1st Battalion, Grenadier Guards. He was gazetted as a Lieutenant-Colonel, a rank for which he felt unworthy. While in Ireland, he fell for the charms of actress Nellie Clifden – the first of many such liaisons.

At Windsor, it was decided that Bertie was of an age to marry. Photographs of suitable European princesses were sent to him but he rejected them all. It was while staying with his sister, Vicky, that he was first introduced to Princess Alexandra of Denmark when visiting a cathedral.

Bertie and Alexandra were left alone, both unaware that a supposed chance encounter had been carefully engineered by his sister. Although not taken by her beauty, Bertie did admit to being impressed with Alexandra's simple, unaffected manner.

Back in Cambridge that autumn, Bertie received a visit from Prince Albert, who berated his son over the Nellie Clifden affair and urged him to marry Princess Alexandra as soon as possible. The Prince Consort returned to Windsor Castle exhausted and within days collapsed with the typhoid fever that was to take his life. Queen Victoria blamed Prince Albert's illness on Bertie's misconduct, writing that she knew "all the disgusting details. I never can or shall look at him without a shudder."

To remove him from her sight, the Queen sent her son on a tour of Palestine and the Near East for several months. To be blamed for causing his father's death must have been a heavy burden for Bertie to bear and he was probably glad to get away.

The following September, the Prince travelled to Brussels to stay with the Danish Royal Family and there asked Alexandra's father for her hand in marriage.

"I frankly avow to you," Bertie wrote to his mother, "that I did not think it possible to love a person as I do her. She is so kind and good, and I feel sure will make my life a happy one."

The couple were married at St George's Chapel, Windsor, on 10 March, 1863. Bertie wanted a big state wedding but Queen Victoria was in mourning for Albert so insisted on a smaller ceremony and she remained in the background.

After a honeymoon at Osborne House on the Isle of Wight, the couple went to Sandringham House, which the Prince had bought for £22,000, and in April took up residence at Marlborough House, which became the focus of London society.

Queen Victoria was reluctant to give him any official responsibilities or involvement in affairs of state. Thus, with an annual income in excess of £100,000, he embarked on a life of pleasure. January and February were spent at Sandringham with house parties and shooting; in March he began a five-week holiday on the French Riviera; in April he returned to London for theatres, parties and dinners, plus racing at Newmarket and Epsom. In July he yachted at Cowes, holidayed in Europe for the summer before returning to Balmoral in the autumn for deerstalking and grouse shooting, then back to Sandringham for his birthday and Christmas.

On average he spent 30 days a year on royal engagements and fulfilling duties for his various patronages. A further 25 days a year were spent attending committee meetings.

Although he loved his wife, now the Princess of Wales, and fathered six children, the Prince enjoyed other female company and had a roving eye. He enjoyed London's nightlife with various society ladies. He gambled, often losing large sums of money, and when an anonymous article appeared in *The Times* denying that the Prince was in debt and actually deserved more money, it was rumoured that he had written it himself. Occasionally his antics got him into trouble and he was once subpoenaed to appear as a witness in a divorce trial.

Shooting was a passion and at Sandringham he kept the clocks forward by half an hour to make the most of the daylight. Although staff often despaired of his behaviour and quick temper, he was much liked for his forgiving nature and generosity.

In October 1871 the Prince was struck down by typhoid fever, the disease that had killed his father. Queen Victoria made her first visit to Sandringham – believing Norfolk to be a wild-looking, flat, bleak county – where for several weeks Bertie's life hung in the balance. The crisis point arrived on the anniversary of Prince Albert's death, and a National Day of Prayer was held for his recovery.

Alexandra nursed Bertie throughout his illness and it brought them closer together. Public affection for the Royal Family increased dramatically. On 27 February, 1872, a thanksgiving service for the Prince's recovery was held at St Paul's Cathedral. Thousands lined the streets to see the heir to the throne and Queen Victoria making a rare public appearance together.

The Prince's life quickly slipped back into its familiar routine, although he appeared to take his official duties more seriously. In October 1875 he embarked on a lengthy tour of India. So great was the success that it set the wheels in motion for Queen Victoria to be proclaimed Empress of India.

Bertie arrived back at Portsmouth after almost seven months away and, after a private reunion with his wife, returned to London. Within an hour of their return, the royal couple attended a concert at Covent Garden, receiving a standing ovation before every act.

The Prince loved the theatre and was particularly fascinated by the actress Sarah Bernhardt. For one night only, he appeared on stage with her, playing the part of a corpse in a Paris production of Sardou's play *Fedora*.

In May 1877 he dined at the home of Arctic explorer Sir Allen Young and met another beauty, Lillie Langtry. Within weeks Mrs Langtry had taken London society by storm, and she became the Prince's lover.

In 1881 Lillie Langtry made her London debut as an actress, playing Kate Hardcastle in Goldsmith's comedy *She Stoops to Conquer* at the Haymarket Theatre. The Prince attended this first performance in aid of the Royal General Theatrical Fund. With Bertie's patronage, Lillie formed her own company and toured England and America, drawing large audiences because of her royal connection.

After Bertie's illness, his relationship with Queen Victoria mellowed, although at her Diamond Jubilee service he said, "I don't mind praying to the Eternal Father, but I must be the only man in the country aflicted with an eternal mother!"

By the 1880s his royal workload had increased and he averaged 42 official engagements a year (compared to the present Prince of Wales, who undertook over 500 in 2018, at the age of 70). As a member of the Royal Commission on the Housing of the Working Classes, he explored the slums of Holborn, Clerkenwell and St Pancras in disguise, and was horrified by what he saw. He spoke out about the situation in the House of Lords.

The Prince celebrated his 50th birthday in 1891, a year that was the worst of his life. He was called as a witness at the gambling trial of Sir William Gordon-Cumming and was publicly criticised for gambling.

Hours before his 50th birthday celebrations, his beloved Sandringham House was badly damaged by fire and 14 rooms destroyed. Water used to extinguish the fire also penetrated into the rooms below. Just days later, his second son, Prince George (later King George V), developed typhoid. Then his eldest son, Prince Albert Victor, the Duke of Clarence, caught influenza which turned to pneumonia. He died in January 1892. Bertie sobbed openly at his son's funeral.

Bertie's yachting and racing exploits did much to win him popularity. He transformed the annual Cowes regatta into a major social event and achieved success in his racing yacht, Britannia. On the turf he had even greater success: his horses Persimmon and Diamond Jubilee won the Derby in 1896 and 1900 respectively. His horses later won the Grand National, the 2,000 Guineas, the Newmarket Stakes and the St Leger.

In February 1898 the last in a succession of beautiful mistresses entered the Prince's life: the Hon Mrs George Keppel (great-grandmother of Camilla, Duchess of Cornwall). Alice Keppel was witty, clever and discreet. She came to be tolerated by Princess Alexandra. Bertie hated being alone, so needed constant amusement, whereas his profoundly deaf wife preferred a simpler life.

Age did little to diminish Bertie's prodigious appetite. He relished what he called "plain English fare" and ate roast beef and Yorkshire pudding on Sundays. He was a heavy smoker – never fewer than 20 cigarettes and 12 large cigars a day – but was a moderate drinker. His favourite tipple was champagne, which he called "Boy". This stemmed from a picnic where the guests were being served by a young waiter. When they wanted their glasses refilled, they shouted, "Boy!" The Prince saw a girl had nothing in her glass and asked what she would like. "I'll have some Boy like everyone else," she said.

On 22 January, 1901, Bertie was at Queen Victoria's bedside at Osborne House when she died. At his Accession Council in London Bertie announced that his first name, Albert, would always be associated with his father and he wished to be known as Edward. Although now monarch and resident at Buckingham Palace, he did not allow royal duties to destroy his social life. There were still nightly entertainments, holidays, racing, shooting, endless parties and, of course, visits to the theatre.

Queen Victoria had done little to prepare her son for the role of sovereign and their characters were very different. While she enjoyed the behind-the-scenes duties, King Edward VII preferred the public appearances, the pomp and ceremony. In 1901 he revived the State Opening of Parliament ceremony, which had been allowed to lapse. He left secretaries to compose his letters but expected to be consulted on all things.

He altered his mother's private rooms, smashed busts of her favourite servant John Brown, and had a bonfire of papers relating to her beloved Abdul Karim, "the Munshi". He gave Osborne House to the nation, turning it into a Royal Naval College and a convalescent home for naval officers.

Two weeks before his Coronation, planned for 2 June, 1902, the King developed appendicitis which turned to peritonitis. Sir Frederick Treves operated on the King at Buckingham Palace and saved his life. The Coronation was postponed until 9 August, by which time the King was looking fitter and had lost six inches from his 48-inch waist.

King Edward's forte was in establishing good relationships overseas. His presence in France in 1903 made the entente cordiale of 1904 possible and he was known as "Edward the Peacemaker". Yet he was fiercely opposed to the Channel Tunnel Bill of 1907.

He pressed for modernisation in the Royal Navy and did much to reform the Army Medical Service. He was particularly interested in medical research and inaugurated the King Edward Hospital Fund. He also funded a tuberculosis sanatorium at Midhurst in West Sussex, where he laid the foundation stone.

On the King's 66th birthday, he was presented with the famous Cullinan diamond by the people of Transvaal. He took a personal interest in the cutting of the stone and the two largest pieces were incorporated into the Crown Jewels – the Sovereign's Sceptre, used at Coronations, and the Imperial State Crown.

Clothes, jewellery and decorations were very important to the King. He was the most influential trendsetter of his day, introducing the dinner jacket and the unbuttoning of the last button of a waistcoat. He popularised the Norfolk jacket and smoking jacket, the Homburg and side creases in trousers. Once, on a week-long visit to Yorkshire for the Doncaster races, he took 40 suits and 20 pairs of shoes!

In 1909 the King's health began to deteriorate. His lungs suffered from years of heavy smoking and he wheezed constantly. He made visits to Brighton and Eastbourne where the air suited him. In Worthing he stayed with his friend Sir Edmund Loder and was known in the town as "Teddy".

In March 1910, King Edward fulfilled a packed diary of official engagements before holidaying in Biarritz, where he collapsed with bronchitis. He returned to London and on 4 May wrote a final entry in his diary: "The King dines alone." Two days later he suffered a series of heart attacks, although he refused to go to bed and remained in an armchair, dressed in a frock-coat. "I shall work to the end," he said. "Of what use is it to be alive if one cannot work?"

The Queen allowed Mrs Keppel, his mistress, to visit him one last time. In the evening he was told that one of his horses had won at Kempton Park.

"I'm very glad," he said, before lapsing into a coma. He died at 11.45pm on 6 May. Pressing a rose into his hand, the widowed Queen Alexandra smiled wistfully and confided, "He always loved me best."

The King's funeral was held two weeks later, with services at both Westminster Abbey and St George's Chapel, Windsor. Big Ben was rung 68 times, once for each year of his life.

The funeral brought together the largest number of European royalty ever in one place, but one figure walking behind the coffin, ahead of nine kings and countless heads of state, drew the most attention. It was the King's much-loved fox terrier. On his collar was inscribed: "I am Caesar. I belong to the King".

A marble image of Caesar was carved on to the King's tomb, curled up at his master's feet.

Chapter 53

George V 1865–1936
Reign: 1910–1936

Known affectionately as "Grandpapa England", by the time of his Silver Jubilee in 1935 King George V was repeatedly referred to in newspapers and books as "The People's King". No monarch before him had ever been so close to the British people and few Kings had so openly expressed such a deep love for their country.

He hated foreign ways and foreign food, once roaring in disgust, "What in heaven's name is this?" when offered an avocado pear. In his adult life he took holidays only in England and when someone once complained about the English weather, he replied, "I like my own country best, climate or no, and I'm staying in it!"

King George V was the founder of the House of Windsor, ridding his family of all German titles during World War I. Thus, his Teck and Battenburg relatives residing in England changed their name to Cambridge and Mountbatten. When the author H.G. Wells wrote that the Royal Family were "uninspiring and alien", the King took great exception to the comment.

"I may be uninspiring," he told a friend, "but I'll be damned if I'm an alien."

In previous reigns the monarch had remained a remote, hallowed figure, but through the medium of radio the gruff grandfatherly voice of King George V was heard throughout the Empire and he became suddenly a warm identifiable presence – one of the family.

When he sent a special message to children during his Silver Jubilee broadcast – "Let me say this to each of them whom my words may reach:

The King is speaking to you" – thousands sitting beside their wireless set felt as if the King really was speaking to them personally.

He travelled widely as royal duty dictated and used the experience to his country's good. In 1901, when Duke of York, he sailed to Melbourne and opened the first Federal Parliament of Australia, also visiting New Zealand, South Africa, Canada and Mauritius in a 50,000-mile trip. On returning home, he made his famous "Wake Up, England!" speech at the Guildhall in London.

During his travels he had seen how other countries were developing commercially and he felt that England was lagging behind. "The Old Country must wake up," he advised, "if she intends to maintain her old position of pre-eminence in her Colonial trade against foreign competition."

His speech shocked business owners who had become complacent and assumed that Britain would always be at the forefront. During a British Industries Fair at Olympia, he was being shown some British-made typewriters and was told that the Swedish government had ordered a large consignment but the British government continued to use imported machines.

"This is scandalous." he said, "Scandalous! If other governments can purchase these machines, why cannot they be used in our own departments? I will have the matter looked into." As a result, the government was shamed into buying British.

Whether touring a hospital or descending a coal mine, King George V was characteristically down-to-earth. On a visit to Bolton Abbey in Yorkshire, he bought a half-share in a pet rabbit with a sad little girl whose brother had threatened to sell it. Looking at a painting by Cézanne at an art exhibition, he called the Queen across. "Come over here, May, there's something that will make you laugh."

Those who came into contact with him saw the human face of the monarchy. Meeting the author John Buchan in 1935, the King told him, "I don't get much time for reading, but when I do I enjoy your books – *The Thirty-Nine Steps* and so on." When Buchan later had a private audience with Queen Mary, she told him, "The King does not get much time for reading and when he does I'm afraid he reads the most awful rubbish."

King George V was the second son of the Prince and Princess of Wales (later Edward VII and Queen Alexandra) and was born on 3 June, 1865 at Marlborough House in London. He was baptised a month later and given the names George Frederick Ernest Albert. He was educated by private tutors and at the age of 12 became a cadet at the Royal Naval College,

Dartmouth, along with his elder brother Prince Albert Victor. They were nicknamed "Sprat" and "Herring" from the punning title of their father, the Prince of W(h)ales.

The two Princes had a disciplined regime, rising daily at 6 am for drill, followed by traditional lessons and sports. Prince George distinguished himself in rowing and was to have a lifelong love of the sea, taking part in the annual Cowes Regatta in his first yacht *Corisande*. The navy discipline was to remain with him for life. Like his father he became a stickler for punctuality, keeping clocks at Sandringham half-an-hour fast to ensure that guests were not late for meals. He began his breakfast as the clock struck 9 am and he always went to bed at exactly 11.10 pm. He loved ritual, routine, and maintaining traditions, many of which Queen Elizabeth II continued.

At the age of 14 the Prince joined *HMS Bacchante* for three years of "mental and moral" training, after which it was said that his knowledge of the British Empire was "nothing short of encyclopaedic". It was a demanding and strenuous life with no concessions made to royal status. He began keeping a diary detailing his life on board the *Bacchante* resulting in an eloquent record of the voyage.

"Looked out on the waters as the ship ploughed her way through them," he wrote on 4 October, 1879, "and all the stars glittered in between the spaces of the sails and rigging, and everything was silvered over by the light of the moon." Like his grandmother Queen Victoria, George kept up his diary daily until three days before his death.

The tour of duty was extensive and when the Prince finally returned to England he wrote, "The sight of the Devon cornfields, grass lawns and woods sloping to the sea makes every heart on board beat more quickly." Despite all the countries he had visited, England still gave him the greatest thrill.

After a brief period of study at the University of Heidelberg, the Prince returned to sea and took command of the gunboat *HMS Thrush*. Years later he told a group of cadets: "I think that I am entitled, from personal experience of 20 years at sea, to impress upon you three simple qualities which I am sure, if conscientiously acted up to, will go a long way to ensuring your success. The qualities to which I would refer are truthfulness, obedience and zeal. Truthfulness will give those placed under you confidence in you; obedience will give those placed over you confidence in you; and although I have mentioned zeal last, it is by no means the least important, for without zeal no sailor can ever be worth his salt."

In January 1892 Prince George's elder brother, Albert Victor, died suddenly as a result of influenza during a pandemic. It was a tremendous shock to the whole country and George was united in grief with Princess Mary of Teck (known as May), who had been due to marry Albert Victor in February. The pair grew closer and in 1893 announced their engagement, which was greeted with universal approval. The couple married on 6 July that year in the Chapel Royal at St James's Palace.

Now the Duke and Duchess of York, they spent their honeymoon at Sandringham, which George described as "the place I love better than anywhere in the world". They were given York Cottage on the estate as a country home and later Marlborough House became their London residence.

Between 1894 and 1905 the couple had six children: Edward (later King Edward VIII and Duke of Windsor), Albert (later King George VI); Mary (Princess Royal); Henry (Duke of Gloucester); George (Duke of Kent) and John, who died in 1919 aged just 13.

Mabell, Countess of Airlie, a lady-in-waiting, wrote that George had an uneasy relationship with his children. "His manner to them alternated between an awkward jocularity of the kind which makes a sensitive child squirm from self-consciousness, and a severity bordering on harshness."

In private he was very sensitive and his official biographer revealed that George would break down and cry whenever saying goodbye to family members and his voice would crack with emotion during speeches that he felt passionate about. To cover up this softer side of his character, he could at times appear brusque and offhand.

After Queen Victoria's death in 1901, George and May were created Prince and Princess of Wales and added to their already punishing schedule of official engagements. They embarked on a seven-month tour of "British Possessions", of which a contemporary commentator wrote: "This probably did more to cement the Empire and to stimulate enthusiasm for Imperial progress and prosperity than any act of diplomacy could possibly have achieved."

Despite their success overseas, the Prince missed his children and wrote home to his mother, Queen Alexandra, "Of course, our tour is most interesting, but it is very tiring and there is no place like dear old England for me."

The death of his elder brother had placed the Prince in direct line of succession to the throne. Thus, when Edward VII died in 1910, George took his father's place. The couple were crowned King George V and Queen Mary on 22 June, 1911, and at the end of that year set sail for India for the spectacular Delhi Durbar – a state ceremony watched by 70,000 spectators, during which Indian Princes and the Viceroy paid homage to the King.

A series of benefits for the country were announced, including better education, a more democratic form of government, and Delhi became the capital of India instead of Calcutta. An impressive diamond tiara was made for Queen Mary to wear for the ceremony, which in recent years has been worn by the Duchess of Cornwall. The awning beneath which the King and Queen sat during the Durbar now forms the canopy above the thrones in the ballroom of Buckingham Palace.

Back home in England 10,000 people were rendered homeless by floods in East Anglia, the *Titanic* sank, and war clouds were slowly gathering over Europe. In 1913 the King and Queen visited Berlin and were given an enthusiastic welcome that seemed to dispel any threat of war, and the following year they entertained the Kaiser on board the flagship *HMS King George V*. But just three days later on 28 June, 1914, Archduke Ferdinand was assassinated at Sarajevo, which was the spark that lit the fuse of World War I. Within weeks Austria-Hungary declared war on Serbia, and shortly afterwards Germany declared war on Russia. On 4 August, 1914, Britain entered the conflict.

At the end of November the King made the first of many visits to the battle zone in France, toured military hospitals and joined the fighting forces on land and at sea. In 1915, while inspecting troops on the Western Front, he fractured his pelvis when his horse reared in fright. It was an injury from which the King never fully recovered. Frequently his own life was put at risk on these visits and worry over the war took its toll on his health. "Very often I feel in despair," he wrote to the Queen, "and if it wasn't for you I should break down." His beard grew whiter and he began to smoke noticeably more cigarettes.

During the war the King gave £100,000 to the Exchequer to help England's crippling costs and tightened the purse strings at Buckingham Palace, which he referred to as "my house in Pimlico". He banned alcohol in the royal households, although it was widely understood that when he left the dinner table saying that he was going to his study "to attend to a small matter of business", that business was a bottle of port.

Meals were frugal and the American Ambassador complained that at a Buckingham Palace dinner he was given one egg, a slice of bread and a glass of lemonade. Instead of having clean napkins every day, Queen Mary agreed to use napkin rings for the first time.

When the Armistice finally came in 1918, King George wrote, on 11 November, "Today has indeed been a wonderful day, the greatest in the history of our country." That Armistice Day, the King and Queen appeared on the Buckingham Palace balcony and shared in the jubilation with the thronging crowds. There were tears in the King's eyes as people sang the National Anthem with more fervour than he had ever heard before. From then onwards it took on even greater significance for him.

Once, after a concert at the Royal Albert Hall, he said to the musicians, "I do wish you would not play *God Save The King* so quickly. You hurry through it as if you wanted to get it over. You see, it means a great deal to me. I look upon it almost as a hymn."

After the war, the King employed many ex-servicemen in the royal household, hoping to encourage other employers to follow suit. He unveiled numerous war memorials, including the Cenotaph in Whitehall, initiated the annual Remembrance Day ceremony, and was present as an unknown British soldier was laid to rest in Westminster Abbey to represent all those who had died through war without being identified.

Life settled into a more comfortable pattern with the ensuing years of peace. He loved the theatre, although nothing too highbrow, and his favourite musical was *Rose Marie* which he went to see several times. He took an interest in all sports, particularly horse racing. In the evenings, if there were no official functions he enjoyed playing cards with friends or quietly maintaining his vast stamp collection.

When an equerry asked him if he had seen that "some damned fool has paid £1,400 for a stamp", he replied, "I was that damned fool!" He had a strong faith and every year gave out prizes of Bibles to the local schoolchildren at Sandringham, advising them to read a chapter every day. "I don't think you'll regret it when you get to my age," he told them.

When in London, the King rode each morning in Rotten Row before starting work on official business. The King and Queen undertook a full diary of engagements and were concerned particularly with the welfare of the people. When, for example, the King opened a small block of houses for working men and their families, he complained about the design. Each house had two fireplaces which, in his opinion, meant twice as much fuel would be used.

Working men, he insisted, had to spend their money wisely and coal was expensive. He suggested that a single fireplace should be installed in an adjoining wall that could heat two rooms at the same time. His idea was followed up and eventually patented. When the King visited Wales and became aware of large-scale unemployment, he donated £750,000 to help colliers of the Rhondda Valley.

In private, the King remained happiest at Sandringham. He had a pet parrot called Charlotte, who was allowed to help herself to food from the breakfast table, and Bob, a Cairn terrier. He enjoyed working on the estate, clearing bracken and ivy, but hated the sound of motorcycles in the countryside and loathed anything being moved in his rooms. When a housemaid slightly altered the arrangement of furniture in his sitting-room, he had a photograph taken so that the exact position could be noted and adhered to.

Always smartly dressed, invariably in a frockcoat, and trousers creased at the sides never at the front, the King expected his sons to follow his example. He insisted that they wore morning coats whenever they visited him, and white tie and tails, plus the Garter Star, at dinner even if no other guests were present.

He used the same collar studs and hairbrushes for 50 years and was not impressed by changing fashions. When he saw a courtier wearing trousers with turn-ups, his reaction was, "I was not aware that my Palace is damp." He was also horrified if he ever saw a man not wearing a hat outside, although he did not approve of bowler hats, which he thought only suitable for rat catchers.

At the Goodwood races in 1928 he caught a severe chill which led to a serious congestion of the right lung. As the autumn days went by this worsened into pleurisy and throughout November crowds gathered silently at the gates of Buckingham Palace for news bulletins to be posted. With each hour his condition appeared to deteriorate. His eldest son Prince Edward was called back from Dar-es-Salaam and by mid-December an operation became necessary to withdraw infected fluid from the lung. It was not until 6 February, 1929, that the King was strong enough to travel by ambulance to Bognor for a period of convalescence at Craigweil House, the home of Sir Arthur du Cros, founder of the Dunlop Rubber Company.

Every bedroom of Craigweil House had a sea view; the main reception rooms looked down on to the promenade, and sea water was piped into the bathrooms. Ideal for a king who loved the sea and with the bracing Sussex air his health began to improve. On Easter Monday he made his first public appearance, sitting out of the wind to listen to the Kneller Hall Band. On hearing the National Anthem he said, "I used to hear that good old thing almost every day, but I have not heard it now for five months. It is rather moving to hear it once again."

In July he returned to London to resume official duties and attended a thanksgiving service to celebrate his recovery. The town of Bognor was granted the suffix Regis as a sign of the King's gratitude.

The following year he was well enough to take part in the annual regatta at Cowes and was delighted when his yacht *Britannia* won the race. It was his 200th win and all the crew received double prize money to mark the yacht's double century. Having recovered from a serious illness, the King was now regarded with even greater affection by the British public. The introduction of an annual live Christmas Day broadcast on the wireless in 1932 only added to his popularity.

At the beginning of his Silver Jubilee year, the King briefly took up residence at Compton Place in Eastbourne to build up his strength. He and the Queen could frequently be seen strolling along the promenade between the Wish Tower and Holywell in fine weather. A plaque now marks the beach chalet that the royal couple used during their stay and another plaque at St Mary's Church in Eastbourne's Old Town records the pew where the King and Queen sat.

The highlight of Jubilee year came on 6 May, 1935, when the Royal Family drove in procession from Buckingham Palace to St Paul's Cathedral for a service of thanksgiving, with thousands of people from all over the world lining the route.

"A wonderful service," said the King on the steps of St Paul's, "just one thing wrong with it; too many damn parsons getting in the way." For a whole week he and the Queen toured London to thank cheering crowds, and appeared several times each night on the balcony of Buckingham Palace in response to the never-ending chant of, "We want the King!"

King George was very moved by the public displays of affection. "I had no idea they felt like that about me," he told his resident nurse. "I'm beginning to think they like me for myself." It was a full year of engagements and the 70-year-old monarch even continued to ride on horseback for Trooping the Colour but cancelled the State Opening of Parliament due to the sudden death of his closest sister, Princess Victoria. On Christmas Day he broadcast for the last time.

On Friday 17 January, 1936, nine-year-old Princess Elizabeth was playing in the snow at Sandringham when she looked up to see her grandmother, Queen Mary, crossing the lawn towards her. With characteristic calmness the Queen explained that the King was very sick and she took Elizabeth to his bedside. The next day young "Lilibet" and her sister Princess Margaret Rose were taken away to Royal Lodge at Windsor.

A public announcement said only that His Majesty was suffering from a cold but at 11pm a further bulletin stated that "there have been signs of cardiac weakness which must be regarded with some disquiet." During the night he was given oxygen and the following day's bulletin said that the King's condition gave cause for anxiety.

On 20 January, King George held a Privy Council meeting to appoint Counsellors of State to act on his behalf while he was unwell but, propped up in a chair, he was too weak even to sign his name. His condition deteriorated further throughout the day and people gathered silently outside Sandringham House and Buckingham Palace. All wireless programmes ceased, save for regular updates. At 5.30pm: "The condition of His Majesty shows diminishing strength." At 9.24pm: "The King's life is moving peacefully towards its close." Finally, just after midnight: "His Majesty the King passed peacefully away at a few minutes before 12 . . ."

For the people of Britain a measure of comfort and stability died with him on the accession of Edward VIII, of whom King George V had written to Prime Minister Stanley Baldwin, "After I am dead, the boy will ruin himself in 12 months." Shortly before his death he had confided in his old friend Blanche Lennox, "I pray to God that my eldest son will never marry and have children, and that nothing will come between Bertie and Lilibet and the throne."

Both his prophecy and his wish were to come true.

Chapter 54

Edward VIII 1894–1972
Reign: January 1936–December 1936

"Hark the Herald Angels sing,
Mrs. Simpson's pinched our King.
Now she knocks on Edward's door,
She's been married twice before."

In school playgrounds across England at the end of 1936 children parodied a familiar carol. At Madame Tussaud's waxworks in London the figure of Mrs Wallis Simpson, dressed in scarlet satin, had to be closely guarded for fear that a member of the public might attack it. Even today, Edward VIII is still synonymous with having given up the throne for the woman he loved and the subsequent repercussions.

When Prince Harry, Duke of Sussex, announced in 2020 that he and his American wife, divorcee Meghan Markle, were giving up their royal duties and planned to set up home outside the UK, the media immediately drew parallels with the Duke of Windsor.

At a charity dinner that January he said that he was speaking "not as a Prince or a Duke, but as Harry", that it was not a decision he had made lightly, but he had "found the love and happiness I had hoped for all my life." Echoes of Edward VIII's abdication speech over 80 years earlier were very clear.

Edward VIII was born at White Lodge, Richmond Park, on 23 June, 1894. The first child of the Duke and Duchess of York, later King George V and Queen Mary, he was then third in line to the throne. After visiting him in the nursery, his great-grandmother Queen Victoria remarked, "He has fine, powerful lungs!" The child was christened Edward Albert Christian George Andrew Patrick David, which encompassed family names with those of the Patron Saints of England, Scotland, Ireland and Wales. To the public he was known as Prince Edward and to the Royal Family he was simply David.

The Prince's early childhood was spent at York Cottage on the Sandringham estate, with occasional visits to Windsor, Balmoral, and Osborne House to see "Gangan" – Queen Victoria. Soon he was joined in the nursery by brothers Bertie (later King George VI), Henry (Duke of Gloucester) and their sister Mary (Princess Royal). Then later brothers George (Duke of Kent) and John (who died at the age of 13).

The children were reared by nurses and nannies, seeing their parents only twice a day, a practice not confined to the Royal Family at this time. Prince Edward had a nanny who he later described as "sadistic and incompetent". She worshipped the young Prince but would pinch him and make him cry whenever he was in the presence of his parents, as if to prove that he loved her more than them. Equally, she neglected his brother Bertie.

The children were quarantined with German measles when Queen Victoria died. Their parents immediately became Duke and Duchess of Cornwall, and later Prince and Princess of Wales, and soon departed for an eight-month tour of the British Empire.

On their return, life changed for Prince Edward. The nanny disappeared and a footman, Frederick Finch, took charge of the boys. He was strong on discipline and the Prince later revealed that, if he ever misbehaved, Finch "applied a large hand to that part of the anatomy nature has conveniently provided for the chastisement of small boys." A former schoolmaster, Henry Hansell, was employed as tutor and the two men ensured that their royal charges had a strict and regimented routine.

The Prince spent an hour with his mother each evening, when invariably some practical activity was encouraged so that the time was not wasted. She taught him how to crochet and do needlepoint, which he continued to do throughout his life for relaxation. The importance of good manners was impressed upon the boy and his father made him memorise the lines:

"I shall pass through this world but once. Any good thing, therefore, that I can do or any kindness that I can show any human being, let me do it now. Let me not defer nor neglect it, for I shall not pass this way again".

In 1903 the family moved to Marlborough House in London but Edward hated the noise of the city and longed for the peace of Norfolk. In those days, however, the family had much more privacy and Henry Hansell was able to take the young Princes to the British Museum or the Tower of London unrecognised.

At the age of 13, Prince Edward began training at the Royal Naval College at Osborne "with tears drenching my new blue uniform". He was frequently bullied, once having red ink poured into his hair and on another occasion his head was deliberately trapped in a sash window. Academically he had poor results and found it hard to accept the philosophy that "the navy way was the right way and all other ways were wrong." In May 1909 he transferred to Dartmouth, where he found a greater degree of comfort and freedom. On Sundays he explored the beautiful Devon countryside and indulged in cream teas.

He was on leave at Marlborough House a year later when his grandfather was taken ill with bronchitis. A view from his bedroom window one morning of the Royal Standard flying at half-mast on the roof of Buckingham Palace told him that King Edward VII was dead. From that moment he became Heir Apparent, Duke of Cornwall and financially independent.

On his 16th birthday that year he was created Prince of Wales. In 1911 he attended the Coronation of his father, King George V and was invested with the Order of the Garter at Windsor, followed by his Investiture as Prince of Wales at Caernarvon Castle in July. Politician David Lloyd-George taught him sufficient Welsh to be able to make a speech.

Already uncomfortable with royal pageantry, Edward decided that he preferred the comradeship of the navy and went back to sea as a Midshipman on the battleship *HMS Hindustan* for three months, before continuing his academic education. After studying for a time in France, in October 1912 he became an undergraduate at Magdalen College, Oxford, where he hoped to be treated like an ordinary student, although he was the only undergraduate to have his own bathroom.

Naval training had left him ill-equipped for an academic life and study became a drudgery. After less than two years he left University and joined the 1st Life Guards. Within weeks World War I began.

Prince Edward then joined the Grenadier Guards and was further detailed to the King's Company, in spite of his 5ft 7in height. When his Battalion went overseas, the Prince was left behind amid fears that he could be taken prisoner. Eventually he was sent to France but was 30 miles from the front line doing clerical work.

After bombarding his father with letters requesting permission to take on a more active role, the Prince served under Major-General (later Field

Marshal) Lord Cavan in the Guards Division and saw action in Egypt and Italy but was still protected. "I was being kept on ice against the day that death shall claim my father," he wrote, "I found it hard to accept the unique dispensation. Oh! Not to be a Prince."

When the war ended, the Prince did not leave the army immediately but was attached to the Australian Corps in Belgium and visited Occupation troops in Germany. "My education was widened in war," he wrote afterwards, "not through book or theory, but through the experience of living under all kinds of conditions with all manner of men."

As King George V's health started to deteriorate, Edward began undertaking Royal duties in earnest. At the suggestion of Lloyd-George, the Prince embarked on a series of tours of the British Empire to prepare for Kingship. An old courtier gave him what he considered to be the best two pieces of advice: "Never miss an opportunity to relieve yourself; never miss a chance to sit down and rest your feet."

Prince Edward set up his first home at York House, St James's Palace in London before making tours of Canada, America, Australia, New Zealand, Japan and India. Between the ages of 25 and 31 he visited 45 different countries, travelling 1,500,000 miles, mostly by land and sea, farther than any Prince of Wales before him had ever been.

During periods at home in England the Prince's life became a social whirl, with sometimes four parties in one evening. He loved the theatre, dancing and music, he hunted, went steeplechasing and played polo, all as an escape from official life and stiff formality.

The Prince appeared to be able to burn the candle at both ends and maintained a full diary of official engagements. On a wall at York House he kept a map of England and stuck in pins to mark all the places he had visited. If a specific area had no pins, then a visit was hastily arranged. "In this way I came to know my country, from Land's End to Caithness, from Rothesay to Dover," he said.

Unemployment, especially in mining communities, became his greatest concern and he took a keen interest in the poor housing conditions in the many slum areas that he visited. He had long discussions with the Prime Minister, Ramsay MacDonald, in an attempt to improve matters. The outcome was not always favourable, as it was felt that if the Prince drew attention to unemployment or poor housing it could be seen as a criticism of the government.

Sir Frederick Ponsonby, Keeper of the Privy Purse, once complained that Edward was making himself too accessible, saying: "The Monarchy must always retain an element of mystery. A Prince should not show himself too much. The Monarchy must remain on a pedestal. If you bring it down to the people, it will lose its mystery and influence."

Edward did not agree. When visiting poverty-stricken areas, he refused to travel in the Rolls Royce provided for him, considering it to be inappropriate.

In April 1930 the Prince was given a grace-and-favour house as a retreat from official duties. Fort Belvedere near Sunningdale became his passion and he spent every spare moment renovating the house and garden. The following year at a houseparty in Melton Mowbray he met Mrs Wallis Warfield Simpson – a meeting that would change his life forever.

Over the next few years their paths continued to cross at social events. The forthright Mrs Simpson spoke her mind, even if it meant disagreeing with the Prince. Surrounded by people who generally kowtowed to him, Edward saw this as a refreshing change. As Mrs Simpson's second marriage disintegrated, their friendship slowly blossomed into love and she became a regular visitor to Fort Belvedere.

On 20 January, 1936, King George V passed peacefully away at Sandringham. Queen Mary took hold of her eldest son's hand and kissed it. Edward was now King. The next day he flew to London to present himself before an Accession Privy Council. It was the first time a King had ever flown.

His father's body was taken by train to London to lie in state in Westminster Hall. On top of the coffin had been placed the Imperial State Crown and as the gun-carriage bearing it crossed the tram lines where Theobalds Road meets Southampton Row, the jeweled cross on top of the Crown shook loose and fell on to the pavement.

"It seemed a strange thing to happen," Edward wrote, "and, although not superstitious, I wondered if it was a bad omen."

King Edward VIII did not adjust easily to his new position or the fact that life could not go on as before. When he one day walked to a meeting wearing a bowler hat, carrying an umbrella, instead of travelling the short distance by car, there was a national chorus of disapproval. He aimed to be considered as "Edward the Innovator" but in reality he said he was a King who "collided with the Establishment." If he tried to change or modify royal traditions, he faced a wall of opposition.

"I wanted to be a successful King, though a King in a modern way," he wrote in retrospect.

There was an uproar from the Royal Mint and the General Post Office when the King requested that his left profile, which he considered to be his best side, should be used on coins and stamps. It is customary to reverse the profile with each new reign. Edward VII looked to the right, George V to the left, therefore all insisted that Edward VIII must face to the right.

"It is my face that is to be used," the King retaliated. "Isn't it only reasonable that I should at least have the privilege of deciding which side is to be put on public display?" The fight continued. Although the GPO conceded, no coins were ever minted.

King Edward VIII received much criticism because he refused to follow the traditional path laid down by Queen Victoria. Instead of holidaying at Balmoral in August, he wanted to play golf at Biarritz. The younger generation saw him as a refreshing change but old courtiers continually stood in his way.

Within days of his accession the Archbishop of Canterbury, Cosmo Lang, intimated that Edward should end his friendship with Mrs Simpson, but having discovered that the life of a monarch is a lonely one he turned increasingly to her for companionship. They took a month-long cruise together in August 1936 causing speculation in the American press.

In October Edward moved into Buckingham Palace, a building that he never liked and later admitted, "I never got over the feeling of not quite belonging there." That same month Mrs Simpson's divorce petition was heard at Ipswich Assizes. The King told newspaper magnate Lord Beaverbrook that he wanted Wallis protected from publicity. Consequently, the British press had a "gentleman's agreement" to report the case without sensation. The American newspapers, however, were already predicting that Mrs Simpson would marry the King as soon as her divorce was finalised.

Within days the Prime Minister, Stanley Baldwin, visited the King to express concern about the rumours appearing in foreign newspapers. "I am beginning to wonder whether I really am the kind of king the people want," Edward confided in his legal adviser Walter Monckton.

He continued with his diary of public engagements but two days after laying a wreath at the Cenotaph on Armistice Day matters came to a head. He was warned that the British press could no longer maintain a discreet silence about his relationship with the "lady from Baltimore" and that Mrs Simpson should be sent abroad immediately to avert a scandal.

Whoever the King married would be Queen and it was felt in 1936 that neither the Government, the Church, nor the British people would tolerate a twice-divorced woman as Consort. After a quiet family dinner one evening, Edward revealed the full situation to his mother. Queen Mary tried all in her power to persuade her son to change his mind, but he was determined to marry Wallis Simpson no matter how great the cost.

The business of kingship continued and Edward VIII made an important visit to Wales. It was at Caernarvon that he was crowned Prince of Wales and fittingly it was in Wales that his official duties in the UK drew to a close. For two days he toured the mining villages of South Wales, a region gripped by poverty and unemployment, assuring people that "Something must be done".

Back in London it was suggested that the King might consider a morganatic marriage, whereby Wallis would have no title or position and any children the couple had would not be heirs to the throne, but Parliament refused to pass the necessary legislation. The King had two choices. Give up Wallis or relinquish the throne. Edward VIII decided to abdicate.

Incognito as "Mrs Harris", Wallis Simpson crossed the Channel from Newhaven to stay with friends in France away from the impending furore in England. Whenever they could be in contact by telephone, the King used the code name "Mr James" (after St James's Palace). Despite pleading messages from Wallis that "Mr James should not step down", the King was insistent that he was not prepared to give her up.

By December 1936 the matter was coming to a conclusion. Crowds gathered outside Buckingham Palace, quietly singing the National Anthem and "For He's a Jolly Good Fellow". Edward admitted that he was reminded of the words of G.K. Chesterton:

"Smile at us, pay us, pass us, but do not quite forget
For we are the people of England, that never have spoken yet."

Abdication documents were drawn up, passing the throne to Edward's brother Bertie, the Duke of York. The first act of the new King George VI was to create his brother Duke of Windsor. The abdication speech was broadcast from Windsor Castle at 10pm on Friday, 11 December, written by Edward and polished up by Winston Churchill. The Duke of Windsor then said farewell to his beloved Fort Belvedere, was driven to Portsmouth and at 2am on *HMS Fury* he departed from England to begin his years in exile.

The Duke of Windsor and Wallis Simpson finally married at the Château de Candé, Touraine, in a small civil ceremony on 3 June, 1937. No member of the Royal Family was present. On the wedding day itself came the pronouncement that whilst the Duke of Windsor was entitled to style himself Royal Highness, the new Duchess of Windsor was not. The Duke considered it to be a hideous insult to his wife and never forgave the Establishment. Within their own household he always insisted that his wife be addressed as "Ma'am" and referred to as "Her Royal Highness".

Although the Duke hoped that they would one day be able to establish a home in England, the couple found a house in the Bois de Boulogne, Paris, where they lived for the rest of their lives. Now no longer undertaking royal duties, the restless Duke needed to find a role for himself.

His interest in housing and working conditions continued and, in the autumn of 1937, the Duke and Duchess visited Germany to tour factories and workers' housing. With the threat of war in the air, some historians feel that the Duke might have considered himself something of a peacemaker, although the British government objected to the visit.

While in Germany, the couple met Göring, Himmler, Hess, Goebbels and Hitler – names that would soon be hated by the British people. *The New York Times* quoted British MP Herbert Morrison as saying, "Who are the Duke's advisers? I do not know. But either they are very bad ones or he will not take good advice."

As war loomed, the Duke sent a telegram to Hitler in August 1939 appealing for peace. It had no effect. At the outbreak of war the Duke was assigned to the British Military Mission in Vincennes, transferring to the French Armée des Alpes in May 1940. After the fall of France, the Duke and Duchess went to Spain and Portugal before the Duke was finally appointed Governor of the Bahamas, then considered to be the least important of Britain's 35 colonies.

The Duke acquitted himself well. He encouraged an increase in agricultural production in preparation for food shortages and founded an Infant Welfare Clinic, while the Duchess became President of the Red Cross and ran canteens for American servicemen.

Shortly before the end of the war, the Duke tendered his resignation and the couple returned to Paris. In October 1945 the Duke made a solo visit to England and stayed with Queen Mary at Marlborough House. The Windsors visited London together on a number of occasions in the succeeding years and although the Duke saw members of his family, King George VI and Queen Mary were resolute in their determination not to meet the Duchess.

The Windsors divided their remaining years between France and America, spending four months each year at the Waldorf Hotel in New York. They seldom travelled anywhere with less than 30 pieces of luggage, a retinue of staff and their beloved pug dogs.

They moved in café society, frequenting places and functions where they would be treated as royalty. At home they gave lavish dinners, with guests changing places for each course. Golf and gardening became the Duke's passions and he laid out an English style garden with a lawn and herbaceous borders. Their house in Paris was filled with royal mementoes, echoes of a past life. Edward's conversations were peppered with anecdotes beginning, "When I was King . . ."

When King George VI died suddenly in 1952, the Duke of Windsor flew immediately to England to be with his family, and a year later was with his mother when she died. On both occasions the Duchess remained in France. Not until 1967 was she invited to be with the Duke at Marlborough House for the unveiling of a plaque to the memory of Queen Mary.

There she met and spoke with the Queen and the Queen Mother 30 years after the abdication. It was seen as an act of reconciliation. When once questioned about the abdication, the Queen Mother said tactfully, "Really it all turned out for the best."

In his 78th year the Duke of Windsor, a lifelong smoker, developed cancer of the throat. In May 1972 Queen Elizabeth II visited her uncle while on a state visit to Paris. Although by then a very sick man and attached to various tubes, he insisted on dressing smartly and stood and bowed as the Queen entered. He died nine days later on 28 May, and was flown home to England to lie in state at St George's Chapel, Windsor, where some 60,000 people filed past his coffin. He was later laid to rest at Frogmore.

The Duchess, who had once rocked the British throne, stayed as a guest at Buckingham Palace. She was frail, grief-stricken and beginning to show signs of the dementia that would blight the last 14 years of her life. Wallis died on 24 April, 1986, and was laid to rest beside her beloved David in England. Only in death did people begin to feel that perhaps the Windsors had been treated too harshly and that reconciliation should have come much sooner than it did.

With a reign that lasted only 325 days, it is impossible to know exactly what kind of king he would have made, but Edward's sacrifice for love ultimately benefited the British people as the much-loved King George VI and Queen Elizabeth brought stability and dignity to the monarchy that ensured its survival. In the end, England had much to thank the Duke of Windsor for.

Chapter 55

George VI 1895–1952
Reign: 1936–1952

As King George VI and Queen Elizabeth toured the bombed streets of London's East End during the war, offering words of comfort and sympathy, a man who had lost his home in the Blitz suddenly took hold of an equerry's arm and pointed to the King.

"You see him?" he asked, "That's why we sing *There'll Always Be An England*. God bless him."

Hearing these words, the crowd around him cheered in agreement. It says much about the resolve of the British people and their affection for the man who had so unexpectedly inherited the throne. In another street a man shouted, "Thank God for a good King!", to which the King replied quietly, "Thank God for a good people."

When King George VI was born in 1895, his great-grandmother, Victoria, was Queen, followed in the line of succession by his grandfather (Edward VII), father (George V) and elder brother (Edward VIII). There seemed little prospect that he would take on the heavy mantle of sovereignty.

Born at York Cottage, Sandringham, on 14 December – the anniversary of the Prince Consort's death – his father tactfully wrote to Queen Victoria to ask if the baby might be christened Albert. The widowed Queen was delighted by the suggestion and immediately agreed to become the child's godmother, sending a marble bust of his namesake as a christening present. The baby was given the names Albert Frederick Arthur George, but throughout his life was always called "Bertie" by the Royal Family.

In the nursery it was his brother David, the first-born son and heir, who received all the attention. Their nanny adored David and ignored Bertie, resulting in him having a stammer and gastric problems through a poor diet. His parents found outward displays of affection difficult, and Bertie was noticeably shy and withdrawn in their presence.

He was educated by Henry Hansell, a humourless Norfolk schoolmaster, who forced the left-handed boy to write with his right hand. To add to his problems the Prince had to wear painful leg braces to cure congenital knock-knees and at night was strapped into a tortuous contraption to straighten his legs. He cried himself to sleep and as he grew older his stammer became worse.

Bertie led a quiet life, remote from his contemporaries until he was sent to Osborne Naval College on the Isle of Wight as a junior cadet at the age of 13. He was homesick, and bullied because of his stammer, but gradually built up a small circle of pals who remained friends for life. Academically he came bottom of the class in his first year.

Later, the Prince moved to the Royal Naval College at Dartmouth, but his studies were interrupted by the death of Edward VII and the accession of his father as King George V. The ensuing Coronation, and the fact that he caught both measles and mumps during the great epidemic of 1911, meant at the end of that year he was placed a lowly 67th out of 68 cadets.

In January 1913, the Prince joined the cruiser *HMS Cumberland* on a tour of duty to the West Indies and Canada. He was a poor sailor and found himself unable to conquer seasickness. In Jamaica, where the people turned out in force to welcome the English prince and show their support for the monarchy, Bertie was so sick with nerves that he persuaded another cadet to impersonate him and wave to the crowds.

Promoted to midshipman on *HMS Collingwood* during World War I, appendicitis soon forced him to return to England from the Mediterranean. The King's physician, Sir Frederick Treves, advised the Prince not to go back to sea. He worked for a time at the Admiralty and began undertaking official royal duties in England but, ignoring the advice, he returned to the *Collingwood* in May 1916.

During the Battle of Jutland the ship was attacked by torpedoes, but suffered little damage.

"I never felt any fear of shells or anything else," Bertie wrote home. "It seems curious that all sense of danger goes." He appeared to gain strength from the experience, despite being diagnosed as suffering from a duodenal ulcer for which he underwent surgery at the end of 1917.

Accepting the fact that he should not return to sea again, the Prince joined the Air Force, on which the King had recently bestowed the prefix "Royal". He went first to the Royal National Air Service training centre at Cranwell, Lincolnshire, where he learned to fly, before transferring to the Air Cadet School at St Leonards-on-Sea, Sussex, in July 1918. In the last stages of the war he briefly witnessed aerial combat in France.

When the hostilities were over, the Prince joined the Air Ministry staff at Croydon and became the first qualified pilot in the Royal Family, before deciding to complete his education with a period of study at Trinity College, Cambridge.

Increasingly proud of his second son, George V gave Bertie the title Duke of York in the Birthday Honours List of 1920.

On leaving Cambridge, the Duke embarked on official royal engagements. Although speaking in public remained a trial for the rest of his life, a course of treatment with Australian therapist Lionel Logue helped control his stammer. He undertook a number of solo overseas tours, including visits to Africa, Australia and New Zealand.

Back in England after a long tour, he revealed: "I return home a thorough optimist. When one has travelled over the vast extent of the Empire; when one has witnessed what our fathers have accomplished; when one has seen how the great and creative purpose of our kinsmen has triumphed over the most tremendous difficulties, it is impossible to despair of the future of the British race."

He began to take a keen interest in the industries of England, visiting more than 150 factories and becoming President of the Industrial Welfare Society. If workers told him of a specific need, he saw that the bosses were informed and invariably conditions improved. At New Romsey in Kent he established a summer camp where some 200 boys, aged 17 to 19, could spend a week's holiday taking part in a wide range of sporting and recreational activities. Later, the camp transferred to Southwold, Suffolk, which the Duke visited each year to join in the fun.

In May 1920 the Duke met the Earl of Strathmore's daughter, Lady Elizabeth Bowes-Lyon, at a private party. Some 15 years earlier at a children's party, the five-year-old Lady Elizabeth had taken the cherries off her slice of cake and placed them on the plate of a boy sitting beside her. That boy was now the Duke of York. The Duke became enchanted with the vivacious Lady Elizabeth and by 1922 the couple were engaged, although Bertie had to propose three times before he was accepted.

The couple were married on 26 April, 1923, at Westminster Abbey, the first time a King's son had been married in the abbey since 1382. As the bride entered the abbey, she laid her bouquet on the Tomb of the Unknown Warrior. She was instantly popular with the British people and was soon dubbed "The Smiling Duchess" by the press.

Marriage gave Bertie a greater sense of security. "He had few friends," Henry "Chips" Channon wrote, "and was almost entirely dependent on Elizabeth, whom he worshipped. She was his will-power, his all." Setting up home at White Lodge in Richmond Park, and later at 145 Piccadilly, the Duke became a keen gardener and an expert at tapestry and petit point, once making a dozen chair covers as a gift for his wife.

On 21 April, 1926, the Duchess gave birth to their first child, a daughter christened Elizabeth Alexandra Mary. No-one thought at the time that she would one day be Queen. A second daughter, Margaret Rose, followed in 1930.

For relaxation the Duke enjoyed sports, particularly golf and tennis. In 1926 he became the first member of the Royal Family to compete at the Wimbledon Tennis Championships. Playing in the Men's Doubles with his partner, Wing Commander Louis Grieg, they were beaten in straight sets by fellow Brits Arthur Gore and Herbert Roper Barrett.

The Duke continued his interest in England's industries. Once, when visiting a soap factory, he was told that the firm also made glue. He immediately asked to see the department but was told that the stench was unbearable.

"If the place is good enough for the people who work there," he replied, "then it is good enough for me." It was noted that when he spoke to the workers in the factory there was no hint of a stammer. His nickname became "The Foreman".

With the death of King George V in January 1936, Bertie's elder brother David became King Edward VIII. "After I am dead, the boy will ruin himself in 12 months," George V had predicted, and due to his love for divorcée Mrs Wallis Simpson, Edward abdicated on 11 December, 1936. Throughout that year the Duke of York had watched the situation with increasing concern, conscious that he was ill-prepared to reign.

It was as if the weight of the world was slowly descending upon his shoulders. When the abdication became a reality, Bertie, in his own words, "broke down and sobbed like a child." His first deed as King was to create his brother Duke of Windsor. In the royal history of England five previous Dukes of York had unexpectedly become King: Edward IV, Henry VIII, Charles I, James II and George V.

"This is absolutely terrible," Bertie told his cousin Lord Louis

Mountbatten. "I've never even seen a state paper. I'm only a naval officer."

Plans for the Coronation of Edward VIII were diverted to that of his brother and the date of 12 May, 1937, remained unchanged. Bertie chose the name George, the last of his four Christian names, and his became the first Coronation to be broadcast on the wireless. At the end of that day the new King George VI broadcast a message to his 700 million subjects throughout the world.

"If, in the coming years, I can show my gratitude in service to you, that is the way above all other that I should choose." Together, he and Queen Elizabeth brought stability back to the British monarchy.

Scarcely had the King been crowned than the first threat of war began. In May 1939 the King and Queen paid a highly successful state visit to America and Canada, which is said to have contributed to their support for England during World War II. In September 1939 the King broadcast to the nation to inspire unity in the British people. No one who heard his Christmas message that year will ever forget his quotation from *The Gate of the Year* by Minnie Haskins, from which so many gained comfort: "Go out into the darkness and put your hand into the hand of God. That shall be to you better than a light and safer than a known way."

The King was one of the first people in England to receive a gas mask and he made sure that his family was subjected to the same rationing as everyone else. Throughout the war, when the collars and cuffs on his shirts became worn, they were repaired with material from the shirt tails. In Windsor Great Park 30 acres were ploughed up to grow crops and a five-inch line was painted around the baths to indicate the level of water allowed.

The King and Queen remained in London during the week, despite the dangers. When it was suggested that Princesses Elizabeth and Margaret Rose should be sent to Canada for safety, the Queen replied, "The Princesses could not go without me; I could not leave without the King, and, of course, the King will never leave."

The King and Queen visited many of the bombed areas to offer comfort and support, travelling over 52,000 miles in a bullet-proof train. When Coventry was bombed on the night of 14 November, 1940, King George VI visited the devastated city within hours. That same year Buckingham Palace had been hit twice, with one bomb completely destroying the private chapel. The Queen was in the process of taking an eyelash out of the King's eye when a bomb landed.

"Had the windows been closed instead of open, the whole of the glass would have splintered into the faces of the King and Queen, causing terrible injuries," Winston Churchill wrote, adding that they kept the seriousness of it to themselves. That same afternoon they visited those who had been bombed in the East End of London.

To reward acts of heroism, the King instituted the George Cross – the highest civil award for gallantry which ranks alongside the Victoria Cross. In 1943 he paid a two-week visit to Allied troops in North Africa, flying to Algiers under the pseudonym "General Lyon". At his own request the war-torn island of Malta was awarded the George Cross. Churchill wrote that the war drew "the Throne and the People more closely together than was ever recorded".

On VE Day in May 1945, Buckingham Palace became the focal point of celebrations as thousands of people gathered outside chanting "We want the King!" The fact that the Royal Family had not fled from the bombing, had suffered their own losses during the war (including the death of the King's younger brother, the Duke of Kent) and had been subjected to the same risks and deprivations as everyone else had a unifying effect.

A very relieved King appeared eight times on the balcony of Buckingham Palace to acknowledge the cheers of the crowds packed into the Mall.

The British people had taken George VI to their hearts and felt that, by a curious twist of fate, the abdication had given them a much better monarch. He was a devoted family man with a deep religious conviction, and one who had always shown great strength in adversity. Those who knew him admired his gentle nature, wry sense of humour and innocent charm.

Meeting President Truman for the first time in 1945, the King asked for the President's autograph "for my wife and daughters". He was thrilled to meet the cast of his favourite wireless programme *It's That Man Again*, and after grand balls at Buckingham Palace he invariably led guests in a Conga line up and down the corridors.

Although he resumed a full diary of official engagements once peace had returned, his sudden accession and the years of war had clearly taken their toll on his health. In 1947 he made a highly successful visit to South Africa with the Queen and the princesses, but returned to England looking physically exhausted, having lost 17 pounds in weight.

He attended the wedding of his daughter, Princess Elizabeth, to Prince Philip of Greece that November, and in April 1948 took part in a national day of celebration to mark his silver wedding anniversary, but he had begun to suffer from severe leg cramps as a result of arterio-sclerosis.

In March 1949 the King underwent surgery to prevent blood clots. Heavy smoking was considered to be a contributory factor to his condition.

Although he appeared to recover, the symptoms later reappeared.

On 3 May, 1951, the King opened the Festival of Britain on the south bank of the River Thames. He looked pale and drawn – the first public indication that all was not well. He began to wear make-up at evening functions to hide his pallid complexion. Eventually, a leading chest surgeon, Clement Price Thomas, examined the King and made a firm diagnosis that it was lung cancer. The true nature of the disease was kept from the King and he was told simply that there was a blockage in his left lung which would necessitate its removal. The operation was carried out on 23 September at Buckingham Palace. During surgery some of the nerves of the larynx also had to be removed and there was a danger that he might only ever speak again in a faint whisper.

Two months later the King was photographed for the first time after his operation, looking much fitter, at his grandson Prince Charles's third birthday party. On 2 December, 1951, a day of national thanksgiving was celebrated to mark the King's recovery. The Royal Family spent a quiet Christmas at Sandringham, the King having recorded his traditional Christmas Day message in advance. To avoid the stress of a live broadcast, and because of speech difficulties, it was recorded in short sections. He was in high spirits and looked forward to revisiting South Africa in March 1952, confident that the warm sun would speed his recuperation.

On returning to London in the New Year, King George was given a thorough medical examination and was pronounced fit enough to wave Princess Elizabeth off at London Airport as she boarded the BOAC Argonaut airliner Atalanta that was to take her to Kenya on the first stage of a royal tour to Australia and New Zealand. On 31 January, the King stood in the bitter cold with Queen Elizabeth, Princess Margaret and the Duke and Duchess of Gloucester to wave what turned out to be a final farewell to his elder daughter.

The King returned to Sandringham and on 5 February, 1952, felt strong enough to participate in "Keepers' Day", the end-of-season hare shoot, and retired to bed that night weary but happy. In the early hours of the next morning, King George VI passed peacefully away in his sleep.

"During these last months the King walked with death," Winston Churchill told Parliament, "as if death were a companion, an acquaintance, whom he recognised and did not fear. In the end death came as a friend."

At the funeral in St George's Chapel, Windsor, Churchill's wreath stood out from all the others. In the shape of the George Cross, it bore the simple inscription: "For Gallantry".

The nation mourned not just the passing of a King, but a man who symbolised all that England had come to expect from its monarch – courage in the face of adversity and duty before self-interest. Qualities that his daughter would come to emulate.

Chapter 56

Elizabeth II 1926–present

Reign: 1952–present

There have been few more poignant photographs taken of Elizabeth II than those in February 1952 when she alighted from an aircraft and stepped on to English soil for the first time as Queen. A group of Privy Councillors, headed by Prime Minister Winston Churchill, assembled at London Airport to greet their new monarch as she arrived home from Nairobi. Each man was overawed by the dignity and composure of the small figure, dressed entirely in black. Placing duty before grief, she had clearly accepted her destiny.

When Princess Elizabeth was born, she was then third in line to the throne and not expected to succeed. Her uncle David was to become King Edward VIII and it was assumed that he would marry and have children of his own, who would push her even further from the throne.

Yet the abdication of Edward VIII, and the early death of King George VI on 6 February, 1952, meant that Elizabeth was now Queen. She was just 25 years old. No one could have foreseen then that Queen Elizabeth II would become our longest-reigning monarch (69 years in February 2021) and has now lived longer than any previous monarch of England (turning 95 in April 2021).

Over those years, she has lived the most extraordinary life. It would be nigh on impossible to calculate how many millions of miles she has travelled, how many people she has met, or how many events she has witnessed, but it would be arguably more than any other person in history.

Early on in her reign, during a tour of the Commonwealth at the end of the Coronation year, the young Queen travelled 43,618 miles, made 102 speeches and listened to 276 more, heard the National Anthem sung at 508 events, was curtsied to 6,770 times and shook hands with 13,213 people. Some 270 more overseas tours followed across the decades, visiting more than 120 countries, the equivalent to travelling around the circumference of the earth 42 times. The Queen made her last foreign trip in 2015 and then, with her 90th birthday approaching, decided to leave overseas tours to the younger generations of her family. Only reluctantly did she then begin to hand some of her day-to-day duties over to her children, yet she still maintains an extensive diary of official engagements that would almost certainly tire someone half her age.

On a tour of the United Kingdom in 2002 to mark her Golden Jubilee, the Queen went to 70 towns and cities in 50 counties over 38 days. Ten years later, to celebrate her Diamond Jubilee in 2012, the Queen visited 10 different regions of the UK in 25 days, undertaking 83 public engagements during that time. In 2019, at 93, she attended 295 official engagements.

Princess Elizabeth was born on Wednesday 21 April, 1926, the first child of the then Duke and Duchess of York, at 17 Bruton Street, London, the home of her maternal grandparents. She is our only monarch to have been born in a private house. It was later destroyed by German bombs during World War II, and only a simple plaque remains to mark where the Queen's birthplace once stood.

Fewer than eight years had passed since the end of World War I, and this royal birth was a joyous event for the people. There was an insatiable appetite for photographs of the infant princess and newspapers even reported that, when the Home Secretary visited, the baby yawned!

At a month old the Princess was christened in the private chapel of Buckingham Palace and given the names of three Queens of England, Elizabeth Alexandra Mary. When, as a young child, Elizabeth tried to say her own name she could only manage "Lilibet", which she is still known as today to her family and closest friends.

On 21 August, 1930, a sister, Princess Margaret Rose, was born at Glamis Castle. The two remained close and spoke daily in person or on the telephone, wherever they happened to be in the world, until Princess Margaret's untimely death in February 2002.

As children they were popularly known as the "Little Princesses" but inevitably the focus was on Elizabeth. Her face adorned stamps, her figure astride a Shetland pony was displayed at Madame Tussauds, a song was written in her honour. Everything from chocolates to hospital wards were named after her; artists painted her portrait; she posed for a sculptor and by the time she was four, a biography had been written about her.

Princess Elizabeth's early childhood was divided between the family's London home at 145 Piccadilly and the Royal Lodge in Windsor Great Park. It was an idyllic time for the princesses, with acres of gardens in which to play and a menagerie of animals to look after.

Although Pembroke corgis featured in their lives, notably Jane and Dookie, the family at the time owned three Labrador retrievers, a Tibetan lion-hound, a golden retriever and a black cocker spaniel. The princesses were also given a pony each, plus 15 blue budgerigars to care for. This resulted in Elizabeth's lifelong passion for horses, dogs and birds, including racing pigeons.

Unlike today's royal children, Princess Elizabeth did not go to school. Instead she had private lessons from a governess, Marion Crawford, with specialist subjects being taught by visiting tutors. She studied music and learned to play the piano, became fluent in French, and also had dancing and swimming lessons. Her only qualification on paper was a certificate for life saving.

It was through Marion Crawford that the princesses gained a glimpse of the outside world, as she took them incognito to museums, art galleries, the theatre, the zoo, and even on buses and the London Underground. Occasionally they were recognised and had to be rescued by detectives, but largely they went unnoticed.

Once they called into the YWCA for a cup of tea and queued in line with everyone else with their trays. Princess Elizabeth left her teapot behind and the woman behind the counter bellowed, "If you want it you must come and fetch it yourself!"

Following the abdication crisis and accession of her father, the family moved into Buckingham Palace in 1937. Princess Elizabeth became Heir Presumptive and the carefree days came to an end. In addition to a standard education, the Princess was now tutored in affairs of state. Her training as Queen had begun.

On an official weekend visit to the Royal Naval College at Dartmouth in July 1939, the fair-haired nephew of Lord Louis Mountbatten captivated Princess Elizabeth. The 18-year-old Prince Philip escorted the two princesses around the college grounds, and Princess Elizabeth watched wide-eyed when he devoured a whole plateful of shrimps at tea.

Within weeks of the visit, England was at war and the princesses were incarcerated at Windsor Castle for their safety. Philip was posted as midshipman on the convoy battleship *HMS Ramillies*, where Elizabeth began writing to him and sending him food parcels and socks that she had knitted.

Although there were fewer hardships for the Royal Family, life was nevertheless greatly restricted and they were subjected to the same food and clothes rationing as everyone else. Like many of her generation, the Queen is today very conscious of waste and goes around turning off any unnecessary lights. She also keeps scraps of paper and used envelopes for scribbling notes, and makes economies where possible. Her clothes do not adhere to fashion, so can be worn for many years, and items from buttons to hat trimmings are re-used wherever possible.

During the war, the princesses had to make their own entertainment and became adept at jigsaw puzzles, which the Queen still enjoys. They also produced their own pantomimes at Christmas with performances in the Waterloo Chamber at Windsor, for an audience of some 600 people, raising almost £900 for the Royal Household Wool Fund.

On her 16th birthday Princess Elizabeth was given her first official appointment and was made honorary Colonel of the Grenadier Guards. She was also required to register for national service at the local labour exchange. Eventually she joined the Auxiliary Territorial Service and donned uniform as a second subaltern. She was posted to the No 1 Mechanical Transport Training Centre at Aldershot where she completed a course in driving and car maintenance, where she enthusiastically learned how to strip and service an engine. "We had sparking plugs all through dinner last night," her mother once complained.

When the war ended, it was the Royal Family on the balcony of Buckingham Palace with Winston Churchill that became the focus of the VE Day celebrations. Princess Elizabeth was allowed to join the thronging crowds on the streets of London unnoticed, later declaring: "I think it was one of the most memorable nights of my life."

As the world slowly recovered from the six hard years of war, in 1947 Princess Elizabeth joined her parents and sister on a highly successful tour of South Africa. Spending her 21st birthday in Cape Town, the Princess broadcast to the Commonwealth, making a pledge: "I declare before you all that my whole life, whether it be long or short, shall be devoted to your service."

Having now grown up, her love for Prince Philip had grown, too, and on her return from South Africa the couple became engaged. They were married at Westminster Abbey on 20 November, 1947. After a honeymoon at Broadlands and Balmoral, the new Duke and Duchess of Edinburgh moved into their first marital home at Windlesham Moor in Surrey.

They also spent some months in Malta when Prince Philip was with the Mediterranean Fleet. It was the closest that Princess Elizabeth ever came to being a housewife and Maltese shopkeepers were conscious that she was slow counting out cash, not realising that she had little experience of handling money.

In the early summer of 1948, it was announced that the couple were expecting their first child. Prince Charles was born at 9.14pm on 14 November, 1948. Their second child, Princess Anne, was born two years later on 15 August, 1950, followed by Prince Andrew in 1960 and Prince Edward in 1964.

Although these should have been carefree times for the young couple, the health of King George VI began to give cause for concern. In 1951 he underwent a lung operation and Elizabeth and Philip moved into Clarence House to be close to Buckingham Palace. That year, the Princess deputised for her father at Trooping the Colour and began to take on an increasing number of official engagements. As the King's health appeared to improve, Elizabeth and Philip undertook an official tour of Canada and the United States in October 1951, and on 31 January, 1952, set off for another royal tour of East Africa, Australia and New Zealand.

Far away in Kenya, Princess Elizabeth was watching wildlife in the African bush at the moment her father died, unaware that she was now Queen, and almost certainly sitting in a tree at the moment of her accession. At 2.45pm local time, 11.45am in Britain, the Duke of Edinburgh broke the news to his young wife. News she bore with typical courage and calmness. When she was later asked what name she would choose as Queen, she replied, "My own name – what else?" She cancelled the remainder of the tour and returned immediately to England.

That year, in her first Christmas broadcast, the young Queen asked that her people would pray for God to grant her wisdom and strength, and renewed her promise to faithfully serve Him, and us, all the days of her life. On 2 June, 1953, she was crowned in Westminster Abbey, the first Coronation to be televised live. The reign of the second Queen Elizabeth had well and truly begun.

Her reign is now unparalleled in English history. No other period has witnessed such a diversity of events, seen so many technological, scientific and medical advances or made the breakthroughs in the field of communication. What is most remarkable is that the Queen has managed to uphold the ancient traditions of monarchy while being at the forefront of our modern world. From the first man on the moon to the first doctor to perform a human heart transplant, there are few pioneers that she has not met. She has witnessed industrial and technological developments at first hand on regular tours of factories and laboratories.

As Head of the Commonwealth she is constantly in touch with world leaders. As Defender of the Faith she is fully aware of all church situations. Her long involvement with the services ensures that her finger is on the pulse of military matters. Her many charitable patronages keep her informed about a wide range of human concerns and conditions. She has met regularly with the 14 Prime Ministers of her reign, from Winston Churchill to Boris Johnson, and is more experienced in government than many politicians.

Above all, no other monarch has been more accessible. A full diary of official engagements enables her to meet as many people as possible, from all walks of life, not just the great and the good. In 1958 she abolished the stuffy presentation of debutantes at court, and instituted informal lunches that allow her to meet a wider range of people from vastly different backgrounds. She entertains nearly 50,000 commendable people at a series of garden parties each summer and holds numerous receptions throughout the year for a variety of good causes.

The Queen may never have given a television interview, as such, but she has given regular access to the cameras when she feels that a documentary might offer a greater understanding of the monarch's day to day life and work.

One of the most engaging was *The Queen's Green Planet* (ITV, 2018) when she was filmed in conversation with Sir David Attenborough as they walked around the garden of Buckingham Palace. The programme highlighted the Queen's Commonwealth Canopy project, which aimed to plant forests in 53 countries to help combat climate change. To mark the 65th anniversary of her Coronation in 2018, the Queen was also filmed as part of a BBC documentary chatting about her memories of that eventful day and was reunited with her two crowns.

The annual Christmas Day broadcast brings the Queen directly into millions of homes throughout the Commonwealth and she fully appreciates the importance of the media and communications. In more serious times, the Queen has made significant broadcasts to the nation, such as during the Gulf War of 1991 and after the death of Princess Diana in 1997. During the Covid-19 pandemic, three-quarters of the UK's viewers tuned in to watch the Queen's inspirational address, offering thanks, encouragement and support. "I hope in the years to come everyone will be able to take pride in how they responded to this challenge," she said. "And those who come after us will say the Britons of this generation were as strong as any. That the attributes of self-discipline, of quiet good-humoured resolve and of fellow-feeling still characterise this country. The pride in who we are is not a part of our past, it defines our present and our future. We should take comfort that while we may have more still to endure, better days will return: we will be with our friends again; we will be with our families again; we will meet again."

On the 75th Anniversary of VE Day in May 2020, the Queen broadcast to the nation at 9pm, the exact time that her father had broadcast to the nation in 1945. "Never give up, never despair," she encouraged as the country was still facing its battle with Covid-19.

"Today it may seem hard that we cannot mark this special anniversary as we would wish. Instead we remember from our homes and our doorsteps. But our streets are not empty; they are filled with the love and the care that we have for each other. And when I look at our country today, and see what we are willing to do to protect and support one another, I say with pride that we are still a nation those brave soldiers, sailors and airmen would recognise and admire."

On a lighter note, the Queen was featured in a short James Bond film for the London 2012 Olympics Opening Ceremony when she made a spectacular entrance, apparently parachuting into the stadium from a helicopter. The Queen received a standing ovation from the spectators and universal praise from across the globe for her humour and willingness to surprise. She had even kept the filming secret from her own family.

The Queen is not, however, a natural performer. On a visit to South Africa in November 1999 she met nine young prize-winners of an essay competition. Having organised the group into a semi-circle, she confessed, "This is one of the worst parts of being Queen, having to pose for photographs."

Following the death of Princess Diana in 1997 there were attempts to make the monarch appear less remote. The Queen looked uneasy as she emerged from her car outside a hamburger bar in Ellesmere Port and toured shops selling trainers and kitchenware. She appeared even more uncomfortable in a stage-managed photo shoot, sitting at a table taking tea in a small Glasgow flat. The Queen's daily work has always brought her into contact with people from all areas of life, and such clumsy attempts to portray her in "ordinary" situations were unnecessary. The experiment failed, and instead photographers were allowed greater access to simply portray the Queen being herself.

Photographers are now permitted to mingle with guests at functions and in our newspapers today we see far more pictures of the Queen laughing than we have probably ever done before. Instead of stiffly posed photographs, we have seen the Queen chatting happily with a pink-haired female rock singer at a reception and doubled up with laughter when a parade by the Grenadier Guards was disrupted by a swarm of bees in April 2003.

On a visit to Canada in October 2002 the Queen awarded a former champion cyclist, Louis Garneau, the Order of Canada in the grounds of Rideau Hall in Ottawa. Mr Garneau then asked if he could have a photograph taken and the Queen replied, "No problem." He put an arm around Her Majesty's shoulder and the monarch posed with a broad smile as his wife took a snap.

Although the Queen was criticised in the days following Princess Diana's death because of her decision to remain in Scotland rather than return to London, her natural instinct had been to stay and comfort her grieving grandchildren whose mother had just died. She later said that there were lessons to be learned and, although the Queen will never attempt to emulate the late Princess's style, there has been a greater public display of emotion in recent years.

On 7 November, 2002, tears streamed down the Queen's face during the minute's silence at a remembrance service at Westminster Abbey, having just planted a small wooden cross bearing a scarlet poppy in the Field of Remembrance. It was the first time she had attended the ceremony, which the late Queen Mother had performed annually for more than half a century, and the Queen felt the loss of her mother that year very deeply. The public's hearts went out to the Queen that day in her grief.

Because her face is so familiar to us, we all feel as if we know the Queen personally. We see her daily on our money and stamps. Her regularly updated figure at Madame Tussauds is one of the most popular exhibits seen by thousands of tourists daily. She has sat for over 150 paintings during her reign, the most famous of which must be Pietro Annigoni's famous 1955 portrait of her wearing the blue robes of the Order of the Garter, which now hangs in the Fishmongers' Hall in London.

Yet, when you meet her in the flesh, she can be disarmingly direct. On a visit to Italy in October 2000, her final engagement was a visit to the

Convent of Santa Maria delle Grazie in Milan. Standing before one of the world's great paintings, Leonardo's recently restored *Last Supper*, the Queen put on her glasses and asked: "Now, where's Judas?"

The Queen has had a long association with many organisations throughout Britain, some for more than 70 years. She has been a member of the Women's Institute since 1943 and attends a meeting most years at West Newton near Sandringham, often handing out cakes during tea. The list of her patronages runs to several pages.

In fulfilling her duties, the Queen also provides employment for many hundreds of people and likes to think of them as one big family. Below stairs the staff often refer to their boss affectionately as "Mother" because of her concern for their welfare. Nothing in the royal household escapes her, and when a footman was rushed to hospital the Queen sent him a basket of fruit. The accompanying card in her hand said "from Mother".

As well as giving all her staff gifts at Christmas, each also receives a pudding. When it became publicly known in 1999 that the Queen had ordered 1,411 Christmas puddings from a well-known supermarket, within hours the shelves were empty. A Buckingham Palace official revealed that it was not a case of the Queen being thrifty, but that she had been enthusiastic about the taste.

Many of the Queen's official engagements centre on centenaries and anniversaries and her attendance is always the highlight of any event. In 2011 she made a state visit to the Republic of Ireland, the first visit of a reigning British monarch to that country for 100 years, which was widely praised, and led to a two-day visit to Northern Ireland in 2012.

The Queen attended Protestant and Roman Catholic church services, meeting with leaders from both sides of the religious divide. During the visit she shook hands with Sinn Féin's Martin McGuinness, a former member of the IRA. It was a meeting that would once have been unthinkable, the IRA having assassinated the Queen's cousin Earl Mountbatten in 1979, but the simple handshake was seen as an act of reconciliation.

On more than one occasion the Queen has made the point that hers is a job for life. She enjoys the tradition and continuity of her role and has rarely failed to keep an appointment. When she caught chickenpox in 1971 she was reluctantly forced to cancel her public engagements.

"It seems a ridiculous disease to catch, especially when it isn't even from one's own children," she wrote to Prime Minister Edward Heath. "The doctors say that I have had chickenpox quite mildly for a grown-up – but it is not much consolation when one is covered in spots!"

When she tore the cartilage in her right knee on a private visit to Newmarket, the Queen spent three days at the King Edward VII Hospital, London in January 2003, and had keyhole surgery. But she was soon back fulfilling official duties and even dealt with government papers from her hospital bed.

From a very early age, Queen Elizabeth II's life has been dominated by a sense of duty to her country. She has been there in times of triumph, and she has also supported the nation in times of disaster. Few will forget her poignant visits to Aberfan in 1966 and Dunblane in 1996. In 2017 she appeared close to tears when meeting with survivors of the Grenfell Tower fire. At a service for those killed in the 2001 World Trade Centre atrocity in America, it was the well-chosen words of the Queen that touched so many hearts: "Grief is the price we pay for love."

The life of Queen Elizabeth II has been filled with extraordinary contrasts. On the one hand she has her various obligations as monarch, as Head of State, as Head of the Commonwealth, and as Defender of the Faith. On the other she has responsibilities and commitments as a wife, mother, grandmother and great-grandmother, and must reconcile herself between the two.

"We're not expected to be human," the late Queen Mother once said, revealingly describing royal life as "an intolerable honour". It is a life where duty must always take precedence, where standards must be forever maintained. Times may change, but the Queen tries hard to remain reassuringly the same, never giving in publicly to emotions, never letting her dignity or her poise slip.

When Prince Charles was a young boy he once pressed a sticky boiled sweet into his mother's gloved hand just seconds before she was due to get out of the royal car and shake hands with waiting dignitaries.

Any other mother would have quickly admonished her son, but the mischievous Prince had to wait until they returned home before being scolded. A discreet change of white gloves and Her Majesty stepped serenely from the car to greet her hosts as if nothing had happened.

Although the work of the Royal Family continually evolves, the Queen has been able to achieve a balance between approachability and inscrutability. We all feel that we know her so well, yet she has retained an imposing mystique.

Mindful of the occasional need to transform, she has always fought against change simply for the sake of it and has kept as many of the old traditions as possible. The Queen has an eye to the future, but always makes a nod to the past. When two official photographs were issued in February 2012 to mark the Diamond Jubilee, the observant noticed that Her Majesty was wearing exactly the same diamond collet necklace and earrings worn by Queen Victoria in her official Diamond Jubilee photograph of 1897. It was a very typical gesture.

When isolated during the 2020 Covid-19 pandemic, the Queen was photographed speaking to Prime Minister Boris Johnson on the telephone. What stood out was that she was speaking on a dial telephone that had been installed in the 1960s. In her private apartments, old-fashioned two-bar electric fires stand in the fireplaces to heat the rooms. "If something still works well, there is no need to change it," has clearly been her motto.

In April 2021, the Queen faced her biggest challenge with the death of Prince Philip just months before his 100th birthday. After 73 years of marriage, it was a huge loss but one that she faced with typical stoicism. Within days, she was back at work. It was business as usual.

At the age of 21, Elizabeth publicly devoted her life, "whether it be long or short", to her country and the Commonwealth. In a mercifully long life, as both Princess and Queen, she has indeed sacrificed herself to duty and service, and has never broken that promise.

Index

A

Adelaide, Queen, 374, 376
Æthelfrith, first King of Northumbria,
15
Albert, Prince Consort, 381, 382, 383,
386, 387
Alexander III of Scotland, 142
Alexander III, Pope, 73
Alexandra, Princess of Denmark, then
Queen, 389, 393, 396, 398
Alfred the Great, King, 17, 23, 24, 25-
29, 31, 32, 35, 51, 53, 62, 68, 71, 83
Alfred, brother of Edward the
Confessor, 66, 71, 73
Alphege, Archbishop of Canterbury,
53
Andrew, Prince, Duke of York, 425
Anne of Bohemia, 161
Anne of Brittany, 197
Anne of Cleves, Queen, 226
Anne, Princess, Princess Royal, 425
Anne, Queen, 138, 314, 317, 324, 326,
327, 330, 331-339, 340, 342, 346, 349
Anselm, Archbishop of Canterbury, 98
Arthur, of Brittany, Prince, 121
Arthur, Prince, 122
Asser, Bishop, 25
Atheling, Edgar, 78, 84
Athelstan, King, 34, 35-39
Austen, Jane, 188, 359, 369

B

Bacon, Sir Francis, 212, 259, 268
Baldwin, Stanley, 403, 409
Balliol, Edward, 153
Balliol, John, 142
Barry, Charles, 377
Becket, Thomas, 107, 108, 109, 113,
116, 168, 171
Bede, the Venerable, 29
Bedingfield, Henry, 251
Benedict III, Pope, 19, 26
Benedict X, Pope, 77
Bernhardt, Sarah, 391
Blondel, 117
Bloodaxe, Erik, King of Norway, 39

Boleyn, Anne, Queen, 221, 225, 226,
242, 243, 249
Bonaparte, Napoleon, 358, 368
Brandon, Lady Frances, 236, 237, 238
Brown, Gordon, 125
Brown, John, 383, 384, 392
Bruce, Robert the, 142, 147
Bruce, Thomas, 311
Buckle, Henry, 311
Burnet, Gilbert, 308, 327
Bute, Earl of, 356
Butler, Lady Eleanor, 195, 198, 205
Byrd, William, 259
Byrhtnoth, Ealdorman of Essex, 51

C

Cabot, John, 216
Caesar, Julius, 29
Calvin, John, 253
Cambridge, Duke and Duchess of, 324
Campion, Thomas, 259
Canute, 52, 55, 56, 57, 58, 59, 60-64,
65, 68, 71, 83
Caroline of Ansbach, Queen, 343,
346, 350
Caroline of Brunswick-Woltenbuttell,
Queen, 367, 368, 369
Carr, Robert, 272
Catesby, Robert, 270, 271
Catherine of Aragon, Queen, 213, 221,
224, 225, 226, 233, 241, 242, 243
Catherine, of Valois, Queen, 177, 178,
180
Caxton, William, 193
Cecil, Robert, 262, 267, 269, 271, 273
Cecil, William, 261
Charles I, King, 228, 272, 277-287,
288, 290, 291, 298, 299, 301, 303,
311, 313, 325, 353, 416
Charles II, King, 137, 200, 280, 287,
288, 291, 292, 294, 296, 298-310,
309, 311, 313, 314, 315, 325, 326,
332, 333, 341
Charles the Bald, 19
Charles V (Habsburg ruler), 223
Charles V, King of France, 242

Charles VI, King of France, 177, 181
Charles, Prince, of Wales, 419, 425, 430
Charlotte, Princess (daughter of George IV), 367, 368
Charlotte of Mecklenberg-Strelitz, Queen, 355, 356, 365
Chastellain, Georges, 173
Chaucer, Geoffrey, 151
Churchill, John, 333, 334, 335
Churchill, Sarah, (nee Jennings), 332, 333, 337, 338
Churchill, Winston, 410, 418, 419, 421, 424, 426
Columbus, Christopher, 216
Conrad II, Roman Emperor, 62
Constantine II of the Scots, 33
Cook, Captain James, 357
Cornwallis, Lord, 357
Cranmer, Thomas, 225, 228, 231, 244, 246, 247
Crawford, Marion, 423
Cromwell, Oliver, 168, 284, 285, 287, 288-297, 298, 300, 301, 302, 303, 313
Cromwell, Richard, 295, 297, 301
Cromwell, Thomas, 222, 225, 226, 227, 243, 288
Cyneseige, Bishop of Lichfield, 40

D

D'Aubigny, Philip, 128
David I, King of Scotland, 103
David II, King of Scotland, 153
Dawson, Carl, 208
de Breaute, Faukes, 130
de Burgh, Hubert, 129, 131
de Bury, Richard, 151
de Glanvill, Ranulf, 120
de Grey, John, Bishop of Norwich, 123
de la Pole, Michael, 160
de Lusingnan, Hugh, 122
de Montfort, Simon, 131, 132, 133, 139, 140
de Mortimer, Roger, 147, 152, 153
de Rivaux, Peter, 130
de Vere, Robert, 160, 161
Delaware, Lord John, 94

Des Roches, Peter, 128, 129
Despenser, Hugh, Earl of Winchester, 147, 148
Devereux, Robert, 256
Devon, Earl of, 28
Diana, Princess of Wales, 426, 427, 428
Dickens, Charles, 220, 247
Disraeli, Benjamin, 383
Donald of Strathclyde, 33
Donne, John, 274
Dowland, John, 259
Drake, Sir Francis, 258, 259, 261
Duchess of Kent, (Victoria's mother), 380, 381
Dudley, John, Duke of Northumberland, 233, 238
Dudley, Lord Guildford, 238, 239, 240
Dudley, Robert, Earl of Leicester, 254, 256
Dunston, Abbot, later Archbishop of Canterbury, 39, 40, 41, 42, 46, 51

E

Ealdorman Sigehelm of Kent, 33
Ealdred of York, Archbishop, 84
Ealswyth, Queen, 27, 28, 31
Edgar the Peaceful, 40-45, 46, 59, 61, 70
Edgar, Marriott, 76
Edgiva, 33, 39
Edith, (aka Matilda) married to Henry I, 43, 97, 98
Edmund, King, 35-39, 40
Edmund Ironside, King, 55, 56-59, 61, 78, 84, 97
Edmund, St, 23
Edmund, (son of Edgar) 43
Edred, King 35-39
Edward (aka Black Prince), 152, 156, 158, 171
Edward I, King, 86, 132, 133, 136-143, 145
Edward II, King, 143, 144-149, 151, 152, 153
Edward III, King, 148, 150-156, 158, 162, 165, 175, 179, 189, 206, 211
Edward IV, King, 184, 185, 186, 186,

188-195, 196, 203, 205, 212, 213, 416

Edward V, King, 194, 196-201, 205, 206, 213

Edward VI, King, 226, 229-235, 243, 244, 245, 250, 253

Edward VII, King, 287, 384, 387-394, 396, 398, 406, 413, 414

Edward VIII, King, 201, 398, 404-412, 413, 416, 421

Edward the Confessor, King, 66, 68, 69-75, 77, 78, 79, 83, 86, 133, 134, 135, 138, 170, 309

Edward the Elder, King, 31-34, 39, 86

Edward the Martyr, King, 34, 44, 46-49, 86

Edward, Prince, Earl of Wessex, 13, 425

Edward, son of Henry VI, 182

Edwy the Fair, King, 40-45

Egbert, King, 13-15, 17

Egwina, Queen, 31, 36

Eleanor of Castille, Queen, 139, 140, 142, 145

Eleanor of Aquitane, Queen, 105, 111, 115, 120

Eleanor, La Belle, later Queen, 129, 132, 138

Elfleda, (wife of Edward the Elder), 31

Elfleda, (wife of Ethelred the Unready), 55, 56

Elfrida, Queen Consort, 43, 44, 46, 47, 50

Elfwine, 66

Elfwinn, 33

Elgiva of Northampton, 63, 65

Elgiva, 38, 41

Eliot, T.S., 113

Elizabeth I, Queen, 211, 226, 231, 248, 249-263, 264, 274, 279, 281, 289, 329

Elizabeth II, Queen, 13, 42, 88, 97, 128, 157, 229, 249, 363, 402, 412, 416, 417, 418, 419, 421-431

Elizabeth of York, Princess, then Queen, 194, 206, 207, 213, 218, 220

Elizabeth, Queen, the Queen Mother, 373, 412, 415, 422, 428, 430

Elton, Sir Geoffrey, 230

Emma, of Normandy, Queen, 53, 55, 63, 65, 71, 83

Ethelbald, King, 17-20

Ethelbert, King, 17-20, 22

Ethelfleda ("the white duck", wife of Edgar the Peaceful), 43, 46

Ethelfleda, (wife of King Edmund), 38

Ethelfleda, Lady of Mercia, daughter of Alfred the Great, 32, 33, 36

Ethelgiva, Abbess of Shaftesbury Abbey, 27

Ethelhelm, 22

Ethelred the Unready, King, 21, 43, 47, 48, 50-55, 63, 68, 71, 83

Ethelred, King, 20, 21-24, 27, 32

Ethelsine, 54

Ethelwald, 22, 32

Ethelwulf, 17-20, 21, 26

F

Fairfax, Sir Thomas, 290, 291

Fawkes, Guy, 270, 271

Ferre, Sir Guy, 145

Fitzherbert, Maria, 366, 367, 368, 370

Florence of Worcester, 59

Forkbeard, King Sweyn, 52, 61

Francis I, of France, 223, 242

Frederick, Emperor of Germany, 116

Frederick, Prince of Wales, 352, 353, 354

Fuller, Thomas, 136, 144

G

Gaimar, Geoffrey, 60, 66

Gaveston, Piers, 145, 146, 147

Geoffrey of Anjou, 97

Geoffrey of Coutances, Bishop, 84

George I, King, 339, 340-347, 348

George II, King, 341, 348-353, 355

George III, King, 286, 354-363, 364, 374

George IV, King, 364-370

George V, King, 395-403, 404, 406, 407, 408, 413, 414, 415, 416

George VI, King, 150, 201, 398, 405, 410, 411, 412, 413-420, 421, 422, 425

George, St, 114, 151

Gibbons, Orlando, 259,
Gladstone, William, 278, 385
Glydwr, Owain, (Owen Glendower)
168, 170, 174
Godiva, Lady, 67
Godwin, Earl, 65, 66, 72, 73, 77
Godwin, Edith, 77
Godwinson, Tostig, 79
Gormley, Antony, 113
Greville, Charles, 374
Grey, Lady Jane, 233, 234, 236-240,
244, 247
Grey, Lord, 376
Gruffydd, Ap, Llewelyn, 141
Guthfrithsson, Olaf (King Olaf I of
Dublin), 38
Guthrum (Danish leader), 27, 28, 32
Guy (of Ponthieu), 77
Guy, Bishop of Amiens, 76

H
Handel, George, Frideric, 335, 346,
351
Hansell, Henry 405, 406
Harding, Professor Steve, 37
Hardrada, Harald (the Ruthless), 78,79
Harold, Earl of Wessex, 73
Harold Godwinson, King 14, 73, 76-
81, 83
Harold Harefoot, King, 65-68
Harry, Prince, Duke of Sussex, 324, 404
Harthacanute, King, 65-68, 71, 78
Hatton, Christopher, 254, 255
Hawksmoor, 335
Heahmund, Bishop of Sherbourne, 24
Heath, Edward, 429
Henrietta Maria, (Queen), 279, 280,
283, 284, 298, 311
Henry I, King, 95-106, 124
Henry II, King, 70, 75, 105, 106, 107-
113, 115, 116, 120, 195
Henry III, King, 74, 75, 128-135, 138,
139, 140, 145
Henry IV, King (Bolingbroke), 160,
161, 162, 163, 165-171, 172, 174,
175, 189
Henry V, King, 118, 163, 172-178
Henry VI, King, 179-187, 189, 192,

196, 203, 207, 212
Henry, VII, King, 200, 206, 207, 211-
219, 220, 221, 237, 267, 353
Henry VIII, King, 34, 48, 74, 190,
199, 211, 214, 220-228, 229, 231,
237, 238, 241, 242, 243, 249, 250,
253, 267, 271, 288, 289, 353, 416
Henry I, King of France, 82
Henry VI, Emperor of Germany, 117
Henry of Huntingdon, 52, 59, 60, 73,
95, 104
Henry, Bishop of Winchester, 104
Henry, Earl of Lancaster, 148
Holland, Henry, 366
Holinshed, Raphael, 178, 199, 228
Holloway, Stanley, 76
Hood, Robin, 114
Howard, Catherine, Queen, 227
Howard, Lord, 258
Hyde, Anne, 313, 326, 331
Hywel, Welsh King, 44

I
Innocent III, Pope, 123
Innocent IV, Pope, 131
Ironside, Edith, 56
Isabella of France, 161
Isabella, daughter of Philip IV, later
Queen, 146, 147, 151, 152, 153
Isabella, of Angouleme, 122, 128
Isabella, Of Gloucester, 122
Ivar the Boneless, 22

J
James I, King, James VI of Scotland
262, 264-276, 278, 279, 340, 349
James II, King, 280, 299, 303, 308,
311-322, 323, 325, 325, 329, 331,
333, 416
James (III), the Old Pretender, 329
James IV, King of Scotland, 242
James V King of Scotland, 227
Joan of Arc, 181
John of Gaunt, 155, 156, 158, 159,
162, 165, 167, 179, 189, 211
John, King, 118, 120-127, 128, 175
Johnson, Boris, 426

Johnson, Samuel, 347
Jones, Inigo, 275
Jonson, Ben, 259
Judith, Queen, 19, 20

K
Karim, Abdul, 384, 386, 392
Kent, William, 346

L
Lackland, John, Prince, 118
Langley, Philippa, 208
Langton, Stephen, 123
Langtry, Lillie, 391
Latimer, Hugh, 246, 247
Laud, William, Archbishop of
Canterbury, 282
Leo IV, Pope, 19, 26
Leo IX, Pope, 83
Leo X, Pope, 225
Leofric, Earl, 72
Leofsige, 54
Leopold, Duke, of Austria, 117
Lloyd-George, David, 406, 407
Longchamp, William, Bishop of Ely,
118
Louis VI, King of France, 99
Louis VII, King of France, 111
Louis VIII, King of France, 125
Lovell, Viscount, 217

M
Macauley, Thomas, 327
MacDonald, Ramsay, 407
Maclise, Daniel, 194
Magnus, King of Norway, 78
Malcolm I, King of Scotland, 38
Malcolm, III, King of Scotland, 91, 97
Margaret of Anjou, later Queen 182,
183, 184, 191
Margaret Rose, Princess, 402, 416,
417, 419
Marlowe, Christopher, 259
Marshal, William, 129
Mary (Daughter of James V), 227
Mary of Modena, Queen, 315, 318, 333
Mary of Teck, then Queen, 398, 399,

400, 402, 404, 408, 410, 411
Mary I, Queen, 74, 233, 238, 239,
241-248, 250, 251, 252, 253, 324
Mary II, Queen, 314, 317, 320, 323-
330, 332, 334, 337
Mary, Queen of Scots, 232, 257, 258,
264, 265, 266
Matilda, Daughter of Henry I, 97, 100,
101, 102, 103, 104, 105, 109
Matilda (of Flanders), Queen, 83, 86,
89, 95, 98
Matilda, Queen, married to Stephen,
104, 106
Mawr, Rhodri, 141
Melbourne, Lord, 383
Michieli, Giovanni, 247
Milton, John, 279
Monmouth, Duke of, 315, 316, 317,
333
Monteagle, Baron, 271
More, Sir Thomas, 194, 199, 200,
202, 222, 225
Mortimer, Edmund, Earl of March,
165, 169, 175
Mortimer, Roger, Earl of March, 161

N
Napier, Sir Charles, 375
Nash, John, 366
Nelson, Lord Horatio, 358, 372
Neville, Anne, Queen, 185, 202, 204,
206
Neville, Richard, Earl of Warwick,
184, 185, 189, 190, 191, 192, 203
Nicholas II, Pope, 83
North, Lord, 355, 357

O
Odo, Bishop of Bayeux, 85, 86
Offa, King, 15
Orosius, 29
Osburga, Queen, 18, 19, 21, 22, 26
Otto the Great, 33

P
Paris, Matthew, 124, 131, 132, 134, 138

Parr, Catherine, Queen, 227, 232, 237, 243, 250, 251
Paul, IV, Pope, 253
Peel, Sir Robert, 385
Pepys, Samuel, 178, 296, 300, 302, 307, 308, 309, 311
Percy, Henry (Hotspur), 169, 174
Peter of Blois, 110
Philip II, King of France, 112, 115, 118, 121, 123
Philip of Spain (married to Mary I) 245, 246, 251
Philip, I, King of France, 87
Philip, Duke of Edinburgh, 418, 423, 424, 425
Philippa of Hainault, Queen, 152, 156
Pitt, William, the Elder, 356
Pitt, William, the Younger, 356, 358, 366
Plantagenet, Geoffrey, 102
Pugin, Augustus, 377
Pusey, William, 63

R
Raleigh, Sir Walter, 255, 256, 259, 272
Rattlebone, John, 57
Reynolds, Joshua, 359
Richard I, King 114-119, 121, 122, 137
Richard II, King, 156, 157-164, 165, 166, 167, 168, 173, 175, 211
Richard III, King, 195, 197, 198, 199, 200, 201, 202-210, 211, 212, 213
Richard, Duke of Normandy, 71
Richard, Duke of York, 179, 180, 183, 184, 188, 189
Richard, Prince, Duke of York, 197, 198, 203
Ridley, Nicholas, 246, 247
Rishanger, William, 139
Rizzio, David, 264, 265
Robert, Duke of Normandy, 91, 91, 95, 96, 97
Robert, Earl of Gloucester, 103, 104, 105
Roger of Howden, 112
Rostron, Arthur, 117

Rous, John, 202
Ruthven, William, 266

S
Saladin, 116, 117
Scharf, Sir George, 163
Scott, Sir Walter, 183
Seymour, Edward, 231, 237, 238
Seymour, Jane, Queen, 226, 231, 249, 250
Seymour, Thomas, 232, 237, 238, 250, 251
Shakespeare, William, 59, 125, 164, 165, 169, 170, 174, 189, 200, 202, 259, 279, 332
Sheffield, John, 332
Sidney, Henry, 234
Sigeferth, 56
Sigereric, Archbishop of Canterbury, 51
Simnel, Lambert, 217
Simon of Durham, 36
Simpson, Wallis, 408, 409, 410, 411, 412, 416
Siward, Earl, 72
Smollett, Tobias, 162
Sophia Dorothea of Celle, Queen, 341, 347, 348
Speed, John, 208
Spenser, Edmund, 259
Spry, Dr JH, 171
Stephen, King, 101-106, 109
Stephenson, George, 358
Stewart, Henry, Lord Darnley, 264, 265, 266
Streona, Eadric, 54, 57, 58, 59
Stuart, Frances, 305
Stubbs, William, 89
Swift, Jonathan, 335, 336, 337, 339
Swithin, Bishop of Winchester, 26

T
Tallis, Thomas, 259
Tennyson, Lord, Alfred, 108
Thackeray, William Makepeace, 344
Thomas, Duke of Gloucester, 166
Thomas, Earl of Lancaster, 145, 147

Thorkelsdottir, Gytha of Denmark, 77
Torigny, Robert de, 96
Towed the Proud, 68
Tresham, Francis, 271
Tryggvason, Olaf, 51
Tudor, Owen, 178, 180, 184
Tyler, Walter (Wat), 159, 166
Tyrell, Sir Walter, 93

V

Van Dyck, Anthony, 275, 281, 298, 299
Van Somer, Paul, 275
Vanbrugh, John, 335
Vergil, Polydore, 215
Victoria, Queen, 229, 363, 370, 371, 378, 379-386, 387, 388, 389, 390, 391, 392, 405, 409
Villiers, Colonel Edward, 332
Villiers, Elizabeth, 326, 330
Villiers, George, Duke of Buckingham, 272, 273, 274, 279, 281
Villiers, Lady Frances, 326, 332
Vitalis, Orderic, 77, 90

W

Wallace, William, 142
Walpole, Horace, 336, 342, 347, 355
Walpole, Sir Robert, 343, 344, 345, 350, 352
Walsingham, Thomas, 175
Walter, Hubert, 123
Warbeck, Perkin (imposter) 200, 217, 218
Washington, George, 357
Watt, James, 358
Wellington, Duke of, 358, 364, 370, 375
Wentworth, Thomas, 282
Whitgift, John, 253
William I, King (the Conqueror), 13, 77, 78, 79, 80, 82-88, 89, 90, 95, 101, 102, 107, 340
William II, (Rufus), King, 89-94, 95, 96
William III (of Orange), King, 299, 319, 320, 321, 323-330, 332, 333, 334, 337, 353

William, IV, King, 371-378, 382
William of Malmesbury, 33, 35, 47, 50, 54, 89, 90, 94, 96
William of Poitiers, 76
William, Son of Henry I, 97, 98
Wolsey, Cardinal Thomas, 222, 225, 228, 242
Woodville, Elizabeth, Queen, 190, 195, 196, 205, 213, 217
Wren, Sir Christopher, 200, 324, 329, 335
Wulfrida, Abbess of Wilton, 43
Wulfstan, Archbishop, 58, 63
Wulgeat, 54
Wyatt, Sir Thomas, 245, 251

About
Paul James

Paul James is the author of 94 books, ranging from a detailed study of the Royal Household to a book of children's games fronted by the late Duke of Edinburgh. Other books include biographies of the Princess Royal, Princess Margaret, Princess Alexandra, Diana, Princess of Wales, and the first ever biography of Prince Edward – which have sold in more than 100 countries. Non-royal books since 1979 encompass everything from humour to quizzes, health to history, children's fiction and non-fiction; he has ghost-written books for a number of well-known personalities, and has acted as researcher/advisor for several publishers and TV companies.

As a broadcaster, he has taken part in over 1,000 radio and television programmes; as an entertainer he has regularly performed a comedy act all over the country since 1978 and, as a journalist, has written for many newspapers and magazines. Since spring 1992 he has had feature articles on royalty in most issues of *This England* magazine, including the long-running series *Royalty Remembered* and *A Royal History of England*. Paul James lives beside the sea on the beautiful Sussex coast.

THIS ENGLAND

The magazine in which *A Royal History of England* was published is a quarterly that gently celebrates the very best of our country. With beautiful photography and well-written, interesting features we explore the country's past, present and future, using a wide network of fantastic contributors. Each issue focuses on a diverse mix of heritage, history, humour, travel and our unique customs and curiosities. Find out more at www.thisengland.co.uk. To subscribe call: 0800 074 0188